Memoirs of Life in Korea

THIS 1th EDITION PUBLISHED IN 2012
by The Korean Doctors' Weekly
Hanju Bldg., 4F, 324-1 Sangsu-dong, Mapo-gu, Seoul, 121-829 Korea

Memoirs of Life in Korea

By O. R. Avison, M. D.
Edited By H. W. Park, M. D.

Phone | 02-2646-0852
Fax | 02-2643-0852
E-mail | books@docdocdoc.co.kr
Homepage | http://doc3.koreahealthlog.com

ISBN 978-89-91232-41-9

• 에비슨전집 3 •

Memoirs of Life in Korea

By O. R. Avison, M. D.
Edited By H. W. Park, M. D.

Contents

Part 1
Medical Missionary, Dr. Oliver R. Avison

Part 2
Political Upheaval at the end of Chosun Dynasty

Part 3
Every Sides of Korea

About Dr. Oliver R. Avison's Memoirs

After Dr. Avison's beloved wife, Jennie passed away in September, 1936, family members around Dr. Avison suggested him to write the memoirs on Korea. Due to this request, it seems like Dr. Avison started writing the memoirs on June, 1940, when he was 80 years old. It is assumed that the memoirs was mostly written in St. Petersburg, Florida, where he stayed after his wife Jennie passed away and was also assisted by Dr. Avison's granddaughter, Mrs. Vernon Crawford, who lived in Atlanta, Georgia. Mrs. Crawford is Helen Dell Avison who is the oldest daughter of Dr. Avison's third son, Dr. Douglas B. Avison.

The original title of this Memoirs is <Memoirs of Life in Korea>. The memoirs is about 670 pages long. It has several characteristics.

First, the Memoirs was not a complete one. It is clear that the chapters were unorganized. There are sections that seems like it was added later and some parts were not complete.

Second, Dr. Avison wrote 448 pages first and then added extra 200 pages later.

Third, the several unofficial Memoirs was distributed to Dr. Avison's descendants. Dr. Avison himself edited the memoirs with a pen by adding and deleting few contents and this edited version was also copied and later distributed

Incomplete version of the Memoirs by Dr. Avison is not organized. If it was published through official route, the whole contents would have been polished.

I also thought carefully how to organize the Memoirs and decided to arrange it as followings.

First of all, it can be assumed that 'Some of Korea's gifts to the world,' which Dr. Avison wrote at the beginning of the Memoirs, shortly described what he felt about Korea and the world after spending 42 years in Korea. Although it is a short passage, considering its content, it seems it has been placed in the beginning of the book as <Introduction to Memoirs>. Also, because Dr. Avison was a medical missionary, I organized a part called <Part 1. Medical Missionary, Dr. Oliver R. Avison> and added another section on Korean politics called, <Part 2. Political Upheaval at the end of Chosen Dynasty>. Finally, <Part 3. Every Sides of Korea> is organized about Korean traditions and etc.

The Memoirs was translated into Korean and published in 2 volumes by me in 2010 at the anniversary of his 150th birth. In this Korean translated version, it includes a section about the early medical education that has been revised, which is from articles called <Avison Baksa Sojun(A Short Biographical Sketch of Dr. Avison)> that was published serially in the Gidok Shinbo (Christian News) in 1932.

Dr. Oliver R. Avison

We rarely realize the presence of a forest due to its enormity. As a result, we often focus on few trees instead of the whole forest. Dr. Avison is like this case.

Dr. Avison, who was a medical and educational missionary, came to Korea when the Chosen dynasty was desperately reaching out for survival under the world powers and made a huge contributions on the introduction of Western medicine and higher education in Korea. Although he was not a clerical missionary, he successfully carried out his duty as a missionary more than anyone else through medical service and education.

Looking back on history of Yonsei University, which now meets its 127th anniversary, Dr. Avison's role stands out. The name Yonsei University was made of first letters of two institutions, Severance Medical College and Yonhi University, in January, 1957. These two schools at the time was each established by Dr. Horace N. Allen (1885) and Mr. Horace G. Underwood (1915).

Current Severance Hospital has its root at Jejoongwon, the first Western-style hospital founded in Korea in 1885. During a political Coup D'Etat which occurred on December 4th, 1884, Mr. Yong Ik Min, the nephew of Queen Min was injured by sword. This incident turned out to be an unexpected opportunity for Dr. Allen to treat him, and as Mr. Min reported full recovery after 3 months, Dr. Allen's relationship with the royal family was suddenly elevated to an unexpected state.

It was a great opportunity for Allen as a missionary. He submitted a proposal for founding hospital to the Government and took responsibility of Jejoongwon by King Gojong's patronage. It was formally opened on April 10th, 1885. Medical education was stated clearly as a purpose of founding the hospital. However, immediate medical education was not held since it focused more on medical treatment and also lacked on student registration system, enough space for students and textbook preparation, etc..

Official medical education started with help of Dr. John W. Heron and Mr. Horace G. Underwood. As a result, Korea's first Western-style medical education institution, Jejoongwon Medical School opened in March 29, 1886. Mr. Underwood assisted Drs. Allen and Heron and taught premedical courses such as physics, chemistry, and etc. Medical education held at the time did not exactly resulted in producing a real doctor.

After Dr. Allen temporarily resigned from his Missionary work on September of 1887, and Dr. Heron died from dysentery on July, 1890, Jejoongwon was faced with lots of problems on its management. Also, Dr. C. C. Vinton who was assigned as Heron's replacement in April, 1891, had a conflict with the Government. The conflict was an important issue which was later linked to fate of Jejoongwon. For two years long, Jejoongwon faced dangers of continuation.

Mr. Underwood who used Jejoongwon as a shield to continue on his missionary work, married to Dr. Lillias S. Horton, one of the lady physicians of Jejoongwon. In 1892, while staying in the States as sabbatical, he was invited from Dr. Avison, a professor of University of Toronto's Faculty of Medicine, who led the missionary meeting at the time. At the end of September, Mr. Underwood visited Toronto and shared his experience to professors and students on his missionary work in Korea. He also asked Dr. Avison whether he would like to take direct action on foreign missionary works. This suggestion later influenced Dr. Avison's decision on his missionary work and was appointed to Korea as a medical missionary from the Board of Foreign Mission, Presbyterian Church of U. S. A. on February 6, 1893 and landed Korea on mid-July.

The year after his coming to Korea, Dr. Avison had a 6-months negotiation with the Government. With this, Jejoongwon reorganized as a private missionary institution in September, 1894.

Later, Mr. Underwood and Dr. Avison began to work together. In 1900, when Mr. Louis H. Severance was questioned by Pyeng Yang's missionary on donation towards new Hospital building, Seoul Station missionaries, including Mr. Underwood, supported Dr. Avison. As a result, Jejoongwon was rebuilt on September, 1904 as Dr. Avison hoped and renamed as 'Severance Hospital', after the donator. Jejoongwon medical school was renamed as Severance Hospital Medical College.

On June, 1908, the first 7 medical school graduates became Korea's first medical doctor by Dr. Avison. Severance Hospital Medical College later was renamed as Severance Union Medical College and became the centre of Korea's medical education.

Meanwhile, in 1906, Mr. Underwood hoped establishing a Institution for higher education in Seoul. However, lots of missionaries were against the idea due to existence of Soongsil College at Pyeng Yang. This time, Seoul Station missionaries, including Dr. Avison helped Dr. Underwood out. Mr. Underwood's hope became real when the Department of College, Kyungsin School was established on March, 1915. Mr. Underwood was assigned as the President and Dr. Avison as the Vice-president.

Dr. Avison first worked on promoting the college status after being assigned as President after death of Mr. Underwood in 1916. As a result, it was approved as a foundation and private a Yonhi College by the Japanese Government General of Korea. From then, the Department of College, Kyungsin School started to use the name, Yonhi College (or Chosen Christian College, or C.C.C.). Next, enough space and securing teachers was the problem. The expense was donated by Mr. Underwood's elder brother, Mr. John T. Underwood. Dr. Avison purchased a 290,000 pyeng land at Yonhi-Myen Goyang-gun, Kyunggi-do at September of 1917. This place is where the current Yonsei University stands. (134 Shinchon-dong, Seodaemoon-gu, Seoul).

Likewise, Dr. Avison, while being assigned presidents of colleges for 18 years, prepared the ground not only for Korea's Western medicine but also for higher education. There has been demands for a joint of two institutions since these were all supported by the Presbyterian Church and especially, considering Dr. Avison's position as a president both schools.

After 3.1 Independent Movement, Dr. Avison was busy establishing the Korean University. He was considering expanding Severance and Yonhi. However, Japan was against the plan. Instead of approving it, Japan established Keijo Imperial University in 1924.

By 1926, the plan for jointing both colleges set forth and debate on the joint settled down for the first time on June, 1929. Later, several resolutions on the joint were presented but were not able to make further progress due to interference by Japan.

After liberation in 1945, lead by Mission Board, debate on joint came to the fore again. On May, 1949, there was a progress on the joint issue when Yonhi University decided to accept students of premedical course of Severance Medical College. The Korean war, 1950, which broke hearts of all Koreans, became a huge opportunity for promoting joints of two schools. During before and after re-construction period, both schools had meetings again and as a result, Severance Medical College and Yonhi University was merged as Yonsei University. It was right after Dr. Avison passed away on August, 1956. Unfortunately, it is hard to assume that Dr. Avison was aware about the establishment of Yonsei University since he was ill for few years.

Looking carefully at the history, if pioneer missionaries like Dr. Allen and Mr. Underwood paved the road, Dr. Avison was the person who actually managed the plan and made Yonsei University to become an actual organization. If it wasn't for Dr. Avison, Korea's medical and higher education would have been different today.

Then, what is the background that made Dr. Avison possible to contribute to Korea by carrying out both medical and higher education?
Let's take a look into several aspects.

First, looking at his natural personality, he was always a positive individual and never rushed through his work. He also rarely got upset or mad. One Korean student said that although he was a foreigner, he was a warm hearted individual like a traditional Korean grandfather.
Once he set up his goal, he worked hard and organized his plan carefully. He made his own decision to design his life. He worked at a factory when he was young and after he graduated from high school, he became a teacher, and then a

pharmacist, finally as a doctor and a professor, he paved his own road for his future. Leaving all the glory behind, however, he came to Korea as a medical missionary. Of his 96 years of life, he spent the longest time in Korea.

Second aspect is his tolerance in religion. He was flexible in religious beliefs. A tolerance that his father showed when he was young, later influenced his idea on religion for the rest of his life. One of the most important challenges he faced as a missionary was the fact that he applied for Presbyterian Church instead of his original religious background, Methodist Church.

However, Dr. Avison did not cling to denominations and only focused on emphasizing on "business of God" and changed his position to Presbyterian Church from Methodist Church under influence by the Secretary of Board of Foreign Missions, Presbyterian Church, Dr. Frank F. Ellinwood. Later, Dr. Avison united different Protestant sects and had no difficulty running the missionary business. He was a pioneer of ecumenical movement in Korea.

> The word union in the name signifies that different missions joined in providing operating funds, doctors and nurses in harmony with Dr. Avison's original plan and Mr. Severance's earnest desire.

Third is his belief in true missionary work. Dr. Avison, through his whole life, showed his love to God by loving his neighbours, also known as 'serve god and love your neighbors.' This was different from what clerical missionaries believed because they payed more attention to respecting only God and as a result, payed less attention to their neighbours who were suffering from various diseases.

As to this belief, Dr. Avison wrote as following.

> I regret to admit that a considerable number of missionaries still regard many mental conditions as evidence of the factuality of evil spirits.

> Some of them seem to think that the lessening of the incidence of contagious diseases in Korea is due to the spread of Christianity per se.

> I would be one of the last to decry the value of Christ's teachings and example, though I am skeptical of the literal accuracy of some of those reports of what Christ did and taught on certain occasions, I am, however, a physician and more or less of a scientist, and must perforce accept the truth of what has been shown to be true by thousands of investigators and medical practitioners.

Fourth aspect is his love for Koreans. When Dr. Avison came to Korea and what he saw at the time was devastating. However, after meeting with different kinds of people for 40 years, he figured out that Korea was nationally and spiritually decayed in many aspects. Therefore, he believed that educating younger generation to strengthen knowledge was necessary and taught medicine and science at two schools. As a result, he was able to witness young students later becoming scholars, doctors, lawyers, and others and came up with a conclusion stating that all human beings are equally intelligent.

He was sure that there will be positive effects in future and encouraged Koreans to continue on their education. He helped Koreans in many angles to gain back their national power, when Koreans at the time, did not have enough power to fight back in Japanese policy, using his extraterritorial rights.

Fifth is his belief in education. As a medical missionary, he always thought through how to make actions in Korea. He thought it was impossible to make improvement in sanitary conditions with only few foreign doctors around. In the end, it was necessary to educate enough numbers of Korean doctors. He believed that after training enough talented people, missionaries have done enough work and needs to step out from it and leave the future to new generations.

> Every missionary, whether they are a doctor, a nurse, a teacher, a priest, needs to understand that one day, they need to take the road to the 'exit' door when their job is finished.

All the efforts Dr. Avison made to accomplish this goal was to naturalize Western medicine after all. He published Medical textbooks written in Korean on nearly all subjects with help of Messrs Pil Soon Kim, Suk Hoo Hong, Jong Eun Hong, and others. Also, different from what Drs. Allen and Heron's period did, he made graduates to earn their own Medical License, which was the first one in Korea. In other words, medical education in Korea now became in more than just education, but was able to make official social contribution through out the country. Furthermore, these people were able to give services at schools and train future doctors, which later became roots of Western medicine to grow naturally in Korea.

Dr. Avison's purpose of C.C.C. was to produce talented individuals who can lead the country by devoting themselves to their studies and polish up their unique skills, based on Christianity. Following this spirit, many talented Korean educators were invited as professors to C.C.C. It is clear that their contribution to Korea after liberation was influential to development of Korea. What Dr. Avison did was not to conquer Koreans but to share his knowledge and form a equal relationship with Koreans to work together to spread God's will.

In 1934, Dr. Avison resigned from his post and gave the position of the President of Severance to a Korean. When the time came, he wisely stepped out of the game. Then, he left Korea on December, 1935. According to the report at the time, Dr. Avison left Korea to see his family back in his hometown before he settle down in Korea. However, right after he returned, his wife Jenny suddenly passed away and Korea's national situation was unstable, and as a result, he was never able to come back to Korea again.

> I have not gone back to Korea. I probably will never do so, but my heart is with its people as was that of my wife as long as she lived.

Dr. Avison returned to his hometown in 1936 and died after 20 years, in 1956. Over 50 years have passed already. Dr. Avison's statue, which is his alter ego, stands in the center of Severance compound and memorials commemorating him are held annually. However, as time passes by, it is a shame to see that memoirs of Dr. Avison are being faded away. I truly hope that Dr. Avison's great accomplishment and his spirit stated in this memoirs becomes a valuable foundation for the development of Korean society.

February 19, 2012
Hyoung Woo Park, M. D., Ph. D.

* Professor, Departments of Anatomy and Medical History, Yonsei University College of Medicine
* Former Director of Department of Medical History (1996-2000)
* Former Director of Department of Anatomy (2004-2008)
* Director of Dong-Eun Medical Museum (1999~　)
* President of Korean Society for Medical History (2009~2012)

Preface

I am writing this preface on my eightieth birthday June 30, 1940. My life has been eventful. Every man's life is eventful, but because more than half of mine was spent in a far-off and but little known land in Asia, my friends have for years been urging me to write a book about it. It was easier to me to decide to go to Korea than it was for me to agree to write this book but, perhaps, it will be less difficult to do it than to keep on finding excuses for not doing it.

I might have won out in this "war of nerves" had not some of the important Koreans joined in these demands. They urged that my contacts with the King and Government of Korea as well as with the representatives of Japan and the Western powers had given me an insight into some of the affairs of that glamorous country that were not available to most of the other missionaries and foreign residents. Perhaps this is true. Whether it be so or not, I at last yielded.

But I am an old-time writers - I was trained in composition at a time when long and involved sentences were in style and it is not easy now for me to alter this long established habit and I fear this lack of facility in modern writing will lessen the interest of those who prefer short sentences, colorfully written and full of action. Color and Action! How often these words have been dinged into my ears by my critics - friendly critics who are anxious to have these memoirs find many interested readers. They have constantly held up to me their ambition that I shall produce a best seller - the book of the year - but how hopeless such an achievement appears to me! Such as it is, however, I commend it to you, hoping that, at least, it may be sufficiently interesting and sufficiently convincing in its appeal to gain increasingly large support for the missionary cause to which I devoted more than forty-two years of my life. It will have at least one virtue - all the events related actually occurred; there are no fabricated stories. There may be inaccurate explanations and erroneous interpretations of what I saw for these are unavoidable as long as human fallibility exists.

Korea has a past history of great accomplishments in the fields of science and invention, but, from various causes, she slipped back into a state of mental and national decadence. In the last fifty-five years, however, she has emerged, from this condition and is now manifesting even greater mental and moral progressiveness than she did even in those far-off eras of cooperative greatness.

If this book makes you acquainted with this group of human beings whom having fallen out of the forward-moving procession and stayed out for centuries, are now becoming revitalized, and if it stirs you to a search for the causes of national decadence and renaissance, one of the chief hopes of the writer will be realized. If it proves to be sufficiently interesting to attract enough purchasers to save its editors and publishers from financial loss, he will be thankful; if it goes beyond this and adds something to the meager financial resources of a pensioned missionary, he will be elated; if it increases interest in foreign missions so that more and better qualified individuals are led to give themselves to the cause and others are interested to the point of giving more liberally to the various Boards of Foreign Missions, he will be gratified. If it should help the Western Nations to see that Korea should be set free from the domination of Japan so that the native genius or her people may once more serve the world, it could be a real boon both for Korea and for all mankind.

As for my beloved wife and me, we lived our lives in Korea just day by day without any thought of ever writing a book, only thinking how best to relieve the sicknesses of the people and stem the overwhelming death rate that was decimating the population and, while doing that, to establish institutions in which the younger generations could be trained to carry on what we could only begin. She stayed with me throughout our period of service on the field but passed away suddenly a few months after our return to the American continent. Had she lived longer she would have been my best mentor and critic. She could have brought to my mind many occurrences which would have given greater force to my writings and perhaps have eliminated some things which are of lesser value. While I frequently use the first personal pronoun singular, I want it to be understood that whatever I did that proves to be of value to the people was made possible by her unceasing cooperation and unfailing confidence in me.

Though she was the mother of ten children (of whom seven lived and are doing their share of the world's work), and for many years had to be their only school teacher, she supervised Biblewomen, visited Korean homes, and kept her own home a happy one for all her family.

Now, having undertaken to write these memoirs, I stand embarrassed at the shear mass of material that make up the content of those forty-odd years of work in the Capital of Korea, from it I must select those incidents that are most illustrative of the characteristics of a people whose modern history is saturated with dramatic, I might almost say tragic, interest. Although, for the sake of historical accuracy, I must confine my account to events with which I was personally connected, I must admit that the efforts of other missionaries, teachers, business men and the official representatives of the various foreign powers had far more to do with the kaleidoscopic changes through which Korea has passed during the past half century. Mine is but the partial record of one man and one family in the effort to help in the restoration and rehabilitation of a nation that has been ground between the upper and lower mill-stones of, first, powerful and unscrupulous neighbors, and, second, its own inexperience and political ineptitude. Beneath it all lies the proven fact of Korea's splendid physical virility and a temporarily dormant but now awakened intellectual capacity equal to that of any or its neighbors.

Introduction to
Memoirs

Introduction to Memoirs

The modern history of Korea has been one of "fightings without and fears within". Korea is so situated geographically that it became the pathway between China and Manchuria on the one side and Japan on the other. In later years, Russia was added to the list of those who needed a way out to the world from her Asiatic possession - Siberia. Being thus the connecting roadway between the Asiatic continent and its neighboring island Kingdom (Japan), it naturally bore the brunt of all wars between Japan and the continental nations as well as of wars between all those other powers and Korea herself. No doubt those almost continuous wars over centuries of time can be blamed, for the dwindling of Korea from its former position of prominence to what it was when it was first opened to intercourse with Western countries.

I have selected from Dr. H. N. Allen's *Chronological Index*, in which he sets forth, in terse word, some of the chief event in the foreign intercourse of Korea. In his preface he makes some very important statements - a few of which I am quoting as being especially significant to my readers and to students of the Orients (bracketed lines are my own remarks).

"Korea's foreign intercourse is a growth of the present generation" (By present generation' Dr. Allen was evidently thinking of only the members of Western nations living in Korea at the time).

"Twenty years ago (probably about 1876) Korea was properly and popularly known as the 'Hermit Nation'. Such intercourse as she had had with the outside world prior to that time was in the nature of the perfunctory exchange of enforced ceremonies accompanied with force or misfortune."

"It is a somewhat unique experience, this watching a nation being 'born again' and as I chanced to be here almost from the beginning of the free advent of western foreigners, I am frequently asked questions as to dates and occurrences that sometimes require considerable looking into dusty records before answering properly …"

Dr. Allen then goes on to say "Although the Royal Geographical Society has decided that Korea should be spelled, with 'K', the British and some other governments still use 'C'. The government of the United States uses 'K', hence I have done the same".

"To anyone who may chance to look through this 'Index' consecutively, it will be readily apparent how large a part missionaries have had in opening up the country, expecially those of the Catholic Church whose history is written in the blood of martyrs".

Students of Korean History owe Dr. Allen a vote of thanks for his work in producing this *Chronological Index* for it saves a great deal of research for those who want only a sufficient knowledge of what occurred at specially important crises to guide them in appraising the various stages in the development of this nation which, though small, has contributed to the World's progress by the additions it made to knowledge in the departments of art, science, inventions and literature.

This book which I am now writing, does not set out to be a history of even the brief period of my personal acquaintance with Korea and its people. It merely relates some of the occurrences in which I had the privilege of participating. It happens to coincide with a very important period in the modern history of Korea, and as I spent more than forty years as a medical and educational missionary in daily communication with all classes of the people - from the King to the humblest in the land - my closest friends, including missionaries, representatives of foreign governments and many Koreans, have insisted that I might be able to throw some light on things that happened and even suggest the causes that lay behind them and the devious paths along which Korea travelled and also travailed through this interesting period. This book is not planned, therefore, to be a history. It is merely a more or less disconnected narrative of some of those events.

If what I have written seems sometimes to throw blame on individuals and groups who intended only to do something helpful and appears to praise some who ought not to be praised, I am sorry. Everything I mentioned happened. My interpretations of the happenings may be faulty, but I write of them as they appeared to me at the time they occurred.

I can give so better introduction to this story of life in Korea than to begin with the following sketch of what it did to forward civilization in its earlier days, beginning with a brief account of its origin.

Origin of the Korean People

Many have tried to solve this problem but so far no one has done it conclusively.

Koreans claim their national life goes as far back as 2333 B. C. when Tangun appeared on the Everwhite Mountain in the Northern part of present day Korea. The country, then known as Chosun (pronounced cho' - sun'), a descriptive title made cut of two Chinese characters - "Cho,", which means "morning" and "Sun" which means either "bright" or "calm". What a beautiful name for a beautiful country! The country to the South of the Everwhite Mountains had other names but when the Yi dynasty was formed in 1,392 A. D., this one was given to the whole combination of small states. Its people liked the name and kept it until the close of the China-Japan war in 1895.

But where did Tangkun (Pronounced Tang-goon) come from? History does not tell but Dr. Hrdlicka, the well known anthropologist of the Smithonian Institute, Washington, D. C., believes the Koreans originated somewhere in Western Asia, probably in the country of the Tartars, who, for some unknown reason, began to trek eastward. This, in the course of ages, brought them through Mongolia to Manchuria where, after prolonged contacts with the Chinese, they proceeded into the peninsula to the south where Tangkun established the nation we now know as Korea. We do know that Tangkun's name is connected with several walled mountain fortresses which many Koreans still visit in their pilgrimages. One of these is on the side of a high mountain in the Western part of Whanghai province. Of course Tangkun is a wholly legendary character, but these putative relics of his reign give some color to the story. Perhaps the best known is a very ancient altar on the summit of a mountain on the island of Kang Wha, some miles from the south of the Han river. The reason given by Dr. Hrdlicka for believing the Koreans were originally of Tartar stock is based on the usual color of their beards - when they have any - and on the occasional color of their hair.

The Chinese have black hair and black beards without any tendency toward brown but the beards of the 'Koreans are nearly always tinged with brown and less often their hair also shows a reddish tinge. Also, the Chinese have oval eye openings which tend to turn upwards at their outer extremities while, in the Koreans, these features are much less definite and are often quite lacking.

However this may be, the history of Chosun (Cho' - sun') under Tangkun and his immediate successors is not very well known. The next important ruler was Kija, a Chinese statesman who came to Chosun in 1,122 B. C. with 5,000 followers and, having gained possession of the country, made Pyeng Yang his capital. He surrounded the city by a stone wall, part of which still exists with some of its arched gateways. These ancient arches were so well constructed that at the end of more than 3,000 years they are still practically perfect. Kija'a capital was not on the exact location of the present city but immediately south of it.

This great ruler is credited with the introduction of many of the arts and with the culture of his day, some relics of which are still found in his capital - expecially a well near the present railway station which still contains usable water and also a rather fine mound, said to be his grave, located on a hill within the bounds of the present city. At the head of this mound is a stone tablet which bears an inscription stating that this is Kija's tomb. The grave is surrounded by a wall and has around it the usual stone images and in front of it the stone table on which offerings are placed.

In the years following Kija the kingdom of Chosun had many contacts with China. The Chinese script was adopted and utilized by those who had time to study it and through it much of the learning of China became available to Korean Scholars who contributed largely to the literature of the East. The three great religions of Asia, - Confucianism, Buddhism and Taoism - are introduced during the sixth century. Shamanism (the worship of the spirit of Nature) was not challenged by proponents of any of those three religions. The net result of this was that though Shamanism adopted many of the tenets of the newer religions, it was never ousted by them and the religion of the country became a good deal of a conglomeration.

The records of China show that when the Great wall of China was being built in the beginning of the third century many Koreans helped in that monumental work.

Some of Korea's gifts to the world

- The Magnetic Compass

Korean History says the Magnetic Compass was used in Korea before the I2th Century and that in 1,100 A. D. Arab traders with Korea obtained it there and took it back home with them.

The Arabs claim to have introduced it into Europe and it was used by Columbus in his voyage to America in 1,492 so Korean records cf its discovery by them may be true.

- Modern Method of Printing

About the middle of the twelfth century Korea gave the world a new method of printing. Up to that time all books had been either written by hand by the Chinese brush pen or printed from wooden blocks in which the characters had been laboriously cut by hand.

But amongst all who worked so hard and so slowly at making those blocks was a brighter man, a thinker. He struck on the idea of cutting each character on an individual little block which could then be put in whatever order was desired till a page was set up. When the printing had been done the little blocks could be separated and laid aside to be used again.

What a great idea it was! But what a tiresome job it was to cut the great number of characters needed. Several thousands of characters, all different were required to complete one font, and several fonts were needed to compose even one page of a book.

Some more thinking must be done. If only a way could be found to make these little printing units of something that could be moulded and hardened. Yes, why not? Porcelain was the immediate answer. One by one the moulds were made, the clay packed in and baked. Some perfect ones turned out but many could not be used because they were twisted in the baking but enough good ones were turned cut to enable pages to be set up and printed, but the loss was too great and too much labor and time were spent in making the type.

More thinking - and the idea of using bronze was tried. The bronze type came out of the molds in perfect form and were durable. The great problem had been solved and printing made easier and quicker.

One day in Korea, Mr. Homer B. Hulbert, one of the first three American employed by the Korean Government to teach English said to me, "Avison, do you know that the first successful effort to print books from movable metal type was made in Korea?"

"No, I had not heard of that." "Well," he said, "I found an account of it in an old history of Korea. The Koreans accomplished this long before Gutenberg was born but for some unknown reason they lost this art and for centuries have been again using the old and slow method of making blocks."

"I talked about it with some old Korean Scholars who told me that there were plenty of those old porcelain and bronze type in a certain royal storehouse."

"I got His Majesty's permission to search for them and found them in an old storehouse in the palace. I took some of them away with me and when I went to America I put them in the Museum of Natural History in New York City."

Once when I was visiting the British Museum in London my curiosity was aroused by seeing a tripod in the middle of an otherwise empty room. On it was a book. Going over to see what it as that was thus set apart I found a book printed in Chinese Characters and on the accompanying tag were these words - "The oldest book in the world known to have been printed from separate metal type - Korean." What a surprise and what a joy to me to find it there in so conspicuous a setting!

At a later time, the Japanese, who after their annexation of Korea spent much effort in searching for and putting old Korean things into Museums, found specimens of these old type, both porcelain and bronze, and placed them in the small special museum which they set up in the North palace.

I have seen them there often and have taken pleasure in showing them to foreign visitors to Seoul, as a proof that the Koreans had, at one time, been among the brightest of the Oriental nations. It would be a pity not to help such a nation, to rise again from its lethargy.

The same printing problem presented itself to Gutenberg a century and a half later and he practically found the same answer.

In later years of course a different type metal was developed that was both better and cheaper than bronze.

For some reason not known this method of printing fell into disuse and as late as the 19th century printing by wooden blocks was being done. There must have been cogent reasons for this. One probable reason is that the blocks could be stored away for future use in reproducing lost pages in the exact form as the original or in reproducing entire books.

- A Suspension Bridge

In the latter part of the 16th Century, about 1585, when Hideyoshi was the Emperor of Japan, or rather its Regent, he sent a large army to invade Korea in an effort to force it to assist him in his war against the Chinese.

The Japanese forces consisted of a combination of army and navy. The navy of course consisted of small wooden boats propelled by cars. When the Korean king refused to help the Japanese, they drove the Korean defenders far to the North, almost to Pyeng Yang. The Koreans, however, made a turn and began enforced march Southward.

Reaching the Imjin river[1] which flows into the Yellow Sea farther south than Songdo, they found the tide out. At that point the river flows between high banks and when the great tide on the West side of the country is in, the river rises rapidly till the water is almost level with its banks and that was the time when crossings could be most easily made by the many ferry boats always to be found there. But when the Korean army arrived the tide was out. The river ran far below them and the banks were steep, muddy and slippery. Even if they got down there the banks there were no boats to take them to the other side. Even though they found a way of crossing the river they would still have to climb the steep slippery bank, on the other side to gain the roadway to the South.

By that time the pursuing Japanese might be at their heels with the tide in and crossing would be easy - what could they do?

A bright idea struck one of them. In Korea there is a vine called 'chik' whose branches trail along the ground and climb trees. Its stems are very fibrous and tough and are often used for making ropes. Why not make long cords to reach

---

[1]   That river is now spanned by a railroad bridge and always when I have crossed it on a train I have thought of the predicament the Korean army was in when it got there and found the tide out. No wonder they felt they were trapped!

across the chasm and having anchored them on each side lay branches of trees across these so as to make a swinging bridge on which the crossing might be made? The first strand to be carried across by one man swimming could be a light one and this could be followed by a stronger one. Many men made the job of producing strong cables one of hours only, and soon the suspension bridge was completed, and the Army got across in time and destroyed the bridge.

- Iron Clad Boats

Even when the Korean army succeeded in getting backs to its starting place, the country was still endangered by the presence of a thousand Japanese boats that far outnumbered Korea's naval forces. What could be done?

A Korean Admiral, Yi Soon Sin, is credited with the nev idea that solved their problem. Why not make a new kind of boat, covered with iron plates, with which to attack the Japanese wooden structures? These were quickly built in the shape of a turtle with iron sheets overlapping each other in imitation of the shell of the turtle. Soldiers protected by these would have a great advantage over their enemies. Only a few were produced, but they were filled with great numbers of torches, to be lighted as they drew near their opponents and flung into their wooden boats. This new method of attack succeeded wonderfully well. The wooden boats of the Japanese took fire and fighting became impossible.

All who could escape did so but many Japanese boats and lives were lost. The morale of the Japanese was destroyed and they withdrew from Korea as quickly as possible.

On some of my visits to the South, I was taken by my missionary friends to the site of this wonderful sea battle. The remains of old forts are still to be found at various places on the shores of that great bay and on islands in it, showing the scare of great battles.

Even to this day Admiral Yi Soon Sin is regarded by the Korean as the saver of their country, and not long ago, while I was still in Korea, his home at Hansan in Southern Korea was made into a shrine where many souvenirs of that war are stored and to which pilgrimages of Korean patriots go though over three hundred years have passed since the idea of iron-clad boats was first put into effective use.

The library of the Chosen Christian College, a union missionary institution in Seoul, recently received a gift of some 12,000 Korean books nearly all of very early times, printed from wooden blocks or produced so far back in the past that they were not even printed but were written by hand with a Chinese brush pen.

In this collection are several books of original letters written by famous men, signed by themselves and amongst these are some written by Admiral Yi Soon Sin himself, reporting the matters described above.[2]

An Explanation of Some Terms Used in These Memoirs

Lest my readers find it difficult to understand my many references to the Mission, the Mission Board, etc., I think it best to explain the relation to each other of the various organizations mentioned in these memoirs.

Each of the religious denominations in the U. S. A. and Canada divides its mission work into two classes - Home Missions and Foreign Missions. I was a Foreign Missionary of "The Presbyterian Church in the U. S. A." generally referred to as the "Presbyterian Church North" to distinguish it from "The Presbyterian Church South" - differentiated by using only the letters U. S. instead of U. S. A.

The general Assembly of the Northern Presbyterian Church appointed a Board of Foreign Missions to conduct its work in foreign lands and this body is spoken of as "The Board" or "The Northern Presbyterian Board." when it is necessary to distinguish it from boards of other churches. The Southern Presbyterian Church has no Board of Foreign Missions. It conducts its mission work by means of an Executive Committee.

The Board selects and sends out missionaries and, in general, controls their policies.

The Missionaries of any given church are organized into a Mission for the country in which the work is carried on so the organizations connected with the Foreign Mission work are.

1. The Home Church in a given country.

2. The Board appointed by that Church (or its General Assembly or General

2   Among some 12,000 Korean books donated to the library of Chosun Christian College may be found illustrations of ancient types of printing. Some of these were written with a Chinese brush pen, others were printed from wooden blocks. Several volumes of these contain the signatures of many of Korea's scholars and heroes. In one of these is a letter from Admiral Yi Soon Sin with his signature which of course is highly valued by all concerned with this College.

Conference, etc) to conduct and control its Missionary enterprises.

3. The Missions is composed of those members of a Mission allocated, to one division of the country in which the Mission is working. These missionaries generally reside in one or more central cities and, carry on their work there and in the country around them under the direction of the Annual Mission Meeting.

In Korea the following named groups of Missionaries worked, sometimes cooperating with, sometimes opposing one another.

- American Presbyterians - North and South.

- American Methodists - North and South (recently amalgamated)

- Canadian Presbyterians - afterward the United Church of Canada.

- Episcopalian - English - Society for the Propagation of the Gospel, S. P. G.

- Roman Catholics - French, German, American, Irish.

- Baptists - Only two irregular groups not directly sent out by the Baptist Church in America, both weak and one of only short duration.

- Salvation Army - British

- Seven Day Adventists - American

- Holiness Mission - American.

- Pentecostal - American

- Young Men's Christian Association - American Y. M. C. A.

- Young Women's Christian Association - American Y. W. C. A.

- Some other small independent groups that lasted only for a short while.

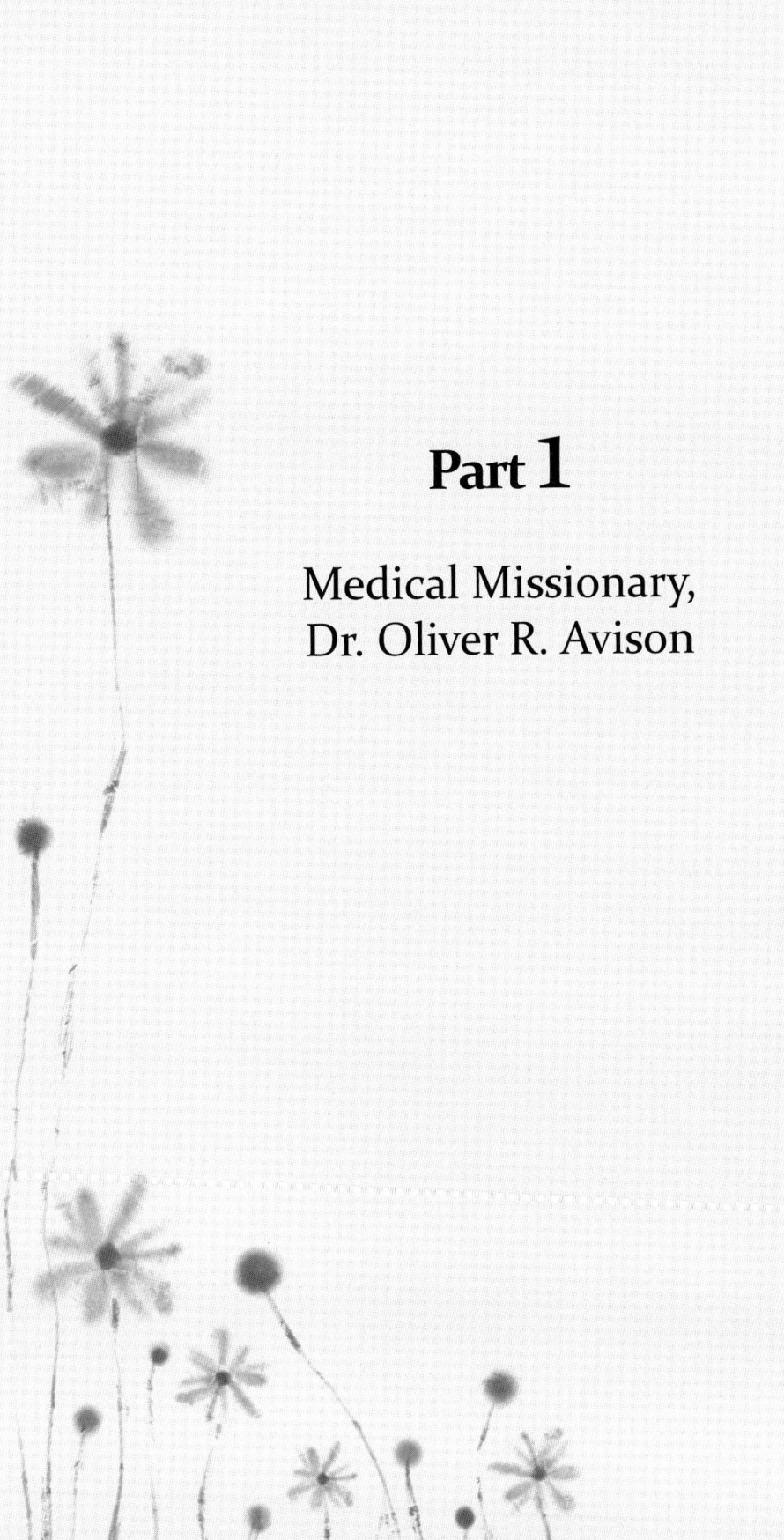

Part 1

Medical Missionary,
Dr. Oliver R. Avison

Chapter 1

Memoirs of early life
from birth to time of going to Korea

My hometown

I was born June 30, 1860, in the West Riding of Yorkshire, England, in a small hamlet called Jagger Green, located on a plateau on which was one of those broad heather moors which have made Yorkshire famous for the beauty of its landscapes. This hamlet overlooked a valley in which was located the large woolen manufacturing plant of Messrs. John Shaw & Son, known as the Brookroyd Mills, in which my father worked from his sixth year until he grew to manhood and had a family of three children to care for. During those years he had worked his way up till he had becomes Superintendent of the Finishing Department that takes the cloth from the looms and prepares it for the market. Though he stood high in his class of workers he saw little opportunity for raising his family to an easier and better way of living.

However, my earliest recollections are not connected with my birth-place but with the village of Brookroyd in the valley below to which place the family had moved so as to be nearer my father's place of work. There I first attended school. It was known as a dame's school, and was held in a private home in the small block in which we lived. I do not recollect what we were taught there, but I do remember the "dunce cap" which everyone had to wear who could not do his lessons or who misbehaved in any way. Sometimes he would have to stand in a corner with his face to the wall - at other times he was made to stand on a bench and, if he had been very bad, he was made to stand on one foot. Of this kind of punishment I bore my share, and so have never forgotten it.

A glance at these pictures will suggest my humble origin. This home like most English houses, was built of stone. Its front door overlooked a small walled-in garden beyond which was a little creek. This garden stood out in my memory as a rather extensive place, but when I went back after forty-three years, alas, how small it proved to be! We children used to cross the little stream on its single plank bridge with much fear. One unlucky day I fell off the bridge into the water, striking my elbow in a stone and dislocating it. I still shudder when I recall the terrible pain that accompanied there placement of the bone.

This little house was like all those occupied by the working classes in that part of England. It had one large living room on the first floor with two bedrooms upstairs. The floor of the lower story was covered with stones, known as flagstones - large, flat and smooth, but not particularly well matched. These were kept clean by diligent scrubbing, after which fine, clean sand was sprinkled over them. To satisfy the ideas of the housewives these floors had to be not only scrubbed, but also sanded. At one side of the room was a large fireplace, the fire serving both for heating and cooking. It is not necessary to describe how cooking was managed at a fireplace of that kind. However, I remember that the food cooked on it was very satisfying, especially the roast beef and Yorkshire pudding of old England, which, of course, constituted a considerable part of the family's food. My parents used to say that English beef differed from American in that the latter contracted when roasted, whereas the former expanded.

As I write, one of the happenings in that house comes vividly before me. The stairway to the second floor, closed off from the living room, led directly to a bedroom above and there was a fireplace in this bedroom to heat the entire upstairs. My mother left us children alone in the house one day and some of the neighboring children came to play with us. No doubt we were as boisterous as children left alone usually are. Like all boys of my age in that neighborhood, I wore a dress covered with a long pinafore and in running about upstairs, I went so close to the fireplace that my pinafore touched the flame and immediately was ablaze. There was a great uproar among the children but I had enough self-possession to gather my pinafore above the flaming part with my hands and run downstairs and outdoors where help reached me before any harm was done, except the destruction of my pinafore. By the time my mother returned and my father came home in the evening the story had grown considerably and I remember how pleased I was to have everybody speaking of the remarkable presence of mind I had shown. Why, any ordinary boy would have been burned up! This incident had a considerable influence on me later because I felt I had to live up to the reputation I had gained.

Another boyhood recollection is that of my weekly Sunday journeys to a church in the neighboring village of Stainland. My oldest sister took me across the fields to the little church where we attended Sunday school and afterwards the preaching service which followed. After Sunday school we gathered in the little churchyard and, sitting on the flat gravestones, ate our lunch. This usually consisted of a sort of pastry called "fatty-cake." It was made of biscuit dough rolled out thin, with sugar and currants sprinkled over one half of it, and then the other half turned over, making a semi-circular cake like a pastry. How good it was! I would have preferred to go home then but that was not permitted for after eating our pastries, we had to go to church again. Though I do not remember a single word of what was said in either the Sunday school or church, no doubt the good word shad some influence on my religious ideas. I do remember one incident, however, which showed that my sister, at least, had taken some of the touching to heart. On a certain Sunday, while crossing a field, I noticed a small twig lying on the ground and stopped to pick it up. My sister immediately made me throw it down saying, "It is not right to gather sticks on Sunday." But then, she was nearly three years older than I.

In Brookroyd we lived in a house close to the bank of a small stream. Just across the stream was a stone mill which had not been used for a long time. Around it had grown up blackberry bushes and other shrubbery. We children frequently went to play around or in the mill. It was generally regarded as haunted and this thrilled us, though we never saw any ghosts and in time began to doubt this tale. The memory of the old mill and its specters, however, has remained with me and I regard it as one of the factors in my mental development.

Genealogy

I can remember both of my grandfathers, but I have no recollection of either of my grandmothers. On my father's side my grandfather was George Avison who was connected with woolen manufacturing like most of the men of that section. He died before we left England but my memory of his is not very clear. My father used to tell one story about him that has always stayed in my mind. When the woolen mill would shutdown temporarily for some reason the old gentleman would return to his home, dress up in his best clothes and go downtown. When asked why he did this he said, "There is no use in both being poor and looking poor." So, whenever the work closed down, instead of making a poor mouth of it, he took the opposite course, making himself look as prosperous as possible. Though I remember little else about him, I have always remembered his unique method of making the best of everything when anything untoward had occurred. If I remember rightly, this grandfather had eleven children - seven boys and four girls - my father being the youngest member of the family. I have no vivid recollection of some of these, but others I remember well. With the exception of my father, all the members of the family were musical - members of local orchestras, and leaders of choirs. Yorkshire is celebrated for its musical talent. Queen Victoria used to send there every year for a brass band to play for her in the palace and one of my father's brothers was a member of the band. These bands were not made up of men who gave their whole time to music but of those who made it their pastime. They were all men working in the woolen mills who, loving music, gave much of their spare time to practising. While neither my father nor his children had any special musical talent, they all appreciated it and many of his grandchildren have shown considerable ability along this line, and this seems to have come from far back in the Avison family. In most of the hymn books of today a tune called "Avison" can still be found. It was written by one Charles Avison, a member of the family who lived at Newcastle, Yorkshire, during the reign of Queen Elizabeth. Strange to say, the words of this hymn were written by a man named George Rawson and one of his descendants, Kathleen Rawson, became the wife of my son Dr. Douglas B. Avison.

I had often wondered about the origin of this name, Avison, because so many asked me whether I was not a Swede till an old friend of mine, Professor Shuttleworth of Toronto, Ontario, looked up the origin of the name AVISON and reported that he had found the following quotation in an English book of heraldry:

"This surname, at first sight, invites the hasty conclusion that it belongs to the class of nick-names, with a suggestion of foreign origin. 'The son of Avis' is plainly put in just so many words, thus apparently pointing to a direct personal name, but, as will be shown, the origin is local, or locational, and has no relation with avis, a bird. It seems to be a form of Anglo-Saxon name variously spelled as Haweis, flaws, Hawes, Hawisia, Hawice, Hawaiess, Haweyse, etc., all of which are used to designate, generically, the various species of haws, and best characterized by the English hawthorne - Grataegus oxayacanthus. The very general use of this bush as a hedge renders haw and hedge almost synonymous. A hedge implies a limit or boundary, also an enclosed space, such as that surrounding or adjoining a house, as in the garth of the haigh, or haugh, of Scotland. The idea of protection stands prominently forward and this carries with it the suggestion of a home. It may be assumed that the name AVIS is a corruption of Hawis - a change favored by the neglected aspirate as well as the transposed w - and that those who originally bore that name were so called because they resided in a locality in which the hawthorn formed a prominent feature of the landscape, or surrounded the home."

The article went on to say that men having these names were to be found as far south in England as Cornwall and that they were to be found in all walks of life - from the nobility to the humblest - some had been great loyalists while others had been equally great rebels. The name is found in English court records as far back as the time of King Alfred. However, the heraldry record says that the family seems to have had its origin in Yorkshire and there most of the Avisons are to be found.

Why Oliver? Why R?

The name "Oliver" had been given to my brother who had been born and had also died before my birth, in honor of Oliver Cromwell, the soldier; Oliver Goldsmith, the author and minister; and Oliver Wendell Holmes, the poet - three men whom my father greatly admired. When his first son died in early infancy and the next child was a boy, my father, determined to have an Oliver in the family if possible, gave me the name in the hope that I would be like at least one of his favorites. However, I failed to choose for a career anyone of the occupations of those whose name was given me.

As for the "R," it is simply an insertion. As a school boy, I noticed that nearly all the boys had two given names and that their three initials made a nicer appearance than my two, "O. A."; so I began to experiment with the letters of the alphabet not only to see which one would look best between the "O" and "A" but also be most easily written in combination with them. After much typing, I chose "R." Without securing anyone's permission, I began using it regularly as part of my signature and, after more than sixty years of undisputed use of it, I would scarcely recognize my signature without it.

My maternal grandfather was Joseph Bray, but I do not remember what his business was. Many years after our family had gone to Canada, he left his English home to join us. I remember how he jocularly described his trip across the ocean as "crossing the big pond." He lived in our home for several years, passing away after I had grown to young manhood.

My maternal grandmother's maiden name was Sykes. I do not remember her and have no knowledge whatever of her family, though I have since met many people of that name and found that all of them came from Yorkshire, in or near Huddersfield, which was the chief town of the district in which I was born but I have never been able to trace any connection between them and my mother's family.

One of my sons recently (during the summer of 1938) visited Yorkshire and tried to find some of his father's people. In doing so, he found them still occupying places in varied social strata. The one he liked best was a public accountant who, my son told me, greatly resembles my son Raymond. From him he learned that one Avison lived in "the big house," the manor, and one was a surgeon in Buckingham Palace. I think that is a good point at which to drop the consideration of my forebearers and possible family connections.

Both my parents were brought up in a district where schools were very rare, and where none but people of means could have the privileges of learning and, probably, it was this dearth of educational opportunities that made my parents anxious to give their own children as good an education as their circumstances would permit. Like all other sons of working men of that day my father had to go to work when a mere lad. He entered the woolen factory when only six years of age, working the twelve hours a day which were the daily labor hours at that time. He grew up with a great fondness for books, avidly reading everything that came his way in the form of biography, history, and poetry, and learned by rote many of the best poems of that day. I have heard him tell how he and another young mill worker used to go out to neighboring towns to give whole evenings of entertainment, each alternating in the recitation of poetry. On one occasion when his chum was unable to go with him, he supplied the entertainment for the whole evening. This love for reading continued through his entire life and, even while I was still a boy, he was regarded as one of the best read men in the neighborhood in which we lived. While he did not avoid fiction his mind was largely stored with the more serious writings of his time. One of his favorite poets was Charles Mackay, a contemporary of his father, and I, too, learned to admire his writings, some of which helped materially in the formation of my ideals.

During those days many of the great economists of England lived and wrote.

It was the time when the invention of machinery for spinning, weaving and other kinds of work required in the woolen manufacturing industry, threatened to replace large numbers of workers. It was also a period of great controversy between the owners of the plants and the workers who were thus displaced by this new machinery or feared they might be displaced in time.

As a boy, I used to hear my father discuss these questions with guests in our home. He used to tell how, because of these conditions, his father became a member of the radical party and how he also became imbued with so-called radical doctrines. The manufacturers and nobility were naturally Tories or Conservatives; the workers were just as naturally members of the Whig or Liberal or Reform Party and staunch upholders of the doctrine of free trade. Even in his later years my father never lost those early impressions and continued, throughout his life, to vote for the Liberal Party, even in Canada, though many of his best friends in later years were not only Conservatives but also representatives of the Conservative Party in the Dominion Government. Even when I was quite a grown boy in Canada, the mills were still working eleven hours a day: the Liberal Party had advanced their claims for more leisure time by only one hour in all those years between my father's boyhood and my own. As I listened to those conversations it was but natural that my political and economic ideas should be largely molded by the viewpoints so forcibly expressed by my father viewpoints learned from the school of his own and his parents's bitter experiences.

Immigration to the 'New World'

Feeling the common urge to better his condition, my father had been considering the question of emigration to one of the British colonies and, before I was six years old, he took us all to the United States, intending to settle in Illinois where one of his closest friends had preceded him, though he had first planned to go to New Zealand. Whether this would have turned out better I do not know. Years ago New Zealand adopted an entirely different economic policy from that of any of the other British colonies and became the most prosperous of all the colonies or dominions, having less unemployment than they and almost no poverty. However, as it came about, we actually settled in Canada.

In February, 1866, we sailed from Liverpool for New York on the steamship "City of Boston." We were but emigrants, of course, and never got a glimpse of the first-class accomodations. My recollection of our sleeping quarters is of bunks two stories high and so broad that we children had to creep over one another and lie in rows. There was scant airspace and several other families occupied the same room. The voyage lasted fourteen days. As I now think of those two weeks, it seems as though the days were nearly all stormy and that the ship rolled and tossed continually. To the great discomfort of everybody, nearly all of the occupants of those quarters were seasick most of the time. But, no matter how sick we were, the captain often compelled us to go out on deck to get fresh air. We would have much preferred to stay quietly where we were, for our going out did not depend upon the steadiness of the ship or the absence of winds but upon the presence or absence of rain. On one occasion when we were on deck the ship rolled so that the waves swept over the deck and washed an old lady down the hatchway to the room below. As this led the captain to give us all permission to go below deck we did not regard the old lady's accident as an unmixed evil. Following the good old English custom, Plum-puddings were served as the main dish of every Sunday dinner. We all had as much as we could eat and nothing more to our taste could have been served. I suppose that is why, even after seventy-five years, I can see those puddings and almost taste them as I think back to that wonderful but fearful journey.

"The City of Boston" was regarded as one of the best ships of her day but, alas, she was lost on her return trip. The only report as to what happened to her came from a note found in a corked bottle that was picked up in the wide waste of waters. It said, "The 'City of Boston' is on fire and we have no hope."

In due time our ship landed in New York at the Immigrant Station on a little island just off the lower end of Broadway, called Castle Garden. My only recollection of the occurrences there was of the long delay caused by the examination of the immigrants so that we did not land until late in the evening. My father had decided not to stay in New York but go right on into Connecticut where one of his brothers was living so we immediately took a train for Winnipauk, now called South Norwalk. It was pouring rain and the night was dark when we arrived there and, as no word of our coming had reached my uncle, no one met us at the station. But someone directed us to his house and we started out on foot along the muddy roadway. Walking was very difficult and some of us lost our overshoes in the clay mud. Two of our family were younger than I and Father and Mother had to carry them all the way. Though my mother declared several times she could go no farther we pressed on and reached the house.

Two of my father's brothers were living there together. The oldest one,

Thomas, was married and had several children. The second one, George, was still unmarried. Uncle Thomas was a sober man and had a good home but Uncle George, an old soldier, had acquired drinking habits and drinking always made him vicious. My memory of him is chiefly of the times he came home drunk. We dreaded his corning into the house because he would seize one of us children and dash him to the floor.

Uncle Thomas had married an American lady and had given up his British citizenship. Those who change their opinions or nationality sometimes become over-zealous for their new loyalties, and so it was with my uncle. He was far more American than those born to the soil. I remember on one occasion when my father was trying to put the baby to sleep by walking around the room with it in his arms while he sang a well known patriotic song beginning with the line, "There is a land, a well-known land, though it is but a little spot, ⋯" My uncle jumped up and, in a low voice, forbad his brother ever again to sing that British song in his house. This so angered my father that the two brothers almost had a quarrel for my father was thoroughly British.

Settlement in Canada

We did not remain with these relatives long as my father wished to visit one of his brothers in Canada. On reaching Brantford in Western Ontario, where my uncle James was living, we found that he, like my father and other uncles, was in the woolen manufacturing business, all of them having become "boss finishers." He had lived in Massachusetts before taking up his residence in Canada and had there married an American wife but had retained his British citizenship.

During our visit to Brantford, we were taken to see the Indian Reservation situated just outside the town. I must have heard tales of Indian raids before we left England, even though I was very young, for I can still recall how I shrank back in fear as we drew near the Indian encampment lest they come out after us and perhaps scalp us.

While we were in Brantford I first began to realize the difference in the use of words in England and in Canada. When my cousins would say, "Would you like to go down to the shops?" they meant, "Let us go down to the mitts." To me a shop meant a place where goods are sold but I found my cousins called that a store, while that which I had always heard spoken of as a mitt was known to them as a shop. I was alert to grasp all such differences. We found their way of counting money very different from ours. We were puzzled by the words dollar and cent and were unable for a considerable time to count our money or even to pay for what we bought without help. But while our cousins laughed at us for the strange words we used, they tried patiently to teach us how to speak Canadian. Another difficulty was with the letter h. It was quite a while before we were able to put our h's in or leave them out in accordance with Canadian usage. Our parents never reached a point where they were quite sure when to sound them and when not to. As for myself, after twelve years of constant attendance at Canadian schools and graduation from high school, I made a slip when I attended the model school of the county. Having been asked one day to dictate a paragraph to one of the classes, I suddenly dropped an h to the great amazement and amusement of the children and to my own chagrin. Though I turned it off with a laugh, I realized how difficult it is to get away from the pronunciations we have learned in early childhood. Even today, I suppose, I am not entirely free from such a danger though very rarely does it now occur.

When my uncle learned that our father was intending to go to Illinois, he began trying to dissuade him from going there, declaring that Canada was a much better place to live in. He pointed out that there would be many difficulties to meet, particularly for one who had never done any farming, which work my father was planning to undertake. As uncle said he could get my father a good position at his own kind of work father at length yielded to his urging.

This changed the entire course of my life. Had we gone to Illinois, I should probably have been a somewhat rabid American, whereas I am still a loyal British subject. I am not a fanatical Britisher, however, for I have lived so much among Americans and have had so many business dealings with them that I know them well and have a sincere affection for them and a high regard for their nation.

The position in woolen manufacturing which my uncle James secured for my father was in a little village called Weston, situated about eight miles northwest of Toronto on the Humber River. This river provided the power for the running of the mill which was the chief industry of the village. There my father followed the good old English custom of going for a "walk" every Sunday morning, often taking us children with him. I was going to say a "stroll" but that term is not correct when applied to the walks taken by English people. Often we really walked miles and seldom strolled. A favorite route was out along the Grand Trunk Railway, across the railroad bridge which spanned what seemed to me then like a deep chasm, at the bottom of which ran two rivers. I can remember how I clung to my father's hand as we stepped on the bridge, never daring to look down between the ties lest I should be overcome with dizziness. Some years ago, while visiting Weston, I set out to find the bridge and cross it to get that thrill again but, though I found the bridge, I sought in vain for the deep chasm. As for the bridge, it was a comparatively short one, spanning two small streams at a height of not more than fifteen or twenty feet and there was no thrill. What a disappointment that was!

In Weston I had my first experience with Santa Claus. I remember how strange was the story of St. Nicholas and his reindeer and how, on that first Christmas Eve in the Western World, my sister and I determined we would stay awake and meet the old gentleman as he came down the chimney with his pack. But we fell asleep and awoke the next morning only to find that he had come and gone without our making his acquaintance.

One of the homes in which we lived had an orchard, some trees bearing luscious cherries and the barn behind the orchard was a grand place to play in. In it I had an experience with a hatchet very different from that of George Washington. A cousin of ours, who was a cabinet-maker, used the barn as a workshop. I was greatly interested in what he did and watched him use various kinds of tools amongst which was a sharp hatchet. One day I wanted to split a piece of wood so I took the hatchet, and not being able to make the wood stand up by itself, I sat on a stool and placed the block between my knees. I raised the hatchet and brought it down-no, not on the block of wood but on my left knee cap. At first I was surprised; then when I saw the blood flowing I flung the hatchet from me and fled to the house, crying. Pus formed, "proud flesh" grew on it and I was kept from school. Neighbors came in, each with a good cure for "proud flesh." I remember one of these as an astonishing example of the crude ideas of only a few decades ago. We were told to secure some fresh cow manure and put it on the wound like a poultice, which would quickly destroy the proud flesh. Of course we tried it but without the favorable results. In the course of time the wound healed but the scar still remains to remind me of the foolishness of a small boy that "knew it all."

A very important political event occurred while we lived in Weston. By the confederation of all the Canadian Colonies of Great Britain, all of Canada, except Newfoundland, was organized into one Dominion. Newfoundland is still a separate self-governing colony of England and not a part of the Dominion of Canada. The Confederation Act was agreed to by the Colonies of Cape Breton, Nova Scotia, Prince Edward Island, Lower Canada (Quebec), Upper Canada

(Ontario), and British Columbia, with all the territory between them and to the far north left unorganized. This had been approved by the Government of Great Britain and the new setup was to go into operation on the first of July, 1867. July 1st, has ever since been celebrated as Dominion Day just as July 4th is kept in the U. S. A. as Independence Day. It was a very important event because it was the beginning of that self-government in Canada which has gradually developed until now the autonomy of the Dominion has been so enlarged as to constitute it a separate nation within the bounds of the British Empire. This is true to such an extent that Canada now not only has control of her own taxation but of her customs regulations also, and within the sixtieth year of her establishment as a Dominion, has set up her own diplomatic agencies in various countries, thus gaining recognition as being on an equality with the other recognized sovereign countries of the world. This is an entirely new political development in world history. Never before has it been considered possible for apart of an empire to be recognized by that empire and by other nations as an independent and sovereign nation while still owing allegiance to the head of the mother nation; so it can be said that what took place in Canada in the first day of July, 1867, marked one of the most far-reaching epochs in both ancient and modern history. It was my privilege to witness the first celebration of that event and I am glad that I was old enough to take in its significance. I have lived long enough to see the successful carrying out of the principles then established over a period of more than seventy years and their extension to other parts of the Empire. These separate parts of the British Empire are now spoken of as together constituting the British Commonwealth of Nations.

How well I remember the first Dominion Day celebration in Weston, July 1, 1867! The whole village spent the day on the commons. What fun for all! For the first time I saw young men trying to climb a greasy pole, while others tried to catch a greased pig - and I saw many pastimes entirely new to recent comers from the old country. Dominion Day is still celebrated in Canada much as Independence Day is observed in the United States of America. The difference between the two is that the fourth of July in the United States commemorates the separation of the American Colonies from the mother country and the first of July commemorates the uniting of the Crown Colonies into a practically independent Dominion still retaining a vital connection with the mother country. The seventy-four years that have elapsed have shown the wisdom of Canadian Statesmen, led by Sir John A. MacDonald, Conservative, and Sir Oliver Mowatt, Liberal, who devised the Constitution of the Dominion so that it pleased the people of Canada and also met the approbation of the statesmen of Great Britain and developed a loyalty not of submission but of collaboration.

My Elementary Education

It was in Weston I got my first realization of war, though I had heard my father reading aloud in the evenings from a history of the slavery war in the United States and had been impressed by the fact that closely related people, even brothers and fathers and sons, had fought on opposite sides, sometimes meeting one another in battle, in the struggle between North and South. The accounts of this kind of war, involving such awful things as were set forth in that book, produced in my mind a horror for war itself which has affected all my thinking ever since, though I have not become what is known as a Pacifist, and now the threat of war by hands of Irish patriots in the United States was facing Canadians! Even as early as 1867 many of the Irish were clamoring for separation from Great Britain and had formed themselves into groups of Fenians[3] to make troubles for the British Government. They believed that many of their countrymen in the U. S. A. would join them if they actually got over into Canada and so they threatened an invasion of Canada. They tried but failed for they were driven back by a volunteer Canadian army when they attempted to cross the Niagara River and the incident, as far as outward manifestations were concerned, was closed. But the feelings of Canadians toward the United States Government were considerably aroused. They felt that it had committed an unfriendly act toward a country at peace with it, in having permitted a group of its citizens to drill openly and prepare munitions for an armed attack. I was but a boy at the time but I was affected by all the expressions of resentment I heard from my parents and neighbors. It required many years for this resentment to die down - indeed, the Canadians of that generation never really lost it. It was very different today, for only feelings of ardent friendship are felt and the closest possible alliance that does not interrupt relationship with Great Britain is warmly welcomed by all Canadians

---

3   The term "Fenian" was applied principally to a group of Irishmen who, being enthusiastic advocates of home rule in Ireland, had banded themselves together to set up trouble in Canada for the British Government, in the hope of forcing a settlement in England of the question of home rule in Ireland.

As most of the Fenians were Roman Catholics, these occurrences also served to emphasize the opposition of Protestants in Ontario to Roman Catholicism. This opposition was led by a society of extreme Protestants known as Orangemen.[4] The organization grew to be very influential in Canada, especially around Toronto and throughout Protestant Ontario.[5]

These events which occurred so near together had much to do with my mental development and, presumably, I might have been a rabid Orangeman had my father's opinions been less broad than they were. His conversations, to which I so often listened, were free from fanaticism and were always for peace and unity.

One of the pleasure of those days was to go on a business trip to Toronto with my mother and father in a light wagon. When crossing some weak-looking bridge my father would start a discussion as to whether it is better to drive quickly across a bridge that looks frail, or to cross it slowly. I would begin thinking pro and con. My father would express his own opinion, or illustrate by driving both ways in order to let me note the different effects. Afterwards I noticed that, in travelling over dangerous bridges, trains go across slowly, so I came to the conclusion that this must be the safer plan. By asking me those questions my father was endeavoring to train me to think for myself and to encourage me to form my own judgment as to why certain methods of doing things were better than other ways.

It was in Weston that I began my school life in Canada. The first day I went to school a class was conducted in writing and the teacher asked me what hand I wrote. When I answered by holding up my right hand the teacher and pupils laughed. I saw no reason for their laughter until it was explained to me that she did not want to know with which hand I wrote but whether I wrote in large letters or small ones. Even at that early age I learned that there is such a thing as technical language and that if I desired to get on well with my studies I must first learn to know what was meant by the words used.

---

[4]   The name originated from William Prince of Orange, who had defeated the armies of the so-called Pretender to the throne of England on July 12, 1689, a Roman Catholic who planned to make Roman Catholicism the national religion of England.

[5]   Seventy years after the attempted invasion of Canada, that animosity has not entirely disappeared and many of the descendants of the Orangemen still celebrate the 12th of July every Year. They parade the streets and denounce Roman Catholicism according to the methods practiced in the days of Fenianism, endeavoring to keep alive the sentiment against Catholics. But these parades are now largely a matter of custom. The Catholics turn out to see them and though the paraders look very fierce it is all a semblance and, as soon as the day is over, all meet together again as good friends and neighbors.

Like most other schools of the time, we had frequent visitors who would examine our writing or hear us recite our lessons. Then the teacher would ask the visitor to say a few words to us. I noticed that each one referred to his own boyhood days and always said that discipline was more rigid when he was young. Children had to obey their parents and their teachers then but, alas, in these modern days, he would say, obedience to authority is scouted and children do much as they please. He would then go on to say this might lead us into a great deal of trouble and he would exhort us to avoid these evil ways and learn to be obedient to those in authority. As I listened I thought he certainly had not had much experience with my parents. And now, after seventy years, I find visitors to schools still making the same old speech and still feeling that modern children are going to the dogs!

It was in Weston I learned to swim. My father did his best to overcome my fear of the water by taking me on his back and swimming across the river, but that was of very little help. I really learned to swim when I went out with a crowd of boys and followed the gang where I would not have dared to go alone so, when I was but a small boy, I learned to swim and dive like the rest. I had my first experience herewith an ice-jam in a part of the river which was very narrow. Though I was but a little fellow, I watched with great interest the efforts of the men to relieve the jam in order to avoid the piling up of the water which would threaten the mill. How the fears of the people rose almost to a panic as the efforts of the men seemed to be futile! What a thrill came as a piece of ice was set loose, for it might relieve the whole jam! Watching the process we observed a real feat in engineering and that work so interested me that I thought then I would become a civil engineer.

While we were in Weston hard times struck the woolen industry and the mill had to be shut down. I was too young to understand this fully but I knew my parents were very anxious. The owner decided to transfer his machinery to another town and asked my father to go with him so we had the excitement of moving to the new location, a town called Campbellford, not far from the mouth of the River Trent. This river was large, as compared with the Humber, and I greatly admired the length of the main bridge. I was thrilled by the depth of the water which was held back by a large dam just below the bridge to provide waterpower for the various mills built further down stream. My father rented a small house on the commons not far from the mill and there we lived and had a garden and kept cows and hens.

The River Trent provided good fishing - black bass, rock bass, Pickerel, and pike - and I took a great interest in this sport, I heard, too, of the great musk-ellunge which inhabited the waters of the lake higher up. These were said to be several feet long, and to weigh thirty to forty pounds. I never had the chance to catch these monsters of the deep, for so they seemed to us boys, though I did see some that had been caught and so knew that they really existed.

In Campbellford I had my first contact with death for I was drowned there by proxy. As I was late getting home from school one day my mother began to worry and, when a neighbor ran in to tell her boy had been drowned in the river, she ran frantically to the spot. A crowd had already gathered and men in boats were searching the deep water above the dam for the body. According to report I had been seen floating on a raft that I could not control. Then, suddenly, I appeared in the crowd! What had happened? A boy had been seen as was claimed, but he was not Oliver - he was Oliver's chum, and he was really drowned. His body was found next day. The funeral was held in accordance with the custom of those days. As abundance of refreshments, solid and liquid, were on the table for those who attended, often a funeral became an orgy. It is a matter for congratulation that feasting is no longer a part of such a solemn ceremony.

While in the Campbellford school the first 24th of May that I can recollect approached and, with it, my interest in Queen Victoria was first aroused, for the 24th of May was her birthday. I was told by the other pupils that it would be a school holiday but, lest the teacher should for any reason overlook it, we all sang out in school:

"The 24th of May is the Queen's birthday!
If you don't give us a holiday, we'll all run away."

To my surprise, the teacher showed no signs of irritation although this was done during a school hour. She just smiled and said nothing. The day arrived ultimately and was celebrated with an unlimited use of fireworks, plenty of ginger beer and other popping drinks. On one occasion when I had a coatpocket full of firecrackers a mischievous imp threw a lighted cracker into that particular pocket. You should have seen me jump! It certainly gave my mother a' job to remake that pocket. No, all the pranks and thoughtlessness of youth are not of recent development!

Evidently Queen Victoria was greatly beloved, for I noticed that many men when speaking of her would start by saying, "The Queen, God bless her ---"

One particular experience in that school either made manifest my natural bend or helped to develop a state of mind, I do not know which. A quarrel had arisen between me and my closest chum, Walter Farrand, the son of the owner of the woolen mill in which my father was a superintendent. This quarrel gave the other boys great delight, and they egged us on. Finally, they decided for us that things had come to such a pass that the dispute could only be settled by fighting. This was to take place behind. the school building that afternoon immediately after school was dismissed. I had no particular desire to fight - indeed the quarrel did not call for a fight - but the other boys were determined to have one. Though Walter was set against it, I declared myself ready to go on with it, for to call it off would have been too great a disappointment to the other boys.

So, shortly after four o'clock, we faced each other and the boys surrounded us in a ring. Just then the principal came around the comer, wanting to know what we were doing. Naturally a quick retreat took place but not before he had ordered us to see him the next day. The following morning he called us up before the whole school and asked us what it was all about. Walter declared that no fight was to have taken place while I insisted to the contrary. The principal dismissed us with a warning and we retired to our seats. Fortunately the matter caused no break in our friendship. I have wondered whether my actions on that occasion were the result of plain obstinacy or of a feat of public opinion if I should decline a fight that the rest of the boys felt ought to take place. Whatever it was, I was always more careful afterwards about consenting to follow a course contrary to my own judgment.

Mr. Farrand seemed to be a restless man, for, not having developed a better business even in this new location, he again decided to move. This time my father declined to go with him and soon found a position in the village of Lanark farther east. His new work was not in a rented mill, but in one owned by the manager and that gave it a greater promise of permanency.

Several things happened in that village which affected my attitudes and ideas. One was a very severe thunderstorm in which the lightning struck one of my friends and rendered him unconscious. Though he recovered the experience left me with a fear of lightning that I did not overcome for many years.

Another occurrence was an epidemic of scarlet fever that carried off some of my playmates. In that day the germ theory was unknown, even to physicians, and the real causes of so many epidemic diseases were therefore undiscovered secrets. As a preventive measure everyone carried on his or her person a piece of camphor and I was careful to follow the custom, but even so I contracted the disease and was quite sick though never in any danger, I believe. My parents took care of me without the aid of a doctor and the other members of the household went about their business as usual. Onion poultices were applied to the soles of my feet to draw the inflammation from my throat and similar applications were made to my neck. These were regarded as very effective. As a matter of fact, the inflammation began to leave my throat soon after the application of the poultice and of course it was taken for granted that the lightness of the attack was due to the camphor I carried around. Perhaps if I had carried a larger piece I might have entirely escaped the disease!

While going to school in that village I had the good fortune to study under a principal who believed, that children should be given special training in the four elementary principles of arithmetic, addition, subtraction, multiplication, and division. Every afternoon the more advanced pupils were sent down to one of the lower rooms where the teacher gave us practice in performing those fundamental exercises rapidly and still more rapidly. Problems in addition, for instance, were placed on the blackboard and the pupils were asked to add the figures as fast as the teacher's pointer was passed up the line. The speed was gradually increased until we could add a line of figures as fast as the teacher could point to them. When we had become proficient in adding one line at a time we were taught to add two lines at a time. Later we did three columns at once, and by that time remarkable proficiency in adding had been gained. We were then put through the other arithmetical processes in a similar way. I found this training a great advantage to me in after years, for I could always finish my problems in arithmetic much more quickly than others who had not had it and so was able to keep at or near the head of my classes in mathematics. Later, in the practical application of arithmetic to business problems, I found I could sur- pass most of my fellows in everything pertaining to the use of figures, I have of- ten wondered why this training is not more emphasized in all schools. It makes the pupils not only quicker in figuring but, in my estimation, it sharpens their faculties for the quick consideration of all other kinds of problems.[6]

My life in that village did other things for me for which I have been very grateful. We were Methodists but there was no Methodist Church in that com- munity which was largely Scotch. There was a Presbyterian Church, of course, and two others, Congregational and Episcopal. My father chose to attend the

[6]   This idea is controverted by present day psychologists who claim that a speed ability in one line does not give one greater facility in other realms of thought. I think this is contrary to experience.

Congregational Church. At that time there was no interchange of pulpits. Ministers of different denominations did not meet together even on the platform of the town hall. On one occasion, however, the temperance people of all the churches joined in holding a community gathering in the town hall to which the ministers of the three churches were invited. They accepted and, for the first time, those ministers sat together on one platform. Each gave an address and it was interesting to hear all three refer to the new experience they were having, and each asked his parishioners to take note that, whatever differences existed in their theological views, they were united in their opinions concerning the dire effect of alcoholic liquors. Since then, the churches have moved, forward toward greater unity, though they are far from that degree of oneness that is imperative as well as desirable if they are to win the world to Godliness. The broadmindedness of my parents is shown by the fact that after we moved into a house about a mile outside the village limits we attended the Episcopal Church which was the nearest one and the one with which most of our immediate neighbors were connected. The effect on me was that, though, when we moved to another town, we returned to the Methodist fold, I, without compunction served that connection and went to the mission field with my family under Presbyterian auspices when my own denomination could not send us out.

The new house, outside the village limits, was near a country school, and so we children were not entirely deprived of educational facilities. There I had my first taste of life in a "little red school- house." Not far from the school was a large tamarack swamp, and one of the most interesting relaxations of the pupils was to wander through the swamp in search of tamarack gum, which we brought home in great chunks. This kept us well supplied with chewing material long before Wrigley or any other gum manufacturers had discovered that fortunes could be made by supplying the world with something to keep their jaws going between meals.

Though our teacher was a very pleasant young woman, she tried to rule the school with a severity to which she was quite unaccustomed in other walks of life. During one noon hour we pupils had all gone to the woods in search of gum and had wandered, far without realizing the distance we had gone so that it was mid-afternoon when we returned. The teacher told us we would have to stay after four o'clock to make up for the time we had lost - a decree to which we could not reasonably object though we did not like it. Just after four, however, a young man from the farmhouse where the teacher boarded drove up to the school, expecting to have the pleasure of taking the young lady home. The moment we saw him enter we realized that this was an opportunity for us to escape. Jumping up we seized our caps and made for the door. The poor teacher! She saw the uselessness of trying to call us back and went home with her friend and we never heard anything more about making up the time we had lost, she afterwards became the young man's wife.

Worker of Woolen Mills

The mill in Lanark being a small one, and my farther being always on the lockout for opportunities to improve his financial condition, it was not surprising that before long we moved to the town of Almonte, some twenty miles away, where there were several large mills. I was then about nine years old. I entered the public school at Almonte, and before I was eleven was advanced to the senior class. Even at that early age we were initiated into the mysteries of vulgar fractions and decimals, into proportion or the "rule of three", and into the "rule of practice."

I began to grow weary of school life and felt a strong impulse to become a factory worker and begged my father to take me into his department at the mill. Though he was very much averse to this, as his own experience had taught him the great value of an education, he finally yielded to my wishes. My mother fitted me out with the overalls which were commonly worn by the mill workers and I proudly donned them. Father preferred to have me work under some other superintendent than himself, so I was put to work on a picking machine. A picking machine consists of a cylinder studded with spikes which revolves rapidly inside a casing similarly studded. My work was to feed into this machine portions of wool that were knotted together and could not be put into the general mass of wool until they had been combed out. We also fed into it pieces of cloth which had been cut off the ends of bolts in order to even them up for nothing that would make cloth could be thrown away. By this process the fibers of the wool were broken up into shorter fibers so that cloth made from it would not be as strong as that made from the original wool but when it had been well worked up and mixed with a quantity of long-fibered wool, it made yarn almost as strong as that made only from new wool.

I began work at a daily wage of forty cents or about ten dollars a month. I worked eleven hours a day, six days in the week, a total of sixty-six hours each week. I often think now of those days when I had to rise early enough to get my breakfast and be down at the mill at half past six in the morning even though I was only eleven. We worked until noon and then had an hour to go home to dinner. We had to be back to start at one o'clock from which time we worked without intermission till six thirty in the evening. At the end of the workday we went home for supper and such amusement as we could get out of the remaining hours before bedtime. We had to go to bed early in order to be ready to rise with the early morning bell and so go through the routine of another day with Sunday our only day of rest.

After working for some time on the picking machine I was advanced to a position on a spinning machine or jack, and my wages were increased to forty-five cents a day. This machine occupied a space about sixty feet long and fifteen feet wide. At its back were placed great cylinders of the carded wool that had been made up into fluffy rolls about half an inch in thickness, each roll to be spun into yarn out of which cloth was woven. The jack consisted of a stationary section holding the spindles which revolved very rapidly and twisted the carded rolls into yarn. Another operation of the machine was to wind the yarn on the spools. In this rapid twisting of the yarn, if there was too much tension on the spool, or if any strands of yarn were weaker and unable to stand the normal strain, the yarn would break. It was the business of bobbin-boys to watch for these broken strands. Each boy had to watch a section and pick up the ends and put them together so that the two ends would be spun together without leaving a knot. Sometimes, when the machine was running well and the wool was of good long fiber, the breaking of threads would be infrequent and we could, sit down and talk together and rest. This work required more skill than my former work had done and I felt I was making an advance.

The boys with whom I worked had had almost no education. They could barely read and write, and. had very little knowledge of arithmetic and I had already become a senior in the public school before coming to the mill, they regarded me as well educated and asked me to organize a night school for them. After talking it over with my father I consented, and a class of eager pupils was soon enrolled. Both teacher and pupils had already worked eleven hours each day, but three evenings a week the class met at my home and worked diligently at the three R's for two hours. As I look back on those busy days and evenings I realize the physical and mental strain of those long hours but at the time it did not feel so hard. The boys learned quickly for they were in earnest and I, too, gained much for teaching others develops the teacher as much as it does the pupils. As the class advanced to the study of fractions I reviewed my own former problems so that when the time came for me to return to school I was ready to catch up the work just where I had dropped it when I left to enter the mill.

My next advance in the mill came when my father decided to take me into his own department. There I was taught to run a machine called a shearer. When the cloth has been woven both surfaces are rough, and the pattern can be but dimly seen and it has to be put through several processes before it is ready for the market. These are all performed in the finishing department over which my father was superintendent. After the cloth has been fulled till it becomes thickened and firm in texture, it is gigged so as to raise a nap on its patterned surface and then is run through a shearing machine which cuts off the nap in the same way that a lawnmower cuts grass. This leaves a smooth surface with the pattern showing distinctly, I received fifty cents a day for this type of work. As other boys doing similar work were paid sixty cents, I thought I should get that rate but, though I petitioned several times for it, my father refused to raise my wages lest it might be said he was advancing his own son too rapidly. This argument didn't satisfy me but I had to put up with it.

I worked in this mill altogether about two years, during which time I saw the eleven-hour-day system changed first to a ten-and-a-half-hour- day and later to a ten-hour-day. These changes were brought about after considerable discussion between the owners of the mills and the workmen. Although my father's position as superintendent was but little below that of the owners, he took sides with the workmen in favor of shorter hours, I can even yet remember the arguments he used in talking with the masters. He said the men became very tired before the end of the eleven hour day so that the latter part of the afternoon was a period of slow production and, if the hour of work should be shortened, the men would carry on throughout the entire day with greater energy and production would be increased. It was hard to convince the masters whose profits depended upon the speed of production but, in time, they agreed to try out the shorter day. It was decided that during the first five days of the week the hours of work should remain the same but on Saturday afternoon work should stop at half-past three, bringing the average to ten and a half hours a day. The reason for adopting this method instead of reducing by half an hour each day was that the workmen themselves preferred to have the weekly three hours of freedom all at once so they might have enough time for outdoor sports or other forms of recreation. After a few months it became evident that my father's argument was being justified for the production was actually greater than it had been under the old system.

Within a comparatively abort period the workmen applied for a still further shortening of hours of work to an average of ten hours per day. This petition was granted all the more readily because of the results that had come from the first test. Under the ten-hour system production again rose beyond that of the ten-and-a-half-hour system and everyone was pleased. This time the cut was made by starting work in the morning at seven o'clock instead of half-past six, greatly relieving the pressure on all the workers.

One Saturday afternoon, when we were about to leave the mill, my father surprised me by saying, "Well, Oliver, this will be your last day here." I asked him why it was to be my last day, and was I being dismissed. I wanted to know what for. "Well," he said, "I have been watching you and have come to the conclusion that perhaps you have had enough of this and will be glad to get back to school again. I have noticed, too, that you are not as strong as you were. You are pale, and I think a rest will do you good. You have stuck it out pretty well." I said. nothing in reply but I felt a great thankfulness welling up within me for I had certainly had all I wanted though I had never grumbled.

The following Monday morning when the milkman, a farmed named John Watson, came around with the day's supply of milk and saw me playing outside instead of being at the mill, he wanted to know what I was doing at home. When I told him I had stopped work and was to return to school, he said, "That's fine! There's nothing like an education for a boy! If you get an education, you'll be able to make your living without having to take off your coat." That was his highest conception of the value of an education end I am not sure but what I agreed with him at the time. For a long period and through long hours of toil I had been asking my living with my coat on. The thought of being able to get a better living without such long hours in the midst of so much dirt strongly appealed to me and I suppose that thought is still a powerful incentive to many young men to get an education.

School Life Resumed

When I returned to the school the same principal was there, an old Scotsman named John McCarter, and his greeting was: "Well, Oliver, so you have come back, have you? Now I wonder what class we are to put you in. Let me see. You were in the senior class when you went away but, after being away so long a time, I am afraid you will have forgotten a great deal, and so, perhaps, you had better drop back into the junior class." I heard this with a sinking heart, for I naturally hated to be put back but, without letting him see my disappointment, I took my place with the juniors. Of course he did not know I had been teaching a night school and giving special attention to arithmetic. When the Arithmetic class I was called, he would write a problem on the blackboard. Then each pupil having worked it out on his slate as quickly as he could would lay his slate face down on the master's desk. Gradually the slates were piled up and, when the tine allowed for that problem was ended, the master turned the slates over and marked the first one that was correct with the number "1" in the corner of the slate. The next correct one was marked "2" while those that were incorrect were all marked one number higher than the total in the class. At the end of the class period, the numbers were added and the pupil with the lowest total was given first place. It happened that my slate went in first almost every time and was always correct.

One day a problem was given that stumped every member of the class but me. I worked it out quickly and put my slate on his desk. After waiting several minutes the master looked at my slate and seeing it was correctly worked, almost threw the slate at me and said, "Go to your seat and come up with the senior class tomorrow." That was one of the proudest moments of my life. I walked back to my seat with my head high, I fear. My hours of night school teaching had turned out to me my salvation.

But more was yet to come. This teaching had either sharpened my wits generally or the long vacation had increased my zest for studying, and as a whole I stood high. As the early summer passed and the time for the entrance examination into the high school approached the master stopped at my desk one day and said, "Oliver, have you been thinking about trying the examination?" "No," I answered, "not very much." "Would you like to try it?" I replied that I would if he thought I should. "Well, I think you had better try it," he said. And once more I had a thrill only a degree less than that of the other occasion.

Go on to the High School

Examination time came. I had worked hard. Surprisingly to myself I not only passed but took first place, I hope I am not boasting - I had studied faithfully, probably more earnestly than those who had done nothing else while I was away from school.

My first teacher in the High School was Mr. Wilkie, a small man but a very energetic one, and not very attractive to boys in the "teen" age. One day he got into a dispute with one of the larger boys about some prank the lad was playing. Mr. Wilkie attempted to punish him but the boy seized him and threw him down on one of the desk seats. When the teacher arose from that undignified position he was of course deeply humiliated. I was divided between my admiration of Jim Miller's prowess and my sympathy for the embarrassed teacher. It was the first time I had ever seen such an occurrence but before I finished my high school course I saw it done again - though not by the same persons. It happened only when a high-strung teacher lost control of his temper in his handling of a boy who realized his own strength and felt he was being unduly shamed.

At the end of that school year Mr. Wilkie resigned in order to complete his theological studies in Knox College, Toronto. Then he married one of the public school teachers of our town and they went to India as missionaries. I did not see them again for several years after my graduation as a doctor, and they were on their first furlough. By that time they had several children and when the time came for them to go back to India they left all of them in the care of one of his sisters in Toronto and, asked me to be their medical adviser. I was glad to do this for one who had been my teacher when I was a boy. The parents served many years in India and he died there. The widow returned to Canada to live in Toronto with one of her daughters. I saw her last in 1936.

But it was the headmaster, Mr. P. C. McGregor (P. stood for Peter but he was always referred to in conversation as P. C. without even mentioning his surname which was Campbell, so you can guess his origin). He, of all my teachers, most influenced my thinking process. He came from a farm home in Lanark County between the county town Perth, and the village of Lanark where we had lived before. He was a graduate of Queen's University, Kingston, Ontario and though he never proceeded to any higher degree than B. A., he became one of the most famous high school teachers in Canada. While a student he had suffered from an inflammation of one knee which left it stiff and for years after he came to Almonte he walked only with the help of clutches, but fortunately the stiffness gradually lessened so that he later got along very well with only a stout walking stick to help him.

Very fortunate were the students who were privileged to study under his guidance. His whole thought in life was controlled by two very powerful

Principles: religion and politics. In religion he was a Presbyterian and in politics a Liberal, both of which beliefs prevailed in the neighborhood in which he was born and in the university which he attended. In his teaching he did not ever knowingly attempt to influence his pupils along these lines but none of us could remain unaware of his convictions. As for me, I did not receive any impulse toward Presbyterianism, though the principals of both the public and high schools were Scotch and earnest disciples of John Knox. Perhaps my escape was due to the fact that my father was strongly Methodist and just as firm a believer in its doctrine of free will as they were in predestination.

On the other hand, my home training led me to become a Liberal in politics so that P. C.'s interpretations of current events and history fell on prepared ground and I steadily increased in my leaning toward political liberalism.

While I was a schoolboy in Almonte, probably the most important measure to come up in the Dominion Parliament was the method of financing the building of the Canadian Pacific Railway. Both Conservative and Liberal members agreed on it as necessary to the development of the country, but they clashed on the question of "how." The Conservatives, then in power under the leadership of that greatest of all Canadian Conservative politicians, John A. MacDonald, contended for its construction by a private company assisted by the government but the Liberals were convinced that it should be entirely a government project. The discussion was taken up even by schoolboys who, of course, knew little about the matter except as they heard their elders quarrel over it. P. C. was strong for the Liberal's idea of government construction and probably because of that I became an ardent supporter of that method. When the time for a decision by Parliament came the Conservatives won and the Canadian Pacific Railway Company was organized. A recital of the details of that arrangement does not fall within the lines of these sketches but they were so favorable to the Company that it became one of the wealthiest transportation corporations in the world and, though the competition of the Canadian Government itself which subsequently paralleled all its railway lines as well as its steamship lines under the name of the Canadian National Railways, greatly reduced its volume of business, it still carries on and ranks as, perhaps, the largest company of its kind in the world.

My father was a strong advocate of temperance which in those days was interpreted to mean total abstinence from the use of all drinks containing alcohol. In this respect he differed from many of his fellow countrymen in Almonte. But he had seen some of his brothers succumb to the drinking habit and had come to the conclusion that the safety of the Avisons was to be found only in leaving it alone. However, home-brewed beer, or home brew as it was called, was not then regarded as an alcoholic beverage and my mother kept the family supplied with it. Every day it was served with the noon meal and we children got our share and liked it. Then one evening on returning from his day's work, my father went down into the cellar, brought up the keg of homebrew and carrying it out into the back yard, emptied it into the drain. Shocked, we all cried out against such a waste of good beer and wanted to know why he had done it. He explained that, after having taken his usual mug of home brew for dinner that day and was walking back to the mill, he overheard two men, whom he had just passed, saying "Did you notice the smell of liquor on Simeon Avison's breath? I thought he was a total abstainer and a temperance lecturer. His breath has given him away this time; - he is just a plain hypocrite." This remark, not intended for his ear, affected him so deeply that he decided he would never again touch even homebrewed beer or allow any member of his family to do so if, by so doing, anyone might mistake him for a drinker or if it in any way interfered with his influence as a temperance lecturer in all the districts near our town and his enthusiasm had imbued every member of his family with the desirability of avoiding alcohol in any form so one day, very shortly after I had learned to write and was only tall enough to reach up to the table, I signed the pledge and felt that I had taken a very important step in life.

My father's love for the best literature naturally led him to instill into his children's mind a similar love for good reading. Though none of us ever became such readers as he, we, from our earliest years, learned some of the best poems and sometimes recited them in public. Once I told my father that before I rose to recite and even when I first began to speak I always trembled and thought I could not go on but, by the time I got through the first verse all fear left me and I was able to proceed with ease. His reply that this was generally true of good speakers was very encouraging. However, I cannot say that I have ever become an orator.

During those years of my boyhood father was not a member of the church though he attended its services regularly, taking us with him and mother. We children were always taken to Sunday school too any my mother and sister united with the Methodist Church when I was still too young to think of it. I wondered why my father had not joined with them and why I myself had never been baptized though I was about twelve years old. The reason for this was cleared up, however, when on one occasion I ran across an old diary of mother's. In which he wrote of his early days when he had been reading Voltaire and the book of other "free-thinkers" and radicals. He was much impressed by their arguments and in time professed himself as an agnostic. He didn't throw away his belief in God entirely - he just didn't know. In that state of mind he could not be a church-member though he continued to attend the services and was glad to see his family taking an interests in religion.

When we moved to Almonte he evinced even more personal interest in church work, attending Sunday school and said nothing to others about his personal religious beliefs, so all his friends regarded him as a nominal Christian at least. The superintendent of the Sunday School, who was the leading lawyer of the town and his close friend, evidently thought of him as such for he asked him to become teacher of the Bible class. I remember my father telling me of this and expressing surprise at it. As he was well-read in general literature as well as in the Bible and was a born teacher, his class became very popular. Then one day he surprised me by saying he was going to join the church and would be glad if I would go in with him. That was happy to do. Because I had not been baptized in infancy, as previously explained, I knelt at the altar and received baptism. I must have been then about fourteen or fifteen years of age. Up to that time we had never had family devotions, and did not have grace at table but that very Sunday my father began these rites and they were continued till his death. In fact, this event marked a great and pleasant change in the tenor of all our lives.

Almonte is situated on the Mississippi River - no, not the large river you are thinking of. There are two Mississippi Rivers on the American continent - one in the United States and one in Canada. The one to which I have referred is smaller in every way than the one which flows south into the Gulf of Mexico, but it has reaches of smooth water full of fish and stretches of rapids and falls which make it more interesting and more romantic. Those drops in level make possible the development of great dams which serve as sources of power for driving many woolen mills. Almonte was built where there is a series of such falls and rapids and many woolen mills were erected there, making it, as already stated, the center of the woolen industries of Eastern Ontario. The sources of the river were in the rocky heights to the south and west of our town where extensive forests were still being felled by lumbermen. These were mostly sons of farmers who, in the winter seasons, when farming operations were at a standstill, eked out their incomes in this way. The trunks of these trees were cut into logs which were left round to be sawn into boards or lumber or, if very long and free from many knots, were squared and called, timbers. Both of these were hauled by horses to the banks of the nearest streams large enough to float them. When spring melted the snow and ice and thus caused the water to rise, they were rolled into the streams and piloted down to the main rivers. The men kept up with them and made sure none of them were left on shoals or trapped in the many small inlets. As they moved downwards they put up their tents near the larger villages, most of which had been built where falls and rapids provided waterpower for various purposes, and it was in such places that the lumbermen were kept busy guiding the logs down the slides that carried them past the natural obstructions.

The coming of the logs down the Mississippi every spring was a great event for the boys of the town. Every boy became a lumberman and each provided himself with a pike firmly fastened to one end. This pike had two sharp prongs, one in the direction of the pole for pushing, the other at right angles to it for pulling. Out on the logs we want. What fun it was! The round logs would spin as our bare reel struck then and then we must either try to stay on or jump to another log with the chance of being dumped into the river in either case. That often happened, but who cared? We swam to another and manoevered into a position that made it possible to climb on it, but at other times the log would roll so as to make it is impossible to mount it from the water. Our clothes? Oh, yes, they got wet but our mothers knew about that and had old suits ready for us to wear at such times. There were contests of skill - who could stay on his rolling log the longest? For indeed escaped a ducking in the end. The long square timbers generally floated with one edge up, and though they didn't roll much it was difficult to keep from slipping off their sloping sides.

A visit to the lumbermen's camp was great fun. The cook was nearly always a Lower Canadian(Quebec) who spoke the English and French languages half and half with a dialect peculiar to the habitants. They were generally good natured and glad to see us and well knew what we wanted when we called - a thick slice of that newly baked bread covered with a deep layer of hard butter and washed down with a bowl of strong tea, unspoiled by either sugar or cream. At home a meal like that would have been scorned but, out in the woods, after a scramble on the logs, it was sweet to our keen appetites.

A boy in such a town who couldn't swim was to be pitied. Two of my school chums were in that class and I tried to teach them but each of them nearly drowned me. Once a group of us had gone to swim and were diving off a raft of logs into very deep water. One of those two lads arrived a bit later and, having stripped on shore, ran over the logs to where we were and without a word to us jumped into the deepwater. At the moment I was standing on the boom(a string of single timbers chained end to end to hold the logs at a given place) and knowing George couldn't swim, I watched for him to rise to the surface. Strange to say he rose only till his hair floated on the surface. With a cry of "save the boy," I jumped in and swimming to his back put my hands around his neck and hoisted his head above water. Then I seized him around the waist and swam to the boom. Others had noticed what was happening and when I got near the boom, they dragged him out. When asked why he had jumped. into the deep water, he replied that he thought he might be able to swim if he got into water beyond his depth!

My experience with the second boy was different. After school a group of us decided to go for a swim in a part of the river where there was a comparatively small but deep swimming hole some distance below the town. John wanted to go with us so, as we were passing his home, he asked his father's permission. His father, turning to me, said John could go if I would agree to take care of him. "You know, Oliver, John cannot swim so I am putting a great responsibility on you. - You must take care of him," he said. So off we ran to catch up with the other boys, it was quite a long walk, - or would have been had we been going to get the milk for the house - but what boys ever thought if far to go to a favorite swimming hole?

It didn't take us long to strip and get into the water. All the others could swim and at once dived into the deep part but I led John, much bigger than I, into a shallow place where I could help him. This shallow place was on a ledge of rock that at one side fell suddenly off into deeper water. We got nearer its edge than we knew and suddenly, as John took a step backward., he found himself sinking. He threw his arm about my neck desperately, and down we went together to the bottom, I expected to rise at once as usual but we didn't rise. I worked to unloosen his grip on me and at last succeeded. We rose promptly and as we reached the surface I swam toward his back and, putting my arms around his waist, drew his head above water. I shouted to the other fellows to save him but they were absorbed in their fun and, when they did hear me, they thought we too were playing and paid no attention to us. I worked toward the edge of the pool and a boy sitting there, seeing what was up, reached out to get hold of John and ere long had pulled him ashore. We were both puffing hard and as much alarmed, of course, but I was glad to be able to hand him over to his father alive later on.

Primary School Teacher

I completed my high school course in Almonte and then attended the Model School in Perth, the county town. It was the first session of that school and so it had no previous record to guide the actions of either teachers or students but, when we left it, we were the holders of third class certificates which qualified us to become teachers in public or grade schools.

I began watching the papers for advertisements for teachers and at length saw one for a country school near Smith's Falls, some twenty-five miles from Almonte. I sent an application to the school committee and received a reply asking me to go to see them. They had chosen me out of thirty applicants, they wrote, but felt it would be better for us to meet each other before a final decision was reached, I was to go by train to Smith's Falls and get directions there for the remaining three miles which had to be made on foot unless I could get a ride with some farmer going out that way, "hiking" we call it today.

On arriving at Smith's Falls, I found the bookstore where I was to make enquiry and there learned how to find the home of Mr. William Graham, the chairman of the school board. I then walked the three miles only to find that Mr. Graham had his sons had all gone to town where they expected to meet me.

"You must have passed them on the way," they said at the farm house, "but come in and wait. You cannot get home today as there are no more trains so you will have to stay here till tomorrow anyway. You will be very welcome."

The men soon returned and supper was served. As evening came on I noticed some neighborhood people coming in by twos and threes and all were doffing their wraps and I asked if there was a party on for the evening.

"Yes, indeed, there is a Halloween party. Don't you know it is October thirty-first? All the people of the countryside will be here." And so it turned out. There was a houseful and it was a big farmhouse at that. All who came at first were evidently from similar farmhouses, but later a young man and two ladies came in whose dress and manner proclaimed them as from a town. They and I were the only ones from outside the district. There was plenty of fun for all - Halloween tricks and plays and then to finish the evening there was the inevitable game of forfeits, less played now than then, I think. It was carried on until all in party had given a forfeit, something personal, and then the important feature of the game began. Each person had to redeem his or her forfeit. A judge was chosen, one known by previous experience to have a faculty for dealing out thrilling judgements which must be carried out before the one concerned could redaim his or her property. At last it came the turn of Miss Jennie Barnes, one of the young ladies, or girls I should say from the town. The judge, being blinded, was supposed to know nothing about the identity of the claimant except the sex. This being made known to him, he directed her to kiss the man in the room she liked the best. The poor girl, under sixteen by three months, was embarrassed. She didn't know the young farmers very well and didn't want to kiss any of them; she didn't like to kiss the young man who had brought her from town - that would be too much of a give-away; the only one left was the stranger. He was just past seventeen, smooth faced, rosy complexioned. She could kiss him with the least danger of comment. So she approached the blushing young fellow and did her stunt. She did it well too! Her face was flushed as she claimed her forfeit admist loud applause. And I? How did I feel? I make no confession.

After a time my forfeit came up. I fear the judge had got an inkling of the ownership, for he declared the owner must be immediately married to Jennie Barnes. This brought on louder applause than ever. A guest was chosen to act as minister, all usual formalities were attended to and the mock wedding proceeded to a finish. The bridegroom did his duty by kissing the bride who blushed more rosily than ever. Was it all prophetic? Or was all that followed just a natural sequence of events ? The young couple actually became man and wife nearly eight years afterwards and lived together more than fifty - one years.

The school committee consisted of only three members, Mr. Graham, Mr. Davidson (both present that evening) and Mr. John McDonald. Evidently Mr. Graham and Mr. Davidson had consulted together during the evening, for the next morning they told me their decision was favorable but suggested that we go together to see Mr. McDonald before completing the engagement. When we reached his farm we found him busy plowing and waited till he reached the fence where we were standing. A very interesting dialogue followed.

Mr. Graham : Good morning, Jock, an' hoo are ye the morn's morn?

Mr. McDonald : I'm varry weel, thank ye.

Mr. Graham : Ye weren't oot to the pairty last nicht, Jock, but Davidson and I talked with the young teacher and decided he was a'richt, so we've bro't him over to let you see him.

At that, Jock, a great big Scotchman, looked me over just as he would have looked over an animal that was being offered him for purchase. Then he said,

Mr. Graham : Nae, nae, he'll never dae. He's too wee. The last teacher, ye ken, was run oot by the scholars and he was bigger than this yin.

Mr. Graham : O, well, Jock, that means naething, ye ken. It isn't a' in the size. We like this young man's looks an' his ways.

Mr. Graham : He's sma' but you've heard that sometimes the best goods are found i' the sma' packages.

Jock : A weel, that may be sae. But I canna agree tae it. You're twa an' I'm only yin, so if you want to hire him, I can't hinder ye. But, if he comes rinning over the hills some day with the scholars chasin' him don't cum to me aboot it.

Myself : Well, Mr McDonald, I may be small, but you'll never see me running over the hill with the boys after me. You can be sure of that.

So I was hired. The contract was drawn up and singed. My year's salary was to be $240.00 out of which I would pay for board and lodging, buy my clothes, etc. I went back to Almonte, Proud and happy, for I was now a teacher and so a man! I was to begin work the second of January, 1878.

I arranged to board at Mr. Graham's home at $2.50 a week, so some of my salary would be left for the purchase of clothes and other necessaries. On January first I went to Mr. Graham's home to be ready to begin my work on the second. They had some New Year guests from the town for the dinner, including their relatives, Mr. and Mrs. Barnes, parents of the Miss Jennie already mentioned. The river, several hundreds of yards away, was frozen over and the men had gone down there to play croquet on the ice so I went down to get acquainted with them.

The school was a stone building with only one room but it had over forty pupils in it, representing all grades of the public school and a few old ones who were in the first and second years of High school. Many of the students were older than I as they farmed in the summer and attended school only in the winter. They looked me over as carefully as I did them. I don't know what they thought when they saw a fair complexioned, light haired boy who had never yet shaved, only some five feet two inches in height and weighing less than 100 pounds, standing in such a relation to them. I knew that I watched them to try to judge their attitude. I smiled and after a brief greeting said we would go on with the school work and a bit later we would get acquainted with each other.

They turned out to be a friendly bunch and in the three years I taught there we had good times in the school room and out doors. All, including the teacher, took their lunches to school and so had time to play together at noon. The boys and girls and the teacher joined in rounders(the forerunner of present day base-ball), in football, etc., and all enjoyed it, but when the bell rang and we entered the school room all knew that it meant steady work all the time.

Only on one occasion did I have even a semblance of trouble. I was hearing a class recite on beaches in front of the teacher's desk when two lads sitting at one of the desks rose up in a quarrel. The bigger one, a son of one of the trust-ees, started a fight right there in the school, I quietly asked for an explanation and this fellow noisely told his side of the quarrel.

"Well, George," I said, "this is not the place for a fight. Sit down and wait till after school and then we will see about it." Both sat down, but soon began again, without a word I jumped over a bench and made my way to where they were standing.

"George," I said, doubling my fist, "if you don't sit down, I'll knock you down."

George, much bigger than I, was so surprised, that he sat down without an-other word, and after school, when the whole matter had cooled off, everything was settled and with no blows. After that time, George became my protector and would have fought anyone who might treat me roughly. The idea of the "wee schoolmaister" knocking big George down had taken him completely by surprise. After I left that part of the country I did not see George again for many years. Then on one of my returns from Korea on furlough I met him. He had be-come a burly farmer with many children and I was already getting gray. During that summer, Smith's Falls was having its old boy's reunion and there was a great, gay time. One evening my wife and I walked down the principal street - a very wide one - where a big community dance was being held. Farmers from all sections were there. Suddenly we met a big man who stopped us and said "I guess you don't remember me. You used to be my teacher at Hutton's Schoolhouse." "Why, of course I remember you," I replied, "You are George McGillvray." At this he laughed heartily and said, "Do you remember that day in school when you were going to knock me down ?" And again he laughed, "I've never forgotten it," I said, "and I would have done it too." "Those were great days," he remarked, "and we all liked you."

School teaching has its drawbacks as a profession, but I know of no greater pleasure than to meet, many years later, the pupils one has taught and hear them say "we all liked you."

I remained there three years except that within that time I engaged another teacher to take my place temporarily while I went to Ottawa, the Dominion capital, to study in the Normal School for a higher grade teaching certificate which would enable me to secure a better paid position.

I have already told of my first meeting with Miss Jennie Barnes and said she was related to the Graham family in whose home I boarded all the time I taught in that little schoolhouse. Mr. Barnes was a blacksmith and carriage builder and his shop and home were near the entrance to the town, and so the Grahams found, it convenient to leave their horses in his blacksmithy on Sundays while they went to church. They were Presbyterian and their church opened its serv- ices at eleven a. m. The Barnes' were Methodists, however, and that church began at ten-thirty a. m.. To oblige their boarder, the Grahams brought him up with them coming earlier so that I, a Methodist, could go to my own church. Because of this difference in time of opening, the services also closed at differ- ent times. I always left the church with the Barnes family and went to their home to wait for the Grahams to come a half hour later. Thus, every Sunday I spent a half hour with Jennie who usually played hymns on the organ while the rest sang, all but the mother who was busy preparing the noon meal. In this way I became better and better acquainted with the family and with Jennie!

I made one great blunder while I was at Normal School in Ottawa during part of my third year. I didn't write Jennie very often and, she concluded my acknowledged affection for her was not so strong as we had both thought it was, and so when I returned, it was to a very cool young lady. It took a lot of explain- ing and a good deal of time to restore the former happy relations, for another young man, living in the town, had done his best to win her while I was away. Even up to the time I left the neighborhood at the end of my third year in the school, I had not succeeded in completely reestablishing myself in her affections.

Apprenticeship for a Pharmacist

When I left Smith's Falls I returned to my home in Almonte and reentered the High School to prepare for matriculation in the University of Toronto where I planned to fit myself to become a college teacher, but before I had finished this preparatory work a reconsideration of my aim in life made me realize that I was not sufficiently enthusiastic in my wish to become a professional teacher to make me go through all the necessary years of college, coupled with the task of earning my living and my college expenses all the way through. What then? Some kind of a business life seemed to be most feasible - but what? Something more than buying and selling would be to my taste and, as I had been much interested in chemistry all through my high school life, a business that would combine the further study of that subject with the making of a living would be ideal. No sooner had I come to that conclusion than an "ad" appeared in our local paper announcing that an apprentice to the drug business was needed by a drug store in Smith's Falls. The owner was Dr. J. S. McCallum whom I had known while I was teaching school. I called on him at once and he engaged me with no further ado as an apprentice for three years at a rate of remuneration that seems ridiculously small in this day - first year, board and room only; second year, the same plus $100.00; third year, an additional $100.00. That meant board and lodging and $300.00 for three years plus an opportunity to learn chemistry, botany, medical materials, manufacturing processes, compounding prescriptions and business methods. The hours of work were from seven in the morning to nine at night, six days a week, with only time off for meals but it offered what I wanted, - a combination of scientific studies and business with a living thrown in. Besides and this must not be forgotten, Smith's Falls was the home of Jennie Barnes.

When I entered on this apprenticeship a very competent businessman and well qualified, druggist, Duncan McIntyre, was in charge. The doctor was busy looking after his patients and writing prescriptions and the fact that all his prescriptions were compounded there gave his clerks an unusually good training in that line of work as he was very particular not only about their accurate preparation, but also about the cleanliness and neatness of the finished package. My work the first year was to get to the store in the morning early enough to do the sweeping and dusting before either of the other men arrived. The cleanness and neatness of the entire shop, outside and inside, the windows and their contents, and above all, the drug bottles on the shelves, occupied by first hours of the day.

After that I could wait on customers and in between I could read the text books that dealt with the various subjects of the course. I soon determined that we ought to manufacture our own tinctures, ointments and various powders and, as my first efforts made it evident that my products were as good as those they had been buying from the regular wholesalers and manufacturers, I was given a free hand at this work and very soon was allowed to compound the doctor's prescriptions.

The chief hindrance to my complete contentment was the fact that almost every night I had to stay in until the store closed which was never earlier than nine o'clock, so that I had not much time in which to carry on my courtship. The location of Jennie's home was but one block from our corner so every morning when she was sweeping the sidewalk in front of her home I managed to be outside too and we waved good morning to each other. Her mother was on my side - very much so - and when I called in an evening - often as late as nine-thirty, much consideration was shown me by the understanding mother. Instead of expecting me to leave at ten o'clock, which was then considered the proper hour for beaus to depart, the mother would come into the parlor carrying a tray on which was pie or cake and something nice to drink. Placing it on the table she would smile, say good night, and quietly leave the room. What a treasure of a mother she was I. She certainly knew which of the boys who came around she wanted for a son-in-law!

Before the end of the first year the head clerk decided to "go West" to Winnipeg, the capital of the newly organized province of Manitoba. I rather hoped I might be given his post in view of the work I had done, but the doctor explained that, as he understood the pharmacy law of the province, he would have to keep a legally qualified pharmacist in the store. This was not a fact, as he discovered later, because he, being a physician, was regarded by the law as competent and legally qualified to be a druggist. A qualified druggist was engaged but he proved to be less than competent as a business head and a few months later the doctor let him go and put me in charge with an apprentice under me. That pleased me because I escaped all the menial work and could give all my time to management and study.

I am not boasting when I say the business grew rapidly and the profits increased, as I developed the manufacturing end more and more. The duplicating of many of the patented remedies and the sale of these under our own labels was bound to bring good financial returns. Though I could not use the names of the originals, I could intimate that our products would do all that the patented, remedies did. At the end of the year the doctor gave me a small present, over what my contract called for. I had hoped for a greater recognition of my efforts but made no comment, - a false pride kept me from telling him what I was thinking.

Graduation from Ontario College of Pharmacy

Before the end of the three years I had completely routed my rival for Jennie's hand, and a few months before I was to leave for Toronto to attend the College of Pharmacy, we pledged our faith to each other, I reported this to her father according to the customs of the day, though he didn't need to be told. and I didn't need his assurance that he approved it. However, he had to raise some questions as a matter of form.

"Well, Oliver," he said, "'I have suspected this for some time and I can't say I disapprove it, but you are about to go to a big city where you will see many fine ladies. You may change your mind when you go cut into the world. Hadn't you better put off this engagement so you will be free to choose some one else in case you change your mind?"

I just smiled at this and declared, I would risk it, and. so would she. We had talked that over together and knew, after more than six years of close companionship that we were fully satisfied with each other.

"Well," said he "if you feel that way about it I have no further objection, I just felt I ought to give you this bit of friendly advice. Her mother and I both look upon you as a son anyway."

In a few months I would be a qualified pharmacist if I passed my examination and I had won my bride to be, so I did not regret the change I had made in my plans three years before. You may wonder how I could go through college in so short a time so I had better explain the modus operandi of those early days.

The main preparation for the druggist was his three years' apprenticeship under the tutelage of a qualified pharmacist. During that time he was supposed to study the various subjects on which he would be examined and know them sufficiently well. But many were not well prepared and found themselves unable to pass the examinations which were given in Toronto by a board of examiners appointed by the Council of Pharmacy, a body elected by the votes of all qualified druggists in the Province.

One of the manufacturing druggists of the city, Mr. E. B. Shuttleworth, who had been well trained in England in chemistry and all the subjects required by the Pharmacy Act, seeing the need, opened a short term school in which capable teachers would give an intensive course for a period of months to all who desired to attend the classes before attempting the examinations. This course was intended to supplement the more or less superficial courses of study many of the young men had had during their period of apprenticeship when so much of their time had been given to business. This innovation proved to be so valuable that the Council of Pharmacy had made attendance on these courses compulsory and undertook the selection of its teachers. Mr. E. B. Shuttleworth was appointed Principal, and its courses were gradually improved. and lengthened. It was at that early period that I attended it. Not only were lectures given but laboratory courses in chemistry, pharmacy, and compounding of prescriptions were established as well as a course in microscopical examination of drugs by which the identity and purity of drugs could be determined.

I enjoyed, these studies and. gave them my full attention. I was fortunate too in gaining the friendship of the principal. At the examinations that followed, the completion of the course of study, the work I had done during my apprenticeship in Smith's Falls stood me in good stead. I received 3 gold medals in special subjects, and also the gold medal for general proficiency.

Professor of Ontario College of Pharmacy

Dr. McCallum had asked me to return and continue as manager of his business with an offer of a good. salary at once and a partnership at the end of a year and I expected to accept it, but I had barely made a start under this proposition when I received a telegram from Principal Shuttleworth offering me the post of teacher of Botany in the School of Pharmacy at a salary of $600.00 a year. Two sessions of the school were held each year and three lectures a weeks were given in Botany, supplemented by a weekly tramp into the woods with the students to gather and classify specimens of plants and flowers as a practical laboratory course in that subject. All the rest of the time would be at my disposal.

When I showed this telegram to my employer he shook his head and asked me what answer I would give. Of course it was not a big thing but it seemed to me to open up a new vista of possibilities and I told him it was very tempting to me. He then made me several offers of better salaries if I would stay with him but in the end I went to Toronto. My father-in-law to be was evidently pleased with the opportunity for advancement this might give me and heartily approved my decision.

This advanced and practical study of botany fascinated me and every Saturday afternoon a group of the students accompanied me in search of plants, especially medicinal ones. We covered all the open ground and woods north of the city at the same time that Ernest Thompson Seton was studying the wild animals of the same section and writing his first book about them - "Wild Animals I Have Known."

Admission to Medical School

At the end of the first term, the teacher of Materia Medica (Pharmacology it is now termed) had to leave for California because of ill health and the principal asked me to take over that subject in addition to the botany, It added $600.00 to my annual salary and put me on Easy Street financially, so I felt, more than ever assured I had chosen wisely when I gave up my work in the drug store, In addition I had received several offers of good auxiliary positions in city drug stores, I told Mr. Shuttleworth of these and asked his advice as to which I should accept. His answer surprised me.

"If I were in your place I would not accept the best position in a drug store in Toronto."

Amazed, I asked for an explanation. His reply was equally astonishing.

"You are now receiving a good living salary and have plenty of spare time. There are two medical schools in the city, Toronto and Trinity. Go and find. out which one will give you the most credits for what you have done and. are doing in pharmacy, examine their courses care-fully and consider the relative abilities of their teachers. Then sign up as a student in one of them in the end you will get your M. D. That will be much better than being a druggist and will not interfere with your teaching in the College of Pharmacy."

I could but answer that I had never intended to be a doctor. He brushed aside that objection by saying that even as an M. D. I need not go into medical practice. If I decided not to do so I would still be the gainer because with the double qualifications I could, command a position in Pharmacy that would carry me to the very front of that profession. He went on to say that when he was a young man in England he was offered an opportunity to study medicine after he had become a pharmacist. He had refused it and. had been sorry ever since. Had be accepted the otter he would have been much farther ahead now than he could over expect to be within his lifetime.

I took his advice and after conferring with the deans of both medical schools, I decided. on attending Toronto which would give me a year's credit for my work in Pharmacy, and. as it seemed. to me had. the best staff of teachers. This would enable me to graduate in three years instead of the usual four. So again the course of my life was changed, and just as unexpectedly as before.

I worked as hard at my medical studies as I had done at my pharmaceutical course and. at the end. of the first year stood first in the class and received. a scholarship of $50.00 which was of great use in the purchase of additional textbooks.

Then the Professor of Materia Medica in the College of Pharmacy resigned because of illness and the principal offered me that position. As it would add $600 a year to my income I gladly accepted it.

Marriage with Jennie

Then I began to realize I was lonely and to think how nice it would be to exchange my boarding room for a home but would an income of $1,200 a year warrant such a procedure?

I wrote to Jennie and asked her opinion. She consulted her parents who said it was enough for a modest home. That was fine - would she marry me the corning summer holiday? She would, and the wedding took place July 28, 1885.

We went to Ottawa for a part of our honeymoon. My former competitor for Jennie's hand had found another nice lady and married her before we had reached that point and they were living in Ottawa. They called on us the first morning after our arrival and insisted that we leave the hotel and go to their home. After much persuasion we agreed though it certainly seemed odd that this should have happened. Then we all laughed over it and this took away the restraint we might otherwise have felt. We soon returned to Smith's Falls and spent the rest of our honeymoon camping on the familiar Long Island in Rideau Lake.

In the fall we rented and furnished a home in Toronto and I pursued my regular work in a very contented frame of mind.

Those who read these memoirs may think getting married on an income of $1200.00 a year was risky, but we found it quite enough though it would not be enough in these days of 1940.

At the end of my second year, I again stood first and received the usual scholarship of $50.00 and might have done so the third year had I continued to study as hard. as I had done before. But I found, my strength lessening and feared I might break down so, after consultation with my wife, I decided to reduce my hours of study to a point which, while insuring graduation would likely lower my standing at the end of the year. It turned out that way. Though I graduated, I stood, only third in the class but with good, health instead of a broken constitution.

During the third year of my medical course a group of second year medical students asked me to give them a special course of lectures on pharmacology.

"Why," I asked, "you have a regular course on that subject, haven't you?"

"Yes," was the answer, "we have, but the teacher has been giving the same lectures from the same notes for the last thirty years and. they are entirely out of date. Why, the boys who have had his course have told us to be prepared, to laugh at certain places when he repeats his old joke. We know of your teaching at the College of Pharmacy and would like to get your lectures and are prepared to pay you."

Though I thought this was rather piling it up on me, I asked where such a course could be given for I could not, of course, use one of the lecture rooms without the permission of the secretary of the college. They said they would attend to that. When, a few days later, I met the secretary he stopped me to say he had heard of the boys' request and I was free to use the main lecture room. So I became both a student and teacher in the same institution.

My Medical College years were marked by some unusual events, only a few of which there will be room for in my story, but they are of interest because I helped to change many regrettable customs in the schools and this led to other very important developments in my life.

The mischievous spirit that is supposed to prevail in all colleges had been augmented to a point that caused all medical students to be regarded with suspicion. This came home to mein a very humiliating experience. Another student and I went together in search of a room. We found one that suited us but when we were just completing the bargain, the landlady suddenly said, "You're not medical students, are you?" We admitted we were but why had she asked.

"They are a bad lot," she said, "I wouldn't have one in my house at any price. I am sorry, for you two look like nice young men."

"Well, there are, some bad ones among us," we said, "but we will not cause you any trouble."

She would not risk us, however, and we had to go on searching for a room.

Some of the students came to the classes intoxicated, and. at times created so much trouble that the teacher had to dismiss the class. It was the custom for the students to sponsor an annual dinner to which other medical schools were asked to send representatives. Liquors were served in abundance and by ten o'clock many of the hosts and some of the guests were under the table, some vomiting and some sleeping. A few of us who didn't drink alcoholics got together and organized a temperance society and. it soon become evident that a majority of the students felt as we did for they joined the organization and before the end of two years the anti-liquor group were able to veto the serving of alcoholic drinks at any representative gathering of students and to send only non-drinkers to represent the school at the dinners of other colleges. As the two medical schools were only a block apart the organization included both.

Organizing the Y. M. C. A.

Then a student named Robert A. Hardie suggested that the two Medical schools should unite in organizing a Y. M. C. A. with the aim of developing a Christian fellowship. The Liberal Arts Department of the University of Toronto already had a very successful "Y" with a building of its own on campus. It had sent one of the University graduates to Korea as an evangelistic missionary and was supporting him there, - Mr. James S. Gale. He was not an ordained minister but as a lay Christian was conducting a very successful work. Another Toronto layman, Mr. Malcolm Fenwick, had also been sent out by a committee made up of wealthy men of several denominations. The letters of these two were enthusiastic and Hardie felt a strong desire to be sent out as a physician to be associated especially with Mr. Gale.

He succeeded in interesting a number of students in the idea of organizing a medical "Y" and one evening a group met at my home to consider the suggestion. We met, considered, decided, organized, and even elected the necessary officers all in one evening so it can be seen that Hardie's enthusiasm had borne fruit. We arranged to hold our meetings in the medical schools just as the temperance meetings had been conducted there so as to connect our work definitely with the schools. The first meeting after organization was held in the large theater of the Toronto Medical School. I was appointed to open the meeting with prayer and as I looked up the tiers of seats at the large number of men gathered - mostly out of curiosity - I felt rather strange as, without doubt, that was the first public prayer to have been offered in it. The new venture was successful and quite often some member of the faculty would address us.

Just as might be expected, Hardie, after a time, suggested that this "Y" should send him to Korea to join hands with Gale. A broad smile of incredulity met this suggestion but one after another became converted to the idea and a committee was appointed to obtain information about the cost of travel to Korea and the cost of living there. Reports were obtained from Gale and Fenwick and their estimates were so low that the project began to seem feasible. But Hardie soon followed my example and brought a wife to the city and that was an unexpected, complication. The other two men were unmarried and were living in the country in Korean homes and eating Korean food. Hardie, with a wife and probably a family would need a home where they could live more in accordance with Canadian standards.

However, the time came when all arrangements were completed and the long journey to Korea was made possible for the Hardies. The family- the doctor, his wife and little girl spent a few days with us before they started off. They left for Vancouver on an evening train and I drove them to the railroad station in my carriage. This item of information is introduced only as a setting for an interesting occurrence at the end of their missionary career.

At that time, August, 1890, we had no thought of going to Korea ourselves, it was not till January, 1893, that this question came up for consideration, but that summer found, us in Korea.

The Hardies continued work there until April 27, 1935 and, when they were about to leave Seoul, they spent the last few days in our home in that city and again I drove them to the railroad station - almost forty-five years after they left Toronto. It wes rather unique that the same person who saw them off on their trip from Canada should, so many years later, have seen them off on their return journey to Canada. I used a carriage on that first occasion, but an auto at the second. one. Even in America the auto had not come into being in 1809, and not even a horse carriage was in use in Korea, but in 1935 autos had become common in both countries.

Professor of Toronto Medical School

I graduated a year ahead of Hardie and was at once appointed to the University Medical Faculty to teach pharmacology and, at the same time, I opened up practice in the city. Then I was really busy, giving nine lectures a week at the College of Pharmacy and four at the Medical College besides getting started in practice. However I continued my connection with the medical "Y" and also became medical officer for the Central City "Y" and a member of its Board of Directors; I was a member of the Official Board of Sherbourne Street Methodist Church and a local preacher or, in different phraseology, a lay preacher; every Sunday afternoon I taught a Bible Class in a branch of the Sherbourne Street Church, and every Sunday evening helped to carry on a service for a new branch church over the Don River; and each Thursday evening I served as leader of a Band of Hope in the east end of the city for the City Mission which headed the slum work in the whole city. So not much unoccupied time was left on my hands.

Having bought a small home on the eastern end of Carlton Street I opened practice there after graduation. Two needs faced me at once. The first was caused by the customs of city medical practitioners in that day. Every doctor wore a black Prince Albert Suit and a silk top hat and it would be infra dig for a doctor connected with the University to visit his patients not properly attired. The second was that every doctor had a horse and carriage, I bought the suit and hat but had to put off the horse and carriage till I could afford them. The first time I donned the black suit and went down the streets of the city I was self conscious to an extreme degree, but it soon became a matter of course, in a comparatively short time, too, my father-in-law sent us a nice carriage and I spent my last dollar for a horse and harness. How we were in the swim of a city medical practice and I was ready to become the trusted family physician of the highest of the high!

And, as a matter of fact, it was not very long, before I was summoned to attend at the birth of a son to the Mayor of the city. To be sure, I was not his first choice. He had been married twice and his first wife had died at the birth of their first child so this time he had chosen the most moted surgeon in the city, determined that no unnecessary risk should be incurred. But alas! When the time came this surgeon was busy with another case and could not be there. He suggested to the anxious husband that he call me in his place. Proud moment! I had known both the Mayor and his wife but had not expected to meet them under such circumstances. Everything passed off smoothly and when I was about to leave the house I told them I would report to their doctor who would doubtless call during the day.

"Oh, no," they said, "You are to continue to attend. We are quite satisfied with your work."

"But," I answered, "I am only a substitute for Dr. Cameron who was kind enough to recommend me to you and I cannot keep the case."

"We do not know the etiquette of your profession," they said, "but we know we want you to see the case through."

"Well," I answered, "that will be between you and him. I shall call him up and tell him how things are with his patients and that you will expect a call from him as soon as he is free. Any change must be made after consultation between you and him."

"All right," said the Mayor, "I will call on him myself and tell him what we want."

"But," I said, "in any event, he must visit your wife, and if, then, he wishes me to continue, he can ask me to do so."

During the day Dr. Cameron called me up and, after saying he would call at the patient's home that evening, asked me to meet him there. This I did and, having complimented me on my work, he asked me to carry it through. Of course I agreed to do so and after that, until he left for Korea I continued to be the family physician of the Mayor of Toronto. My punctiliousness pleased Dr. Cameron and he sent me many other cases which he was too busy to look after. It does pay to treat one's fellow practitioners and everyone else with utmost consideration.

At the end of my first year as a teacher in the University, I was appointed to the Board of Examiners. This pleased me very much as it was a real mark of confidence in my judgment. I had already been on the Examining Board of the College of Pharmacy for some years but this was the University.

After the Hardies had actually gone to their missionary work the Medical "Y" had to face the problem of their maintenance. Funds were so short in the "Y" treasury that I had to personally pay the bill (some $200) spent on their final outfitting. I had expected to be recouped but alas! the treasury was kept constantly empty by our effort to provide for their upkeep in Korea and I at last realized that I had made my first considerable contribution to the missionary cause, for there never was enough to repay the loan.

Do you know that when I realized this I got a thrill out of it? We had. had for some time a plan for our missionary giving through our church that I felt would keep these offerings steadily enlarging as time passed and our income grew greater. It started with $5.00 each for my wife and me and $1.00 for each year of age for each child. These amounts were to be increased by adding a dollar to each of these gifts as every year went by. We felt it was good for the children to make such a contribution, expecting that when they left home they would go on doing the same. The amounts had to be changed when we have ourselves to the work and Korea, because our missionary salaries would not allow us to give so much, but the system, with necessary alterations, was continued.

My experience of giving is that it is better to decide on how much one will give in any one year and then lay that amount aside to be used in some regular way or else set up an account based on that figure and keep it audited at regular intervals so as to always know whether to increase or decrease contributions and keep them on an even keel. The old method of tithing is a pretty good standard. My wife and I decided early in our married life to adopt this method and did so through the course of our years together.

Appointment as a Medical Missionary to Korea

Before we start looking into those early days in Korea, it might be better to go back to the starting point, my home on Carlton Street, Toronto, Ontario, where I was practising medicine. You can be sure it must have been a strong conviction that caused two people as old as we were, 32 and 30, with a family of three living children and another corning, to make such a radical decision and leave our beautiful Canada and wonderful Toronto. Our future in this fair land looked promising indeed, for at the end of six years I had a practice that was yielding more than enough to support my family and as a teacher in the Medical Faculty of the University had just received notice of my appointment for another five year period. Our decision to separate ourselves from our homeland and all those other things was indeed a momentous one.

Both my wife and I had grown up in religious, though not fanatical, surroundings. From our young days, we had been members of the Methodist Church of Canada and had started married life together in the Sherbourne Street Methodist Church in Toronto. That was quite a wonderful church and we soon became members of a very active society of young people who studied missions in Japan where that church was supporting a young lady missionary, a member of the home church. This was probably the starting point of our missionary thinking for it was then we began our plan of missionary giving which has already been referred to.

Some five or six years after my graduation from the Medical School, Rev. H. G. Underwood of Brooklyn, New York, the first Protestant clergyman to begin work in Korea, visited our city at my invitation, for the purpose of arousing greater religious zeal amongst the medical students. His visit not only did what we desired for the students but also stirred Mrs. Avison and me so greatly that we decided to offer our services to the Methodist Church of Canada if they would send us to Korea. Unfortunately the Canadian Methodists had no work in that field, the country in which our chief interest lay, and it seemed we would not be able to go. Mr. Underwood, without consulting us, had given our names to the Presbyterian Board of Foreign Missions in New York as that Board was then looking for a doctor to fill a special place in their Korea Mission which he thought I could fill satisfactorily and they at once asked me to go to New York for a conference with them and this led to our appointment.

Another factor in our decision to go into foreign mission work was my continued interest in promoting the work of the Canadian Colleges Missionary Association. Our little Medical Students' Association had grown to a point where it touched the student bodies of all the colleges in Ontario and was supporting a travelling secretary to keep up interest in the work. Dr. Hardie, who had been sent out as noted above, united after a few years with Korea Mission of the Southern Methodist Church of the U. S. A. and then the Colleges Mission devoted its strength to arousing missionary enthusiasm in a more general way. The great influence of our organization may be judged by the fact that nearly all the members of the Association became foreign missionaries, one by one.

Probably the deciding factor in our acceptance of the appointment to Korea was what the New York secretary, Dr. F. F. Ellinwood, said in answer to my question as to whether he thought they could make a good Presbyterian out of me. He said they didn't want to make me into a Presbyterian - they wanted me to take some good Methodist fire out to Korea and set ablaze the work of the missions out there. I felt that if that was the spirit of the Presbyterian Board I could work under its direction. Before leaving Toronto, however, I transferred my membership to Old St. Andrew's Presbyterian Church on the corner of the next block on the same street, of which church I am still a member and elder after forty-eight years.

Chapter 2

Our Early Days In Korea

Leaving from Toronto

When I left for New York our two older children were in quarantine at our home with scarlet fever. On my return I found the third child, a boy of a year and a half, had contracted the disease but we went on with our preparations to leave Canada. This case was complicated with abscess of the ear and pneumonia so that the child's life was despaired of during the whole period of our preparation for the long journey. The many friends who were opposed to our new plans used his sickness as an argument against our going saying that we were flying in the face of providence. Our answer was that if he died, his illness need not influence our going so we would continue getting ready to go and, if he lived till we got to Vancouver and the boat would take him on as a passenger, we would go right on to Korea, but if they refused to take us on the boat because of him we would regard that as a sign that God was preventing our going.

When all was packed and we were ready to leave Toronto, he was so weak that we were much disturbed about taking him on the two hundred mile train trip to his grandparents' home, but he made the trip safely and during his stay there rapidly gained strength so that on our arrival in Vancouver the question of boarding the ship did not arise.

Our journey across Canada was uneventful except that the newly made roadbed of the Canadian Pacific Railway was neither very solid nor very smooth. It was late spring and there had been heavy rains, and at one place the railway ties with their iron rails were floating and as the train moved forward they sank to the ground and then rose again behind us. As we were on the last car I went out and stood on the rear end platform and it was a strange sight to see the rails thus sinking and again rising to the surface as we passed over them. As the train sank it maintained its place on the rails and the water rose nearly to the top of the steps while big waves rolled over its surface. Then we crossed the wide prairies, miles and miles of them, without seeing a house or even a hillock. Houses were scarce because the railroad was new and the great distances still prevented settlers going so far in search of farms even though the government offered them free of cost.

Then came the mountains. Who can describe their greatness, their rocky ruggedness, their grandeur? But the roadbed was new here too and its roughness gave us many jolts. However, all those minor unpleasantnesses were passed and suddenly the air became more balmy. We could already feel the effect of the warm Japan current off the western coast of our continent. The fields were green and the flowers were in bloom.

We arrived in Vancouver just as it was beginning to recover from the fire which had recently devastated it. As yet it was only a big village but the great Vancouver Hotel, built and run by the Canadian Pacific Railway, rose on the highest point in the city for, though small, it was even then spoken of as a city. To this hotel we went to wait for a week for the sailing of the big C. P. R. steamer, the "Empress of India", that was moored at the big dock.

"Has Mrs. Gibson arrived?" we asked at the hotel desk.

"Yes," was the answer, "she came some days ago." Mrs. Gibson was the mother of Mrs. J. S. Gale of Korea, widow of the late Dr. J. W. Heron and, as she was going there for a long visit, she had been consigned to our care by the New York Board. We were a bit anxious to meet her and learn what to expect in the way of companionship. Would she help us or would we have to do all the helping? She turned out to be a large handsome woman, a real Southern aristocrat with all the friendliness that authors of tales of the South have always attributed to the white people of the South and we at once knew we were going to enjoy her.

Shortly after our arrival in Vancouver we went down to the docks to see our ship. How big she seemed! Six thousand tons! How fine she looked in her new coat of white paint and what beautiful lines she showed ! We went on board to see what she was like inside and how it felt to be there. But vile smells greeted us as we began to go down into the sleeping quarters which grew even worse as we got farther down. All ships in those days had that stifling odor because of poor ventilation - it was a regular ship smell that got one ready to be sea-sick even before the moorings were loosened and the ship slid quietly away from the dock.

We spent our few days of waiting in seeing the new Stanley Park which had in it giant trees like those in California, and the many other natural beauties of what has since grown to be a real city and a great port. Across the bay rose the high mountains even yet covered with snow in spite of the Japan Current that made it possible for the city and its surroundings to manifest all the glories of early summer. There on top of the nearest mountain are 'the sleeping lions' so famous in the tradition of the Indians.

Sailing from Vancouver

At last the time for our departure came and we went aboard early in the afternoon to get settled in our cabins while the boat was still moored. Our family of five needed plenty of bed space so we had a cabin to ourselves. How comfy it was! Who could get sea-sick on so big a ship? Before evening the ship left the dock and lo, it was as quiet as the hotel we had just left! But as evening came on and we passed through the narrow strait into the broader bay where the waves came in from the ocean it became a bit rough, a good introduction, I thought, to the wide ocean we should soon be crossing. But as we went farther on, the waves grew higher and shook the ship as though it were but a skiff. Ah, what was that strange, uneasy feeling that welled up within me! It could not be - but, yes, it was and only one hour out from port!

At length I was relieved and felt better and went to find the family. The children were all right, but my wife, had she been sick?

"No," she said, "but I wish I could be, I have such a headache and am so dizzy."

Fortunately a time came when we got used to the rocking motion and began to enjoy ourselves. But why dwell on these details? There were many rough days as well as many fine ones in our two weeks' voyage across the Pacific.

We had not been aboard long when a finely dressed officer approached us who turned out to be none other than Dr. Herbert A. Bruce, one of the brightest of the many bright young medical students to whom I had taught Pharmacology in the University of Toronto. He had graduated a year before and after serving an internship in the hospital had then taken this appointment as ship's surgeon to give him an opportunity to see something of the world, gain some further experience as a surgeon and enable him to pay off the debt which gives many a medical graduate a pain in his head during his early years of practice when paying patients are so few. What a pleasant surprise for me! It was the rule of the ship in those days for the surgeon to act as host to the passengers and Bruce was it. As he was good looking, upright in his bearing and a fine specimen of young manhood he soon became very popular, especially with the young ladies, who never have been able to resist the combination of a good looking young man and a brilliant uniform.

It was a pleasure for me to accompany Bruce on his daily rounds of the lower quarters of the ship where most of the Oriental passengers and members of the crew lived during the voyage for it was all a new experience to me. The climax of interest came when a sick Chinaman, long resident in the Western Hemisphere, died on his way back to China. It is the belief of the Chinese that a man's soul never leaves his native land and that if he leaves the country of his birth and dies in a foreign place, the soul cannot rest unless the body is brought back to the place of its origin. For this reason it is the great desire of a Chinaman, who has left his own land, to get back there before his death. If he should die on his way his body must be taken on to his destination or the separation of soul and body will never occur. So the shipping company, to get the business of China men returning to their homeland, had made a contract with the Chinese in America and Canada to deliver body of every Chinaman that sailed back to China, dead or alive, in China. When one dies on the ship, therefore, his body had to be embalmed so that the contract could be fulfilled. I helped Dr. Bruce do the embalming of this case which was the only one during that voyage.

It was very different when a Singhalese gentleman died on the same voyage for these people have no such belief and we had the unique opportunity of seeing a burial at sea. This man being a British subject, his body, to which lead had been attached to sink it, was covered with the Union Jack and placed on a board that projected over the ship's side. After the reading of the Anglican burial service the board was tilted so that the body slipped quietly into the sea leaving the flag behind it. I had always thought that a burial at sea would bea very grim sight, but, conducted in this way with the crew and passengers standing around quietly as at any funeral on land, there was nothing of the disagreeable - it was similar in every respect to the lowering of a body into a grave in a cemetery.

When we left Victoria our boat was headed northwest which seemed strange to us as our first port in Japan, Yokohama, was considerably south of west.

When we expressed our surprise to one of the officers, he pointed out that the nearer we get to the North Pole, the shorter the circles around the globe become so that the shortest distance to Japan is to go northwest for a certain distance and then veer to the southwest till we reach Yokohama.

This route took us within sight of the Aleutian Islands which we could see clearly and, with the use of a good telescope, we could even see the seals clambering over the rocky shores.

Then it grew colder, snow fell and the ship's ropes were covered with ice. The cold weather continued almost till we reached Japan - but it became suddenly summery one day before we entered the port. What a change took place overnight! We went to bed Saturday night covered with heavy blankets and awoke Sunday morning with a warm summer sun shining in through the portholes. We had worn thick winter clothing on Saturday and on Sunday the lady passengers wore out in thin white dresses. What had happened? We had suddenly entered the western branch of the Japan Current. It had divided into two branches, one running north along the coast of British Columbia in which we sailed at the beginning of our voyage and the other flowing north along the coast of Japan. It was an eye-opening experience to us, inexperienced travelers that we were.

Arrival in Japan

That day we sailed into the harbor of Yokohama and gazed for first time at the famed hills of Japan. The port was spacious, the hills brilliant in the June sunlight and as beautiful as we had been led to believe but - there seemed always to be a "but"- the beauty of the surroundings was soon spoiled by the coming to the anchored ship of men and women in their sampans, most of them completely naked. Mrs. Avison's first reaction was a feeling of repugnance and then a realization that she had been deceived by all she had read about the advanced civilization of Japan. If this that she saw was to be described as advanced civilization what had it been like before?

Soon we were on a sampan on the way to the landing pier where we speedily passed the customs examination and got into the strange jinrikshes pulled by men. This method of transportation intrigued us but when we came to a long hill on our way to the Bluff, where we had been told we would find the foreign houses in one of which we were to stay while in Yokohama, I couldn't bear the idea of letting a man tug and puff to pull me up the long slope, so out I jumped and started off on my own much to the surprise of the little man who seemed to fear he was going to lose a fee.

The Bluff was at the top of a steep hill, a section of the city considerably higher than the shore and was at that time the residential district for nearly all the foreigners who lived in Yokohama. We were taken to the house to which we had been directed and were made very comfortable. But, oh, the heat i It seemed to smother us. It was greater than anything we had experienced in a Canadian midsummer.

I was very much pleased to find a young doctor there whom I had known as a student in the university. He had gone with his wife as a missionary to South China, but the health of the family had broken down and they were now on their way back to Toronto with but little hope of ever returning to the Orient. This was not very stimulating to us though we hoped for better things.

We expected to find letters from Korea advising us as to the time they expected us to arrive in that country but day after day passed without any word coming. This delay gave us a good opportunity to visit and learn much concerning places of interest in and around Yokohama. Some of it was gratifying and some of it very discouraging. Some missionary friends living there took us one day to the red light district of the city where we saw things we had never expected to see in even a heathen land. The business pertaining to that section was carried on with a great amount of publicity. As we returned home from that trip we decided that our ideas of Japanese civilization would have to be greatly changed.[7]

We also visited Tokyo, leaving the three children in the care of a Japanese amah(nursemaid) who was said to be reliable. The Canadian Methodists had established a mission in Tokyo some years before and we knew some of their missionaries and had introduction to others. We got into separate rikshas and naturally expected they would keep together. Interested in the curious scenes around me I did not notice that when my man turned a corner suddenly the other rickshaman did not follow us. Turning around to point out an interesting sight to Mrs. Avison, I found I was alone and my rickshaman did not know what had become of the other one. The only thing I could do was to give him the ad-

---

[7]   Beautifully dressed young women sat inside show window. Gentlemen who passed were invited to enter. No one seemed to regard it as disgraceful or a cause for wonderment.

dress of the Canadian mission home where we knew a young preacher who had visited us frequently at Smith's Falls, Canada. On our arrival, Mr. Crummy was greatly troubled since I did not know by what streets we had come. We started out together to search for her but failed to find her anywhere, so were turned to his home and found her there. She had been greatly alarmed at finding herself alone but fortunately she knew the address of the friend to whose house we were going.

We waited some six weeks in Yokohama for a letter from Korea in answer to several requests for directions we had made but no reply had come, and this worried us for we were anxious to get to Korea without much more delay as our fourth child was expected within a few weeks.

Arrival in Pusan(Fusan)

At last we determined to wait no longer for letters but to move on toward our destination. We took passage on a very nice steamer as far as Kobe and there transferred to a much smaller boat, the "Higo Maru," which was then lying in the harbor loading cargo for Korea. Instead of landing and going ashore, we went directly to the boat and there awaited its sailing.

The ship smelled so strongly of dried fish that we were sickened. As the sleeping accomodations on the lower deck were small and stuffy and the dining room was hot and poorly ventilated we took chairs up to the outside deck and remained there all night for we felt better there as far as air was concerned than we had been below. But with evening came the mosquitoes, and they came in droves, so we were glad when next day the boat weighed anchor and we set off on the last of our journey to our future home.

After calling at Nagasaki we crossed the Korean Straits and as we neared Fusan I watched eagerly from the prow of the boat for the first sight of the land which had called us. I had read descriptions of the approach to this port and so knew what to expect - great rugged rocks with no intimation of anything like a harbor till we got to its very entrance and passed through a channel guarded on each side by rocky pillars that stood up like tall sentinels. Having sailed through that passageway at slow speed, almost immediately an extensive harbor opened to view. Presenting a magnificent spectacle of mountains in the background with only a strip of low land along the shore. Here the town of Fusan spread out along the widest part. On it were one-story houses with tiled roofs and an occasional taller building. Many small Korean huts with thatched roofs were grouped in villages along the narrower strips of land while high hills and higher mountains, showing no signs of habitation, rose behind, unwooded and uncultivated. On the whole, it was not an inviting prospect.

We had been told that at least one of our missionaries was stationed there and at length, on one of the hills, a foreign style bungalow came into sight which turned out to be what we were looking for. Leaving the family on the ship, I went ashore in a Korean sampan and made my way up to the house by a rough and crooked pathway. It was the afternoon of Sunday, June 16, 1893.

On reaching the home of Rev. W. M. Baird I found a small group of foreigners gathered there for Sunday worship. They were Rev. Dr. and Mrs. Baird, Dr. and Mrs. Brown, members of our mission and a few members of the Australian Presbyterian Mission whose homes were some two or three miles away. I was warmly welcomed by what I thought must be a very lonesome little group. Next day I took Mrs. Avison and the children up to the Bairds' as the ship was to remain in the harbor a day or two.

On Tuesday I met there the Rev. and Mrs. Bunker, Methodist missionaries from Seoul, who were on their way to Japan. When they saw me and learned that we were on our way to Seoul, they expressed surprise and asked if we had not received a telegram at Yokohama advising us to remain in Japan until fall. Of course we could not have started, had we received such a telegram. They told us all the foreigners in Seoul had gone to the hills to escape the intense heat, except Rev. and Mrs. Underwood who were staying in the city because they were having their house repaired and were unable to go away.

What were we to do? Here we were in Fusan on our way to Seoul with no one to receive us as the Underwood's house was not in a condition for guests. We were advised not to go on to Seoul till some other arrangement made. But what arrangement could we make?

"You will be welcome in our home if you can put up with the few accomodations we have," the Bairds said.

But their house seemed to be already filled, Dr. and Mrs. Brown were living in two rooms of the house while their own house was being built. But the Bairds said they would vacate both their studies, one on either side of the hallway, and make us as comfortable as they could.

How glad we were to accept this generous offer I Mr. Baird went with me to the ship to help bring the family ashore and before evening Mrs. Avison, the children and all our baggage had been brought up and installed in the two rooms in which beds had replaced the desks.

Under such circumstances we began our missionary career in Korea. That evening, Mrs. Baird asked if we had brought mosquito nets with us. We hadn't thought of a need for such things and they seemed concerned for, said they, we would surely need them. Cheerfully I said we would manage some way that one night and we could go down to the Japanese village next day and buy gauze to make up into nets. But as darkness came I heard a loud buzzing in the air and a wave of mosquitoes filled the rooms.

We had put the three children to bed in one room while we were to occupy the other but there was no sleeping for any of us that night. After killing the mosquitoes in our room, I went to the other room and killed them there, and back and forth I went throughout the long night.

In spite of all my efforts the children's faces were swollen and their eyes almost closed because of the myriad bites.

We lost no time the next day in going to town to get netting. We could find no foreign netting in the stores and were compelled to buy two large green nets, one of which would just fit in a Japanese room. These we hang over our beds and there was room enough inside them to allow walking clear around the bed. But, somehow the mosquitoes got inside the nets that night and again we got little sleep. In time we learned better how to use the nets and were able to keep the troublesome insects on the outside.[8]

Although the Baird house was on a high hill overlooking the harbor the heat was intense. We wore as little clothing as we dared, but still had on too much.

On the Sunday afternoon after our arrival, just a week from the day when we entered Fusan harbor, our fourth child was born. We had left Japan when we did hoping to arrive in Seoul before Douglas came, but our temporary stay in Fusan seemed providential.

A few days after we moved into the Baird home, Rev. Samuel A. Moffett came unexpectedly from Seoul to spend the summer with the Bairds.

"You are more than welcome," said the Bairds, "but we have no unoccupied bedroom; we can put a mattress on the wide ledge of the bay window of the din-

---

[8]   Do you remember the vivid description of New England mosquitoes given Josh Billings? "They could climb the trees and back" and "Happy little critters singing as they toil." How apt! New England must have imported the japanese variety.

ing room for you if you don't mind putting up with such an arrangement." He decided to stay and so every room in the house except the kitchen was used as a bedroom.

During our stay in Fusan I went with Mr. Baird to many places in the neighborhood and gained an insight into his missionary work. Naturally my lack of understanding of the language was a handicap and it was not long before Mrs. Baird suggested I should use part of my time with a Korean teacher and Mr. Baird said I could use his teacher and helper, Mr. Koh, whenever he had some free time.

I well remember the first lesson I took. We sat on the floor of the little Korean room with a low table between us and looked at each other. I knew no Korean and Mr. Koh knew no English. How were we to begin? Mrs. Baird had given me one Korean sentence to start with. It was Korean for the question "What is this?" (E-gut moo-uh-se-o? literally "this thing, what is it?") I took up a book which was on the table and asked the question. He replied "Kugut chak-e-o." Literally "that thing, book it is." Naturally I took the answer to mean that the name of the article was "chak-e-o." Then I took up a pencil and asked the same question. My teacher answered, "Ku-gut yon-peel-e-o." Every time I asked him a question, he ended his reply with "e-o" and when I got through with my first lesson, I said to Mrs. Baird, "it seems queer to me that the name of everything ends in e-o." She laughed and said, "Oh no, you didn't understand - the name of the book is 'chak' and the 'e-o' at the end means 'it is.'" In English we would simply say 'a book,' or 'a pencil,' but the Korean idiom always includes a verb at the end. This verb, 'e-o,' means, 'it is,' and the complete answer is 'It is a book,' or 'It is a pencil.' Thus I had my initiation into the intricacies of the Korean language.

One of my trips into the country during our stay in Fusan was to the old Korean village of Pusan. 'Fusan' is the Japanese name and Pusan is the Korean, P instead of F. A point of great interest there was an old fort which had been built by the Japanese three hundred years before, during the Hideyoshi invasion. It was now a grass covered hill and nothing remained of the fortifications excepting the excavations at the top of the hill and some rough stone walls.

Mr. Moffett accompanied us on this trip and as we gathered flowers along the way we discovered that both of us were interested in botany. For eight years I had been a teacher of botany in the College of Pharmacy in Toronto, and he had been particularly interested in that subject during his college courses and so we decided to collaborate in a study of the flora of Korea, gathering specimens, drying them and classifying what we found. That promised to be an enjoyable and worthwhile avocation, but we both soon became absorbed in our real tasks and, excepting in a very desultory way, never had leisure to carry out our plan. Botany is an interesting subject but it takes a lot of time to do anything profitable with the gathering and classification of plants and I soon found that between studying the language and looking after the sick, there was not much time for a vocations.

Arrival in Chemulpo

We remained at the Baird home until the end of August when, as the summer was practically over, we felt we should continue our journey to Seoul. We had learned through letters from Mr. Underwood that the missionaries were returning from the hills and it would be possible to find a place in which to stay temporarily. We took passage on the 'Genkai Maru' and on going aboard found that Dr. Horace N. Allen, the first Protestant foreign missionary to take up work in Korea, was on board en route to Seoul. He was returning from America where he had gone as companion and guide of a group of Korean officials who had been sent by the king to Chicago to attend the World's Fair, "The Great White City." We were pleased to have this early opportunity to get acquainted with this pioneer physician.

The trip to Chemulpo required only about two days from Fusan. The captain of the 'Genkai Maru' was a Scotsman named Thompson. As a matter of fact, all of the captains of Japanese passenger boats in those days were foreigners though the other members of the crew were Japanese.

Mr. Underwood was at Chemulpo to meet us and help us on the trip up the river and then to the capital. We went ashore to Steward's Hotel where I made the acquaintance of the Chinese proprietor, E. D. Steward, the man to whom all foreigners looked for help on their arrival at the port. For many years he had served as a steward on Pacific Ocean ships and when he decided to leave that service and become a hotelkeeper he adopted the title 'steward,' which he had always been called on the ships, as his family name. He took the initials of his Chinese name (E-Dai) for his given name, and so he was known as E. D. Steward. The ground floor of his hotel was occupied by a general store in which all the clerks were Chinese who spoke Pidgeon English, and the upper story with its simple but clean furnishings was a haven for weary travellers.[9]

Mr. Underwood had learned that the river boat was to sail about midnight so arrangements were made for us to goon it to the nearest port to Seoul and we boarded the boat in the early evening. The cabin was a low room in which one could just sit on the floor without striking one's head on the ceiling, but could not stand erect without having to duck. As there were no sleeping cabins, all the ladies were assigned this room, while the men sat through the night in chairs on the open deck. It was tiresome, but we arrived at the port of Mapo in the early morning. As the trip was made during the night we missed the fine scenery and a sight of the big island of Kangwha where, in 1867, the Koreans had given battle to the American ship Shenandoah in an effort to prevent the Americans reaching the capital when the U. S. A. attempted to force Korea to make a treaty with her. The Koreans had fought bravely using cannon which they had made on the model of guns previously taken from French ships when the French made an unsuccessful attempt to reach Seoul in 1866. Mr. Moffett was at Mapo waiting for us. Having arranged with Korean boatmen to take us all on shore, he came out in a sampan to meet us. As we were about to step into one of these, the boatmen demanded double their usual price and pay it in advance. Mr. Moffett had arranged all these matters before coming aboard but when the men saw that the people to disembark were strange foreigners they repudiated the bargain.

Mr. Moffett, having argued with them for a few minutes without making any impression, called to one of the coolies on the shore to come to the side of the boat, and hopping on the shoulders of this man was carried to the shore while the rest of us prepared to follow his example. Then seeing they would lose their job altogether, the boatmen begged us to let them land us at the usual price. We complied very quickly because we were unaccustomed to being carried on a man's shoulders and preferred to land in the ordinary way.

[9]   Pidgeon English is understood by natives in the port towns of nearly all Asiatic countries. It is a combination of broken English, broken Chinese, and broken several other tongues, by means of which Western traders communicated with the Orientals. The word Pidgeon is itself an example of broken English being a corruption of the word "business" in the attempt of the natives to say that word, and so Pidgeon English is simply business English.

Arrival in Seoul

Carrying chairs (sedan chairs of various types) had been provided for our travel to the city. In those days the most common mode of travel was by these chairs. There were many varieties of them, but they may first of all be divided into two kinds - those carried by two men and those carried by four - designated as two-men chairs and four-men chairs.

Soon we had our first sight of a walled city. Through its West Gate we passed into a narrow street that led to the home of Dr. C. C. Vinton who was to entertain us until we could furnish a house which had been already rented for us. The house was of Korean architecture exteriorly but inside was of foreign style as it had been built for the residence of Mr. Möllendorff, a German who had come from China to head up the Customs Department of the Korean Government when it entered into treaty relations with the Western Nations. It was located on the north side of the city, a mile away from the homes of any other foreigners.

As our large family could not be long accommodated in Dr. Vinton's home with their several children needing the rooms we occupied. A call was sent out to all the missionary homes for the loan of any furniture they could spare as none of our furniture had yet come. Every family contributed something - a cookstove, a table, a bed or a chair and before long we had enough to make housekeeping possible.[10]

Servants had been engaged for us - a Japanese amah(nursemaid) who could speak a little English, a Korean man who said he could cook foreign style, and a Korean outside man to supply fuel and run whatever errands there might be.

During the interval between landing in Chemulpo and settling in the new house, Mrs. Avison had become ill and had to go to bed as soon as we got into the house. The Japanese amah didn't know how to dress 'foreign' children. She put the left shoe on the right foot, she put the girl's clothes on backward; many things were done in a queer way, all of which didn't help Mrs. Avison to get well. The Korean cook did not know how to do any foreign cooking - he couldn't even cook an egg. The outside man stole our fuel for his own home and things went generally wrong.

---

[10] Though our own furniture had been shipped from Canada months before, it had to go to New York by rail, across the Atlantic Ocean to London, through the Mediterranean Sea, the Red Sea and Indian Ocean, past Singapore, up the China coast and via the Yellow Sea to the Korean port of Chemulpo and then overland to Seoul and had not yet arrived.

A Chinese Cook

A Korean language teacher had been secured for me and he came every day to take up much of my time, hence I could do but little to help in the house. Mrs. Avison grew worse and I became desperate. At length I decided to get a trained Chinese cook if I could find one. I applied for help to an English- speaking Chinese servant in the American Legation.

"Did he know of any Chinese cook who was out of work?"

"Can do."

"Is he a good cook?"

"Yes, he cook for a German family in Wonsan."

"Is he honest?"

"Oh, yes, if he steal anything, I make good."

So I told him to send the cook to me.

He knew a little English and when I asked him if he could cook dinner by himself if I showed him where the supplies were he replied "Can do." I took him to the store room and left the keys with him and by and by we were called to dinner. He surely could cook! The meal consisted of soup, an entree, main course, salad, and dessert, and it certainly did taste good. It was the first time since our arrival in the new home that Mrs. Avison had been able to enjoy her food. One afternoon Mrs. Avison while still in bed, said she wished she had a nice piece of steak, so I called the cook and told him that Mrs. Avison would like a nice steak. "Can do," he said, and in a short time he returned with a piece of steak, nicely cooked and very tender, and Mrs. Avison ate it all. With this change in diet she was soon on her feet and able to teach the amah what to do for the children.

Though I had given the cook no money during his first week, he had provided us with plenty of good food and I knew that a time of reckoning would come. It did. On Saturday evening he brought in his account book, listing the various purchases for the week. He did not know how to write except to make figures so he had drawn pictures of the various items purchased, eggs, chickens, and the like. It was the strangest looking account I had ever seen. The prices of each item was listed and the total for food ran to much more than our salary for the period. So I said, "The meals are good. The cooking is good. But the cost is too much. From now on I will give you a certain amount for one week and you must not spend more than that amount." We came to an agreement and he remained with us for a considerable time, always providing good food and keeping within the limit set. A good Chinaman can do.

One day he came to me and said he wanted more help in the kitchen. He wanted a boy to clean things up and scrub the floor - he was a cook and not a kitchen servant. I said that the outside man would clean the floor for him. He did this for a time and then one day, without further conversation, I found a young Chinese in the kitchen attending to the cleaning work. I called the cook and told him I could not pay for an extra servant in the kitchen and he must use the outside manas I had already said. He replied that the boy was his nephew and wanted to learn how to cook. "No pay him any wages." And so I agreed to the plan.

Not long afterwards the outside man was missing. The cook then said, "Chinese boy can do." The lad did the chores and carried the fuel and all went well. We paid him the wage of an outside man and he did the kitchen chores for nothing.

Another day the man who did the bedroom and laundry work was missing - the houseboy. The cook said, "No mind. Chinese boy can do." So the chap did the work of two servants.

When the Japan-China War broke out the old cook came to me and said he must go back to China. He had "one piece wife" there. He must go to see what was happening to his family. I said we could not let him go for we had to have a cook. Again he replied, "China boy can do." So we let the old cook go to China and the Chinese boy became cook. We secured a Korean man as "boy" to do the housework and the young Chinese cook really "could do."

Thus I learned something about the far-sightedness and strategy of the Chinese. All the time he had had in view his desire to go back to his family and yet make suitable provision for us and for his nephew.

Roles of Missionary's Wife

I suppose you are wondering why we had to have so many servants. That is a fair question for American people to ask because in America a house and family such as I had could manage with only one. Several reasons for this apparent surplus for servants may be given but perhaps two will suffice. In the first place the wife of a missionary has to become a language student and do the work of a full missionary. She is expected to teach Bible Classes in the Sunday school and church, to visit the women in their homes and to conduct classes in outside villages. When her husband is a doctor she often has to see the woman patients who enter the hospital, comfort them and often go to their homes after they get well in order to keep up the connection and foster the beginning of a church in the village or town from which the women had come. In the second place the untrained servants of that day were unable to handle more than one kind of a job in the unfamiliar circumstances and surroundings of a home.

The value of the work done by the doctor's wife in visiting the women patients is well illustrated by the following incident.

A middle class woman from a village near Seoul came into the hospital as a patient and, through the teaching of Mrs. Avison and her Bible woman, she had decided to become a Christian. When she returned to her home she was visited by the Biblewoman who brought back a pressing invitation to Mrs. Avison to go to the former's home once a week to conduct a Bible class to which she would invite all the women of the neighborhood. Of course the invitation was accepted and the rooms of her house were soon taxed to the utmost to hold all who wanted to attend.

The son of the hospital gate man then decided he would do a follow up job with the boys of that village by gathering a few of them each Sunday afternoon and teaching them. He taught them to read and used the Bible as their textbook. Before long he had most of the boys of the village attending. When winter came this class, which so far had met out of door, continued to meet in the same way in spite of the cold weather for there was no room in the village large enough to hold them.

Before beginning the next stage of this story it will be necessary to tell how some of the working men spent the winter months when much of the work of the villagers stopped till spring came round. Most of the working people wore shoes made of straw twisted into twine and woven into shoes, soles and all. The straw could not be used if prepared and woven in the warm rooms of their homes as it would dry out too rapidly and break and also the shoes could not be made out of doors where the straw would freeze and break as it was being manipulated. So every winter they dug an oblong pit about sixteen feet square and two or three feet deep and covered it with a roof of thatch supported by poles. Doors were cut in the roof, which could be opened when the weather was suitable to provide the necessary ventilation and light. Inside, the floor was covered with straw mats on which the men sat and worked. That winter, when such a shelter as this had been erected in the village, the men, seeing the boys still meeting in the open air, invited them to come inside and hold their school there. The boys gladly accepted the invitation and every Sunday afternoon during the winter they were made welcome by the men, who got into the habit of stopping their work and listening to the reading, the singing and the recitation.

Years passed and the outcome of this beginning in such a simple way was the development of an organized church of 250 members with its own church building, kindergarten, day school, night school, and all the various organizations of a modern church, all supervised and led by a regular Korean pastor.

The accompanying picture shows this church as its attendants sat for a photo taken on the last Sunday before Mrs. Avison and I left Korea as retired missionaries. My wife, my doctor son and I can be seen in the center of the group. This is just one such group developed as a result of Mrs. Avison's labors in the hospital and a consideration of this will help you to understand why she could not do her own housework and carry on her missionary visitation and classes and also act as a teacher to her children in the years before schools for the children of Westerners were established.

In December our boxes of furniture arrived at the port of Chemulpo and were loaded on two-wheeled ox carts (each wheel made of wood and not perfectly circular) and brought over the rough mountain roads to our home in Seoul, nearly thirty miles inland. There was great rejoicing when we heard of the arrival, accompanied by a considerable amount of trepidation for we feared for the condition of the contents. Mrs. Avison was particularly anxious about the piano which would be one of the first brought to Korea.[11] Many accidents might have happened to it en route - by train, by ship, and finally by ox cart. When the shipment arrived at the house the piano box was the first to be opened and Mrs. Avison at once sat down to try out the keys. To her delight and ours, every note was perfect. The first tune she played was "Praise God from Whom All Blessings Flow," and we all gathered around and sang it lustily. As for the rest of the contents of the boxes, crates, and barrels, we found only one broken piece - just one fruit jar!

---

[11]   The instrument had been carefully prepared for the long journey and great care had been taken to stretch all of the wires so that they would not easily get out of tune. After a period of forty-eight years, it is still one of the best in Korea.

Getting acquainted with Seoul and learning the Language

As my official appointment to a specified task in the missionary enterprise had to await the action of the Mission, which would not meet for nearly two months after our arrival in Seoul, I applied myself in the meantime to studying the language and getting acquainted with the city in which I rather hoped I would be permanently located.

The need for active language study was made strikingly apparent by a very early incident, I received an urgent call to go to a nearby house, supposedly to see a sick woman. On arriving I found her already dead and the body covered with a sheet according to the usual custom of Korea and of our own country as well. Though her family knew she was dead when they called me they had heard such wonderful stories of what the western doctors were doing that they hoped I might even be able to bring her back to life. My slight knowledge of the language was much strained in my effort to explain the limitations of my skill but I managed to make them realize that this was beyond the power of even a foreign physician.

This experience, however, made me all the more anxious to learn the language as fast as possible for what can any one do in a foreign land till he gets to a point where he can understand what the people say to him and be able to reply in the language with which they are familiar?

My fellow missionaries knew this and had engaged a language teacher for my wife and me before our arrival. He lost no time in calling on us, bringing Mr. Underwood with him to introduce him and act as interpreter. His surname was Yi (Yee) and it was not necessary for us to know his given name because he must always be addressed as Yi Sun Saing (Sun Saing meaning teacher), one of the highest titles in Korea where scholarship is regarded as of even more importance than official rank and where ability to read and write the Chinese Script was the supreme test of scholarship.

There was a great paucity of helpful textbooks and I had to depend on Mr. Yi's teaching ability. He came to me every forenoon to give me such instruction as could be imparted by a teacher who did not understand his pupil's language any more than the pupil understood his. As he had at one time been teacher to Mr. H. B. Hulbert who had drilled him in methods of teaching he was perhaps a better instructor than the average, so I had no reason to complain and in time I was able to speak haltingly and to understand fairly well what people said to me.

Mr. Hulbert had taught Mr. Yi certain words important in his own work and he took pleasure in using them on me and I must say he made them an effective means of teaching me some of the grammar of the language and some pronunciations. One of his favorite words was "aspirate" which he pronounced with great difficulty but with great satisfaction to himself as "ash-pi-Reg-Ituh". Though I never gained anything like a complete use of Korean, I did get enough to make myself understood in the range of subjects included in a medical course and in delivering addresses to the students and in the churches.

Professedly Yi was not a Christian but I learned after awhile that he was secretly a member of the Roman Catholic Church and that his daughter was being brought up by the sisterhood to become a nun. I soon realized there had been something in his past that he was hiding from me and from others too. Though he was introduced to me as Mr. "Yi," I was told by some who were acquainted with his past that his real surname was "Pee" and that he had changed it back in the 1860's when ruthless persecution of all Christians was carried on by the regent Tai Won Koon. At that time he lost his courage, denied his faith and even betrayed some of his friends to the police. Then, ashamed of what he had done, he tried to conceal his identity by changing his surname from Pee to Yi. Though he never went back to the idolatrous customs of his fellow countrymen he did not again openly avow his Christianity until near the time of his death many years later. I found that if any one spoke the name Pee in conversation about him a hush immediately fell on the group if he appeared.

Yi Sunsaing[12] came to my home every morning except Sunday and we sat down for the forenoon to wrangle with words and phrases and then I spent the afternoons in trying to make sense out of the voluble speech of the men and women who came to the clinic and thought I should understand their long and rapidly spoken sentences. At first I could only get a word here and there of what they said but as time went by my ears seemed to open and gradually my brain grasped an occasional sentence and I gained courage.

One day I suggested to my teacher that he go with me to the clinic in the afternoons but he shook his head and though I urged him he, for a long time, kept on declining. I wondered why but one day was shocked to discover that while he was willing to come to a foreigner's home, which he could do without being observed, he didn't want to be seen on the streets with one. Apparently his need

12   "Sunsaing" means 'teacher' and it was generally used for literary men. For some reason this man's given name was never used and even I, his loved pupil, never knew it.

for money compelled him to associate with us but he did not have much love for us in his heart. However, one day he consented to go with me. I did not at first observe that he was taking me through narrow, unfrequented lanes but when I did notice it and suggested that we take the more direct route by the main street and save time, he paid no attention to my suggestion.

This continued for some time until one morning, without any request from me, he led me through the main street to the hospital. I made no comment and he made no explanation but it soon became evident that he had lost his fear of me and had really become my personal friend for never again did he avoid being seen with me in public.

After nearly six years of this daily intercourse, we were ordered to Canada because of the ill health of both my wife and myself and he and I, who had learned to love each other, must part for at least some time. The morning of our departure came. Our trunks had been shipped ahead of us and we were to be carried in sedan chairs over the three miles to the Han River where we were to board a small river steamer for the port of Chemulpo. My teacher came to the house early in the morning to say the last good-bye. When the coolies had been loaded with our baggage, I tried to bid him good-bye but he would not have it so - he was going to accompany us part of the way. So the family went on ahead in the chairs and we two followed on foot. He took my hand and so, hand in hand, we walked through the main street of the city and I had full proof that his affection for us and his trust in us was genuine. Though I suggested, every little while, that he leave us and return to his home it was not till long after we had passed through the city gate and were well on our way to the river that he at last stopped to say good-bye. As he uttered the Korean phrase which meant "go in peace" followed by the English words "good-bye," the tears welled up in his eyes. Sadly he turned and began his return to the city while I too had moisture in my eyes. As we were going to Canada without any certainty of returning we were greatly moved by this evidence of our teacher's devotion. When we did return, eighteen months later, he again became our faithful instructor and friend.

‣ Chapter 3 ◂

A Strange Career in Korea

The First Medical Missionary in Korea, Dr. Horace N. Allen

The most interesting personage to me as I entered Korea was Dr. Horace N. Allen, the first Protestant Missionary to reach that land and remain there so I think it but right to give him the first place in my series of stories of men, women and events.

In October 1883 a young doctor and his wife left Toledo, Ohio, for Medical Mission Work in China. He spent nearly a year in Shanghai, studying the Chinese language but grew discouraged at not receiving an appointment to a definite field of work. When he learned that his Board in New York had decided, after the signing of the Treaty between Korea and the United States in 1882, to establish Mission Work in that newly opened land, he cabled to them offering his services there. He was appointed July 22, 1884 and became the first Protestant Missionary to Korea.

Leaving his wife in Shanghai he reached his new field September 20, a date which thus became memorable in the history of Missions in Korea. On reaching Seoul, the capital, he went at once to the home of the American Minister, General Lucius H. Foote, from whom he learned that no mention of Mission Work had been made in the Treaty with Korea and so his coming raised a problem that might easily produce disagreeable reactions. Much would depend on the tact of the American Minister and the first comer.

Though the American Minister was unable to give him any assurance in regard to beginning Missionary Work he suggested that he might appoint him as medical officer to the Legation, a position that would give him a definite standing in the community and at the same time, without raising the question of missionary work at the outset, enable him to give medical service incidentally to any one who might apply for it.

He bought a Korean house next to the legation building and, after preparing it to fit the needs of foreign occupants, went back to Shanghai for his family and soon afterward returned to Seoul.

His coming to Korea just when he did was either fortunate or providential for it was not long before an event occurred which settled without any controversy the question as to whether missionary work would be permitted or proscribed in Korea.

Treatment of Mr. Min by Dr. Allen during the Emeute of 1884

The Korean government had decided to revise the Postal System and have that service conducted on lines similar to those of western nations.

A young man, Hong Yong Sik, son of a noble family, who had studied in Japan and was already interested in government reform was appointed Postmaster General and arrangements had already been made to inaugurate the new system December 4, 1884, by a banquet to which many high Korean officials and the foreign diplomats were invited.

In the meantime a number of the younger Korean nobles who had studied-in Japan and had learned there a good deal about the governmental systems of the U. S. A. and Europe, had organized themselves as a Reform Party which had for its object the overthrow of autocracy and the substitution of a limited monarchy. Its leaders having failed to interest the King and Queen in their plans, decided that force must be used to effect their purpose. Choosing the occasion of the banquet as the time for throwing the Conservative group into confusion, they planned to force their way into the palace and then, taking their Majesties into custody and by pressure obtaining the King' Signature to a royal edict announcing the new form of government they would form cabinet composed of themselves to bring about the new form of government.

At that time their Majesties were in residence in the East Palace or Tong Kwan and the banquet was held at the new post office headquarters outside the palace entrance.

While the feast was in progress a cry of fire in a nearby building was raised and all was soon in disorder and in the confusion that followed a party of the reformers made an attack on the group to create a state of alarm that would enable them to enter the palace and carry out their scheme. The new postmaster was killed in the confusion and the leader of the Government, Prince Min Young Ik, favorite cousin of the Queen, was severely wounded on his face and arms. He himself had been a member of the reform party, as had been Hong Yong Sik, the postmaster general, but had refused any resort to force. He had advised the reformers to take a slower but surer (as he believed) method of making the desired changes. The revision of the postal system had been done a this insistance and in pursuit of that policy.

The court physicians were called to treat the Prince's wounds but, quite ignorant of anatomy, they were unable to stanch the flow of blood which endangered his life. Some one suggested calling the American doctor and in desperation he was sent for. Dr. Allen, finding a severed artery in a deep sword cut on the Prince's arm, did not take long to expose it and ligate it. Lo! the bleeding at once stopped! It was a miracle! The efforts of the native doctors, however, had so contaminated the wound that suppuration set in and only by means of constant attention was the arm saved. But saved it was and established was the reputation of the foreign doctor. In Dr. Allen's own words.

"the medical sucess in this instance prepared the way for the opening up of the missionary work proper - that early success with the prominent native prince caused the natives generally to come for treatment of all sorts of ills, real and imagined. As a consequence I asked for and obtained the use of a building in which to see and treat these people. This, the first modern hospital for the Koreans was named by the ruler Kwang Hei Kwan or house of civilized virtue."

Another result of this incident was the appointment of Dr. Allen as medical officer to the royal court and, of course, he became physician to all the Western Legations that had been established in Korea.

All this meant that he and his wife were accepted socially also by the entire foreign community and afterward this social recognition was extended to all the missionaries who soon began to arrive. Such recognition had not always been given to missionaries in other countries but in Korea the business people and officials of the Legation have throughout all the years accepted them as social equals, a boon to all concerned.

Founding of the First Western Hospital in Korea, Jejoongwon

During those early years the official representatives of America found it necessary to return to the U. S. A. frequently yon business connected with the establishment of better relations with Korea and with those other countries which, having established treaty relations with her, were concerned to see that they got their share of favors. It was natural that, on such occasions, this half official, half missionary should be entrusted with the work of the American Legation and as one reads Dr. Allen's notes in his Chronological Index one finds it hard to distinguish in which of the two functions he was acting at any given time.

Dr. Allen became American Diplomat in Korea

The King also asked him at various times to accompany delegations of Koreans to the United States - now a deputation to the American Government and again as adviser of a group going to the Chicago Exhibition in 1893.

One is puzzled sometimes to know whether he was acting as a missionary doctor, a community physician, or the medical attendant of the Korean Court. He was naturally more or less troubled to determine just how much time he should spend in activities that interfered with his work as a missionary doctor - Were his energies being too much scattered? He decided they were and, after much consideration, resigned from his connection with the Mission.

Later on he was reappointed by the Board of Foreign Missions but, after a second trial, again retired from missionary work and that retirement became permanent.

His first position in the U. S. Legation was as Secretary but, because the Minister and Consul were so often absent, he, as substitute for first one and then the other, often really knew more about governmental affairs than they did. This led to his promotion step by step, until he became Minister Resident and Envoy Extraordinary and, when the Legation was raised to an Embassy, he became the first American Ambassador.

My first acquaintance with him was in August, 1893 when he was returning from the trip to the "White City," as the World's Fair in Chicago was called. He had gone there as the King's representative to assist the Korean deputation and advise them how to meet the many difficulties they would certainly encounter.

When we were leaving Fusan for Seoul we boarded the S. S. Genkai, always referred to as the Genkai Maru (maru meaning ship), we met Dr. Allen as he returned from America and during the two or three days of our trip to Chemulpo and the night on the river boat to Mapo (the river port nearest to Seoul and only three miles from the city) we got to know him quite well.

It was on this return to Seoul he decided to resign from his position as Court Physician feeling that, as an official of the American Government, he might at sometime or other find himself much embarrassed if he had to take issue with His Majesty or His Ministers.

So the next time he was called on to attend the King he asked me to accompany him and be introduced to His Majesty and from that time for fifteen years I was a frequent visitor at the palace.

During his period as American representative he certainly found himself in many interesting but difficult and embarrassing positions. The large number of American Missionaries, about 150, must have caused many of his embarrassing moments.

Had they all been wise it would have been easier for him and them; but how could we expect wordly wisdom to be always found in religious enthusiasts?

Some of these, no doubt, felt that, as he had been a missionary, he should always decide in favor of the missionary when one of them got into a dispute with a Korean citizen, a Korean official, or a representative of some other country. Some of them too, expected him to support them in trying to help Christian Koreans who, depending probably on securing the missionary's help, had evaded his duties as a Korean citizen.

Dr. Allen, because of his missionary experience, knew the ins and outs of such things and, while he sympathized with those who wanted his help, showed his sagacity by carefully discriminating the cases brought to his notice and giving or refusing this help accordingly. Though the reasons for a refusal were always, or nearly always, explained in a sympathetic fashion, the complainants were sometimes aggressive, saying to others that Dr. Allen had no use for missionaries since he had taken up with politics.

I quote the following from Dr. Allen's book "Things Korean."

While, as a rule, our missionaries combine commonsense with superior mental qualities, among so many there must be some exceptions. One man lost his patience while a guest at a Buddhist temple and began smashing the little plaster idols with his cane so that he together with his innocent fellow missionaries were excluded from visiting that place for some time. This was a somewhat noted case at the time since the British representative urged drastic punishment on the ground that his government would never allow any interference with the native worship in India and that we ow edit to ourselves to take the same course in this newly opened country, I did not have to do more than consult with the missionary and with his associates who deeply regretted his lapse, to get from them jointly a promise that nothing of the kind should occur again. However, the man, not now in Korea, did break out again and wrote a letter to the Emperor calling upon him to repent of his sins and asking to be allowed to preach repentance to him. As the letter was written by an ignorant native scribe who used terms that amounted to an unintentional insult to His Majesty, the matter was referred to me and again I was obliged to get another joint promise of good behavior.

Remarking on the frequent complaint that missionaries are persons non grata to other foreign residents he has the following to say -

Let a gentlemanly missionary come to this community, Possessed of some talent that makes him a desirable acquisition, whether it be a good voice for singing, the ability to make music upon some instrument or skill in some good vigorous game of athletics; let him even be a good story-teller or be simply endowed with good sense and good nature backed by learning and he will be taken up gladly and find real human sympathy even though this may not extend to his work for the natives in just the comprehensive manner he might wish.

Further, such a man may find that an important side issue of his work will likely be the giving of sympathy to these fellow countrymen, who have their own trials and discouragements in the new land, and in so doing he may gradually win them to the ideals left behind with the distant home.

A missionary of this description, and I have known such, who has something to give to the community and who is willing to give it, will not be ostracized or lack for sympathy and the companionship of his kind. He will on the contrary be welcomed and be made a part of that little band and it will be for him to say just how much or how many of the attention open to him he shall or may accept.

There are missionary names of good men, some of whom are now long dead, which are revered in the communities of which they were members and to whom more than one prosperous and successful business man of substance and position in the community looks with deep regard as to one who had given him real help in climbing out of the rut of personal gain and creature comfort or what may have passed for pleasure.

A body of one hundred and fifty missionary men and women, with their large native following, brought plenty of work to the legation; for while the simple and kindly natives accepted Christianity readily, the official class were apt to let pass no chance for personal gain, and the frugal habits taught by the missionaries usually resulted in bringing about a better worldly condition to their followers, making them con-sequently the more liable to magisterial attention. In interfering with these native Christians the officials would sometimes overstep their rights and give good cause for the foreign teacher to take up the case for his native pupil. Sometimes, also, these cases seem to have been welcomed by some of the more indiscreet among the missionaries, who may have thought that the legation officials were in need of stimulating excitement. At any rate, mission cases were almost always "on the docket."

I have entitled this account of Dr. Allen's activities "A Strange Career," because I realized that his experiences in Korea covering a period of twenty-one years had been very much out of the ordinary. Now as I glance over his own writings I find a paragraph headed "A Strange Career" which shows that the title I chose is a very fitting one. I quote that paragraph here:

It is a rather strange termination of a career begun as a medical missionary to have it end as a minister plenipotentiary; yet the change was so gradual as to be little noticeable, beginning with a preliminary service with the Korean Legation in Washington and then step by step from the lowest post in our own service up through all the grades below ambassador. As this service was continuous and all in one country and practically coincident with the whole period of that country's diplomatic relations, it enabled one unconsciously to acquire a useful familiarity with conditions such as would be difficult to secure in a period of shorter service. It also enabled me to hold commissions consecutively under Presidents Harrison, Cleveland, Mckinley and T. R. Roosevelt.

He also had in the same book the following reference to his varied duties.

A Promoter - It was a somewhat unique position in which I found myself upon leaving Korea after twenty-one years' residence there, having to my credit the introduction of the following new departures, all of a useful nature :Protestant missions and Western medical science; modern mining on a colossal scale; steam railways; electric trolleys and water-works, all of which were left in a successful going condition.

During the progress of the Japanese-Russian War, Dr. Allen visited America to lay before his government the situation in the Far East as he saw it. It had become apparent what his view of the situation was - Korea would lose its independence no matter which side won. He also saw clearly that America would lose her position of influence not only in Korea but also in Japan and China.[13]

Not only was he unable to convince his Superior Officers of this but his views brought him into disrepute with the Japanese Government which did not like to feel that America's representative in Korea did not approve either their plans for expansion or their methods of carrying out these plans, and as a result he, in 1905, resigned his post and returned to America where he took up residence again in Toledo, Ohio. His book, "Things Korean," was apparently written in 1915 for the last paragraph reads as follows:[14]

But even if China should escape, who knows but the little peninsula of Korea may not possibly witness another decennial overturn and pass under the guidance of yet another overlord? In 1884 Japan drove China from the peninsula. In 1904-5 Japan drove Russia from the entire Korean neighborhood except in the vicinity of Vladivostock. In 1915 --- The blank will have to be filled in later; may we be spared any military participation in events that may lead to any such change.

13   This was a true foreseeing of what really did happen in a short time.

14   This too soon happened.

Did he foresee what would come after 1915? Apparently he did.

His last years in America were years of suffering from osteomyelitis of the leg. One leg was amputated but the disease was only halted for a time and ere long caused his death.

As a fitting close to these notes I quote a few sentences from the preface to his book "Things Korean" that plainly show his attitude, toward the Koreans and his views on the failure of America to redeem the pledge made to Korea in the Treaty of 1882.

The poor Koreans are now in desperate straits and it has been suggested that this work be devoted to exposing their wrongs in an effort to turn public sentiment in their direction. Such a course does not seem to be advisable at this juncture - rich as are the supplies of materials at hand. Opposition on their part seems at best to be unavailing if not suicidal: they can only make the best of existing conditions.

The sad feature of the case is that we deserted them in their time of need and ignored the solemn agreement we had entered into with them as an inducement for their abandoning the centuries-old position of exclusion and non intercourse and emerging into the dazzling glare of treaty relations. Written into the treaty are the following words.

If other Powers deal unjustly or oppressively with either government the other will exert their good offices, on being in formed of the case, to bring about an amicable arrangement thus showing their friendly feeling.

We paid no heed to this solemn pledge at the critical time of the Portsmouth Convention and must accept the odium attached to such violation of sacred covenants.

Dr. John W. Heron and Foreign Cemetery in Seoul

Dr. J. W. Heron died July 23, 1890, and this was the first death to occur among the foreign residents. It seems odd to those of us who came later that until the need for a cemetery became immediate no efforts had been made to provide a place for the burial of foreigners, though any one giving any thought to the matter would have known that some of the community would certainly die some time and that some one might die at any time.

Dr. Heron was stricken with dysentery in the midsummer of 1890, just five years and one month after he and his wife arrived in Seoul and then the need for a cemetery became immediately peremptory.

A deputation at once set out on a search for a suitable place and several possible sites were found. Application to the Korean Government for permission to purchase one of these was refused because of the objections raised by the Koreans living in the neighborhood. "It was bad enough to have living foreigners around them; as for dead ones, who would venture to arouse the ill will of the spirits or what might not occur when these were allowed to be buried there? It would never do. Who asked the foreigners to come anyway? Let them take their bodies back to America instead of creating a menace to the natives by burying them in Korean soil."

When application for one selected site was refused each of the others was asked for in turn but always with the same result. Many days had already passed. It was the rainy season in the intense heat of July and no ice could be obtained to delay decomposition of the corpse. What could be done?

At length Dr. Allen, who was then acting consul for America, let it be known that he had given the family permission to inter Dr. Heron's body in the garden that surrounded the legation which was owned by the American government and therefore under his control and preparations for the funeral were got under way. The matter was speedily reported to the King who declared that that could not be allowed as no burials, even of Koreans, had never taken place within the walls of the capital.

"But," he was asked, "what can be done?" That was American property and not under Korean jurisdiction. How could they be stopped form thus desecrating the capital?

It was suggested that a royal edict directing the owner or owners to sell to the foreigners whatever site they might choose outside the capital would settle the difficulty in order to preserve the sanctity well outside of the city. This was done and out went the committee again. They selected a vacant hill site along the Han River about four miles from the city but again were met with the refusal of the owners till a direct order from the Government to the owner to sell brought results and the interment of the remains of Dr. Heron took place there without further delay. Whether the local spirits were rendered powerless by the fact that the sale had been made peremptory by His Majesty and therefore the owners should not be blamed does not appear but no reports of any devilish acts against the people of the neighborhood have ever been made. With the passing years many burials have been made there and several times the cemetery has had to be extended by the purchase of adjoining fields and always without any difficulties greater than could be surmounted by giving a little more for them than their market value.

It is a beautiful location and if the place for the bodies they have left behind them is a matter of any moment to those who formerly occupied them, I am sure they could want no more beautiful spot than the hill at Yang Wha Jin overlooking the river and far enough from the noise and hurly-burly of the city.

Chapter 4

Jejoongwon and Dr. Oliver R. Avison

Charging the Jejoongwon

I looked eagerly forward to the meeting of the Mission to be held in October for it would settle the place and nature of my work. During the interval I heard the subject much discussed. Certain of the small group of missionaries then on the field (all of them lived in Seoul at that early date) had explored various sections of the country with a view to establishing one or more stations outside the capital. The leader in this work, the Rev. Samuel A. Moffett, was very anxious to have me appointed to open medical work in the city of Pyong Yang in the far north, where he was opening evangelist's work. It was a very important and strange place but some felt it would not be appropriate or wise to send a newly arrived family with four young children as pioneers so far away from the capital. Personally I agreed with that point of view though I said nothing either pro or con. I felt I should submit to the judgment of those who ought to know where I could most probably render the best service. I tried to be impartial but I fear I was very much like John Wesley when he was planning to take a wife. He wanted to do God's will even in the choosing of a wife and so prayed much about it. He said, "Oh, God, I want even in this to do thy will. Please make me willing to let Thee choose, but, but, O God, Please let it be Hannah."

Naturally one of the first things I wanted to see in Seoul was the hospital about which I had heard so much, and in the development of which I expected to spend my life, the institution given to Dr. Allen by the King for saving the life of Queen's favorite cousin in 1884.

When Dr. Allen was giving the hospital his constant attention and while Dr. Heron lived and also backed up Dr. Allen's ideals, it had served a worthwhile piece of work but after Dr. Allen found himself unable, because of being often requisitioned to assist the Legation, to give his full attention to aid his co-worker, Dr. Heron, died and when their successor did not give it his full attention the number of patients gradually fell off so that medical missionaries came to regard it as an unimportant part of the mission work and were inclined to drop it altogether so for a time it looked as though my appointment to it would not be desirable.

After Dr. Heron died and Dr. Allen resigned from the conduct of the hospital, it was carried on by another doctor in the Mission who was still in charge of it when I arrived.

When I visited it the first time I was greatly disappointed though I had been warned not to expect much as the buildings were all of Korean style and the work being done was practically only that of a dispensary.

During Dr. Allen's period of service in it the work had grown so heavy that the board had sent Dr. J. Heron to assist him. As a matter of historical exactness Dr. Heron had been selected for this post before the removal of Dr. Allen from China to Korea but his sailing to Korea had been delayed and Dr. Allen was the first to arrive and receive the honors that came to him as already described.

After seeing the hospital I looked around the city and found it full of interesting things some of which are described in the following pages.

Rev. Underwood wished very much to see the Mission continue its connection with Royal Hospital believing that, if rightly conducted it would be very helpful in maintaining the King's interest and that of the most influential people in all phases of missionary and when the Mission Board in New York consulted him about the matter while he was in America, he strongly advised them to continue connection with it and urged them to seek a physician who was especially fitted not only to do the medical work but also to maintain Dr. Allen's prestige at court and with the noblity; while at the same time he made the institution itself a directly evangelistic agency.

While this matter was still under consideration, Mr. Underwood, as previously stated, mad a visit to Toronto to address the Y. M. C. A. connected with the two medical school there. It fell to me to conduct him around the city to the several meetings that had been arranged for him and as we moved about, we discussed the medical needs of Korea. He told me about the Royal Korean hospital for which they wanted a physician and also of the dire condition of the people because of a sanitary knowledge, of the terribly high death rate of the people as a whole and the still more terrible infant mortality. I had already told of our decision to go out to those needy people as a result of Mr. Underwood's visit.

However, the frequent absences of Dr. Allen as related and the early death of Dr. Heron from dysentery, the work fell of - probably because neither their successor nor the clerical members of the mission regarded it as an important factor in helping to forward the evangelistic side of the mission work.

Had it not been for the interest Mr. Underwood took in its continuance, it would doubtless have been dropped altogether after Dr. Heron's death.

But Mr. Underwood whose ideas of missionary work were broader than those of most of his evangelistic coworkers believed that ···.

Just before the decision was made, however, a letter from New York to the Mission instructed it to retain its connection with the Government Hospital and to appoint me to conduct it and that settled the question. I was pleased for it put me in a position to initiate a project that I had already envisioned - the training of native doctors with the object of fitting them to carry on a campaign for the introduction of sanitary methods, a work that should naturally be begun in the capital.

So it came to pass that on November 1, 1894, I began my work as physician to the Royal Korean Hospital. What a high sounding name for such an insignificant institution! But it was a place in which to begin - it presented an "open Sesame" to whatever I might want to make of it. There was a small dispensary building where the medical work had been done and where much more, I hoped, could be done.

A Real Pictures of Jejoongwon

It consisted of a one storied building, sixteen feet by twenty-eight feet, divided as in the accompanying drawing.

All outdoors served as a waiting room. The patients entered at 1, or 2, were examined and treated in 3, 4, and 5, then, passing through 3, received their medicines from 6 and went out at 1.

It was a small affair but what a lot it might mean to many suffering people!

The equipment of instruments and the stock of medicines was small but I added some of both that I had brought with me and these gave me a fair start. As for the rest of the buildings, they were sufficiently numerous and large to provide a commodious hospital when the time for preparing them should come. The King contributed W3,000 a year - at that time the equivalent of $1,500 United States currency - for the use of the institution but as the money was paid through the choosas, most of it was eaten[15] by them and but little of it reached its proper goal.

I have said that most of the money was eaten by the choosas but that word will mean nothing to my readers. A choosa is a government official of a low order who, having passed the regular government examination, expects to be given a salaried office and if that is not done he still never expects to do menial work. When the hospital was established under His Majesty's order it opened an opportunity for giving a group of these hungry waiters a place but as no fund was established to provide them with salaries they naturally took what they needed out of the fund given to the hospital and which was transmitted to the institution through them.

As there were then no nurses to help me in my work, I asked the Northern and Southern Presbyterian Missions, both located in Seoul at that time, to try an experiment, I suggested that each of them appoint a single lady, having some knowledge of the Korean language and a flair for medical work, to join the institution as pupil nurses and learn how to assist the doctor and give practical care to the sick under the conditions found in such a primitive hospital. The idea was well received and two of the women, not too old to learn and not too young to meet even the male patients, were duly appointed. They were Miss Martha Tate of the Southern Presbyterian Mission and Miss Victoria Arbuckle of the Northern. They were very helpful to me under the difficult conditions of the time but Miss Tate was soon taken to the southern part of the country where her own mission had selected a separate field for work and liss Arbuckle left Korea to return to America and so the scheme did not have a fair trial.

When I began work in the dispensary I had not acquired enough of the language to enable me to talk with the patients personally so an interpreter was appointed from among the group of choosas to help me. As he understood English fairly well I was able to carry on with comparative ease but he was what the

15   'Eaten' is a word commonly used for that part of a sum of money supposedly given for a specific purpose which is appropriated by the agent for his own use.

Korean called a yangban[16] and so had to get his living without working with his hands. He was apt to address the low-class patients in a supercilious tone to which they did not object because they were used to it but which I did not like. On one occasion he showed his sense of greatness when a boy brought him a note written in the simple Korean script which was then despised by readers of the difficult Chinese characters as fit to be used only when writing to the un-learned and how could he, a choosa, be put into that class. He kicked the messenger and sent him back with the note with directions to tell his master that, he, the interpreter was not a 'sangnom.'[17]

How I Came to be Physician to the King of Korea

Dr. H. N. Allen's success in the treatment of prince Min, the Queen's favorite cousin, when he was wounded during the Emeute of 1884, gained for him the gratitude of the court and the King's complete confidence in Western surgery. From that time His Majesty regarded Dr. Allen as his private physician and showered on him many favors.

In 1893 the United States Government asked Dr. Allen to accept the position of Secretary of its legation in Korea. After accepting that position, he felt it would be inappropriate for an official of the United States Government to hold such a personal relation to the King of the country as he had done and so informed His Majesty. It was just then I reached Korea and Dr. Allen took the opportunity to suggest that the newly arrived physician be asked to succeed him.

I knew nothing of this until one afternoon in October, 1893, within a few weeks after our arrival. That afternoon-while a conference of the men of the mission was being held Rev. H. G. Underwood received a message from Dr.

---

16   This word, yangban, conveys a very distinct meaning to a Korean, a meaning which we foreigners gradually absorbed so that we always used it instead of the English word by which it was interpreted to us, Viz- gentleman, It could be applied, however, either to a man or woman. Yangbans belong to the official class, not necessarily rich and often quite poor. It they cannot get a position suitable to a yangban they live from hand to mouth by borrowing or sometimes even by begging. Most of them have studied the Chinese classics and this puts them into the highly respected group of "scholars." They are neither plebeians nor bourgeois. They may be rich or poor but, in any event, they do not work. They are born into a group above the working class.

17   A sangnom is just the opposite of a yangban. He is a member of the working class.

Allen saying that the King was ill and asking him to get hold of Dr. Avison at once with his evening clothes on and bring him to the United States legation that he might take him to the palace and introduce him to the royal patient.

That broke up the meeting for in those early days, when our number was small, the removal of two members of a conference was a serious matter. Mr. Underwood turned to me with the important question, "Did you bring an evening suit with you?"

An evening suit! The last thing I would have thought of as an adjunct of missionary work! Of course I hadn't brought one, so Mr. Underwood took me to his home to try on his suit. Didn't fit? Of course not, for he was shorter than I and at the same time heavier. My arms stuck out from the coat sleeves, my legs were too long for the pants and my body was too slim for the vest. The difficulty was reported to Dr. Allen who directed a search to be made among the foreign men in Seoul and at length we got a coat and vest from one home and pants from another.

Why all this fuss to get an evening suit? Well, the palace regulations required all who visited the King to be dressed in the official garb of his country. The United States Government had ruled that its officials at foreign courts should have no special attire except the regular full dress suits worn in America at evening affairs and His Majesty had accepted this as the official dress of American representatives. So all Americans who appeared at court even in the day time were expected to dress in that way. As court physician Dr. Allen had followed this custom and I too must do so.

Because of the search for clothes to fit me Dr. Allen and I did not reach the palace till ten p. m. and the only explanation that could be preferred was that the new doctor, not expecting the call, had not been available at an earlier hour.

On entering His Majesty's room I found his face and scalp so greatly swollen that he could not open his eyes to see his new physician. His face was also very red and blistered. I could not yet speak the language but the English-speaking chamberlain, Ko Hui Kyung, was on hand and able to interpret clearly so the conversation proceeded without difficulty.

My diagnosis was made as soon as I saw him for I had treated many cases of poison-ivy infection in Canada and had been warned after my arrival that Koreans sometimes suffered from a similar condition caused by the varnish on their hats which is made from the sap of the poison oak trees. This poison is volatile so, if the hats are not worn till all the poison as ingredient has evaporated, no bad results follow but if worn too soon by a susceptible individual, the specific inflammation is likely to ensue.

My first question therefore was, had His Majesty recently worn a new hat? Yes, he had. The diagnosis was then easy - he was suffering from lacquer poisoning. They all agreed to this but marvelled at the diagnostic skill of the new doctor who had so recently come to their county. But His Majesty was suffering severely and all those around him were filled with anxiety - could I cure it quickly? Yes, I would at once send from the hospital a sufficient supply of liquid medicine to be applied freely and constantly to his face and head so as to keep the skin wet all the time and I would return the next day, hoping to see some improvement.

When I called the following day, the swelling was much lessened, the burning feeling had been relieved and his eyes could be opened enough to enable him to see those around him, including the doctor. There was great rejoicing and the reputation of the new physician was established.

If I had not recognized the disease at once and if the remedy had not been immediately effective, then what? As it was, I had to continue my daily attendance much longer than was really necessary - my patient being such an important personage ⋯ but it was the beginning of fifteen years of a very pleasant relationship with one who was always easy to please and very grateful to his doctor.

Sedan Chair Provided by the King

When I began my work in the Royal Korean Hospital, November 1, 1893, I had the standing of a semi-government official and a sedan chair was placed at my disposal, It was a four-man chair and the carriers wore a special uniform which distinguished them from the common chair-coolies who served the general public. The men were so arranged that the two in front of the chair and the two in the rear were in a single line. As they walked along the streets it was necessary for them to keep constantly on the lookout for rough places, ditches, narrow bridges. etc., and it was the duty of the foremost one to warn those behind him of any such danger spots as he came to them. One of their most common cries was "chosim hayera, kaichuneo" which meant "be careful .here's ditch." When we reached a stopping place they took special care to lower the chair to the ground gently so that the occupant would not suffer a jolt. It was interesting to me to watch them crossing a stream on a narrow one-plank bridge or on stepping stones in shallower streams - they were so sure-footed, I soon learned to trust them fully and was not once disappointed in them.

One of their customs always amused me. As they approached the entrance to my home or any other important place to which I might be going the leader gave a signal cry in time to let the gatekeeper open the big doors of the gate house with a flourish and, by the time they reached it, they broke, into a run and kept up their hurried pace to the every door where I was to leave the chair. When I inquired the meaning of this, I was told it was a token of respect paid only to persons of eminence and that I was to accept it as what they called a "taijup" or "offering of respect" to their master. So I took it and fear I reached the point where I would have missed it had it been omitted and would have felt that proper respect was not being rendered to me. How easily one begins to take on airs and feel a certain amount of homage is due him from his "inferiors!" Or, if his fall from democracy is not so grievous, he soon gets to the point of missing these offerings to superior position if they are omitted. It is not at all strange that an absolute monarch, an autocrat, comes to feel his very person sacred.

Reform of Jejoongwon

My predecessor had devoted his forenoons to other duties and attended the dispensary during the afternoon only and I was told that on rainy days he did not attend at all The reason given for this was that the Koreans did not come out when it rained, so it was not necessary to attend at such times. I studied the attendance records and noted that when Dr. Allen was conducting the work the daily attendance ran from thirty to forty while of late it had seldom exceeded fifteen. I felt that the drop was probably the result of the lack of interest of the doctor and I determined to give a service that would attract the sick in greater numbers again.

As I had to devote several hours a day to language study so that I could eventually work without an interpreter I thought it best to study in the forenoons and spend every afternoon at the dispensary according to the established custom, I posted a notice to that effect, It also said that the clinic would be held on rainy days as well as on fair ones because many surgical dressings needed to be changed daily and there might be others who needed immediate attention whatever the weather. Ere long the attendance was almost as good on rainy days as on bright ones.

Under the new order the records soon began to show an improvement in the number of patients and the presence of my nurses attracted more women so that the whole afternoon was required to give all of them proper attention. During the first six months I had some of the empty rooms prepared as wards and thus began actual hospital work. This required the development of a kitchen and laundry and the securing of women to nurse the female patients and young men to take care of the sick men and boys. The next forward movement would be the provision of an operating room.

Just at that time a call came for me to go on two days' journey into the country to see a very sick man of considerable importance who had, as a last resort, decided to try the foreign doctor after all the efforts of the native physicians had failed. To be called in under such conditions is not a pleasant experience for it always means the patient is very near death but the foreign physician must take those serious cases if he is to gain recognition in a new country so I said I would go. Mr. Underwood went with me as an interpreter. When we reached the home of the patient we found they had indeed waited till after their own Korean doctor had done everything he could 'before calling the foreigner, It had taken two days for the messenger to come and another two for us to go and when we got there the sick man was already dead and there was no patient for us to treat.

However, there was a large town nearby and, learning the usual market, held every five days in the chief towns, would be held there the next day, we decided to attend it for the people would gather there from all the farming and village districts for many miles around and it would be a good opportunity for us to do some missionary work. Mr. Underwood arranged to distribute tracts and preach to groups as opportunity might offer while I set up clinic for any who might want the service that I could give them. We rented a small room overlooking the market where a crowd soon collected around the door so I had plenty of applicants for cures for all kinds of ills. I examined the cases and wrote prescriptions for medicines which Mr. Underwood dispensed. Empty beer bottles served as containers for liquids, dry drugs were given out in paper wrappers, and ointments were served in large empty clamshells. How different all this was from life in Canada 1 But it was very interesting for I was often put to my wit's end to diagnose and provide treatment for the great variety of ailments, I had with me a supply of antiseptics plenty of absorbent cotton and bandages, with scapels, forceps. Of course, some simple dental instruments were included and I extracted teeth, opened abscesses, and scraped out diseased bone cavities with but few complaints from the sufferers who either felt pain less than we do or bore it with more fortitude.

When I needed a rest Mr. Underwood took the opportunity to give out and explain religious tracts and this combination of doctor and preacher worked well.

Before the day ended a young Southern Presbyterian missionary, Rev. William Junkin, unexpectedly arrived in the town. Learning that two foreigners were there, he hunted us up and all three of us used the little room, seven by seven feet, as sleeping quarters that night. After we had prepared our beds on the hard clay-covered stone floor I was surprised to see Mr. Junkin get inside a bag which he drew up to his armpits and tied with a drawstring and then put on gloves which were held tight to the sleeves of his night jacket by elastic bands, I watched him get fixed for the night with much interest and then laughingly asked him what it all meant. He said I would probably know before morning and I did.

As many of the Korean houses are infested by fleas and bedbugs, some of the missionaries carried such night bags with them and thus were able to sleep in the midst of all marauders. Next morning we left Mr. Junkin there to take advantage of the interest our visit had aroused while we started for Seoul.

We stopped at various points on our return journey so that Mr. Underwood's time in coming with me might not be wasted by merely travelling through the country without meeting the people for whom he had a message, so we did not get home until more than a week had elapsed.

Jejoongwon Became a Missionary Hospital

When I went to my clinic next day I got an unpleasant surprise. I found all the space I had selected for the operating room and its adjuncts already occupied by a Japanese doctor. The choosas had found an opportunity to rent the rooms at a profitable rate and to them that was better than bothering with operations. I heard their story in silence and no doubt they supposed the matter comfortably settled but I was thinking it out quietly all the day. I had been there just six months and should already have received half of the annual contribution of

W3,ooo given by the King toward meeting expenses but had received only half of the half. So now, having to face the question of the future development of the institution, I determined to take a stand that would settle whether I was to be continually hampered or be given authority over its affairs. Next morning, on my arrival at the dispensary, I called the chief choosa for a conference at the end of which I told him1 would see the patients that day but in the evening would collect all the medicines and instruments which belonged tome, take them to my home and end my connection with the institution.

This startled him for he feared the King would hear of it and be angry. He begged me not to do that, Promising to get rid of the Japanese doctor at once and see that I received the full amount of the money provided by the King. I answered that I could not trust any one who had taken advantage of my absence to rent to an outsider part of the property given to me to use as a hospital and I would just leave the place in his hands. He was alarmed, because the matter would have to be reported to the King by Dr. Allen, the American Minister, and the choosas would be placed in avery difficult situation. All this he explained to me but I said I was not interested and nothing he could say would alter my decision.

I then wrote to Dr. Allen telling him the circumstances and leaving him free to take whatever steps he might think wise. I also wrote to the Executive Committee of the Mission in Korea and to the Board in New York, informing them of what I had done. The following day a deputation of the choosas came to my home to plead with me again but I told the matter was now out of my hands and any negotiations concerning it must be made with the American Minister. When Dr. Allen asked me on what conditions I would return I gave him my terms as follows :

1. All the choosas but one must be recalled by His Majesty. As the institution belonged to the King I would be glad to have one official there as a liaison officer between His Majesty and myself.

2. All the 35 servants must be dismissed so that I might select my own 35.

3. The entire property must be turned over to our Mission to be remodeled according to the needs of the hospital at the expense of the Mission.

If this were done, we would guarantee:

1. To release the King from any obligations for a financial grant towards te expense of the work.

2. To return the entire property to the King at any time after one year's notice and the repayment to us of all money expended by us in improving the property, remodeling it, etc.

They were completely stunned by this proposition and came tome many times in an endeavor to change the conditions but I always referred them to Dr. Allen. They were very much afraid that it would come to the King's ears, especially as I saw him often and might tell him about it. Or he might ask me whether all was going on well with the work.

After nearly six months of negotiating, Dr. Allen reported that they would accept my terms, but all would leave as they did not think it necessary under the new conditions, to keep even one official there.

In the meantime I had been in communication with the Mission Board in New York which approved all I had done. I asked the Board to provide funds for remodeling and for running expenses and also to send me two good nurses who could not only take care of the patients but also train Korean women to do the practical nursing. I described just the kind of nurses I wanted and got a prompt reply from the Secretary saying my request brought to his mind the story of a minister who, needing a horse, went to a dealer and told him the kind he wished to get. The dealer looked at him and replied. "Why man! There ain't no such horse." So, he went on to say, they would do the best they could for me, but feared they would be compelled to say, "There ain't no such nurse!"

They finally sent me one nurse and a lady physician. The latter was Miss Georgiana Whiting - the nurse was a Swedish woman, Miss Anna P. Jacobson. Both were good but unfortunately the nurse lived only a short time, having contracted amoebic dysentery followed by abscess of the liver from which she died. The doctor contracted matrimony with Dr. Owen of the Southern Presbyterian Mission and went with him to the southern part of the country and I was left alone again.

Once more I called on the Board in New York for help and again they appointed a lady Physician Dr. Eva Field, and a nurse, Miss Esther L. Shields, who were already applicants for missionary work, and they were soon on their way to the field.

It was then 1898 and as both my wife and I were in poor health as also were

Mr. Underwood and his wife, the Mission sent us on a vacation in Japan in the hope that the rest and change would restore us all. The Underwoods had only one child to take but we had six so the trip for us was not going to be an easy one. Our little Martin was but a babe in arms, his brother Raymond was only thirteen months older and Mrs. Avison, already much weakened by illness, could not care for them without help, so we took our Korean amah[18] with us and then, to further ease the boat trip for Mrs. Avison, I put a small rocking chair on the deck so she could have some of the comfort of home, but the boat itself did all the rocking necessary and the amah, this being first sea voyage, was unable to care for the babies and we had our hands full.

We landed at Nagasaki and went into the interior to a health resort. There were hot springs there that were seen only when the tide was out as they were close to the sea and the tide, as it flowed in, covered them up. There were many Japanese bathhouses which were much patronized by the native people. Men and women without distinction would go into the same bath house, strip to the skin and bathe together. There was a very large round tub of hot water in which the bathers sat on a bench that ran around its inner circumference and the bathers, men and women, would sit on it indiscriminately, slap each other's knees and laugh loudly. When I asked as to the character of the bathers, I was told they were of good reputation and that such intermingling was not considered indelicate.

As soon as we could make arrangements for Kagas[19] and carriers our party of eleven, adults and children, took a trip up the high mountains to Jikoku,[20] a place of many hot springs. The surrounding limestone rocks have been so long under the influence of those hot springs that one can thrust a stick deeply into what looks like solid rock and there are areas where one can dig a hole in the ground, put a kettle of water in it and before long have boiling water in the kettle. We saw that done many times. Another nearby spot was smaller and fewer springs and it is named Kojikoku, meaning little hell. We met some American friends there, missionaries to the Japanese. It seemed to be a favorite summer resort for missionaries and some people made a joke of this fact, saying the mis-

---

18   An amah is a female servant whose chief work is to care for children and be the personal helper of the mother.

19   A kaga is a sort of two-man sedan or carrying chair used in Japan for carrying travelers up the mountains chiefly.

20   "Jikoku" means in our language "hell" because of the many hot springs.

sionaries went to hell for a rest.

We, however, got no help there and soon returned to Nagasaki where we learned that the lady physician and nurse for the Royal Korean Hospital had recently passed through on their way to Korea.

We then proceeded to China after that sometimes elusive thing called health and, strange to say, found it in the great city of Shanghai. When we felt we could move on toward home, we took a boat northward to Chefoo and then crossed the Yellow Sea back to Chosun where we found the new doctor and nurse already at the hospital.

In the meantime I had been thinking more deeply about the future of medical work in Korea. I had noted the prevalence of epidemics, the terrible death rate that was decimating the population and the unsanitary conditions prevailing in both city and country. I had also given consideration to the fewness of foreign doctors and the improbability of their number being ever increased to more than thirty or so in the whole country and the impossibility of that small number ever being able to do much toward improving conditions. Unless efforts were made to educate Korean young men as doctors in sufficient numbers to do what the small number of foreign physicians could not accomplish Korea must go on as it was doing - running down. With that in view, I had carefully selected my hospital assistants with the idea of giving them a medical education and at the same time guiding them to a desire to spend their lives and energies in improving the health of their people by careful treatment of their sicknesses and by inculcating the hygienic principles that would lessen the incidence of disease. I had already begun the preparation of textbooks and from them had been teaching my helpers some of the amazing possibilities lying in present medical methods.

▶ Chapter 5 ◀

Sanitary Conditions in Korea

Demonology and Disease

The word "demonology" has two meanings: (1) the theory or study of demons; and (2) the belief that demons or evil spirits do exist and do take possession of the minds and bodies of human beings, causing mental and physical diseases of many kinds.

The first theory - the existence or nonexistence of such beings cannot be either proved or disproved. However, all the evidence for their existence can be accounted for by what we know as the vagaries of the human mind and the more we learn of them, the less do we think of them as due to as invasion of an outside spiritual being. The further we advance in our understanding of mental science, the more do we incline to the idea that mental disorders have a physical basis, In any case, the idea that contagious diseases are due to spiritual invasions has been completely discarded by physicians since the discovery of the germ theory. And those beliefs in evil spirit invasions are not confined to countries which we consider uncivilized. Even in America, in the time of the Pilgrims, this belief in demons led those devoutly religious people to regard men and women, especially women, who behaved incertain ways, as possessed by devils and they actually put many such people to torture and even to death. I regret to admit that a considerable number of missionaries still regard many mental conditions as evidence of the factuality of evil spirits. They were especially convinced of this when some cases recovered after they became Christians when all the methods practiced by their unlearned witch doctors had failed to affect a cure. Some of them seem to think that the lessening of the incidence of contagious diseases in Korea is due to the spread of Christianity perse.

Doctors, however, know that this decreasing incidence of such disease is not due to religious faith directly but to an increasing knowledge of the germ theory of contagion. The contribution that Christianity made was the winning of the confidence of the people in the Christian doctors who told them the facts and proved their teachings by the efficacy of their methods of cure and prevention.

Naturally it was considered necessary to get the spirit to come out of the sick person in order to effect a cure One method of attempting this was the application of a red-hot iron point to certain parts of the bodies of those afflicted by certain types of insanity. These applications were made to the scalp and also to any and every part of the body that the doctor believed to have some connection with the mind I think now of a young lad who, after being so treated without a cure was, as a last resort, brought to our clinic.

His body, from head to foot, was covered with scars and unhealed sores after being so cruelly treated by loving but misguided parents.

However, I am not now trying to write an article about the validity or otherwise of either these beliefs in evil spirit causation or of their methods of treatment ; I am writing an account of a group of sorcerers and sorceresses who believed themselves able to drive evil spirits out of the afflicted or who, without any particular belief concerning the matter, earned a living by practicing certain methods which were regarded as efficacious in such cases.

Sorcerers, called Kyungsa, and Sorceresses, called Mudang(Moo-dang), are very frequently called in to exorcise these supposed evil spirits. These professional exercisers have books on the subject which they study assiduously and many of them doubtless believe in the validity of what they do, even though they do not always succeed in effecting their purposes. Quite frequently the patients are not benefited or their sickness may be even increased. But what of that? Even our own doctors do not always succeed in curing their patients but that does not make them regard their theories of disease as founded on uncertain ideas of their cause. So it doubtless is with those professional exorcists whose methods I am here describing for the information of those who, fortunately, have been delivered from the results of the errors of their forefathers who doubtless believed much as did the Koreans when I first went to that land. It is not that I want to ridicule the people of Korea whom I love for their numerous good qualities, but rather to arouse in my readers an interest in giving to the many yet uninformed or less informed people of the world that opportunity for gaining true knowledge and understanding that all the nations may get the benefit of what we ourselves have gained through the efforts of our predecessors. What I am writing on this subject I have learned partly from the writing of a Korean scholar on the subject. He says it is not exactly known where and when the ceremonies of the mudang cult originated but goes on to say that in olden times the people in Persia believed there was a god who liked to see his worshippers sing and dance before him.[21]

He goes on to say this idea of worshipping extended eastward to China, through Mongolia, then to Manchuria, and finally reached Korea. Others hold that it originated in Korea in the time of the Silla Dynasty. Wherever it first began the ceremonies practised by the mudang of Korea gradually took on the character of Buddhist rites and our Korean scholar believes that as Buddhism flourished most vigorously in Korea during the period of the Silla Dynasty (57 B C - 924 AD) the present practice may be dated from that period. But he also says that while many of the ideas were copied from Buddhist ceremonies as late as 1591, some of them were copied from Taoism which was instituted in China about 450 B. C.

I now quote from the description given by our Korean author:

"For many centuries these mudang ceremonies were considered as religious activities and especially in the time of the Yi Dynasty they were much observed by the Korean people. Only a woman is called a mudang - a man is called kyukja or kyungsa. They claim that by their ceremonies they can invite gods or rather spirits to come into them and, once the spirits have control of them, they can predict something for the future; they can also cure the sick, and cast out evil spirits from men. The mudang mother teaches her daughter

---

21   This custom of expressing religious feelings seems to have been general in the Orient. We find references to this practice in the Bible. In Exodus 15: 20 21 it is written "And Miriam the prophetess, the sister of Aaron, took a timbrel in her hand; and all the women went out after her with timbrels and with dances. And Miriam answered them. "Sing ye to the Lord for he hath triumphed gloriously; the horse and his rider hath he thrown into the sea." In Samuel II 6: 14, 15, 16, it is written "And David danced before the Lord with all his might and David was girded with a linen ephod. So David and all the house of Israel brought up the ark of the Lord with shouting and with the sound of the trumpet. And, as the ark of the Lord came into the city of David, Michael, Soul's daughter, looked through a window and saw King David leaping and dancing before the Lord and she despised him in her heart." It is evident from these quotations that the practices of those whom we despise as heathens are but continuations of original methods of worshipping not only false gods but God himself.

the same doctrine and makes her successor. When the girl is about 15 or 16 years old she begins to study by reading books and by practicing with her mother."

While, as stated, the ceremonies, including dancing and the playing of so-called musical instruments, were at first considered as religious, this idea gradually gave way to quite a different one. All sicknesses and all misfortune came to be regarded as caused by evil spirits which were of the nature of demigods or half gods (believed originally to be the offspring of a deity and a mortal and therefore called demigods) that either entered into the persons who did not sufficiently honor them or, from outside their bodies, exerted a malevolent influence over them. The mudang ceremonies were designed to influence these evil spirits to leave the unfortunate persons or to cease their influence over them. They varied greatly and the rites varied in accordance with the spirit concerned so that it required long study to master the art of conducting them.

The kyungsas and mudangs also claim that they have the power to make unhappy homes happy, ensure happy marriages and the good birth of children, assure riches and prevent disasters. Their objectives are worthy but Un-fortunately they often fail. As these people make their living by those practices they charge fees that vary in amount according to their reputation for succeeding and the degree of wealth of their employers who also give them as good a feast as they can afford. Usually there is one chief exorciser but others of lesser rank may assist in the rites.[22]

Many of the spirits are supposed to be local so that different localities call for different methods which are effective only in those regions. Some spirits, however, occupy more extended areas. The number of spirits is very great, so great that the mudangs are sometimes called "man-sin", a word which means "ten thousand spirits" or as we would say "myriads." They are different for men and women; for houses and gates; for mountains and rivers; for different kinds of rooms in houses; for stones - for trees-for everything. Even the stars represent gods and goddesses in this cult. Different kinds of dress are worn in the performance of different ceremonies. The form of the dresses varies but little, except in color and in materials.

Their musical instruments consist of cymbals, flutes, big and little drums

---

22   Did our doctors inherit this from these healers of long ago?

and clarions. Many kinds of fans are also used. Different dishes of foods are offered the spirits according to their supposed likings, and incense is burned - all with the idea of gaining their good will.

The methods used in conducting the ceremonies differ in accordance with the kind of sickness, or trouble for which they are called.

The mudang wears a special hat and dress and recites passages from the books of rites - after some two or three days of fasting and bathing when preparing for a ceremony she is careful not to look on a dead body and she often passes two or three days and nights without sleep. At the beginning of the performance she takes a fan in one hand and a sword in the other and repeats the special prayers she has selected for the occasion while her companions play on their instruments. She may begin her act by saying such a prayer as the following:

"I humbly offer my prayer to our honorable god; help up with your great power."

Then, after bowing from three to nine times, she says, "The God is within me and I will bless you" or "I will curse you" according to the occasion and declares, "This is the god of creation." Then she throws the sword on the ground. If the edge of the blade faces away from her it is a sign that the desire of the employer will be granted. But if the edge faces her, they choose another day on which to try again. Mudangs are unwilling to accept a denial. Sometimes she stands on the edge of the sword and then claims its failure to hurt her is an infallible sign that the spirit is with her or in her. Then she asks the family to give as much money to the spirit as they can, and when this has been done, she says, "You will be blessed," or "Your prayer will be granted."

They have many ways of casting out spirits or otherwise dealing with them such as beating the sick man or frightening him; scorching or piercing the flesh over the painful part; puncturing a picture of the affected part with a needle which will be withdrawn when the sick one is cured; writing on tablets or pasting paper on the upper part of a gate or door; or making a substitute similar to the affected part and then destroying it. Sometimes they decide the cause of the family trouble is some malign happening to the ancestral tomb and the hand of the family must go to the tomb, search for the trouble and get rid of it. In fact, sickness and troubles are all caused by the intervention of one or more demons which in the nature of things can only be exorcised by payments of money to those who by study and practice have become masters or mistresses of the spirits concerned.

The mudang or kyungsa cult is really a closed profession for the art is passed down by one family to the next in line by the training given by parents to children, and so on.

Smallpox

I had not been in the country long before I noticed that practically all the people I met were pock-marked. This meant they had smallpox. Inquiries revealed that smallpox was regarded as a disease of childhood and was so nearly universal that all children were expected to have it before they were two years old.[23] Inquiry as to the death rate brought out the answer that deaths were very frequent.

One day a woman came to the dispensary for treatment and my questioning of her past history revealed that she had borne eleven children.

"How many are still living?" I asked.

"None-all died in infancy."

"That's too bad. Of what did they die?"

"Smallpox."

"What! All of them died of that disease?"

"Yes, that is true. So many babies die of smallpox that Koreans think it is scarcely worthwhile to count a child as a member of the family until it has safely passed through that disease."

It made me shudder and I came to the decision that we mission doctors must disseminate true ideas about how to control this one disease as the first step toward doing something to stop the terrible infant mortality that was causing a constant decrease in the population. When I asked what Korean doctors did for smallpox patients, I was told they were not consulted because everybody, including doctors knew it was caused by the entrance into the child of an evil

---

[23] Like our measles.

spirit, and what could a doctor do for that? The only thing was to try to placate the spirit and get it to leave the child and thus spare its life. They would place before the sick child food, money, anything of value, and then bow before it in obeisance of the spirit and beseech it to depart. Apparently the spirit was supposed to reside in China but came to Korea at certain times and was dubbed "honorable guest!"

One day when I was walking outside one of the city gates, I saw something that aroused my curiosity. It was a kind of shelf projecting from the wall for several feet. On closer examination I found it to be a board with one end pressed into a niche between two stones of the wall and the other end held up by a stick. On the shelf was something covered by straw thatch. I asked a passerby what it was.

"That? Oh, that is the body of a child that died of smallpox." And he passed on.

Looking about me I saw a straw-covered something tied to the branch of a tree and was told that, too, was the corpse of a smallpox child. Later I asked my language teacher about what I had seen. I asked him if they never buried the bodies.

"No," he replied, "they believe the spirit that killed the child will be angry if its body is buried, and it will enter another child and take it too."

I determined to strive with all my might for the elimination of these false ideas. When I suggested to Korean mothers that they let me vaccinate their babies, they asked me how it was done. They shrank in fear from something that they did not understand and that would cause their babies pain. Besides, they could not believe that such a method could keep out the son-nim or guest spirit.

However, one day a woman, converted to Christianity and therefore more trustful of the Christian doctor, brought her baby to the clinic and asked me to vaccinate it. Gladly I did so and told her to bring it every day to let me see that all was going well. The little sore soon got well of course and when, as time passed and the child's second birthday went by and no smallpox had occurred, and when still more time passed and the child's smooth skin was left unmarred other mothers, seeing this, brought their children for similar treatment. None of the vaccinated children contracted the disease thus the devil of smallpox was destroyed by a bit of vaccine. That evil demon was shown to be a more spector - a phantom - and the way was opened to bring other epidemic diseases into the same category.

I was a missionary and perhaps what I am writing about evil spirits and how faith in them was destroyed by the application of scientific methods of preventative medicine may distress some religionists who will refer me to the Biblical teaching regarding evil spirits and the fact that Christ is reported to have cast out devils by a command and to have caused them to enter into swine and drive them to a species of madness, I am an evangelical missionary and I want to give full credit to the gospel of Christ as a message of hope for spiritual degenerates and a reviving of the spiritual and mental powers which in turn wonderfully influenced the bodily functions of men and women and I would be one of the last to decry the value of Christ's teachings and example, though I am skeptical of the literal accuracy of some of those reports of what Christ did and taught on certain occasions, I am, however, a physician and more or less of a scientist, and must perforce accept the truth of what has been shown to be true by thousands of investigators and medical practitioners. That is just what the women of Korea did when they saw the demon of smallpox wilt before the scientific use of vaccine. Their faith in the reality of at least one evil spirit was shattered. After a time vaccination became obligatory and now, after less than fifty years, Pock-marked persons are becoming rare.

Asiatic Cholera

The next epidemic that I had to contend with was Asiatic cholera. It followed close on the heels of the Japan-China war The Korean Government heard of the prevalence of this disease in Manchuria and, day by day, as word came indicating that it was spreading southward into Korea, they became more alarmed for they had experienced such epidemics before.

The Minister of Home Affairs, honorable Yu Kil Choon (Yu Keel Choon), called me to his office and asked me to take charge of the capital and make an effort to prevent the entrance of the disease into the city or, if it did get into the city, endeavor to limit its ravages as much as possible. He gave me quite a large fund to be used at my discretion, appointed twenty policemen to be under my direction, and authorized me to take whatever steps I might think necessary to curb the spread of the dread disease, I accepted the commission and began to prepare for the campaign.

Realizing that it was not a one-man job, I called a conference of all the missionary doctors and nurses to plan with me the steps to be taken. We could not stop its onward progress from the north because travel could not be stopped but we began preparations for dealing with the first cases which might be reported. It is not necessary for me to go into all the details about the methods we used in the special hospitals which were prepared for the stricken people. That story is told elsewhere.

Knowing that the cholera germ had to be taken into the stomach, along with contaminated food, and that, even if food became infected cooking it would kill the germ, we had big posters written in the simplest language telling people what its cause was and how to avoid it. These contained the following statements:

CHOLERA is not caused by an Evil Spirit.

It is caused by a very small particle of living matter called a germ. When this living germ gets into your stomach, it multiplies rapidly and causes the disease.

You do not have to take CHOLERA if you do not want it.

All you have to do is to kill the germ by cooking your food thoroughly and eating it before it can become contaminated again.

Drink freshly-made rice water. If you drink plain water, boil it and keep it in clean bottles.

As you may have come in contact with the germ without knowing it, always wash your hands and mouth thoroughly before eating anything.

If you do these things YOU WILL NOT HAVE CHOLERA.

These posters were pasted up in all parts of the city.

Of course, all the workers in hospitals and all who visited cholera-stricken homes were carefully instructed in these methods of prevention and not one of the large number of assistants, even the nurses who were in close contact with the patients, contracted the disease. This was good evidence to the people of the reliability of our instructions as presented on the posters.

And what has all this to do with demonology? Well, my Korean hospital assistants told me that the Koreans everywhere believed that the disease resulted from the entrance into the body of a spirit called the Rat Spirit. They believed it to have the form of a rat and that it got into them through their feet and gnawed its way up the legs to the abdominal organs and they attributed the terrible cramps in the muscles to this gnawing by the spirit. As I walked through the streets of the city I frequently saw the picture of a cat pasted on the outer side of the main entrance to the house. When I asked the reason for this I was told that, as the disease was caused by the Rat Spirit, they hoped the cat would catch the rat. People everywhere do foolish things like this because of ignorance and how could ignorance be avoided under conditions prevailing in Korea in that day?

Going through another section of the city one evening, I noticed a straw cord stretched around a group of houses on which were hung pieces of paper with writing on them. In answer to my questions I learned that the houses so encircled were as yet free from cholera, and that those living there had stretched this cord around the houses and hung on it written prayers to the cholera spirit exhorting it not to come within the boundary line. A short distance from the section thus protected I saw a platform some five feet above the ground, with some animals on it and a number of court officials who had been sent into that part of the city by the King to offer those animals in sacrifice to the Cholera Spirit and thus placate it in order to gain protection for that neighborhood.

I might go on telling of the spirits that produced other contagious diseases and mental derangements but I think enough has been said to illustrate the widespread belief in demon possession and the constant struggle of the early missionary physicians to fight this belief and to establish a basis of true knowledge on which to found reliable methods of freeing the people from the terrible scourges which they had to endure so frequently. Having won, to a considerable extent, the confidence of the converts to Christianity our further success would depend on ways of educating the great masses.

To do this we adopted the plan of writing brief pamphlets each dealing with one type of epidemic disease. These pamphlets were printed in simple, terse Korean which could be read and understood by nearly all. Each had a striking title, such as "Smallpox and Vaccine," "Eating Asiatic Cholera," "Mosquitoes and Malaria," "Flies and Typhoid Fever," "Bedbugs and Relapsing Fever," "Body Lice and Typhus Fever," "Contaminated Vegetables and Dysentery." These were handed to patients who came to our dispensaries and when itinerating missionaries were making trips into the country to hold Bible Classes we doctors gave them some of these booklets and urged them not only to teach the Bible but to teach also the public health truths presented in the pamphlets. Thus some knowledge of sanitation and healthful living was given to the early Christians and the churches became not only centers of religion, but also centers of sanitary education. Thus belief in demons as causes of sickness was under way to being overcome by the cure and prevention of those diseases, by attention to cleanliness and by scientific treatment.

Typhus Fever

Those of you who know that the carrier of typhus is the common body louse may be wondering how I, a supposedly clean doctor, should have contracted that disease. That is not hard to explain. In the early days of our residence in Seoul one might see coolies sitting at the sides of the street waiting for jobs, just as they apparently did in Judea, judging from Christ's parable of the owner of the vineyard who went out into the street of the town and found men waiting to be hired(Matt. 20: 1-7). Those coolies in Korea could often be seen whiling away the time of waiting by catching and killing the body lice that lurked in the seams of their clothing. They did not do this furtively for no one thought it strange or evidence of special lack of cleanliness. As a result of this widespread presence of lice, typhus fever was a very common disease.

Suppose a typhus patient was lying sick in a house in which there was only one sleeping room for all the members of a household. The lice on his body would bite him and fill themselves with his blood. Later on they might find their way to other persons and, in biting them, eject some of the sick person's blood at the bitten spot. If you have ever been bitten by a louse, you know that the bitten spot itches fiercely so that the victim, without thought of danger, scratches the place, and in so doing is apt to scrape off some of the skin and thus give entry to some of the contaminated blood. As a result he too becomes sick, for the disease-producing germ enters at the same time. How easy it is for an epidemic to occur under such conditions of living!

Cases of typhus were brought to our hospital quite often and, as we did not then know how the disease was transmitted from the sick to the well, we could not protect ourselves or our coworkers as we can do now so the explanation of how I took the disease is simple.

A Toronto missionary, Miss McKenzie, had been on a trip into the country where she became ill with typhus. Returning to Seoul, she came to our home as her own quarters were uncomfortably small for a sick person. She had lived alone in a couple of small rooms with only an ignorant serving woman to care for her. Before she got back to Seoul her vitality had been much lowered and she passed away in our house within a few days.

At the same time, we had several cases in the hospital so that I was daily exposed to infection and just after Christmas I was stricken with the disease.

As there was no other doctor in Seoul at the time, Dr. X of Chemulpo was asked to care for me and he did so most faithfully. When the time of crisis approached he stayed in Seoul within call and, at the height of the fever, remained in my home day and night.

When I regained consciousness from the delirium I had been in, I found one of the liquids I had been receiving was brandy. How surprised I was to see a whole row of empty brandy bottles standing on a table in an adjoining room - something quite new in our home. When I asked my wife about them she blushed and replied that the doctor had insisted on the use of the brandy as a part of the treatment and I said I could hardly believe. I, alone, had drunk so much. I jokingly asked her whether or not she had been on the same kind of diet to maintain her strength. Dear woman, she had nursed me every day most assiduously and needed every available means of supporting her through the long period of mental anguish and physical effort, for though she had other nursing help at night she slept little. But she smilingly shook her head.

Several of the male missionaries served in turn as night nurses and I was greatly indebted to them for they were most attentive, but often I longed for the more tender ministrations that trained women can give.

Two thoughts dominated me while I was unconscious. One seemed to be caused by the alternate and frequent draughts of medicine and nourishment that were given me so, as they told me afterwards, I held my teeth together with so much strength that they were compelled to insert a rubber tube into my mouth through a space where a tooth had been extracted. In my mind I distinguished between two liquids - one the nourishment and one the medicine and I had the idea that my throat held two seweres - different one for each kind of liquid and that they directed the tube accordingly. When I became conscious my nurses were greatly amused by this story as, indeed, I was myself. The second thought was evidently the outcome of my subconscious knowledge that I was facing a crisis which might result in my death. This idea took the shape of a dream in which I was lying under a railroad bridge. Two trains were coming from different directions and it seemed to me they would meet on the bridge and, as they clashed, they would fall over the side of the bridge. If they should fall on me I would be killed and that appeared to be the most likely happening. I was unable to move and great was my anguish as I heard the two trains approaching the bridge from each side. But they stopped before meeting and just then I awoke to consciousness and found my wife there with her arms around me. Evidently I had been evincing my great fear. I smiled, and said I was better and asked about the fever. She assured me it had all gone and urged me to go to sleep and rest peacefully.

From then on I kept them busy changing my clothing and bed linen for I perspired most copiously as did all recovering from typhus. Little by little my strength returned and visitors were allowed to come in. One day Dr. Eva Field told me of the death of Queen Victoria - just as a bit of news. She was puzzled when I burst into tears. It was difficult to get her to understand the affection the English people had for the Queen who had been the head of the British Empire for 64 years. From the time I could remember anything she had been the "great Queen" to whom all Britishers looked with reverence and love. We had celebrated every 24th of May of my life as the Queen's birthday and my remembrance of that event went back 33 years. Because of my own illness I had heard nothing of hers and this sudden announcement of her death while I was still very weak overwhelmed me.

Beginning of Pasteur Treatment

While the Russia-Japan war was in progress an event occurred that gravely affected my family and me. Our two youngest children of that time were bitten by a rabid dog. They were then seven and eight years of age and the dog, a small foxterrier, was their own much-loved playmate.

They were frolicking with him as usual one day when he snarled at them, a thing so unlike him that they were greatly surprised. They tried to fondle him out of this strange mood but he snapped at their hands and, having bitten both of them, ran away and hid. Much disturbed, they told their mother of this and she called me.

After treating the bites, I set out to find the dog. He had run into the cellar as though to hide after doing what he knew to be wrong. When I tried to coax him out I noticed his eyes were red and he ran past me and away into the street. This conduct was so unusual that my suspicion as to his ailment was aroused and, calling others, we set out to follow him. He ran to another group of missionary homes and into the basement of one of them. He was evidently mad so we decided to put water within his reach and shut him in. Next morning he was dead.

Feeling sure of our diagnosis we made a search for any other dog that might have bitten him but none was found.

There was no pasteur virus in Korea but on a visit to the Japanese Minister we learned that such treatment were being given at the Medical School and Hospital in Nagasaki, Japan - but how were we to get the boys over there? All the passenger and cargo boats that had been running between Japan and Korea had been taken over by the Japanese military and naval authorities and converted into troop and supply ships for Japan was then at war with Russia so there was apparently no way of taking them across the straits to Japan. We appealed to Mr. Hayashi, our friendly Japanese Minister for help. He was much concerned but made no immediate answer. Then he smilingly said he thought he could help us.

An army transport was due to sail the next day from Chemulpo to Nagasaki, he said, and he would give me a note to the chief Naval Officer of the port asking him to give my boys and me passage on it. He wrote the note at once and with it I took the lads that night to the port so as to make sure of being on the spot in time next morning, I presented the letter and was glad to learn they had received a telegram from Minister Hayashi telling them to expect me. I was therefore hospitably received and instructed to be ready at a certain time to go aboard.

Within two days we were in Nagasaki. The ship officers would accept no money for our passage except a small sum to cover the cost of our food which they said was required by the naval authorities as all the ship's supplies were rationed and had to be accounted for.

I went at once to the hospital and was told treatment could be begun right away and the first was given the same day. Of course I watched their technique closely and asked many questions. After a few days I asked whether they could provide me with enough virus for the remaining days of the treatment - about eighteen yet - so that I could go back on the first boat on which passage could be obtained. Yes, they could do that. Then I went a step further. Could they not teach me the method of preparing the virus so that when I returned to Korea I could introduce this treatment there and save the great expense and loss of time that came with such a trip as I had taken. Apparently this request raised a problem for they took time to consider it. The next day, however, they said it could be done if I would purchase the necessary equipment and take time to watch them prepare the virus.

I did this and then set out in search of some way to get back home. Learning that a number of foreign war correspondents were soon to sail for Chemulpo on a Japanese vessel that had been chartered by a representative of the London Times, I sought the Englishman out and told him my story. He was interested at once and told me to get my boys and apparatus on board as soon as possible as they were to sail that day. What a relief it was to me!

The virus injections which I gave the boys each day naturally gave them pain but when I promised them a certain amount of money for each treatment if they refrained from saying anything but "ouch!" they suddenly became brave and earned their pennies with lips held tight. These treatments were watched by everyone aboard with the greatest interest. Water had to be boiled, test tubes disinfected, hypodermic syringes antisepticized and the place of injection on the boys' backs thoroughly cleansed. In due time we reached home and, because we had accomplished all I set out to do and even more. I was very happy over it. I am happy to say that the boys never showed any ill symptoms from the bites.

Facing the job of establishing a Pasteur department of our own I soon found it was going to take a lot of my time and a considerable sum of money to set it up and still more to keep it going and we had no money for the job. We all felt the job must be undertaken but how?

The unexpected happened just as it generally does when a great need exists.

Because of Russia-Japanese war a guard of Italian marines had been stationed in Seoul to protect Italian residents and Italian interests and they were billeted at the Italian Consulate near the palace where, his Majesty was in residence. One night a palace building took fire and the marines helped to quell it so the next day the King sent a present of money to the officer of the guard to be given to the men who had been so helpful. The officer said he could not accept it as an Italian Army regulation forbade soldiers receiving any such gratitude. The King would not have it returned to him but asked the officer to use it in some way that would give pleasure to the men. It appeared that the officer, was much interested in Pasteur's work on the prevention of rabbies and, learning that our hospital was about to open a Pasteur Department, he called on me and offered us this money to keep us do it - and there we were with a fund to at least make a beginning. An accident, was it? or a special intervention of Providence? or what? Anyway it just answered our need so we proceeded with thankful hearts. First we must begin to raise rabbits as at least one must be killed every day.

A strong dose of the virus must be injected into a rabbit which was then tagged with a date and next day another must be similarly treated and the frist one killed and its spinal cord which contained virus of the highest potentiality extracted and labeled No. 1 with the date. Next day another rabbit must be killed and similarly disposed of until 21 animals had been used. Then the spinal cord in Bottle No. 1 must be thrown away unless there was a patient to be treated and another be labeled No. 1.

The theory is that the strength of the virus is weakened by the drying process; the Calcium Chloride absorbing moisture more and more each day, the virus at the end of 21 days becomes so weakened that it can be injected into a patient without any evil result on his health while it sets up a degree of resistance to the virus. Next day bottle No. 2 is used and so on until in 21 days the strongest virus in the series can be given without danger. Such a degree of resistance has been built up that before the virus of the original can react in producing rabies the resistance of the patient can destroy it.

You can see the theory of decreasing strength of the virus by drying makes it necessary to destroy one rabbit every day and throw away the contents of one bottle every day so that there will always be on hand a full supply of virus of ranging strengths. We kept of this work until the Japanese Medical Department in Korea announced it had established a Pasteur Laboratory and was prepared to supply the virus, free of cost, to all who might need it. We then brought our special work to a close and depended on the government laboratory for a supply for any case that might be brought to us for treatment.

We found the government's virus effective and thereafter always used it. All we had to do was to send a reliable and duly authorized messenger to the proper official and a sufficient supply for a given case was immediately sent to us. For this courtesy we were duly grateful.

Milk

We were surprised, on our arrival in Korea, to be told that milk was unobtainable. "Why?" I asked, "I see plenty of cows drawing carts or carrying loads on their backs. What is done with their milk?" "The cow's milk? Why do you ask that? The calves have to be fed and they need all the mothers can supply." "You" said I, "but when the calf is able to eat other food, do you not milk the cows?" "Of course not. Cows in Korea are beasts of burden just as horses are in your country. Do you milk your horses?"

That was another point of view and I could only say that in western lands oxen used to be used as beasts of burden, and cows too sometimes, but that was long ago, and cows are now kept only for three purposes - to bear calves, to give milk to their owners after the calves can be weaned, and in the end to be killed for their meat and hides.

"Well," I said, "What do you give your babies for nourishment when the mothers' milk is not available and on what do you feed invalids who cannot eat solid food?"

"Babies? Oh, we give them rice water and rice gruel. What else is there? When one has money one may hire a foster mother but that is for rich people. Most of the people are too poor for that."

So! That was the reason for so many puny infants and one of the reasons for so great a death rate amongst young children! "Well, is milk not used at all in Korea?"

"Oh, yes, it is used by members of the royal family and, in order to make it possible for them to get it, it is forbidden to all others." I could understand that but another question immediately occurred to me.

"What about evaporated milk? Can you not get it?" "Yes, but who can afford to buy it? Besides, when we bought it for a sick one, the patient, not being used to it, refused it. Didn't like the taste and that was true of fresh milk too."

So this is what we were going to be up against in the attack we proposed to make against the high infantile death rate I Scarcity of milk, dislike for milk, high cost of milk! Scarcity could be overcome by importing evaporated milk and liking for it could be gradually cultivated. We could, and did prescribe it, not as a food but as a medicine. They were used to taking bad medicine and so they would take the milk if told that it was a medicine. High cost? Yes, but all our American medicines cost much so why balk at providing the best of all medicines? So for the time being the milk problem was on the way to being solved for our hospitals.

It was many years before the demand for milk was great enough to warrant the establishment of dairies. The first dairy established was unhampered by any Board of Health regulations so the milk supplied was as likely to be a cause of illness as to be a means of nutrition unless it were pasteurized. Even then the container was likely to be left open, exposed to dust and flies. And there was no means of refrigeration available for Korean homes.

But time (that blessed provider of all good things) brought a knowledge of sanitation, first to the authorities, who made regulations for the cleanliness of the dairies and proper care of the milk, but the regulations were hard for the ignorant people to carry out. More time (what a good thing there is so much of it!)

and the principles of sanitation came to be understood. Simple methods of carrying them out were devised so that part of the difficulty of getting a supply of milk was overcome. But one great obstacle remained and still exists - a sufficient supply of pure milk is too expensive for families whose total daily earnings will buy only enough to nourish one child.

- Bean Milk

The question of finding a cheap substitute for milk was always in the thoughts of doctors and nurses. It was especially acute in the nursing homes established by missionaries in various parts of the country. Also for a long time it was an unsolved problem for those who were responsible for improving the nutrition of the children in very poor neighborhoods where it was practically impossible to provide a sufficient supply of milk. There are only two ways of helping such poverty stricken homes. (A) The improvement of the economic methods which have brought about such extremes of wealth and poverty as are to be found in every land, whether Christian or heathen, and (B) Providing the underfed with sufficient nourishment, either at cheap rates or as a free gift.

We should all strive to solve the economic problem but while that is being done we must unite in the effort to provide for the proper nourishment of those in the lower levels of our society. So the effort to secure a cheap substitute for milk occupied the attention of all who were interested in the better nourishment of the poorer classes and especially their children.

As has always been the case in matters of food and medicine the chemical research workers in hospitals and schools solved this difficulty by the work they did in the analysis of the soy bean which was one of the chief agricultural products of Manchuria, North China and Northern Korea.

Without going into the details of their work, it can be said that these research workers found in an extract of those beans a fluid product that contained nearly all the constituents of good milk. A very important part of the discovery was a simple method of extracting this valuable substance which could be followed by a person of even small intelligence.

This information was quickly made use of by the hospitals and child welfare organizations in Korea and the preparation and distribution of "Bean milk" became "the regular thing."

Soy bean milk hasn't supplanted the use of cow's milk by those who can afford the latter for milk tastes better and has at least one valuable constituent not present in the bean product.

Forty-five years ago Korea had neither cow's milk nor bean milk. Today it has both in abundance.

Medical Fees

Orientals held the idea, and many perhaps still hold it, that doctors should not be paid for attending patients, only for curing them, and their doctors charge only for the medicines used and not for their services. Under such a method the only way for the doctor to obtain a living is to give the patients plenty of bulky medicine and charge a big price for it.

In our early years we found it necessary to recognize this attitude of mind. We gave liquids in empty beer bottles of one pint and a half capacity, with directions to take it in 2 table-spoonful doses and gave solids in large powders. In all cases we made sure that the doses given would produce noticeable effects in the right direction and have a good strong taste. If the case was a chronic one enough medicine was supplied to last a week with the instruction to come back then and bring their bottles with them. For such a goodly supply we could make a charge large enough to pay at least the cost of the ingredients but, if the patient was too poor to pay even that, the charge would be reduced or even given free of charge. Our main desire was to cure the patient. As for the doctor's time or skill, we learned that if the case were cured a gift of some kind would usually be made. The most common gift was eggs. Eggs are tied up in wisps of straw. These came to us rapidly that our family found it impossible to eat them all and indeed most of them were fed to the hospital patients. Even then the eggs sometimes accumulated so fast that on one occasion, I remember, they made a pyramid about four feet in diameter at the base and three feet high at the point of the pyramid. Then we began to sell the eggs and add the money to the hospital fund.

Live chickens were also frequently sent to us with fish fruit, etc. The patients and their friends doing something to show their appreciation for what was done for them.

One case stands out in my memory as unusual.

In the year 1905 I was called to the home of a rather well to do man, a Mr.

Kim, to see his little son who was said to be very ill. He was a very sick child indeed. He was suffering from scarlet fever and was the third child in the family to have it. The other two had died and, to my great regret I had to tell them that this one would not recover, Indeed he died the next day.

I warned the parents that the other two children, a girl and a boy would likely develop the disease and asked them to call me as soon as the first symptoms were noticed. It was not long till Mr. Kim came to tell me that both were ill. His voice was shaky with fear as he asked me what he should do. The new Severance Hospital had just been completed but had not yet been opened to patients so, after a moment's thought, It old him to bring the patients in at once and we would put them into a section that could be shut off from the rest of the building. He went home and was soon back with the two children, his wife and a couple of servants with enough food, clothing, and bed clothes to last for weeks. I found them all willing to follow directions, give the medicine faithfully and feed them as instructed. Fortunately both these children recovered and when they took them home well, Mr. Kim cheerfully paid the bill we proffered him. On the first day of the next month a chicken was brought as a thank offering. This was repeated every month for twelve years except when we were away on furlough. More than one hundred chickens were brought altogether. When the two children grew up they were sent to Japan to school but every time they came back to visit their parents they were brought to our home to see Mrs. Avison and myself whom they had been taught to call father and mother.

When the time came for the boy's marriage the parents brought him to us to be clad in foreign clothing, as he was to be married according to the American way. The same thing happened when the daughter was to be married. She wore some of Mrs. Avison's clothing and made a pretty bride.

Yet some Westerners say the Orientals do not know what gratitude is! I never let such a statement be made in my presence without correcting it by relating some such incident as the above. Even the King and Queen manifested their gratitude for my care for their health by sending us at short intervals large gifts of Korean articles - some of them very valuable. Had we kept them all, we might have set up a Korean department in a museum but we gave them to visitors from America and other countries who valued them as coming not only from a foreign country but as having been sent from their Majesties to us as an expression of their appreciation of their doctor's efforts for them. The Queen always sent supplies of food and many pretty vanities, bolts of silk and fans of all kinds. Sometimes the King sent money for the hospital and presents of money for our own use. He supplied us with a beautiful jinriksha with the service of two riksha-men, one to pull and the other to push. When not needed for that purpose they did any other work we set for them.

Gradually we introduced the idea of paying money not only for actual medicines but also for the professional skill of the doctors and for many years payment in eggs and chickens has been omitted and money sent instead. Quite recently a wealthy Korean gentleman brought his wife to the hospital for surgical treatment. He engaged a private room for her and a second room next to hers for the servants who accompanied her. An operation was performed that resulted in a cure of her trouble. When she was to be taken home he asked for his bill. He paid the amount and then said he greatly appreciated all that had been done for her and the careful attention given to her by the doctors and nurses. To show this appreciation, he presented the hospital with 2,000.00 Won equal at that time to about $750.00 to be used for poor patients. He said he had observed the great numbers of very sick poor people who were treated without any charge and this had aroused in him a desire to help those people that he had never felt before. Appreciation? Gratitude? Yes, Plenty of both in Korea.

Later on he returned to report the continuing good health of his wife and spoke again about the great number of poor people he saw coming daily, many of whom had to be turned away because all the beds were occupied. He said he saw the need for another building with a large number of beds, all set apart for the treatment of these unable to pay anything and offered to contribute 10,000 Won toward such a building. Some others, hearing of this, offered other smaller sums. Then one day he came again to say he had been thinking further about the work and realized that Severance needed a building for the poor large enough to accomodate one hundred beds and that he would increase his contribution to 100,000 Won or whatever amount it would cost to erect and equip such a hospital of one hundred beds if the institution could secure enough annual gifts to take care of so many patients.

That man was more than generous and grateful. Though he was not a professed Christian he had imbibed the Spirit of Christ which I believe is more nearly Christian than a mere profession of Christ as Saviour.

Yes, medical fees are now paid in cash and often, too, the interest of patients is manifested through gifts such as the above, though not as large in amount, for only a few in Korea are able to contribute so much.

Sad to say it has not yet been possible for the hospital authorities to secure the amount needed to care for so many patients, anxious as they are to do so, and so that proposed gift has not yet become available.

It is known from experience with the thirty bed hospital now in use for the very poor that it costs one Won a day to care for each free patient, including food, medicine and heat so that one hundred patients would require 100 Won a day or 36,500 Won a year which at ordinary exchange would be $18,250.00. With interest at 5% it would need an endowment of $365,000 to produce such an income and that amount calls for very generous givers, In no other way, however, could the Spirit of Jesus be better manifested and commended to the people of Korea. In no other way could the spirit of real religion be so completely developed in them.

Selecting Soldiers

The old method of choosing soldiers was very simple. They were appointed on passing the usual annual literary examination and even their officers were chosen in this way. Thus the army, even as late as 1895, was made up of rough and unlearned men (unlearned in the art of war) but soon after our arrival the King issued an order that all candidates for the army must submit to examination as to both mental and physical fitness. The mental examinations were given by, Koreans appointed for the purpose, and I was called on to give each applicant a physical test and record his condition on specially prepared sheets.

The site for the examinations was an open space just back of the British and American legations which had formerly been used for the kwagas (literary examinations). There was a large Korean house with a porch where His Majesty sat and watched the proceedings and other smaller buildings accommodated the cabinet ministers and army officers, The physical examinations were given in a separate building having several rooms occupied by the officials who acted as secretaries to fill out the reports I gave them. As there were several hundred candidates and all the examinations had to be completed in one day they were necessarily very cursory. Fortunately I had a number of assistants who weighed and measured the men so that my attention could be given to examinations of the heart, lungs and other organs concerned.

Plenty of food was provided and it was a gala day for all examiners and examinees. At the end of the day His Majesty gave an audience to his high officers, including myself. He personally thanked me for my services and I left for home, being glad to have had a part in initiating the first step in the building up of an army of soldiers capable of giving good service.

Identifying Skeletons

The first foreign missionaries to Korea were Roman Catholic priests who entered the country as early as the 1770's, many of them only to die as martyrs to their faith. Even up to and during the time of the Tai Won Kun's regency, the Roman Catholic missionaries suffered persecution. The Tai Won Kun was very much opposed to having any relations whatsoever with foreigners in matters of either business or religion and in 1886 he ordered a group of French priests and their Korean assistants to be executed.

These executions apparently took place on the banks of the Han River at a place called San. I had read of these executions before I went to Korea but had thought nothing more about them until some French priests who resided in Seoul asked me to go to Yong San to help them identify the bodies of three French priests who had been executed some thirty years before and whose bodies had been buried there. They had received orders from the Pope to exhume the remains and bury them in consecrated ground according to the manner prescribed by the Roman Catholic Church. There was a Catholic cemetery adjoining the church grounds near Yong San and in this they were to be reburied. Much to the consternation of the priests, four skeletons were found when the graves were opened. Evidently some one besides the three Frenchmen had been buried with them, perhaps one of their Korean priests who had been executed at the same time.

The French bishop was anxious to identify the French priests so they could be buried in consecrated ground and as I was a doctor, they called on me to help them decide which three of the four skeletons were those of the French priests. Was there some way to differentiate the bones of a Frenchman from those of a Korean? I knew of none unless we could findsome marks in one which did not exist in the other three.

The bones of each skeleton had been placed in order on a long table in a room of the Catholic seminary building. I had thought that as Korean men are generally shorter than Europeans, the shorter length of the skeletons might be a differentiating factor but all four were practically of the same length. The differences in conformation of the skulls was but slight and as all differed a little that did not help us. I asked if they had a record of the ages of the priests. In their opinion any Korean who might have accompanied the priests would probably have been a younger man than they, but the bones did not indicate any such differences in ages.

Next I inquired if they knew whether or not the priests smoked. Probably so, but what would that have to do with our problem for the Korean also would be a smoker. I explained that if they were accustomed to holding a metal mouthpiece between their teeth, it might have worn them down. And if the teeth in three skulls seemed worn down more than those in the fourth one that might help us.

We spent several hours in our investigation and in the end found nothing to prove with certainty that the bones of one skeleton differed sufficiently from the others to make a reliable selection. However, some decision had to be made and we again examined the teeth and decided upon the three skulls in which the teeth were apparently worn down the most. Since then I have often wondered whether three French priests had been buried in consecrated ground or whether, by chance, one good Father had given himself in death, as in life, to a Korean.

‣ Chapter 6 ‣

Building the Severance Union Medical College and Hospital

My First Sabbatical

During our first period of service in Korea, 1893 to 1899, we worked in the native buildings in Kurigai district to which Dr. Allen had moved his hospital, where its name was changed to Chay Joong Won(Jejooungwon). It is not intended here to tell of the work done there, of the lack of equipment and the many inconveniences that made everything difficult, but rather to give some idea of what it meant to erect and equip a modern hospital in a land like Korea, at a time when Western methods of building were but little known and the installation of modern heating, water and drainage systems was totally unknown.

When we had put in only five and a half of the eight years of service then expected of missionaries before they were entitled to a furlough the sickness of both my wife and myself necessitated our returning to Canada on what was called a health leave.

The experience of those years in Korea had shown me the necessity of better hospital facilities if we were to carry out our plans for improving the health conditions of the Koreans so after our arrival in Canada and as soon as my health would permit it, I set out to obtain a plan for a modern hospital to be erected when we found it possible to return to our work.

A series of seeming coincidences followed. I had a good architect friend in Toronto, Mr. H. B. Gordon, to whom I went with a request for a plan. He was already interested in Korea, being a member of a Committee that was supporting

Mr. Malcolm Fenwick there. His first question was one I had not been prepared for: "How much money have you?"

I said, "I haven't any yet."

"Well aren't you putting the cart before the horse? How can I draw a plan without knowing how much money is going into it? That will determine its size and type."

"But," I replied, "if I haven't a plan with its estimated cost, how can I know much money to try to get?"

At that he laughed and asked me how many patients I wanted it to accomodate. "About forty," I suggested.

After some thought he said such a building, Plain and without any frills, might be built for $10,000.

"All right," I said, "please draw a plan for it on that basis."

He said he would get at the work right away and would himself make the first donation by presenting me with the complete plans free of charge.

"Thank you," I said. "You see I have already made a good start in getting the money I shall need even before I have gotten the plan."

Then a young woman who had been one of my patients before we went to Korea called at my home and said that she, having heard I was going to build a hospital in Korea, had brought a little contribution toward it. "It is not much," she said, "as I am only a working woman; it is only five dollars but it is given gladly." Thanking her heartily, I said, "I am now confident I shall get all the money needed. With such a beginning, entirely unsought, I feel sure of complete success." I reported this to the architect who, in agreeing with me, said he believed success always comes to those who begin an enterprise believing in its necessity and trusting in the guidance of God.

Then occurred another event in the series of those coincidences.

I wrote a letter from Toronto to the Secretary of the Board of Foreign Missions in New York saying I had recovered my health and was now ready to take up any work they might have for me to do in the United States. Before this letter had had time to reach New York, one came to me from the Secretary of the Mission Board telling me they wanted to consult me so they would like me to come to New York as soon as I felt well enough to do so.

When I arrived at the Board's office and met the Secretary for Korea, Dr. Ellinwood, he told me the letter from the Mission asked the Board to give Dr. Avison permission to raise ten thousand dollars with which to erect a hospital in Seoul and it was about this he wanted a conference with me.

I told him that, though I had not consulted the Mission about it before I left Korea, I had realized the great need for a proper hospital there and had taken certain steps toward the scheme which I hoped he and the Board would approve. I told him what I had done in Toronto about this plan and he promised to lay the matter before the Mission Board without delay and ere long learned that the Board approved the idea.

Not long after that, when on a visit to the Board rooms, as I stepped out of the elevator into the lobby, I met the Board Treasurer, Mr. C. W. Hand, who was talking with a young man to whom he introduced me. His name, Severance, meant nothing to me then though it came to mean a great deal later on. When the young man had gone Mr. Hand said tome, "You are wanting a hospital and the Board has given permission for it. If you could just get in with that family, they could build it themselves and think nothing of it." "Wouldn't that be nice?" I said. That was in the fall of 1899.

Shortly afterwards I received a letter from a fellow missionary, Rev. F. S. Miller of Seoul, then in America with a sick wife who had been taken to the Sanatorium at Clifton Springs, N. Y., for treatment. He told me that Dr. Ellinwood, the Board Secretary, while visiting the sanatorium had talked with him about he proposed hospital. He Mr. Miller had emphasized its need and said he was glad the Board had given its consent for it to which Dr. Ellinwood said he was afraid Dr. Avison would find it difficult to get the money as he was not acquainted with any monied men in the United States. "Yes, but he's acquainted with a monied God," Mr. Miller had promptly replied.

Encounter with Mr. Louis H. Severance

This was in spring of 1900 and we were just getting ready to return to Korea when a letter from Dr. Ellinwood asked me to defer our going until the autumn as the Board wanted us to attend the coming Ecumenical Conference of Foreign Missions in New York City. He also asked me to write a paper for the Conference on the subject of "Comity in Medical Missions." I had noted in Korea the great desirability for cooperation in Mission Hospitals and was glad to have that subject assigned me.

The conference met during the latter part of April and the first part of May. Its principal meetings were held in Carnegie Hall while smaller gatherings were held in various other halls and nearby churches. Three times a day Carnegie Hall was packed with an audience of five thousand people and all other meeting places in the vicinity were similarly crowded.

My paper was to be read in Carnegie Hall at a forenoon session and as my wife and I sat on the platform and looked on that big audience, I felt doubtful about being able to make all the people hear me. Also after listening to the many profound papers read by celebrated personages from all countries, my own paper seemed to be very simple and altogether I felt quite nervous.

But, when my turn came I moved boldly forward and stepped up on the small elevated dais that raised the speakers up so as to make them fully visible to the whole audience. Looking towards the farthest back row of the second gallery, I said to myself, "I will speak to the man sitting there; if I can make him hear, all others can."[24]

Then throwing my voice towards that point, I read my paper. At least I thought then that I read it and still think I did but some of my friends told me afterwards that though I began to read I became so earnest that I seemed to forget the paper and spoke with little or no reference to it. The main point I pressed was that if the seven doctors assigned to Seoul by the various Mission Boards all of whom were working in the Capital in separate small and poorly equipped hospitals could cooperate and establish one good hospital in the Capital, it could do more good than the seven poor, little, So-called hospitals could accomplish even though only three or four of the seven doctors should work in it. The rest of the seven could work in other parts of the country and greatly extend the scope of their efforts.

At noon, when the gathering broke up, I heard my name called from the center of the platform - "Dr. Avison is wanted here at the middle of the platform."

I made my way to where I saw Dr. Ellinwood standing and he said, "Oh yes, a gentleman here wants to be introduced to you." Turning to a fine looking grey

---

[24] The man in the gallery to whom I spoke in Carnegie Hall apparently heard me though of course I had no particular man up there in mind, for the next time we came to America on furlough, eight years afterwards, we settled for a year in Wooster, Ohio, where two of our children were in college. The President of the College, Dr. Holden, Called on me and took me out for a buggy ride around the town and, in the course of the trip, asked me whether I knew what led Mr. Severance to give me the hospital. I did not. "Well", he said, "I will tell you. When you were reading your paper in Carnegie Hall, I was sitting with Mr. Severance away up in the back gallery. You had not been reading long when he turned to me and said, 'What would you think if I gave that man a hospital?' With what he got up, went down to the main floor, and made his way through the crowd along the side aisle till he reached the platform where he waited till noon to meet you."

haired gentleman, he introduced me to a Mr. Severance. Severance! The name at once struck a chord in my memory. It was the name of the young man I had met in the entry to the Board Rooms the previous autumn when the Treasurer had told me that that family could build the hospital for me without any help from others if I could get their interest. A great hope at once sprang up within me.

Mr. Severance said he just wanted to tell me he had enjoyed my paper and that the two best words he had heard so far at the Convention were Comity and Unity. Both were good but Unity was the better of the two. He then said he wanted to talk further with me soon and we made an engagement for the afternoon of the following Wednesday.

Then I told him I had met a young man of his name, Severance, at the Board Rooms a few months before and was wondering whether they were related. "Tell me what he looked like" he said, so I described him. Smiling, he said, "Oh, that was my son, John."

Do you ask what I thought? Well, I thought this was another of those coincidences. Will you wonder if I say I felt sure that that family was to build the hospital?

On the Wednesday I met Mr. Severance as arranged and, losing no time on preliminaries, he came at once to the point. He said, "I learned from your paper that there are several denominational hospitals in Seoul and I suppose there is no need for another."

"Well, we have seven places called hospitals by their supporters but I don't know what you would call them if you could see them. Not one of them is properly equipped and each is handled by one doctor without even one nurse." Then I repeated what I had said in my paper - "If three or four of those doctors could work together in one properly equipped hospital, they could do more work than the seven are doing under present conditions and, besides, that would set three or four free to go elsewhere so that a great many more sick people could be helped in different parts of the country."

"You are quite right," he said. "Have you any plan in your mind for accomplishing this?"

Now had come the supreme moment. The fact that I had a properly drawn plan was evidence to him of my foresight and I know I had started out on the right foot when I asked Mr. Gordon to draw a plan for me. I look it from my bag and laid it before him.

He looked it over carefully and followed his scrutiny with such a volley of questions as I had never before been subjected to. He worked his way to the very bottom of my thinking processes and questioned me as to the reasons for this and that requirement of the plan. I answered as promptly and clearly as I could and at last he seemed satisfied.

"Well, I must go," he said, "Perhaps we shall meet again."

It was not a very definite good-bye message but I had discerned his earnestness and was happy in the prospect ahead.

At the end of the Conference Dr. Ellinwood asked me to be one of a group of missionaries to go to Schenectady, N. Y. on Saturday night to speak in all the churches in that city, on Sunday, both morning and evening.

Amongst these were Bishop Thoburn of India, Methodist, and Hudson Taylor, head of the China Inland Mission, so I felt I was to be in distinguished company.

Arriving at midnight I spent the night at the home of Rev. Dr. Richard, President of Union College of that city. In the morning my host took me to the home of Mr. Walter Pitkin, Vice President of the Schenectady Locomotive Works, where I was to be entertained during my stay in the city.

Mr. Pitkin was a delightful person, an excellent host and about as keen as Mr. Severance, I learned at the breakfast table that his parents had been home missionaries in the Western States. They had had a very hard time to live and raise a family on their slender salary and he spoke very feelingly (unfeelingly) of the Christmas barrels that used to be sent to them filled with old clothing that seldom fitted or, when it did fit, was far too much worn to be of much service. But those days had gone by and he was now not only in comfortable circumstances but rich and filled with great admiration for all missionaries either home or foreign.

As he asked about my work I told him of its condition and of my effort to get money for a new hospital which I hoped could be a union one. Would he like to see my plans? Yes, he would, so out they came and many questions were asked. Asking questions seemed to be a favorite pastime of big business men. At length he said, "I like your plans. Every inch of space is being used, not a bit of waste room."

Soon afterwards he reverted to the subject and said, "I want to help you build that hospital and will give you $500.00 towards it."

The first gift had been the architect's plans, the second gift was $5.00 and now it was $500. 00 and no one had so far been asked for anything.

But I thought of Mr. Severance. He might object to others giving anything if he were going to donate the hospital himself, so I told Mr. Pitkin of Mr.

Severance's interest. He said he knew Mr. Severance and I might rest assured that, having gone as far as he had done and then hinted that he might see me again some day, he was planning to carry the project through.

"But," he said, "I will give you the $500.00 anyway. There is always a place for more money in a hospital and if, by any change, more should be needed I will gladly give you more."

Blessed assurance!

I returned to New York next day and reported to Dr. Ellinwood who of course was greatly pleased. He then said that later in the month the Presbyterian General Assembly would meet in St. Louis and he would like me to attend it. "For," he said, "there will be a discussion on the value or otherwise of self support in the native churches and, as Korea is taking the lead in favor of self support methods, you maybe needed to speak as one with authority."

I said I would be glad to go though I might not be able to speak as convincingly on the subject as some of the evangelistic missionaries who were closer to the native churches could do.

"In the meantime, we will make speaking engagements for you on the way to St. Louis" he said.

This plan was carried out and I reached there at noon of the first day of the assembly.

Learning that a meeting on Foreign Missions was being held in a nearby church, I attended it and listened to a paper being read by a young woman. During the discussion of the paper I rose and spoke two or three minutes in reference to one of her remarks on a subject with which I had had some experience. When I sat down the chairman, Rev. Dr. Halsey of the Mission Board, told the audience I was a medical missionary from Korea and he would tell tales out of school by making an announcement that the Board had not yet made public. He said a gentleman had recently called on the Board and, after asking many questions about Dr. Avison and his work, had ended by telling them he would contribute the $10,000.00 needed for the erection of a hospital in Seoul, Korea.

Mr. Severance had not seen me again but he had done better - he had given the hospital, It was only $10,000.00 but it looked like a million to me then.

I soon received an official letter from the Board announcing the gift. The letter said Mr. Severance would beat tending the General Assembly and it would be wise for me to meet him and thank him for the gift. The opportunity for my wife and me to meet him soon came and an interesting conversation resulted.

"We want to thank you, Mr. Severance, for this fine gift. It has made us very happy for it will be a great boon to the sick people of Korea."

"Well," he replied, "you are no happier to receive it than I am to give it and I hope it may prove to be all you think it will be."

"You do not know it, Mr. Severance," I said, "but Mrs. Avison and I have been praying for this hospital for about a year and we can do no other than regard this as an answer to our prayers."

"Well, seeing you say that, I will tell you that for just about a year I have had it in mind to build a hospital somewhere but I could not come to a decision as to where it should be till I heard your paper at the Ecumenical Conference a month ago. The thought came into my mind that Seoul was the place for it and so I decided. I trust that events will make it plain that both you and I have been devinely guided."

Fast and Slow

I do not remember that I was regarded in Canada as being overactive except that some of my friends did chide me for running upstairs, always going up two steps at a time and sometimes three. But one day as I was walking somewhat briskly along a Seoul street I met Rev. H. G. Appenzeller. He stopped me and said, "Avison, you walk too fast, you do everything too fast. Why are you always on the run? If you keep up that pace here in the Orient you will soon be used up. It will give you only about ten years of life here. But if you will just go at a more moderate speed you may have many long years of life and be able to do a great work. Take your time, man, - you are not in America - you are in the Orient."

Perhaps he was right for in less than six years the doctors ordered us home to Canada. Both Mrs. Avison and I were unable to carry on any longer without a change and so much doubt was expressed as to the advisability of our returning to Korea, that, after laying out what we must take with us, we separated the rest of our goods into two parts -things which should be sent to us if we were unable to return and things to be left in storage, to be sold in such case.

It is doubtful, however, whether our poor health was caused by overwork and too much speed because our symptoms were those of sprue. Exposed as I constantly was to the contagious diseases of the country, I had suffered from tertian malaria, dysentery, typhus fever, and other illnesses and, though I had always recovered, the general effect was not good and Mrs. Avison was likewise weakened.

Return to Korea

That autumn Mrs. Avison and I left for Korea feeling very happy at this fortunate outcome of our wishes and prayers.

In the meantime the king of Korea had notified the Mission through the American Legation that, in accordance with the agreement already described, he would in a year from that date, resume possession of the property of the Jejoongwon, the Royal Korean Hospital, so we had to set out at once on a search for a new site.

Between Christmas and New Year I fell ill with typhus fever and just when I was convalescing the King sent word that he was greatly pleased at hearing that an American gentleman had donated money for the erection of a new hospital and, in view of that he would like to contribute the site for it. He said he had ordered his financier to accompany me and help me in the choosing of it. We appreciated this for it would make it easier for us to secure it after it had been found. But alas for our hopes! Ultimately we had to find one for ourselves and buy it too, for the king's messenger, a man of great influence, was opposed to things foreign and, though he spent much time with us in the search, he always objected to whatever place we asked for. Mr. Severance became disgusted at so much delay and sent me a check for $5,000.00 with which to buy a site without further waiting, for he was anxious to get the project completed, In sending this check, he said, "Now, Dr. Avison, it is up to you. Do not wait any longer on the King for he seems to be tied up to advisers who do not want you to get what you need. Hurry up!"

That check cheered us wonderfully, for it enabled us to secure the best site we had yet found, just outside the Great South Gate and directly across the street from the main railroad station. Having the plans ready, all we had now to do was to find a builder and make a start. So we thought, but "the best laid plans o'mice and men gang oft agley. (=go often agley)"

A considerable group of our fellow Presbyterian Missionaries had a different idea of missionary work from that held by most of the medical and educational folks and, although the mission had asked that I be allowed, while I was in America, to secure $10,000.00 for a hospital, this group became alarmed when I got it, fearing such a fine hospital as they thought it would build, the finest as yet proposed for any branch of work in Korea, would give the Koreans a wrong idea of Christianity.

They wrote me begging me not to build it according to the plan Mr. Gordon had drawn (which was not at all decorative though correct architecturally) and not to spend so much money in erecting it. They feared "the simple Korean converts would get the idea that Christianity was a philanthropic institution rather than a spiritual development."

They wrote to the Board in New York urging this fear on them and asking them to divide the money, allowing half of it to be used in the evangelistic work, leaving only $5,000.00 for the erection of the hospital, an arrangement that they thought would safeguard the mission work against the danger they feared. Just previous to these events I had taken sick with typhus fever and did not learn of them until I was convalescent.

Those objections were not raised by my fellow workers in Seoul Station where the hospital was to be built, but by a group in the city of Pyong Yang in the North. The Board, glad to get $5,000.00 so easily for evangelistic work, agreed to their request, In the meantime, the Secretary of Korea, Dr. Ellinwood, had died and been succeeded by a new man who "knew not Joseph" and, with his concurrence, the Board voted to divide the fund and duly informed Seoul Station of the fact.

While I was still in bed, too weak to leave it, the members of Seoul Station met in my bedroom to discuss this unfortunate situation. They decided to write a letter of protest to the Board in New York signed by every member of the Station and to send a copy to Mr. Severance to let him know just how Seoul Station members felt.

When Mr. Severance learned of this action of the Board he went at once to them and asked why they had taken this liberty with a gift he had made. The secretary explained that it had been done at the request of the Mission which felt that the evangelistic work needed financial help and that in its opinion $5,000.00 would be sufficient to build the type of hospital that would be suitable for Korea.

"All right," said Mr. Severance, "the Mission should know. But as we are at this time building a hospital and $5,000.00 is thought to be enough for that purpose my gift will be $5,000.00. There will be nothing of this gift left for evangelistic work. I believe in the evangelistic work and give freely toward it but just now we are building a hospital."

This was reported to the Mission in due course and as you will see it had a great effect on the Board's thinking.

Visit of Dr. Arthur J. Brown

In the meantime the new secretary was sent to visit the countries under his supervision - Siam, the Philippines, Japan, and Korea-and study their needs. When he arrived in Seoul I was up and around but still not permitted to engage in regular duties.

Dr. Brown met with the members of Seoul Station to discuss its work with them but as he did not ask me any questions touching the Board's action regarding the hospital, I said nothing to him about it.

The next place he was to visit was Pyong Yang, some 200 miles to the North. The trip could be made either by a coastal steamer .or overland by a combination of walking and pony-back riding by men and in sedan chairs by ladies. As Dr. Brown wanted to see some of the work in the interior he chose the overland route.

For this he would need guides and interpreters and the Station appointed one of the evangelistic workers and me to accompany him.

It was quite a cavalcade that started on the trip - sedan chair with four carriers for Mrs. Brown, a pony for each of the three men, each pony having a ma-poo walking at its head and two coolies to carry supplies of food, bedding, etc. We missionaries were to conduct them to a certain town more than half way to Pyong Yang where a deputation from that city would meet them.

The news of our approach got ahead of us and quite often people would come out of their homes to meet us, bringing their sick to the side of the road or asking us to go into their homes to see such as could not leave their beds. Of course it delayed us to stop and treat those but what else was a doctor for? So stop we did and Dr. Brown took great interest in what he saw. It was all new to him and said he was beginning to feel he was back in the time of Christ who, during his journeyings, frequently stopped to help the sick, the lame and the blind.

One day, as we were walking along the road together, he turned to me and, without any introduction to the subject, said, "Doctor, I was one of the Board members who voted to divide Mr. Severance's gift for the hospital. I thought then I was doing the right thing for I was ignorant of the actual conditions of these poor sick people." While we were in Seoul, I wondered why you did not take me to task about my vote but I took note of all I saw there, of the many people who came to your hospital and of how great their need was and since we started on this trip I have been overwhelmed by the amount of sickness we have seen and noted the hope aroused in the patients and their friends when they knew a doctor was in our party and I have changed my mind. I now see that a Christian missionary doctor entirely fails in his relation to these sick people if he does not give them all the help in his power. I can see too that a Christianity that is only preached falls far short of being complete - it must be practised also if Christ's spirit is to be manifested. I am glad that this opportunity has come to me to actually see the work you and your fellow doctors are doing and I am now sure that not only is the full sum of $10,000.00 needed but that sum is altogether too small. I shall immediately write to the Board in New York and urge them to reconsider the question and grant you the full amount of Mr. Severance's gift.

I heard this with a glad heart and was glad I had let him find out for himself.

In due time we turned our guests over to the contingent from Pyong Yang and began our return to Seoul.

My fellow missionary and I travelled back slowly, stopping at various places - he to preach and I to practice. So, when we reached Seoul, we found Dr. and Mrs. Brown already back in Seoul after their inspection of the work in Pyong Yang. They had returned by boat and so had comeback more quickly than we had expected.

We found not only the Browns there but all the missionaries in the North had come with them and a meeting of the Mission was already in progress in the parlor of my home.

Dr. Brown slipped out of the meeting and asked Mrs. Avison and me to go with him into my study as he wished to talk with us privately.

There he told us that in Pyong Yang he had spoken of his experiences along the way and of his change of mind towards the medical work and bad pleaded with them to join him in asking the Board to reverse its action. When they had remained firm he had suggested that they send a deputation to Seoul with him to discuss it with the Seoul ground and endeavor to present a united front to the Board either for or against the proposition. Not only some but all of them had come with him. Neither side had yielded as yet but the Northern delegation had offered to vote for the use of the $10,000.00 for a hospital under certain conditions:

1. That at no future time should Seoul Station ask for any additional sum for the enlargement of the hospital.

Asking me to think it over carefully and then come into the meeting with a written answer, he left us in the study. Together, my wife and I composed a statement in which I repeated what I had said to Dr. Brown that I could not agree to either of the conditions proposed to me. In regard to the future enlargement of the plant, neither they nor I could judge now of what would be desirable or wise. In regard to the cost of running the hospital, no one could know now what advances would be made in the price of fuel, food, service, or drugs. Already the price of wood had doubled, and the price of one drug, quinine, so much of which was needed for the constant stream of malarial cases that came to us, was three times what it had been. How could they ask me to be so foolish as to make such promises?

I said I would prefer to take $5,000.00 new with an open future, rather than $10,000.00 with a closed future, for with $5,000.00 I could build a smaller hospital and hope for its future enlargement. In regard to the cost of running it, I would not make any promise except to say I would, as I always had done, be as economical as the welfare of the patients would permit but I would never agree to sacrifice the interests of the sick people who entrusted their lives to me in the belief that I would do all I could to help them regain their health. What else could I say?

As soon as I sat down, Dr. Brown cried out, "answered." The meeting was then brought to an end without any action being taken. Dr. and Mrs. Brown went to the home of the lady physician and nurse for dinner and the others scattered to the homes of their hostesses.

Erection of Severance Hospital

In less than an hour American mail was delivered at our home and there was a letter from the Board telling me of the reversal of its former decision so that we would get the $10,000.00 without conditions. I ran over to the ladies' home to announce the news. Finding them all seated at dinner, I waved my letter. Dr.

Brown jumped up and waved a similar one that had just come to him. Did we rejoice?

The next letter from New York informed us that the Board had invited Mr. Gordon, my Toronto architect, to go to Korea to supervise the erection of the hospital and several residences in Seoul and then go to China to do the same for a number of buildings that were to be put up there and once more our hats went up in the air.

There was great rejoicing in Seoul station but the Pyong Yang contingent didn't get over their disappointment until long afterwards when the new hospital had been completed and was in operation. I am glad, however, to say that the day did come when the majority of the members of the Mission changed their attitude toward medical mission work and gave me a practically free hand to carry out my ideas.

While those discussions were in progress I had been looking for another site on which to begin building the hospital as already related, I found a vacant hill outside the South Gate that seemed even more suitable than my former choice. Several letters had passed between Mr. Severance and me concerning the delay in getting started. He had grown restless and had sent me a letter urging me to forget the King's promise to give us a site and enclosing $5,000.00 with which to purchase one and with it I bought this latter site. The deeds for it had just been obtained when I heard that the railway company was about to erect its main station directly across the street and that they had expected to purchase the land which I had just bought. They offered me more money than I had paid for it but I was unwilling to give it up. They then purchased some other fields at the foot of the hill but when they found these too small for their purpose, they sold them to us. I was glad to secure them as I realized our site was going to be too small. In the end we secured over nine acres, quite enough for our institution, without depending on either the King or his agent Mr. Yi. The value of the plot increased as time went by so that what I bought for $15,000 was recently valued at almost $1,000,000. Out of this small beginning a plant was developed which cost several hundreds of thousands of dollars.

We were never told the name of the donor of Mr. Gordon's salary and expenses but some of us thought it would not be difficult to name him who but the giver of the hospital itself?

We had now only to find a reliable builder and get the work started. We chose a Chinese contractor, Harry Chang, who at one time had been a trusted servant at the American Legation where he had learned to speak English. Later he had also learned the building trade by working with contractors for foreign houses and familiarizing himself with all parts of the work. We knew him to be honest and that he would abide by any contract he made and we arranged with him to do all parts of the work except the installation of the modern heating plant, the ventilating system, the water supply and the disposal of sewage, with none of which he had had any experience. These would have to be done by ourselves.

While Chang was busy with the preliminaries, the architect arrived and assumed responsibility so we knew that all would be properly done. He worked out all the orders for the materials that would have to be imported together with all the necessary tools and in due time all came to hand.

By that time it was already 1903 and there was much talk of a possible war between Japan and Russia. This culminated in 1904. Prices of materials then soared and our contractor asked for a consultation with me. He showed me the purchasing price that had enabled him to contract at the rate he had given me and compared them with the prices he had had to pay of late. His loss would almost ruin him if we compelled him to complete the building at those still rising prices but, he said, he would go on with the work if we insisted on it. Feeling that would not be fair, we released him from his contract and asked him to give us a new price. He said the future was so uncertain that he would prefer to give up the job altogether. We agreed to that and undertook to complete it ourselves by day labor.

I immediately reported these things to Mr. Severance and told him we were proceeding on the belief that he would want the work to go on even at the increased cost. I said I understood that he had told the Board, when the question of cutting his donation in half was being considered, that his contribution had been $10,000.00 because Dr. Avison had suggested this amount to him but that he wanted a good hospital, whatever it cost, $5,000.00, $10,000.00, or $15,000.00 I had now to tell him it would cost considerably more than $10,000.00 to build it properly but that I could not name the exact sum. His answer came promptly - "he wanted a good building and was glad we had proceeded as we had done." So the work went on.

One of our medical students who had assisted me in the compiling of textbooks in the Korean language acted as Mr. Gordon's interpreter and all went on without special difficulty until we came to the installation of the heating and plumbing systems. As there was no one in Korea who had any knowledge of such things, Mr. Gordon, Mr. Kim and I had to do this work ourselves. Though I had to spend several hours a day at the old hospital, nearly a mile away, I managed to do a lot of the installation work with the other two men.

The first part of this work was to lay a tile sewer under the floor of the basement so as to insure the free disposal of all sewage and a completely dry basement, It would not do to have either wrong slanting of any of the drains or poorly cemented joints so, having had the trenches dug for us, we laid all the pipes according to the plans and cemented the joints with our own hands. Then all the down pipes from the bathrooms had to be installed. These four inch iron pipes had to be tamped at their joints with solder. None of us had ever done such work but the architect, of course, understood the method so, after a few trials, we were able to make the joints safe even though they were not as smooth as a plumber would have made them. The distribution of the water pipes and the installation of the hot water heating system were not easy tasks for us for we had to cut all the pipes to their required lengths, thread them and make them leak-proof. But at last the work was finished and Korea had its first really foreign hospital building.

When this main building had been completed we still needed separate accomodations for contagious cases and another call on Mr. Severance was made. To this also he responded promptly by sending the money needed.

When all had been completed we had spend $25,000.00 instead of the original $10,000.00 but Mr. Severance was pleased and we felt we were at last prepared to do the kind of work we knew ought to be done in a hospital wherever it might be located.

Residences for the foreign doctors and nurses and some Korean homes for assistants and servants were erected with the money we received from the King in payment for all we had spent on the old hospital.

The new plant was dedicated in the presence of a large gathering of well wishers of many nationalities.

As related elsewhere the first patients admitted were two children with scarlet fever and as the special building for such cases was not then ready for use, they were accommodated in a part of the main building which of course had to be thoroughly disinfected before it was open to the general public. This was a fair example of our policy that nothing was too good in a case, of need

First Foreign Occupants of the New Hospital Building

Soon after opening the new hospital building in Seoul, Dr. Roy K. Smith and his wife came to Korea to work in Chairyung. As no house was ready for them there, it was proposed that they remain in Seoul for a time and study the language. There was no vacant house in Seoul either. But as many missionaries lived in Seoul surely they could be accommodated in some home. There were some as yet unoccupied rooms in Severance Hospital. What about them? Dr. and Mrs. Smith lived in them for some time.

In the intervals between language study periods, Dr. Smith worked in the laboratory as he had taken a special course in that work and had brought some apparatus with him. Thus began the method of laboratory diagnosis which we had not before been able to install.

Dr. and Mrs. Smith are still living in Korea (1941) and not long ago I had a letter from her in which she referred to that early experience. At that time it seemed to them they were having a very hard time but in retrospect she considered it one of the happiest periods of their lives.

Expansion of Severance Hospital

In 1907, Mr. Severance, accompanied by his personal physician Dr. A. I. Ludlow, visited us. He expressed himself as well pleased with what his gift had produced and helped us plan for additional buildings which would cost much more than the amount of his first investment.

The greatly enlarged plant is located on a valuable property covering nine and a half acres and is now surrounded by the ever-extending city. The railroad station is just across the plaza outside our main entrance and all these surrounding improvements have added greatly to the money value of our property.

The group of buildings now consists of:

A.   The original hospital building.

B.   A much larger and even more modern hospital building of four stories connected with the original one by a covered passage to each floor.

C. A new and much larger contagious disease hospital of three stories. (The normal capacity of these three buildings is 200 beds.)

D. A combined moregue and post mortem building in which a large class of students can watch the postmortem examinations.

E. A building of two stories, one housing the new modern laundry and the other the kitchen and nurses' dining rooms.

F. A four story building containing:
    1st floor. The drug manufacturing and wholesale plant which supplies drugs and medicines to most of the doctors throughout the country; the optical manufacturing department; the medicine dispensing rooms, and the clinic rooms for non-pay patients. On the second floor is the X-ray Department, the pay clinics for surgery, Pediatrics, and skin and urinary diseases. On the third floor are the pay clinics for neurology, internal medicine, eye, ear, nose and throat, tuberculosis and obstetrics and gynecology. All these clinics are carried on by competent specialists. The fourth floor accommodates a set of lecture rooms and laboratories for chemistry and another set for physiology.

G. A clinical laboratory building of two stories with complete equipment for all kinds of tests, It also contains the department of parasitology.

H. A building with lecture rooms and laboratories for anatomy, Pathology, and bacteriology, and a sanitary animal housing section.

I. A small Hospital for the acutely insane.

J. A church and general lecture hall that seats 500.

K. A kindergarten building completely equipped for 40 children which is also utilized for a weekly well-babies clinic.

L. A students recreation building.

M. Dormitory and school rooms for pupil nurses.

N. A residence for graduate Korean nurses employed in the hospital

O. Two residences for the foreign nurses connected with the hospital.

P. Five residences for foreign doctors working in the institution.

Q.   Many homes for Korean doctors, evangelists and servants.

R.   A four-story building, three stories for the dental department which has a lecture room, ten completely equipped chair combinations each in a separate room, a dental laboratory, a mechanical room and a director's office. The fourth floor, opening from the larger hospital building accommodates two complete operating rooms, each with an observation gallery for medical students. (These galleries are connected with the main school building by an elevated covered passage so that students can reach their galleries without entering either the hospital or the operating rooms). Also the suite has sterilizing rooms and rooms for preparing and storing nursing supplies.

Three of the buildings have flat roofs so that cases of T. B. or others needing plenty of outdoor sunshine can be sent up there when weather permits.

All those were erected while the author was in charge(1893-1934), the greater part by funds donated by Mr. L. H. Severance and his son and daughter.

As a memorial to them, the Institution is known as the Severance Union Medical College, Hospital and Nurses Training School, or for short the S. U. M. C.

The word union in the name signifies that different missions joined in providing operating funds, doctors and nurses in harmony with Dr. Avison's original plan and Mr. Severance's earnest desire. It is a union effort of six missions- 2 Presbyterian (North and South), 2 Methodist Episcopal (North and South), Australian Presbyterian, and Canadian Presbyterian.

Before Dr. Avison's retirement, Plans were formed for the uniting of the Medical College with the Chosun Christian College under the name of the Chosun Christian University but conditions did not permit carrying out the project at the time and, even yet (1943), it is still a project though not a forgotten one.[25]

Some acres of hill property were purchased from the Chosun Christian College at that time on which to erect sanitariums for T. B. cases and cases of insanity and these also are yet unbuilt.

Just recently, however, an architect has been asked to draw plans for a complete new medical college, hospitals and residences on that site, including the

---

[25]   Now in 1943 it all seems improbable at least until the war is over and those responsible for the future of the work are free to go on with it.

already mentioned sanitoriums.

President Dr. K. S. Oh, a Korean who cooperated with Dr. Avison for more than 25 years, has expressed the hope that the latter may return to Korea to advise them in the carrying out of this long desired scheme.

President Emeritus Avison is already in his 82nd year and though strong enough yet to be more or less helpful, these plans may not materialize in time for him to cooperate in the project in accordance with this kind thought of the new President.

Dr. Avison desires very much to give expression in these memoirs to his great appreciation of the cooperation given by these six missions in bringing the institution to its present state of efficiency, to the Severance family in particular, and to all others who helped in the provision of the necessary funds.

‣ Chapter 7 ◂

Pak, the Butcher and his family,
or Democracy in religion

Encounter with Mr. Pak, the Butcher

Soon after our arrival in Seoul in 1893 the Rev. S. F. Moore asked me to visit a sick Korean man, a Mr. Pak. As I could not then either understand or speak the Korean language Mr. Moore interpreted for us.

The home was not that of a poor man but like most others it was small. The room in which the sick man lay was about seven by seven feet square and of about the same height inside. The floor, covered with thick oilpaper, was warm even though it was only September, being heated by the smoke from the kitchen fire which passed through channels under the floor before it reached the chimney and the patient was lying on a thin padded quilt which allowed the heat of the floor to be comfortably felt. I sat on the floor, cross-legged, not a very convenient posture for a Westerner and very inconvenient for a doctor when examining a patient.

After making my diagnosis and prescribing for the patient I gave way to Mr. Moore who read some appropriate verses of scripture to the man and talked with him for a short time. We visited him regularly until he had recovered. He was not only profuse in his thanks but made us both happy by telling us he had decided to become a Christian. He was in earnest too for as soon as he could go out he told all with whom he came into contact of his newly found faith and urged them to do as he had done.

Not many listened to him for he was only a butcher and in Korea the butchers are a despised class - they are at the very bottom of the social scale. Of course they are important to all who eat meat but most of the people in Korea were Buddhists and, as such were forbidden to kill animals or eat their flesh. One of the most important tenets of that religion is the belief in reincarnation or the transmigration of souls. This belief is associated with the central Buddhistic idea of Nirvana which is a state of spiritual perfection attained only by an individual who, during his earthly life, has overcome all his natural physical desires. He is perfectly negative because his positive qualities have all been overcome. As the attainment of Nirvana on earth is a very difficult process, few, if any, reach it during one lifetime and so the idea of reincarnation follows naturally. The soul is sent back to earth in another body, Perhaps again in human form but more often in the form of one of the lower animals. No one on earth knows whether one of those animals has in it the soul of an ancestor, so, just as naturally as the idea of reincarnation grew up, there came the idea of the sacredness of all animal life. No animal may be killed for in so doing a parent or dear friend may be the victim.

Now as butchers kill animals as a matter of business they may be killing not only their own friends, but also the friends of others, and so, from the Buddhist point of view, they are not fit to be regarded as men. But what of these who eat the killed animals? Well they eat only dead bodies, do they not? The souls have already gone to the world of spirits to be judged again so why not make use of the bodies that are already dead?

A butcher was not allowed to wear a hat or a topknot, the two most sacred signs of manhood in Korea, and our friend Pak not being a man, could not win a hearing from the people generally so he turned his attention to men of his own class who "heard him gladly". Mr. Moore had a group of Koreans meeting in church every Sunday and our friend allied himself with this group. Of course, its members looked askance at the coming into their midst of a man without a hat and this turned into consternation when the butcher's friends began to come to their meetings in such numbers that the group was often referred to as "the butcher church." What a name for a church in Korea!

The original group included some who belonged to the "upper classes" and felt themselves superior even to most of the men with hats or without them who had become Christians, but what were their feelings when they saw these hatless men coming into their midst and being welcomed by their pastor? They were of course embarrassed. If their friends outside laughed at them for taking up with the strange religion how much more did they jeer at them for mingling with the despised butchers?

So they interviewed Mr. Moore. They told him they did not want to cause him any trouble but he could see for himself that the corning into their midst of the butchers placed them in a very disagreeable position. Would he not do something about it?

Poor Mr. Moore I He was facing not one dilemma but several. He did not want to send the butchers away and he did not want the others to leave. Above all, he did not want the Christian church, at its very beginning, to recognize social status as a test of membership but he could not help realizing the deep repugnance the wearers of hats felt toward those without them and he was greatly disturbed.

It reminded me, and perhaps Mr. Moore remembered it too, that Christ accepted an invitation to dine with the socially outcast Matthew, the taxgatherer and his friends whom the Pharisees called "the irreligious and sinners," and thus set an example to his followers everywhere and at all times. After all, it was a question of democracy in religion such as has often troubled the church throughout the ages but on which no church court has yet ruled.

Mr. Moore discussed the matter with his aristocratic friends and tried to make it plain to them that all men are equally the sons of God and therefore brothers of each other and that it would be a violation of this great principle to ask the believing butchers to stay away from the church and he ended by saying "the butchers are not going!" Though this was a great blow to their pride they finally decided to stay and that church grew and prospered. The principle of democracy was thus established in the Christian church of Korea from almost its very beginning and the butchers found themselves in an entirely new relation to their fellow men.

Human Rights of the Butchers

In 1894-95 the China-Japan war was fought and, as had always been the case in such war, Korea, lying between the two warring countries, became the main battle ground though, at the very end, the Japanese entered Manchuria to complete their victory over China. Then, as is not uncommon even yet, war was followed by an epidemic, in this case Asiatic cholera. It first broke out in Manchuria but moved gradually south into Korea. Cholera is not endemic in Korea - that is, it is not native to the country. It always has to come in afresh from outside. Koreans had suffered from it many times in the past and were very much afraid of it as it always took a heavy toll of a people who knew neither how to prevent it nor how to cure it. As it could advance no faster than men could travel, because its contagion had to be carried by people, we had time to make some preparation before it could reach Seoul but every day we heard of its attacking people along the main highway from the north and every day fear grew stronger among the people.

The Minister of Home Affairs, Hon. Yu Kil Choon, called me to his office for a consultation as to the preventive measures to be taken and then asked me to take full charge of everything connected with prevention and treatment in and around Seoul. He gave me a posse of policemen with full authority over them and supplied me with funds for the work. Naturally I felt a heavy responsibility had been put on me for this was to be my first experience with this dreaded disease.

The King too was greatly alarmed. He called me to the palace to ask me about it and then begged me to remain in the palace so as to be near him all the time. Now what was I to do? Ordinarily the King's word is final and a request is an order but this time it could not be for I had promised to superintend the work for the whole city. I explained this to him and told him I would place in the palace one of the young Korean men I had been instructing in the hospital and give him a supply of medicines to administer to any suspected cases until I could myself reach there and also promised to spend every other night in the palace near him. He agreed to this and so that matter, which might have caused a good deal of trouble, was comfortably arranged. Mr. Moore had had to choose between sending away the butchers and risking the loss of the gentry who were attending his church and now I had had to risk offending the King by telling him I could not accede to his demand as I must also care for the common people in the great city. I told his Majesty there were others needing care as well as he, and again this democratic principle prevailed, for the King saw the point and accepted my solution of the problem. Autocracy had received another jolt, a gentle one you may say, and the greater value of the mass had been maintained as against the lesser value of the few. "There are others, Your Majesty!"

The young man whom I sent into the palace was very faithful and won the praise of the King and his courtiers. Fortunately no cases of the disease developed within the palace walls.

I also kept my part of the agreement. Though it was often very late at night when my work in the city allowed me to leave it, I got to the palace every other night. The other nights I spent with my family at our summer home in Han Kang, about three miles from the city, having to walk there generally long after darkness had set in. Naturally my wife was always anxious till I got there for she had the responsibility of caring for our four young children under very difficult conditions.

Going back now to the epidemic itself and to the preparations we were making to handle it, we learned each day that cases were developing nearer and nearer to the capital and the interval was used to organize the whole missionary group in the city into a cholera-fighting squad. Practically all other work was laid aside while the doctors and nurses coached lay workers in the methods to be adopted in caring for the patients, avoiding the contagion of themselves, visiting stricken homes to persuade the people to send their sick ones to the special hospitals set up for the occasion and in doing all that was possible in the way of disinfecting the homes from which cases were removed. Korean helpers for the hospitals had to be secured and trained to serve both as assistant nurses and servants. Directions for reaching the hospitals had to be posted in various parts of the city.

The popular idea was that this disease, like so many others, was caused by the entry into the patient of an evil spirit that could only be avoided or removed by placating it with gifts, sacrifices and worship and this idea, of course, had to be eradicated before much progress could be made towards either prevention or cure. This spirit was supposed to have the form of a rat and had two Korean names; Kwayjil, evil spirit disease, and Chwee Tong, rat disease.

At the end of seven or eight weeks of very strenuous work, the epidemic began to subside and soon thereafter we were able to reopen our other hospitals and the schoolteachers and evangelists resumed their regular lines of work. While much of our effort appeared to have had little result sofar as saving life was concerned, some headway had been made towards giving the people a different idea of the causes of such diseases. The effectiveness of our methods of prevention had been proved by the fact that not one of the workers, who for so long had been in constant contact with the patients, had taken the disease. That alone was worth all the hard work of those weeks. Years of mere explanation would not have been as effective.

We, too, had learned several lessons, one of which was the value of cooperation among ourselves. We had also gained much practical knowledge of how to handle such epidemics and also much of what not to do. We had learned the uselessness of giving the people orders the purpose of which they could not understand and therefore generally refused to carry out. We had also awakened to the fact that we must prepare for an epidemic before it comes and that education of the masses along sanitary lines must not be neglected if such diseases were to be avoided or controlled. The Government, through the Minister of Home Affairs, expressed its gratitude to us and sent a present to each of the foreigners who had participated in the work.

The attitude of the Government and those evidences of its good will led Mr. Moore to come to me with the suggestion that this might be an opportune time for me to ask a great favor from it.

"What are you thinking of?" I asked.

"Well," he said, "I am thinking 6f the poor butchers whose condition is so pitiable. Why not ask the Government to pass a regulation permitting the butchers to do up their hair and wear hats like other men?"

That staggered me and I said, "You believe in asking a great deal when you are at it. I fear you overestimate my influence."

But he persisted so I gave in and suggested that we join in addressing a letter to Mr. Yu. The letter was as follows:

Your Excellency,

It is not necessary to draw your attention to the great disability under which the butchers of Korea live. Though they are useful members of society and not behind other men in intelligence they are not permitted the honorable custom of putting up their hair in topknots and of wearing hats, the symbols of manhood in Korea. We are venturing to hope that this condition may be remedied now when so many broadminded and liberal men hold positions in your government.

We assure you that we represent the views of all the foreign residents in Korea and that all will be greatly pleased to see such an act of justice done to this long-suffering group of your people. We are, dear sir,

Your obedient servants

We were much pleased to receive a reply from Mr. Yu saying they were grateful for the suggestion and would have notices posted at once throughout the country proclaiming the new law. That was done and the notice said in effect "From this time butchers are to be regarded as men. They are hereby permitted to dress their hair and wear hats according to the general custom of Korean men."

Not long after that I saw a well-dressed Korean coming down the street with the stately tread of a gentleman and as we approached each other I recognized my old friend, Pak, the butcher, walking along the street for the first time in his life - a MAN. I found myself wondering what he was thinking about under his hat and whether he realized what had brought to him this great privilege. Was it not due to a recognition, beginning to take hold of the minds of Koreans, of the Fatherhood of God and the Brotherhood of all men.

Then I realised more strongly than before that the work of missionaries is the making of men. It thrilled me as I recognized that this was really the reason for my being in Korea to make men by bringing them into right relations with God the Father and other men their brothers.

Of course, this was a big step in Pak's upward move. As time passed he became a banker and his religious enthusiasm led to his becoming a recognized leader in the church. However when an elder was to be elected in his church and some one suggested that Mr. Pak be chosen, a more cautious man said they must not forget that Pak had been a butcher and it was not fitting that he should be made a ruler over the rest of them and so another was chosen. Later on another elder was to be named and again Pak's name was mentioned but again objection was made. "Let us wait longer," said one, "for it is not seemly. We need a deacon- let us elect him to that office." To those of you who do not understand these distinctions in church officers we may say that an elder is a ruler in the church while a deacon is a worker. So Mr. Pak became a deacon.

Not till twenty-one years after his conversion, was he elected to the eldership but then he became an elder in the largest Presbyterian church in the capital. How slowly prejudice dies even in the Christian church ! I was present at his ordination and, along with others, Placed my hand on his head while the ordination vow was being administered and, once again, I wondered whether he was remembering the day when he was converted, the day when Mr. Moore said, "the butchers are not going," and the day when he first put up his topknot and donned his hat and thus became a man. I think he never forgot those important steps in his life.

The Butcher's Son

The butcher had a son named Suh-yang-ie. Like all the other boys of that time he wore his hair hanging down his back in a long braid just as the young girls did. He went bareheaded too except when the weather was very cold of which time he wore only a sort of cap, for hats were worn only by men.

But when a boy attains the marriageable age, about twelve or thirteen, the first steps are taken to make him into a man. Three things were necessary - his hair must be unbraided and put up as topknot on the crown of his head, he must be hatted, and he must be given a wife.

The first step is to arrange for a wife for him.

They did not tell Suh-yang-ie to go out and find a wife -oh, no, they just told him they were going to find a wife for him. In Korea these affairs are arranged through a "go between," a woman, who makes it her business to know where all the eligible boys and girls are, their position in the community, their financial situation and all the other things required for the making of suitable matches. So a go-between was called and told they wanted a wife for their son. Of course they explained just the kind of a girl they desired :beauty, of course, amiability too, good health and a strong body as she would have to work hard and relieve her mother-in-law of all the arduous toil of the housekeeping and if she had money too all the better.

In time the intermediary reported and as the report seemed fairly satisfactory, a meeting between the two sets of parents was arranged so that the boy's parents could see the girl and those of the girl could see the boy. When all had been found to be satisfactory to both sides the young people were told of the match though probably they did not have an opportunity to see each other until they met to take their places at the wedding ceremony.

In due time, a date was set for the marriage and preparations begun for the event. The boy's hair was put up and he was given his first hat. This was smaller than the regular hat worn by men and was white instead of black. The wearing of this particular type of hat served as an announcement to his friends and the general public that he was engaged to be married.

The details of a Korean wedding will be found in another section of this book so I will recite here only some of those which pertained to this one, which was partly Korean and partly Western.

Mr. and Mrs. Pak, being Christians, decided on a mixture of customs and Mr. Moore performed the part of the ceremony which might be designated as Christian. The small rooms and the courtyard were filled with guests among whom were Mrs. Avison and I. The bride and groom stood together while the minister asked the usual questions and then pronounced them man and wife. The two wore the usual Korean wedding garments but her face wasn't covered with the alabaster-like paste that is usually part of a Korean bride's make-up, I do not know whether these two had seen each other before they met for their marriage but, Presuming that this was their first meeting, according to the general custom, I could not help wondering what thoughts were passing through their minds at that moment and I wonder how you, my reader, would have liked to be married under such conditions.

However, there they were, doing what their parents and their forebears had done before them and it may be presumed that, not ever having expected anything different, they were content to let matters take their usual course. But I could not help comparing this method of getting a wife with the Canadian and American way. It took me nearly eight years of attention to the young lady whose consent I wanted to win and to prepare a home for her - and we enjoyed it all. But, in Korea, the parents took all the trouble and, as for getting a home ready, the bride and groom just went into the home of his parents and he had no responsibility in that matter. How easy it all was - but what a lot of fun they missed! At any rate they had no heartaches until after they were married !However, in the light of my experience, I prefer to have had the years of effort to win her, the happy memoirs of it all and the joy that came into the home that was founded on a mutual love of which we had made sure before it was too late to change.

When the ceremony had been completed and the time had come for the guests to leave the house, Mr. Pak accompanied Mrs. Avison and me to the gate and surprised me by saying, "Doctor, now that I have got my boy married, I want you to take him into the hospital and make a man of him." Make a man of him I Why, had they not just now completed all the steps required to make a man of him? They had put up his hair, they had given him a hat and they had gotten him a wife. What was in Mr. Pak's mind ? "Ah!" thought I, "the butcher, but lately made into a man himself, has got a new idea. He has realized that those things make a man outwardly only and he wants his son to become a man inwardly." So I said I would be glad to do as he requested.

Not long afterwards he was brought to me and I started him of the road to true manhood, I set him at cleaning the hospital floors, making up the beds and doing all the things that would test him and make me sure he had in him the stuff out of which real men are made. Though it must have been hard for him to be set at tasks so unusual to men in Korea he responded finely and in due time I started him on his book studies. For all the details of the years between then and his graduation as a doctor, the reader is referred to the special chapter on "the making of doctors."

The Butcher's Son becomes a Man

It was not till 1908 that I felt sure the seven young men who had persisted so many years in their medical studies were about ready to be sent out as doctors on their own but, in that year, my colleague and I had given them a thorough examination and set June 8 for their graduation.

As this would be the first ceremony of the sort in Korea for physicians trained in their own land by Western standards, we felt that much should be made of it. We had then no big auditorium where such a large meeting as we wanted to have could be held and although it was June, it would not be safe to plan to hold it out of doors in the open. We realized also that we must make sure of the interest and cooperation of the Japanese Resident General without which we would have no authority to grant medical degrees that would enable the new doctors to practice their profession so I asked Prince Ito for an interview.

He received me most graciously and asked what I wanted so I told him of the years of effort we had spent in training a group of Korean young men in the hospital and teaching them the principles and practice of medicine until we had assured ourselves of their qualifications as doctors, I explained that all this would become useless without his interest and help but that if we could be assured of these we would plan to grant them diplomas. He appeared deeply interested and asked what we thought he could do to help. I asked him to lend us some army tents so that we could enclose a large space on the hospital lawn in which to hold the affair and accomodate the guests we wished to invite. This he at once agreed to do.

Then I went on to invite him to be our guest of honor, to present the diplomas to the graduates and to deliver to them an address of instruction. He consented to do all these and I returned home to prepare the diplomas and send out invitations to all the important people of the city both native and foreign.

The time for the rainy season was nearing and rain might spoil it all.

The day before the great event was to take place, I called the seven young men to me and said I would like to have them tell me the thoughts that were in their minds as they came to the end of the many years of study and hard work that had been required to prepare them for what was to take place the next day. It is always interesting to know what young people are thinking of as they approach graduation but of course I was more than usually concerned to learn what these particular young men had in mind. One of them said they had been talking together of this very thing. They felt they had had long and very trying time in spite of their great interest in their studies and often they would have liked to runaway from it all had I not held them to their task. "You know," he said, "according to Korean custom we were all married when we were still young and before we became medical students. Though each of us had a wife and children we could do nothing for their support while we were studying so we have had a very hard time. Now we have been feeling relieved by the thought that we would be able to practice our profession and make a living."

This was just such an answer as I might have expected - indeed, it was what I had in mind when I graduated and it is just what all graduates think when they finish their course, but I was not quite happy over it. Then another of them spoke and said that when they began to think of the years of effort their teachers had put into their preparation in the hope of creating a body of men who would not only be ready to practice but also to teach others they decided that it was up to them to stay right on and help them teach the next class. Then I did get excited as I realized that while makings even doctors I had made seven MEN. For what is a MAN? What is the difference between a man and a mere animal? Is it not that a man has a sense of responsibility for other people such as an animal has not got? These young fellows had got the idea and were ready to live up to it. Of course I was elated for now I would have the beginning of a Faculty of Teachers who could do this in their own language much more effectively than I had been able to do. Now too, I understood what Mr. Pak had in mind when he asked me to take his son and make a man of him. His son had remained with us through all the years and was now a MAN.

For the details of the graduation exercises I must refer to another section of these memoirs. Suffice it to say that though the big tent seated about a thousand people, it was filled long before the hour for the service arrived and hundreds had to be turned away. It was evident that the Korean people were deeply interested in the event, the first of its kind in the history of their country.

The Butcher's Daughter

The butcher, Pak, had daughters also who, by the custom of the country, had no other outlook than to remain uneducated and become daughters-in-law at the age of 12 or 13 in some household where they must be the servants of their mothers-in-law. As a result of this custom there were no schools for girls in

Korea until after the Christian missionaries arrived in 1885 because, said their fathers, it would take the girls all those years to learn to cook and sew and thus relieve their husbands' mothers of the drudgery of housekeeping. And furthermore, they claimed, girls had no brains and you could not teach them book-learning if you tried and, as they had no souls, what was the use anyway?

But the missionaries opened schools for girls though they could get as pupils only the very young girls who were still too young to do much of the household work. Soon, however, some of the Christian parents did send older girls to those schools and among those were two daughters of Pak the butcher who, he felt, should be given as good an opportunity as his son was having. The years passed by and in 1908, the year made famous by the graduation of the first doctors, one of those girls graduated from her school. The principal of the school asked me to preside at the exercises which were to beheld in the church near the school, the largest church in the city, capable of accommodating 1,200 people sitting on the floor as tightly packed as possible and, let me assure you, the church was packed that day for many were anxious to see this notable sight, the graduation of those young women who should long ago have been married, according to the age-old custom of the country.

It was a day of surprises for even me. As I entered the church I saw no curtain down the middle of the church such as had, from the time when the women and men began to attend church at the same time, separated the men from the women. What had happened ? I was told that the people of that church felt that the graduation of Korean girls, even from a junior high school, marked such a great departure from past customs that they might as well inaugurate the new era by breaking down one more barrier to that free intercourse between men and women that they had observed among the Westerners. So, at the instance of the women of the church, the curtain had been removed and, though the men and women sat on separate sides of the room, they felt a great forward step had been taken, It was not long before this action was followed by all the churches of the city and, later on, the new custom spread to all parts of the country.

Another surprise awaited me for, when the graduates came into the church, they were led up to the platform and seated there in full view of all. Such a thing had never happened before so I realized that a new day was dawning in Korea. The exercises then proceeded according to the usual formula - the diplomas were distributed and the usual complimentary addresses delivered.

Then came another astonishing thing. One of the girls was to deliver a valedictorian address - a brainless girl without a soul was to talk to six hundreds of her own kind as well as to six hundred old men, young men and boys. When she got up and stood before the great audience who was she? Who but the daughter of our friend Pak, the butcher? What a change in but a few years!

I cannot now remember what she said but I did think her speech was a good one. I said to myself that she would make a different kind of wife and mother and make a new kind of home and that if we could do the same for every girl in Korea, the need for missionaries in that land would soon be ended. As I looked around the church from my place on the platform, I imagined the men's ears turned forward to catch all the words from the lips of this amazing girl.

Thinking of all that had happened to the butcher in fifteen years proved a rather overwhelming task. He had become a man among his fellow men as had all the butchers in the country; his son had become one of the first group of doctors trained according to Western methods in Korea; and his daughter had stepped out of the ignorance that had been considered the inevitable lot of women and was now capable of taking part in the educational, the social, and the religious work of her country! But the end was not yet.

Dr. Park's Family

After Dr. Pak, the butcher's son, had served his Alma Mater some years as a teacher it became evident that the needs of the growing medical college and the increasing demands of the government for teachers with higher educational acquirements than had been necessary when the work was first started, led him to leave our hospital and teaching staff and go out to practice his profession independently. He chose to go across the Tuman river that separates Korea from Manchuria at the East and settle among the large number of Koreans who had emigrated to the district. There he opened a small hospital and alas organized a primary school and a church, all of which he supported at their beginning. Years passed and he raised quite a large family.

The time came when the church at the Severance Hospital decided to establish a kindergarten for the small children of its members and Mrs. Avison was selected as its principal, It was not long before the parents of the little tots brought to the principal a young woman whom they had selected as its teacher. She was apparently a capable person and, after careful investigation of her qualifications, Mrs. Avison appointed her as teacher. Then Mrs. Avison learned that she was a daughter of our Dr. Pak. She had returned to Seoul and, strange to say, was to become the first kindergarten teacher in the church which had grown up around the medical school and hospital where her father had been first a student of medicine, then a doctor and teacher. And so the original work was bearing still more fruit.

Not long after that two of Dr. Pak's sons came to Severance as medical students.

Mrs Avison and I retired from Mission Connection at the end of June 1932 in accordance with mission rules but I continued as President of the two Colleges until September 1934 when I retired from those positions also with the title of President Emeritus and we still continued to live in Korea. During the fall of the next year, 1935, we decided we ought to return to America (Canada and the United States) and leave the new officers to carry on the work of the colleges and hospital without feeling it necessary to consult me over any changes they might wish to make. We had never visited the most northerly stations of the Mission of the United Church of Canada so we planned to do that before finally leaving the country and when we reached the last of their stations, the one at Lung-ching-toun, some thirty miles within the borders of Manchuria, we naturally expected to visit Dr. Pak's home and institutions which were only about ten miles from there. But heavy rains, lasting several days converted the newly made roads into sloughs which would have proved difficult for us to travel through and with great regret we gave up the idea of attempting it, sorrowing most of all because we could never again see those whose careers had been so closely interwoven with our lives. But one day, in the midst of this heavy down pour, Mrs. Pak appeared at the home of our host.

Though years had passed since we had seen her, Mrs. Avison recognized her even before I did. She fell on our necks (literally) while tears of joy rolled down her cheeks. We asked for Dr. Pak and learned that, realizing that the journey through the mud would be too hard for us, they had planned to come together to see us, but at the last moment, a call had come for him to go to a patient many miles in another direction and so, with great reluctance, he had gone to the sick man's home as was his duty.

In the good Korean fashion she called us father and mother because she knew her family owed everything to the message of God's love which they had heard from us. How glad we were to find that she and her husband had carried us in their hearts through all the intervening years!

▸ Chapter 8 ◂

The Introduction
of Modern Optical Work

The first wearing of spectacles in Korea goes back to very ancient times. So honored did the custom become, probably because they were first worn by old men whose eyesight was failing, that many who did not need to use them took to wearing them, hoping they might be regarded as getting old and wise.

In the early days of the missionary movement we Westerners smiled at the large size of the lenses and the bighorn frames that made them so conspicuous. We avoided glasses as long as we could and, when the dreaded day came that we must wear them, we wanted lenses as small as possible and the thickness and weight of the frames reduced to a minimum. In fact, we were not satisfied until the legs were dispensed with and later the metal rings around the glasses, leaving only the lightest clasps and springs to hold them on the nose. There again Eastern and Western ideas clashed. Which would win out? All who read this will know the answer.

As I went on with my hospital work I found many whose symptoms of illness were caused by irregularities of refraction that demanded properly ground glasses, not simply to enable them to see better but to make possible the cure of many other symptoms.

Therefore, I provided myself with a refracting outfit so that I could determine just what kind of glasses my patients needed. In order to get quick service, I laid in a supply of frames and ordinary lenses for the usual cases of eye defects. As for astigmatism, there were so many varieties and degrees of this trouble that a stock of lenses to meet them all could not be considered. I had to send orders for them to Japan, China, or America.

This work of refraction took so much time that I taught one of our first graduates how to do it. He soon learned the process very well and I set him aside for special work on eye, ear, nose and throat and Dr. Hong became the first Korean to take up a specialty.

He was able to refract for astigmatism and did so, but as I said, his prescriptions had to be sent away to be filled. I tried sending these to the spectacle department of the Methodist Episcopal Mission Hospital in Peking, to one in Shanghai and then to Tokyo; but in every case the time required to fill our orders caused dissatisfaction to our clients, so I tried sending my prescriptions to the United States. Though so far away this actually took less time and we continued to follow this course until I went to America again on furlough.

There I went to the factory of the American Optical Company, with whom we had been dealing, and explained the difficulties we were up against. I suggested that if they would teach me how to grind lenses for astigmatism I would purchase an outfit of machinery and take it with me to Korea. As they would be repaid for this trouble by the increased trade that would come from better and quicker service, they willingly agreed to do it.

Having learned the correct method of grinding lenses, I bought the necessary machinery and at the end of my furlough took it back with me - the first to be used in Korea.

I selected a bright young man and taught him what I had learned. He soon became quite an expert and could take the doctors' prescriptions, grind the lenses accordingly and have them ready in a day or two instead of the six or eight weeks which formerly elapsed before the work could be delivered from the United States.

Our greatest difficulty after the installation of optical machinery was caused by the frequent changes in size and shape of lenses and in types of frames so that we accumulated a considerable stock of unwanted styles and that ate into the profits we had expected to make.

After a few years, our optician left us to set up in business for himself and another had to be trained. At length we found a young man who after learning the trade was willing to buy our machinery and our entire stock of lenses and frames if we would lease him the rooms needed. His offer was so tempting that we accepted it and threw off the responsibilities of this department with its accompanying losses. It turned out to be a good deal for both of us. The optician continued to do work for us and at the same time he greatly enlarged his business with the general public. He trained all his own assistants and, made so much that before I left Korea, he had taken up the full support of a bed in the hospital for indigent patients to show his interest in this phase of our medical work.

Dr. S. H. Hong (Hong Suk-Hoo)

My first introduction to Sukhoo was through a photograph of the first Presbyterian School for boys taken just before we reached Seoul in 1893. He was one of the students, son of a scholarly Korean who was for many years the language teacher of several missionaries. You will note the costumes of the boys, their long white coats, their hair hanging in a braid down the back and tied at the end with a bit of ribbon or string. The whole picture is much like one of young girls of similar age in America at that time so it is not to be wondered at that, when the Board of Foreign Missions in New York received a copy of this photograph, the members thought it was a picture of a girls' school and, in publishing an article in a mission paper on girls' schools in Korea, they inserted this picture over the title "A Girls' School in Korea."

In that school he studied English and the usual subjects taught in the higher grades of public schools in America. When the school was discontinued, Hong entered so-called medical school, established by the Korean Department of Education, and graduated from it. But, as the course consisted only of reading certain Japanese medical books without any access to either hospital patients or laboratories, those who graduated had not practical knowledge either of diseases or of the methods of treating them.

During those years the Jejoongwon (Royal Korean Hospital) had been giving practical instruction to a group of young Koreans and when the first graduation of the Government so-called Medical School took place two of the graduates, realizing they were not prepared either to diagnose or treat diseased, asked to be taken into this group of helpers in our hospital, saying they would remain in the class until it was graduated no matter how long that might be.

We accepted them and, it must be admitted, the reading they had already done enabled them to make faster progress than would otherwise have been possible. It also prepared them to help in the very important work of preparing a vocabulary of medical terms which could be used in the education we were trying to give our hospital assistants. It required many years for us to prepare this vocabulary, subject by subject, and teach all the subjects of a Western Medical course, so it was not till June 1908 that these two young men and five others had been so thoroughly instructed and practically trained as to justify us in sending them out as a fair sample of the type of doctors we were aiming to provide for Korea.

After their graduation all seven offered to remain as assistant teachers. We selected four out of the seven and amongst these were the two Hongs who had previously studied at the Government school which had, in the meantime, been discontinued.

Sukhoo proved himself a very good doctor and also a good teacher and the same could be said of the other three. Unfortunately the other Hong developed lung tuberculosis and died at an early age but by then we were able to fill his place with one of the later graduates and so the work continued with a staff of six men including myself and Dr. Jesse W. Hirst who had been sent from America to help in the work of the hospital and school. By this time, we had gained enough confidence (and shall we say boldness) to call it a Medical College under the name "The Severance Union Medical College, Hospital and Nurses Training School."

It was soon found desirable in the interest of better teaching, to begin specialization and, amongst these specialties, Hong chose that of eye, ear, nose and throat. The writer who had had to be a specialist in every department, undertook to direct him in this until the appointment of Dr. N. H. Bowman to the staff. He had been an eye, ear, nose and throat specialist in the U. S. A. before he was sent to Korea so I turned over this department to him and appointed Hong as his assistant. This was a grand opportunity for the budding specialist who soon became almost as expert as his instructor. When the illness of Dr. Bowman's wife made his return to America necessary and her death soon after prevented his return with his baby daughter, Hong carried on the department with the help of assistants assigned to him.

In time we felt it desirable to send Hong to the U. S. A. for still further study. He first spent a month in the office and hospital of Dr. A. J. McCannell, of Minot Minnesota, Eye, Ear, Nose and Throat specialist, so that he might gain a better knowledge of English as used by medical men and of the actual procedures of such specialists. Dr. McCannell had for several years been a liberal supporter of Hong's work at the Severance Hospital in Seoul.

Then, following arrangements I had made for him he went to Kansas City,

Mo., for a course on the Anatomy of the Head with Dr. J. D. Myers, Prof. of Anatomy in the Dental School of that city. Then he went to New York and pursued his special studies at the Post Graduate Medical School where he earned for himself the reputation of a good student and clever surgeon in his special line of work. He then returned to his Alma Mater and for many years was head of that department. Residents in Korea of all nationalities trusted his skill. After giving the Severance Hospital many years of excellent service, the claims of a large family of dependents called for more money than our institution could afford to pay and he resigned to take up private practice. During the years of service at our hospital and medical school, he had trained worthy successors so that the institution continued and still continues to be well served.

His children grew up around him, most of them, however, devoting themselves to music. A beautiful daughter was educated in Ewha College for Women, two sons studied the violin and became concert players and soloists of repute.

Chapter 9

Making Korean Girls into Nurses

If, under the conditions that existed in Korea in those pioneer days of missionary work, it was a chimerical proposition to think of making Western-type doctors out of the young men, how much more fanciful it was to think of making nurses out of the girls! There was not only a lion in the way - many lions showed their teeth to those who were so rash as to take the first step on the path to that goal.

First, there was the attitude of the fathers. They were opposed to letting their daughters attend any school. "Whoever heard of such carryings on? It's all a girl can do to learn how to keep house before it is time for her to marry. Girls make good wives and mothers without book learning. No, no, it would never do?" When further urged, they said, "Why, girls have no brains and you couldn't teach them anything anyway. Besides, they have no souls, so what's the use?"

Secondly, there was the time-honored custom of the seclusion of women. As soon as a girl reached the marriageable age she was no longer permitted to leave her home except at night and then only in the company of her mother some or other dependable relative or old-time household servant. Perhaps her mother might take her out at night to visit the home of some neighbor for the streets were free from men after dark and the women could move about more freely.

Thirdly, early marriages constituted another lion in the way. Married at the age of twelve to fourteen years the bride went directly from her own home to that of her mother-in-law where she practically became the latter's servant and so had no time to give to the study of books.

Oh, yes, some girls learned to read, to sing, to dance, to drink, but they were of the class whose business it was to entertain rich men. They never married and it would have given an undesirable reputation to our hospital to utilize them as nurses. They were keisangs or dancing girls, and, generally speaking, their reputations were none too savory.

This was the status in 1893. Though some schools for girls had been opened by missionary women, only very, very young girls were being sent to them.

When I asked the young men whom I had employed as assistants at the Royal Korean Hospital to help me find some young to be trained as nurses, they just shook their heads and said it would be impossible. All others to whom I applied for advice also shook their heads but, after some further thought, some one gave me the first hopeful suggestion-perhaps some elderly widows might be willing to help in the women's wards. That suggestion actually opened the door to the wonderful development that has since made the profession of nursing one of the most honored and therefore one of the most popular forms of work that the years have opened to the educated young women of this rapidly advancing country.

Naturally we had many disappointments but these happen in all lines of effort. As an example, I will tell you about one young woman who applied to be taken in for training. One day this girl was brought to me for an interview. She looked very young to be a widow and she had a not too attractive personality. She was evidently very nervous at being brought before a foreign man to be looked her over as keenly as it was necessary for me to do. She stood with head down, twirling a fold of her dress in her fingers as I questioned her.

"What is your name?" No answer.

"Where do you live?" No answer.

"What is your age?" No answer.

"How long have you been a widow?" And still no answer.

"What was your husband's name" Silence.

"Do you want to be a nurse?" Ah! She nodded her head By this time things were becoming ridiculous. The other Koreans standing near began to snicker and I rather curtly asked why. Then one of my young men explained that in Korea women were not supposed to talk to men and as for her not telling me the name of her husband, no Korean woman ever spoke her husband's name. Then the unexpected happened - she began to giggle. And I truculently asked "What can be done with a giggling girl?"

But applicants were scarce and perhaps it would be well to give her a trial, so I told them to take her to the nurses' quarters and do for her the necessary things. When she was brought to me next day clean and neat, her hair smoothly dressed according to Korean style, she looked like much better material than she had done the day before. She was still diffident and awkward in her new surroundings so I told them to show her how to play tennis. knowing that would give her poise at least.

It was both amusing and pitiful to watch from a window out of her sight. She just couldn't handle the racket and, as for hitting the ball, it never was where she expected it to be. But time worked wonders. Her back straightened, her head was held up, she began to look everyone in the face and she could smile. It was quite a transformation. Her instructors taught her to read the easy Korean script which we used in textbooks and they gave her minor tasks in the sick rooms. She became interested in her work and we looked forward to her becoming a creditable nurse.

Alas! One morning when I went to my office, I asked a nurse to bring 'kimsie' to me. After a time the messenger returned to report that she couldn't find her. I sent her to try again. Again she returned without her and said, rather stumblingly, "Last night her husband came." "What do you mean?" I asked, "I understood she was a widow."

"Ye-es," she answered, "she is a - a kind of widow."

"What do you mean by that?"

"Well, you see, her husband got tired of her, so he sent her off and took another wife and then she was just the same as a widow. Then - last night - he came to see what she was doing. He demanded that she come down to the street so he could see her. Of course, after all, she was his wife and so she had to go down to see hem. When he saw her, so clean and neat and pretty, he - he! he! he! he! - he fell in love with her and told her she had to go back home with him. She had to go with him, of course, for she was his wife!"

Well, thought I, if this is what we are to look forward to, what's the use? Then, after conning it over, I said to myself, she had learned much even in so short a time. She will never again be the same as she was when she came to us. She will make a better home and that is what Korea needs. Perhaps we ought not to be disappointed. So we opened the way for another to come in to take her place.

Of course, we knew that all this was only preliminary. Some day we would have a real school for giving nurses training and someday there would be girls better prepared to enter such a school. Already girls' schools were offering more advanced courses than had at first been possible. The ideas of Christian parents as to the future of their daughters we reexpanding and we felt sure that ere long graduates from those girls' schools would be applying for admission to a training school for nurses, It would become necessary to plan a course that would, while giving the necessary practical training, provide an advanced educational opportunity also.

Miss Anna P. Jacobson

Miss Anna P. Jacobson, a Swedish American, was the first nurse sent me from America - for some details of her short life see further on.

Miss Shields came to Korea in 1897 to succeed Miss Anna P. Jacobson who, the first nurse to answer my call to the Royal Korean Hospital, had died after a service of less than two years. While her first work was to be the nursing of our hospital patients, both she and I had keenly felt the necessity of establishing a Medical School for the making of Korean doctors. Miss Shields' health and the exigencies of the mission work in various other sections prevented her taking up the work at the Royal Korean Hospital immediately so at this point in our narrative I will refer briefly in the very early days of foreign missions in Korea. What immediately follows is a quotation from a paper on Early Nurses prepared by Dr. L. C. Block and Dr. I. M. Stewart, members of the M. E. Women's Mission Board:

> "So far as we have learned, Miss Emily Heathcote was the earliest Western nurse to arrive in Korea. She reached Korea in 1891 with Dr. Louisa Cook. Both of these ladies were connected with the English Mission sent out by the Society for the propagation of the Gospel, usually referred to as the S. P. G. Together they established in Seoul the Hospital of St. Peter where they worked for five years and then returned to England."

> "Miss Elizabeth Webster with five sisters of the St. Peter's Community of Kilburn, England, arrived in November, 1892, to work in Chemulpo with Dr. Landis. This pioneer nurse worked faithfully for five years under the English Church Mission in Seoul and then passed away May 17, 1899, after a painful illness of nearly twelve weeks."

"In 1895 Miss Anna P. Jacobson came to Korea as the first of a group of nurses to be sent out by the Foreign Missions Board of the Northern Presbyterian Church in America. She was appointed to work in the Royal Korean Hospital at Kurigai in Seoul as a collaborator with Dr. O. R. Avison and Dr. Georgiana Whiting, the latter of whom came out with her. Unfortunately she contracted amoebic dysentery which was followed by an abscess of the liver. The operation which was performed was unsuccessful and she died in January, 1897, after less than two years and her body rests in the beautiful hillside cemetery on the banks of the Han River, some three or four miles from the capital."

The following tribute to Miss Jacobson's spirit was written in the report from which I have been quoting:

"At one time Miss Jacobson was out in the country by herself to do a little language study without the inevitable interruptions to which she was subject in the hospital. Her room in a Korean house was 6 x 6 feet square and in it were her cot and trunk. Where did she sit? On the bed, of course. And her visitors? Where but on the floor, as they always did for chairs were not a part of a Korean's furniture? One night she had ten callers - open the window, please. Two were sitting on the bed, the rest stood and she sat on the trunk. A line from her own letter picturing this scene reveals her warm affection for the Korean people, especially the children, but you would need to see the sparkle in her eye and hear her chuckle as she told of that evening's reception. Thus she wrote; "As we were talking I saw a little boy on my bed standing with both feet on my pillow. I told him that was not an American custom. I am so glad I have begun to love them with their dirt as well as without it. If I can get them to look upon me as a friend instead of being afraid of me, I shall be satisfied."

After Miss Jacobson's death I at once wrote to the Board in New York urging them to send out another nurse and Miss Shields was sent in response to my plea. Miss Shields was at first sent to Syen Chun and then to other stations where, it was thought she would have more leisure for language study than would be possible in the busy capital. In the meantime we in Seoul decided to try at least temporarily another plan for training nurses. Why not employ some already trained Japanese nurses? Surely the missionaries in Japan could find for us a couple of well-trained Christian young women who had a desire to introduce their profession to Korea. We know very well the antipathy of Koreans for the Japanese but at what point might that dislike be more easily broken down than in mutual work for the sick?

My fellow missionaries agreeing, I entered into correspondence with some American missionaries in Japan on whose good judgement I could rely and in a comparatively short time two young women from Tokyo joined our staff. They had evidently been well trained according to the Japanese hospital standards but seemed very glad to follow our suggestions in making such changes in their methods as better suited our ideas. They were gentle, had the fine Christian idealism, that we desired and were anxious to win the confidence and friendship of the Korean girls and women though they had a keen appreciation of the difficulties they had to face to overcome the prejudice of their pupils and patients against all Japanese. This was an almost irremovable barrier but they faced it and, in some measure, succeeded. But, though they were excellent nurses, they failed at a crucial point - they were neither leaders nor teachers. Of course they did not know the Korean language though they knew a little English. In this they were neither more nor less fortunate than we missionaries but it stood in the way of their success as teachers so, ere long, we had to let them go back to their homeland.

We then realized that we must depend on America or Canada to supply us with teaching nurses, women who would come to Korea with the expectation of making it their home for life.

Suddenly a serious matter occurred. For more than a year my wife's health, as well as my own, had been steadily failing and in February 1899, the doctors decided we must return to Canada. Fortunately new doctor was on his way to Korea and when he arrived, he and his wife were temporarily assigned to the Royal Korean Hospital and Miss Shields was located there to help him. This brought her definitely to Seoul and when we returned in 1900, she continued to take charge of the nursing work and, through the years that followed, she remained with that institution until 1939 when, at the age of 70, she retired. The story of her life and work is really the history of the establishment of nursing as a profession in Korea.

Miss Margaret Edmunds

Before continuing with Miss Shields' story, however, it is but right to tell of the part Miss Edmunds had in actually organizing the teaching of nurses on a definite basis and, in 1908, graduated the first two Korean women who completed the required curriculum of studies and practical work.

Miss Edmunds was a Canadian lady from Petrolea, in South Western Ontario. She had gone to the United States for her training and this had led to her appointment to Korea by the Women's Foreign Mission Board of the Methodist Episcopal Church in the U. S. A. She was sent out with special instructions to organize a school for training Korean young women as nurses so she made this the great object of her life and actually did this in connection with the Methodist Hospital for women in Seoul. I quote the following from are port written by a Korean gentleman many years later:

> "The very year after her arrival she organized the first training school for Korean nurses. This being a new enterprise, Miss Edmunds' task was a difficult one. The age-long custom of the seclusion of women, the scarcity of educated girls, the general ignorance about the nursing work, all these made it difficult to recruit students for the training school. Fully grasping the situation, Miss Edmunds made this her motto, 'Go slow! Be sure!'"

> "There were no textbooks in the Korean language and practically no equipment for the needs of the school, In spite of those problems of the pioneer stage she excelled herself in training the best nurses the situation allowed."

> "In August, 1907, when so many Korean soldiers were wounded in the fight resulting from the forceful disbanding of the Korean army by the Japanese authorities, she and her staff came to Severance Hospital to assist in the emergency care of the victims."

> "Her first graduation of nurses took place in 1908."

There were but two graduates but their names should be recorded in the annals of their profession for they broke through the conventions of their country to braze a trial along which many of their country-women have since traveled in ever extending lines of valuable service.

Miss Edmunds continued her work in Seoul till the year when she married the Reverend W. B. Harrison of the Southern Presbyterian Mission and took her place in his at Kunsan.

Many other American and Canadian nurses came to Korea and did and are still doing notable work in various hospitals but their work will be related by others. It is necessary to confine this story to the work of Miss Shields and the development of the Severance Hospital School for Nurses as, Perhaps, the most conspicuous illustration of the growth of this service in Korea, just as Florence Nightingale began a movement which spread into all parts of the world.

As medical teaching was first begun and most fully developed in connection with the work of the Severance Hospital, it was both inevitable and proper that the chief school for nurses should be conducted in a line parallel with the aims of the school and in connection with the largest hospital operated by the mission bodies and all the more so because the Severance Institution was a union one in which six of the missions cooperated.

Though Miss Shields had come to the field in 1898, she was not able to begin the organization of the School for Nurses until September, 1906, although, of course, desultory teaching was being given through all the years before that.

Beginning of the Severance Training School for Nurses

There had been many conferences in the meantime between Misses Shields and Edmunds. They and all interested in the work, heartily desired to combine the two efforts and build up a Union School so that all the nurses might have the advantages of more specialized teaching and the wider range of clinical experience to be gained by attendance at both hospitals, but difficulties which it is not necessary to detail here, Prevented such hopes from materializing and each school eventually pursued its own course, though some cooperation was made possible.

Reluctance of Nurses to Care for Male Patients

Korean women nurses were reluctant to care for male patients because of the custom of seclusion of women in that country. After a woman reached her maturity, it was not fitting that she should be seen by any men other than members of her immediate household.

I was always hoping something would happen to breakdown this old custom. One day I expressed such a hope to one of the older missionaries who replied, "It will take at least twenty years to break down that custom!" "That looks like along time," I remarked. "Yes", he said, "but the custom is very old and cannot be put aside easily."

But a change was brought about before the next twenty-four hours had elapsed. After the Russo-Japanese War, the enmity of the Koreans for the Japanese was much intensified. Some of the Korean soldiers organized a group to go through the country opposing the Japanese wherever they found them and urged their Korean brethren not to yield to Japanese authority. The members of this band called themselves "he righteous army." Though made up of remnants of Korean regiments and some Koreans in sympathy with every form of opposition to anything attempted by the Japanese, they became in true only a band of marauders, as they traveled over the countryside, followed by Japanese troops determined to exterminate every member. Finally the Japanese succeeded in ridding Korea of nearly all these roving bands, made up of good and bad Koreans, but one regiment of soldiers still occupied a garrison in Seoul. They were located in the barracks just inside the city wall, between the South Gate and the Little West Gate and the Japanese authorities decided to disband this regiment.

One morning a group of Japanese officers arrived at the barracks to carry out this order. Calling up the Korean officer in charge they placed a written order in his hands, demanding that the regiment be summoned to hear the proclamation to disband. The order was written in contemptuous language and it so enraged the Korean officer that when he had finished reading it he tore the paper in two, threw it to the ground and immediately killed himself.

The death of their leader so excited the member of the Korean regiment that, without any consideration as to the consequences, they shot the Japanese officials and this created a riot. Word soon got to the Japanese government headquarters and troops were sent to the barracks.

In the meantime, the Korean soldiers had locked the doors and barricaded the gates, knowing that an attack would surely follow and it was not long before Japanese soldiers arrived and began effort to break into the barracks.

Our hospital was but a short distance from there and about nine o'clock in the morning we heard shots from the vicinity of the South Gate of the riot be tween us and the barracks. Looking out we saw that the upper part of the South Gate was occupied by Japanese soldiers who were turning a machine gun on the barracks. Many people crowding around the South Gate ran towards the nearby railway station just across the street from the hospital. Some entered the hospital grounds to keep from being fired on and from these Koreans we learned what had occurred.

Then we saw a company of Japanese soldiers at the railway station just across the street from our hospital. They had been sent there to open cross-fire on the barracks, In a short time we could see Korean soldiers leaving the barracks and dropping over the city wall. We supposed they were running away as they ran towards the hills south of the city. It soon became evident that we had mistaken their purpose for they had took up positions on the hills higher than the railway station in order to attack the troop of Japanese soldiers there.

From our hospital we could see what was going on and hear the exchange of shots and realized that many Koreans, as well as Japanese, would be wounded. I called my assistants together and asked for volunteers to go out and bring in the wounded Korean soldiers, I said nothing about the wounded Japanese because I knew they would be taken care of by their own ambulance corps. Everyone of my assistants volunteered for this service. Even the men servants around the hospital wanted to go along as stretcher bearers.

The foreign women on the hospital grounds, as well as the Korean nurses, began making Red Cross emblems which they sewed to our shirts sleeves, It was August and we were not wearing coats and being thus marked, we would be permitted to search for the wounded without being molested. In a short time rain began to pour down for it was the middle of the rainy season and a down-pour was an almost daily occurrence.

Dressings were collected for first-aid service and we made our way to the South Gate where the Japanese troops allowed us to pass. The red crosses told them that we were there for only to assist the wounded. Turning from the board street into a narrow lane leading to the barracks, we learned that some wounded Koreans had fled from their quarters and were hiding in nearby Korean homes. At first the owners would not let us enter and refused to give us any information about the wounded men and even when we were able to get information and enter a house, we had difficulty in getting to the soldiers. These refused to let us touch them and would not allow us to take them away because they feared we would take them to the Japanese. Finally however we made them understand that we were there to help them so the stretcher bearers were allowed to remove them from the homes and take them to the hospital. When we reached the hospital grounds, our wives were alarmed to see us covered with blood and our clothes caked with mud. They thought perhaps we too were injured but it was only the blood from the wounded and the mire in the lanes that were responsible for our appearance.

About fifty wounded men were lying in the halls of the hospital, for there had been no one there to care for them. My coworker, Dr. Hirst, had gone on his vacation and was not expected to return until the following evening. Our foreign nurse Miss Shields, was also on vacation.

I sent a note to the Methodist Women's Hospital asking Miss Edmunds to come over and help us bringing as many of her nurses as she could spare from her own hospital. The situation was really desperate. Our male assistants were working as hard as they could, but there were not enough of them and the young women nurses had never looked after male patients. They gathered around and gazed at the unusual sight of so many wounded men. Then they began to realise that the men were Koreans who had been fighting for Koreans, yes even for them and that they must be cared for. One of the Korean nurses broke the age-long custom and every other nurse followed her lead.

We worked all afternoon, for nearly every soldier needed some kind of surgery, In the evening I was amazed to see Dr. Hirst appeared returning a day ahead of his time. He had been in Taiku and was to have returned to Seoul the next day but for some reason had felt he should come back earlier. A bit later who should arrive but Miss Shields? She too had had a feeling that she should come back from her vacation before her time was up. It did not take either of them long to get into uniforms and join us and by midnight every soldier had been cleaned up and given the necessary treatment. All the operations were over and the helpers around the hospital had cleaned up the mess in the halls.

Korean women nurses cared for the wounded soldiers throughout the night and the following day. Then they realized that they had been caring for male patients. They done it once so they could do it again and they did. I had been told that it would take twenty years to bring about such a change but it had been accomplished within twenty-four hours. A great need had shattered a custom centuries old. After that crisis, the question needed no further discussion -our greatest problem had been solved.

It was not long before we received a visit from Prince Ito, the representative of the Japanese Government who passed through the wards to see the wounded and then personally thanked us for what we had done. As he was leaving, he gave us 500 yen to help defray our unexpected expenses. Then a cable came from princess in Japan, head of the Red Cross Society, transmitting the thanks of the Association for our work. Within a few days, a less welcome letter came from the Japanese commander in the city saying the military hospital was now prepared to receive the wounded men and, at a certain time men would be sent to transfer the wounded Koreans to their hospital. Without doubt they wanted to keep these rebels under supervision so that those who recovered might receive due punishment, It was with sad hearts that we prepared these wounded Korean soldiers for their trip to the Japanese hospital and the patient soldiers wept because they were afraid of what might happen to them there and afterwards. The Korean nurses too wept because they sympathized with the soldiers. We all regretted that the men could not have been left in our hospital until they had recovered though, of course, we would have been under obligation to notify the authorities when the time had come for their discharge. Two or three of the soldiers were so ill that we could not permit them to be removed and these were left with us.

But because of this incident, the sick men and boys of our hospital were to have better nursing care throughout all the future for few men make really good nurses. The women had made the great break.

‣ Chapter 10 ◂

Yellow Versus White

Is there any danger to the supremacy of the whites in the world? The white races have ruled the colored for so long a time that they have come to regard themselves as superior to all others in everything that makes for leadership and power. They are unwilling even to consider the possibility of losing that leadership or to admit that the center of power may be transferred to Asia either in the near or distant future. But it has become necessary for the white people to give thought to this matter for within the last few years there has developed a tendency in nearly all the colored nations to question the right of one group of people to be the rulers of all others.

The rapid rise of the Japanese from great weakness over eighty years ago, when Admiral Perry was able to force them to open their country to American trade by merely showing them the few American war vessels that had accompanied him to such a degree of strength that they right to claim special privileges in Asia is cause for concern.

China, too, though slower than Japan to establish herself as a great nation to be feared, is at least successfully defending her right to an independent standing, India is showing her teeth to the long term rulers and is not simply asking, but is demanding from Britain a greater degree of independence - a demand which Britain is preparing to grant. And all over the world such a spirit is developing. What is it that is making these demands of the colored races possible? And what is compelling their white masters to listen to them? It is the spread of knowledge within countries that have been ignorant. There is an old and true saying that knowledge is power. It has proved its truth in the experience of all time, wherever knowledge has been put to use.

But there is another factor to be considered - numbers Knowledge put to use will enable a small number to overpower a larger number with less knowledge but, give the larger numbers knowledge as extensive as is possessed by the smaller number and the many will prevail against the few. It can be put in a mathematical formula.

$$Knowledge = Power$$
$$Numbers = Power$$
$$Knowledge + Numbers = Supreme\ power$$

So the few white people, having had a monopoly of knowledge, have held power and the many colored races without knowledge have been kept under subjection. But the many colored races are gaining in knowledge and they are gaining in power. If the colored races have as good brain capacity as have the whites and they continue developing that brain power as the whites have done, their great numbers will inevitably give them sufficient power in the course of time to overcome the whites. How long will that be?

All will depend on whether the inherent brain power of the colored races is as good as that of the whites and on whether they continue to develop knowledge as fast as do the whites.

Do we white people regard that possibility with complacence? Have the colored races really got as good brains as we have? Usually, when I ask my white friends these questions, they deny that the colored races are our equals in brain capacity, but my answer is that the average inherent brain power of all races is practically the same. The proof of it is to be seen by study of what men of different races and women too, have accomplished where they have been given equal opportunities for study and practice over a sufficiently long period.

A residence of more than forty years in Asia where I was in close contact with Koreans, Japanese, and Chinese, from the highest social ranks to the lowest and most ignorant peasants has given me the answer. I taught young men medicine and science and saw them develop into scholars, physicians, surgeons, ministers, lawyers, etc, and this gave me a good opportunity to form an accurate judgment in regard to their abilities and my answer is as I have stated above, "the average inherent brain power of all races is practically the same." And though women, until missionaries proved it to be otherwise, were considered to be much less intelligent than men they too, when given equal opportunities, have proved themselves fully equal to their brothers in all lines of study.

But more assertions are not convincing to doubters so I will give a few examples of men and women in Korea who have reached to high places in their professions although they started out of the lowest depths of apparent unpreparedness.

Korea was opened to foreign intercourse in 1882 and the first Western physician went there in 1884. Up to that time, there had been no Western schools, no teaching or practising of modern medicine. There was no knowledge of Western science and no use of the English language. This was almost equally true when there in 1893 so that when I decided to teach Western medicine to young Korean men I had to take raw recruits, give them some knowledge of English, some preparatory education, some introduction to the rudiments of Western science, etc, that would enable them to understand what I was hoping to teach them. I decided that this instruction in Western medicine should be given in the native tongue even though there was then no vocabulary of other medical or scientific terms. It was a clear start from the very beginning, but believing from some study of Korea's past history that its people had fundamentally good brains, I felt confident that a medical terminology could be produced and that the greatest good would eventually result if while educating some Korean young men they and we working together, should coincidentally develop the necessary Korean vocabulary and translate medical books as a basis for future advances.

As my object just now is to support my thesis of mental equality of all races and not to describe the methods we followed in medical education, I will skip all these and write only of results.

It took fifteen years of hard and continuous work to bring those seven men to a point where they were fit to be graduated but by that time I was quite sure they knew fully as much of the theory of medicine and had had much more opportunity for practise than I had had when I was given license to practise in Canada, twenty-one years before.

It must be remembered too, that these men started further back than I had done and that they had had only one teacher in all the medical branches while I had been taught by a specialist in each branch. After these first seven men graduated I continued the work, keeping three of the best of them as teachers and adding more to the staff year by year, both natives and foreigners, as I could get them. In 1934, forty-one years after I arrived in Korea I resigned as president and a Korean was unanimously elected to carry on the work by a governing board that consisted of a large majority of Americans and Canadians.

It is now 1941 and during the interval all the foreign teachers have left the institution and the Korean president who followed me is still its head. It is turning out more than forty graduates a year and the quality of these may be judged from the recognition given the institution and its graduates by the Imperial Government of Japan which accepts the school's diplomas and licenses their holders to practise in any part of the Japanese have taken post-graduate work in Canada, the United States and other countries and returned to their own land to practise and to teach.

As for nurses, the story of the establishment of nursing schools and the production of trustworthy and intelligent nurses would make an epic in itself, so I will content myself with saying we had to begin with uneducated widows, as all girls were married at about twelve years of age. Very few could even read or write their own language and there was complete isolation of girls and women from all members of the male sex outside their own families. During the intervening years, however, all obstacles have been overcome and several hundreds of good nurses, educated and intelligent have been trained.

The two hundred-bed Severance Hospital and its Nurses' Training School are now entirely under the direction of Korean nurses and all this within a period of forty years.

The Chosen Christian College, mentioned before, was opened in 1915, with a staff entirely foreign, except for one Korean and one Japanese who had been educated abroad. Today its President is a Korean and all its teachers are either Koreans or Japanese. Many of them hold the Ph. D. degree from American universities such as Yale, Boston, Michigan, etc.

During those forty years schools for girls were conducted some of which developed into high schools. The Ewha College for Women ranks high as an educational institution and its president and teachers are all members of the yellow race. Its president received the degree of Ph. D. and a Phi Kappa Gamma Key from Boston University, President Marsh of that institution told me that Helen Kim (the lady being referred to)was one of the brightest women they had ever had in the University. She was several times one of Korea's delegates to the conferences of the countries bordering on the Pacific Ocean which met to discuss matters of special interest to them, and to the meeting of the General

Conference of the Methodist Church in the United States and to the World Conference on Religion that met a few years ago in Jerusalem. In all of these she was an active member whose words were listened to with respect and interest. Yet she came from the class of undeveloped women - women supposed to be unintelligent and without brains.

The world at large knows of many statesmen, authors, lecturers, bankers, business men and scientists among the yellow and even the black races but to enforce my thesis I will recount a few cases I have known.

Surgeons and Scientists

When I broached the idea of a medical school, even my fellow missionaries were incredulous and asked me whether I really thought I could make good surgeons out of the Koreans. I answered that as for learning to do operations I was sure they could learn to do them all right but as for the more important phase of surgery - the development of that essential characteristic, the ability to determine whether an operation should be done or not - only time show, for that calls but only time would show.

This question was answered before many years had elapsed and it was in the affirmative. I will cite two instances:

(1) Dr. M. U. Koh graduated from our medical school in 1913, only three years after our first doctors were given diplomas and was at once appointed as assistant in the hospital. Some years later, because he had clearly manifested his surgical skill, he was sent to America for special study at the Long Island Medical College from which he received the M. D. degree. When he returned to Seoul he became an assistant teacher in surgery. On one occasion a man came into the hospital with severe vomiting and many of the other symptoms of intestinal obstruction. Two or three of the doctors, including one American surgeon, decided immediate operation was called for and Dr. Koh was asked to perform it. After a personal examination of the case, he made a different diagnosis Pronouncing it a case of ptomaine poisoning which called for medical treatment and not for an operation. His judgment was accepted and suitable treatment given and within two days the patient left the hospital well. An operation under the circumstances would have been not only useless, but also positively

dangerous. This was an instance of good diagnostic ability and also of that other essential for a safe surgeon - good judgement.

(2) Dr. Y. S. Lee graduated from a Junior Arts College in Korea in 1915 and from our Medical School in 1919. That was the year of the uprising of the Korean people against their conquerors, the Japanese, and Dr. Lee fell under the suspicion of the police. Fleeing to China he found a place as an interne in the Peking Union Medical College (Rockfeller Institution) where he soon became Chief Assistant in the Surgical Clinic. After two or three years it became possible for him to return to Seoul and he came into our hospital as Surgical Assistant.

Later we sent him to the Northwestern University Medical College in Chicago where they accepted him as a third year student though they did it with some trepidation. After two or three months, however, they transferred him into the senior class and at the end of that year he graduated near the top of his class. As the University regulations required a residence of two years before conferring the degree of M. D. the Dean told him he could take an appointment as an interne in some hospital recognized by the University and keep up his connection with them by reporting his progress from time to time. Then, if his work was satisfactory, they would confer the degree.

He was given an internship in the Hospital for Crippled Children in New York and he also watched the work in several other hospitals. Having received his degree from the Northwestern University, he returned to Korea and to his Alma Mater in 1926.

The following year he carried on research work in the Japanese Imperial University in Seoul and received the highest degree given in Japan - the equivalent of the Ph. D. degree in the United States. Then he was given the status of professor of surgery in our Medical College.

At a later period he was called to another city in Korea for consultation with two American surgeons who were attending the young child of an American Missionary, suffering from osteomyelitis in her upper right arm. The bone had already thinned to the point where surgical fracture had occurred just below the shoulder joint.

The attending surgeons were preparing to do a radical operation on the bone but Dr. Lee advised against it because so much of the bony tissue had already been destroyed that any further destruction would hinder a bony reunion impossible. He advised a genale cleansing with soft gauze and a mild antiseptic solution, careful packing and use of a splint to prevent the friction that would hinder the formation of new bone to fill in fhe space and produce a useful arm instead of a flip-flop one.

The attending surgeons accepted his advice but asked him to take charge of the case. The father brought her to our Seoul hospital where Dr. Lee cared for her.

Some weeks later when I went into her room she was swinging the arm about and laughing gaily. What the Korean surgeons with both the qualifications mentioned above might be developed had been realized and a Korean surgeon had, by his wise judgment, done what two American surgeons of repute had failed to do. Do you begin to see what I am claiming - a mental caliber that is not confined to members of the white races?

(3) Dr. M. S. Kim graduated from our medical school and then acted as an assistant in the department of physiology for several years. As he had shown a high degree of capability we sent him to the Northwestern University in Chicago for further study in his chosen line. At the end of two years he, received the degree of M. S. in physiology and, after a test of several more months in research work to determine whether he had the type of brain required for carrying on work for a Ph. D. was reported to have stood the test and he began work in that course. When I was in Chicago the end of his studies I called to see him and ask his professor how he was getting on, Dr. Ivy, the head of the department, assured me Dr. Kim would receive his Ph. D. degree in less than six months and that he would then be qualified to teach physiology in any university in the United States. He really finished before the end of six months and is now full professor of physiology in his Alma Mater. He was also granted the highest medical degree in japan on the basis of the research work done in Chicago over and above the requirements for his Ph. D.

Other Fields

But examples of first class mental ability are to be found in others than medical men.

(1) Rev. Dr. Paik received his primary and secondary education in a mission school in Korea. He then came to the United States where he obtained his B. A.

degree from Park College, Mo. earning his living while he studied. Then he entered Princeton University to work for an M. A. in history and at the same time registered in Princeton Theological Seminary for the Th. B. degree, carrying both courses at the same time. After receiving both degrees in the time usually needed for one, he spent a summer at the University of Pennsylvania studying history and followed that with a three-year course io. Bible and church history at yale University where he received the Ph. D. On returning to Korea he became Professor of the Bible and History in the Chosen Christian College and after a year was made Dean of the faculty of Liberal Arts in addition to is teaching work. Asa speaker and teacher he was called to all parts of the country not only by his fellow countrymen but also by American and other foreign groups who always listened with interest to his addresses, delivered in either Korean or English.

When the Board of Foreign Missions of the Presbyterian Church in the U. S. A. was preparing to celebrate its century of service he was asked to return here and spend a year addressing churches in all parts of America.

Just then the military party in Japan was busy trying to conquer China and in the course of that war, still in progress as I write, all foreign trained Koreans, especially those connected with mission institutions were arrested and jailed on various pretexts and Dr. Paik was advised to remain for a longer time in America until this feverishness might spend itself, In order to earn his living he accepted appointment as a Bible teacher in Park College and taught there a year. Then he decided to return to Korea to his family and work. Just at that time I happened to go to Kansas City, Mo.. where I met one of the principal teachers at Park College who told me they had urged Paik to send for is family and continue his work in the College as a permanent teacher as they had never had a better one, but Dr. Paik felt he should give himself fully to the education of his own countryman and so returned but only to be arrested like so many others of his colleagues. He is free again but not yet permitted to teach.

(2) Dr. Lee was graduated from the Science Department of the Chosen Christian College in Seoul in 1919.

After serving two years as an assistant teacher in science, he came to the United States and entered Albion College in Michigan as a candidate for the degree of B. A. to fit him for matriculation into the University of Michigan for a higher degree in mathematics. In due time he received the degree of Ph. D. in mathematics, majoring in Astronomy.

The subject for his thesis was a careful study of a recently discovered star which had not yet been described. This study required three years and at the end of that time he wrote his thesis. The following January he was asked to read it at a meeting of the American Association for the Advancement of Science and on the basis of this they elected him a member of the association. He returned to Korea and is a professor in the Chosen Christian College where he teaches mathematics.

(3) Dr. T. H. Yun known better perhaps as Baron Yun Tchi Ho is another wonderful example of the brain capacity of a member of the yellow race, especially as he was one of the first Koreans to manifest his talents after the opening of the country to foreign intercourse in 1882. His story has already been told in this book so I shall not detail it.

Through everything Yun held on to his Christian convictions and clung stoutly to his ideals, even through an imprisonment of six years by the Japanese. On his release he became president of the Y. M. C. A. movement in Korea, and now at about eighty years of age is still his country's greatest leader. He holds the honorary degree of L. L. D. from his American University and has been chosen this year (1941) to be president of the Chosen Christian College. He surpasses all others whom I know in his ability to give a terse speech in English, in words well chosen, correct in grammar and perfect in its construction.

If my statements concerning these Koreans are true, and many missions and American College will vouch for that the corollary is that the natural brain power of Koreans, who are yellow, is not below that of the whites, and that all that is needed to bring equality in output is opportunity and time for development.

We have already seen such development among the Japanese and are seeing it now in China and in India and it is quite permissible for us to expect to find it true of all nationalities, I now come back to the question involved in our yellow versus white discussion. Is there any danger to the continued supremacy of the whites? To find the correct answer we need to consider the reason for the rise to world power of the white races.

"Knowledge is Power" is an accepted axiom. It has proved its truth in the experience of all time. Knowledge has long been largely the possession of the white race and it has enabled that race to rule the world though they are fewer in numbers than are the colored race. The white-peoples by their knowledge of the sciences - all the sciences - have long ruled the other races despite their disparity in numbers. But, numbers also give power and it is self-evident that if knowledge can be combined with numbers such a combination would give supreme power.

The yellow race have had the numbers and still have them but their lack of knowledge has prevented their having power. They are now gaining knowledge and in the course of time it will be a case of knowledge and numbers against knowledge. Which will win if it then comes to a struggle?

Does that mean that there must of necessity be a struggle for supremacy between the white and the colored races in which the whites will go down to defeat?

Fortunately that is not necessary. One other force, greater than either knowledge or numbers exists. It is loves shown by loving kindness, helpfulness, good will. If as the whites help the colored races to knowledge they will at the same time manifest their good will in fair dealing, in friendly acts, in unselfish attitudes, experience has shown that in return the "fruits of righteousness" will leave no room for a spirit of acquisitiveness, and the question of Yellow versus White will no longer be a cause of fear. The result will be Yellow cum White - a world at peace, the Kingdom of God on earth.

Dr. K. S. Oh (Oh Kyung Sun)

President of Severance Union Medical College and Hospital and Nurses Training School:
One of the Greatest Men of Korea

This Chapter is devoted to one whom I greatly admire and love. The introduction was written by one who knew him from his boyhood, Rev. F. W. Steadman, formerly a missionary in Korea and Japan and now retired and living in Florida.

- Introduction

by Mr. Steadman

First Contact. We were living in Kong Ju, Dr. Oh's home city. One evening our servant came to my room saying that a young man was at the gate asking to see me. I told him to take him to our men's guest room and I would see him at once.

He was a young man who, having walked from Seoul, the capital (one hundred miles), was foot sore and tired. He was on his way to his home in the city and to his father and mother who were waiting for him. His reasons for calling on me were to tell me that he had become a Christian and because of it was to be disowned by his father and was to leave home never to return and he asked me to pray for him. We talked and prayed for his guidance.

He had been a student at a Mission School in Seoul and had while there become a Christian, contrary to his promise to his father and mother when they allowed him to enter the school along with a friend. He had avoided all Christian teaching as far as he could up to Christmas time. He had not even been in the church to attend a service. But there was to be a Christmas concert and his friend urged that he must not fail to attend it. It was not to be a preaching service - no, only a concert - so he went. But one of the speakers told of Christ our Savior and of what it meant to be a Christian. That talk gripped him and at heart he became a Christian. This faith had come to say and now what about his parents? He had written to his father and his father had told him not to return home. Even so he wanted to be at home long enough for his father to understand why he had become a Christian and then he would go out not to return. He was on his way home but had called to ask me to follow him in prayer. We prayed together and he went on home to his parents - nice people whom I already slightly knew. For a week or so I did not see him but I heard that his father had remarked to a friend that the boy was a better boy than before. At any rate he won out and returned to finish up his school work.

When he was free to do so he came to me as a "helper." As such he was helpful on every hand as an earnest Christian. Mrs. Steadman helped him some in his study of English. The Christian people and people in general liked him.

After about two years we found it necessary to return to America and there was no one to take our place in the work. We were in Seoul preparing to leave and Mr. Oh was with us helping in many ways. But after we should leave what? I told him that I could secure him work with the American Electric Company that had recently installed a tram line in Seoul and needed such young men as he and they could pay him more than double what I had been giving him. But his question was "Can I have time for preaching?" "What about Sunday?" "No time for preaching ⋯ no Sunday in that line of work but much better pay."

"Is there not something else for me?" "Oh, yes, if you wish to work with a Missionary, but the pay will be about as it has been." "That will be all right" was his answer and a short time later he was with one of the Southern Presbyterian

Missionaries as a helper and co-worker. A young medical man came from America to that station as a missionary and the two young men became acquainted. The young American doctor's father's sudden death necessitated his only son's return to his widowed mother. He invited Mr. Oh to accompany him to America where he would see to it that he should receive a medical missionary had hoped to do.

On his return he called to see us in Japan.

We think of him as one of the finest young men we have known in any land.

- An Appreciation

By A. I. Ludlow, M. D., D. Sc. F. A. C. S.

The following is an appreciation of Dr. Oh, written by his fellow professor in the Severance Union Medical College in Seoul Korea - A. I. Ludlow, D. Sc. F. A. C. S., Professor of Surgery and Head of the Department of Surgery for thirty years.

On October 4, 1878, in the ancient city of Kongju, the city of a Korean infant announced the beginning of the twenty-second generation of the Oh family. True to the traditions of his ancestors his father had him thoroughly instructed in Chinese. In the fall of 1894 he entered Pai Chai Academy of the Northern Methodist Mission, in Seoul. Not many months elapsed before he was baptized by Rev. H. G. Appenzeller and the subsequent years proved him to be a most sincere follower of the Master.

Dr. A. J. Alexander, a former missionary of the Southern Presbyterian Church, recognized the great Possibilities in young Oh, now a graduate of the academy and offered to take him to America for further study. Oh accepted this opportunity with great eagerness and after spending two years at Center College in Danville, Ky., took a course in Medicine, receiving in 1907 the degree of M. D. from the Hospital College of Medicine (now the University of Louisville).

Inspired with the desire to devote his life to the welfare of his own people, Dr. Oh returned to Korea immediately and a salary of fifty won (25 dollars) a month. In 1910 he was transferred to the hospital of the same mission in Mokpo where also acted as principal of the John Wantkins School, a Junior High or Middle School for Boys.

Within three years, as a result of an appeal from the Severance Union Medical College, Dr. Oh was appointed to its staff as a representative of the

Southern Presbyterian Mission. In this capacity Dr. Oh has been a most valuable asset to that Institution. A year of special post-graduate study in diseases of the skin at the Tokyo Imperial University and his efficient direction of this department at Severance have given him general recognition as perhaps the best authorities on this subject in Korea.

The appointment of Dr. Oh in 1920, as Dean of the Severance Union Medical College marked an important advance in the history of the school. This office he held until 1929 when he went on Sabbatical leave, visiting the United States and Canada and taking postgraduate work in London and Vienna. From April 1931 to March 1932, during the absence of both the president and vice-president, Dr. Oh served as Acting President. He displayed great ability in administration, winning the hearty support and esteem of the entire staff. At the meeting of the Severance Board of Managers on March 31, 1932, Dr. Oh was elected Vice-president, succeeding Dr. J. D. Van Buskirk who resigned reasons of health.

Dr. Oh's activities are far from being limited to his duties in the Medical College. Soon after coming to Severance he was elected a member of the Board of Directors of the Seoul Central Y. M. C. A. and became an active member of the West Gate Church.

It was the considered policy of the school to train officers and teachers with a view to gradually advancing them to positions of authority and responsibility and finally turn it over to them to carry it on.

The appeals of so many beggar boys on the streets of Seoul moved Dr. Oh to special effort in their behalf and in 1920 he was one of the organizers of a society to care for orphans. This work has grown into the Seoul Orphanage Home. It is a joy to witness the devotion of the orphan boys as they rush up to Dr. Oh, shouting "Uncle, Uncle!"

During a recent winter Dr. Oh, leaving the comfort of his home one midnight, searched the haunts of the beggars and rescued ten boys from freezing to death. Such is the spirit of this man whom we delight to honor.

A member of the Mindong Public School Educational Committee, a director of Public Social Work in the city of Seoul, a member of the Leper Committee of Korea, a municipal councillor of Seoul, chairman of the Society for Prevention of Cruelty to Animals, a member of the Union Charity Committee, and a member of the Christian Literature Society's Executive Committee, Dr. Oh exerts a powerful influence for good in the community.

It has been the good fortune of the writer to be associated with Dr. Oh since 1913, in classroom, hospital, and clinic. I am proud to number among my friends this physician, scholar, and teacher, father of the orphans, and friend of the fallen, Dr. K. S. Oh, who follows the example of his Master in going about good.

- The Author's Testimony

My own acquaintance with him began in 1907 when he returned from the U. S. A. where he had received his M. D. degree. He arrived in Seoul while Mr. L. H. Severance was visiting us and Mr. Severance was greatly taken with his general appearance and his evident ability. When Dr. Oh had left us Mr. Severance said to me - "that's the kind of man I hope you can develop in your Medical College." Neither of us then realized that Oh would become the great leader in medicine, in religious work and in education that he now is.

His first position in our hospital was as a teacher of anatomy and assistant to Dr. Ludlow in surgery, I soon discovered we had brought into our institution a man capable of great development and I decided to give him every opportunity for advancement. When he expressed a desire to be attached to the department of dermatology I granted his request and there he shone both as a diagnostician and therapeutist and in time we gave him time off for a year's study of this speciality in the University of Tokyo under the celebrated Dr. Donc. While he was there I visited him and was much pleased to find his professor regarded him as one of his best students and had indeed taken him as a personal friend.

When he had completed his year the University gave him a special degree and license to practise in any part of the Empire. On his return to Severance he was made full professor and chief of his department. When the American Dean of the Severance College went to U. S. A. for his furlough I appointed Dr. Oh as Assistant Dean to act as Dean during Dr. Van Buskirk's absence.

He showed such a special aptness for that work that when Dr. Van Buskirk returned I suggested that he stop the deanship and thus make it possible for me to name Dr. Oh as Dean. In this work he gave complete satisfaction to all in the College.

Later, when Vice President Van Buskirk again left on a health furlough, I appointed Dr. Oh acting Vice-president and when the Vice-president returned I, with the full concurrence of the staff as well as the then Vice-president, decided to advance Oh to that office. All those years he continued as Professor of

Dermatology and during my rather frequent absences on college business he took my place as President.

These relationships were continued until my retirement from the institution in 1939 when the Board of Managers unanimously elected him as President, a position which he has filled ever since - now seven years.

During those years the institution has continued to advance even more rapidly than ever before and now, having been organized in 1900 with a budget of yen 3,000, all contributed from America, it has a budget of 450,000 nearly all obtained in Korea.

By re-reading Dr. Ludlow's contribution to this article you will see that while carrying these heavy responsibilities he was also called on to fill many other important positions.

Chapter 11

Our Retirement from Korea

The time for our retirement from the Mission, according to the rule, was the completion of my seventieth year of life, but the Board had given the Mission authority to extend the period of service by one year at a time up to a total of three years, realizing that certain individuals might still be able to serve profitably in a position no one else was yet as well prepared for. In our case, the Mission asked us to remain on duty one year and then a second and planned to give us an added third term when this authority to extend the period of service was recalled and so at the end of my seventy-second year, June 30, 1932, we lost our place on the active list.

We could have continued our service with satisfaction to ourselves at least. But we had served, the years had passed, the set time had come and now we must retire.

However the Boards of the two colleges of which I had been president ever since their organization were not controlled by the action of the Board of Missions and were not bound by their charter to select their presidents from the missionary groups. They were free to choose anyone whom they considered suitable and they used that privilege to continue electing me for two more years, so I continued as president till February, 1934. Even then, though the new presidents were chosen at that time, they could not act until they had been approved by the Educational Department of the Government and that approval was not given until the following September.

Though many of our Korean friends urged us to remain in that country even when we had no specific duties, we felt it would be better for our successors to have a clear field in making any changes they might want to make in the conduct of the college so we set the earliest date by which we thought we could get ready for our return to Canada - early in December.

What a time we had during the two or three intervening months! Our friends feted us and took hours of time to call and chat. There were places to visit. Some stations of the Canadian Mission we had never seen, and we decided to take time off for such a trip so that we could report to their Board with some degree of knowledge on our return to Canada. This trip was both pleasant and profitable.

As the time for our departure drew near we were overwhelmed with all sorts of entertainments that need not be described, but one of these, given by our Korean friends cannot be left out. It took the form of a dinner given in the rooms of the largest restaurant in the city. While they had invited a large number of our foreign friends the majority of the guests were Koreans from every walk of life. According to Korean custom all the visiting was done before dinner so that after dating, followed by whatever speeches there were, the guests could at once retire.

Before dinner the secretary of His Highness, the second son of the late King, came to me when I happened to be alone for a moment, and handed me the Prince's visiting card. It had a good-bye message in Korean on one side and English on the other. The secretary explained that though the conditions of the country made it impossible for the prince to come to say farewell personally, as indeed it had been the case for several years, he could not let us leave his country without an effort to say good-bye, etc., etc. The messenger hoped I would not let any one see the card that night as it would cause the Prince both embarrassment and pain were the, Police, several of whom were of course present, to find out this effort at communication had been made. As we had been often together during the early years of my life in Korea, but had not met for more than fifteen years, I appreciated this daring attempt to let me know he had not forgotten me.

In due time we were invited to the dining hall - a very large room some fifty by sixty feet square. It was purely Korean in architecture, in its methods of heating and in the setting out of the many tables. As these were only about afoot high, the guests were all seated on straw mats with their legs adjusted in Korean fashion. About two hundred and fifty persons were soon seated with my venerable friend, Yun Tchi Ho, as host. After the blessing all began to eat. The various foods were all placed on the table at one time, a complete assortment for each section of the table, so arranged that the guests might serve themselves in whatever order they preferred the different courses. As for Mrs. Avison and me, we were continuously served by our friends who saw to it that we were supplied with whatever we liked best.

I had noticed that behind us a long screen of many panels, each about three feet high had been placed. The dean of the Faculty of Commerce in the Chosen Christian College drew my attention to it with the explanation that it had been sent in by a wealthy Korean gentleman who said that though Dr. Avison had never met him yet he knew the doctor and all he had done for his country and he wanted to have this article from his own home placed behind him and Mrs. Avison that evening and then sent to their home with his deepest respect and gratitude. Then he went on to explain that each of the ten panels of silk had on it Chinese characters embroidered in silk thread making a total of 400 characters. Though there were so many individual characters as to form and color there were only two different ones as to meaning and these represented Long Life and Happiness. This meant that there were two hundred forms of the character denoting Long Life, and two hundred that represented Happiness. This meant the strongest manner the giver's good wish for us. Our host told us there were very few of that particular kind of screen in existence. It was one of the greatest honors ever paid to us to have one of the twenty millions of Korean people, whom we had not even known, assure us of his understanding of what our lives in a strange land had meant.

At the end of the delicious Korean meal speeches were made by representatives of schools, newspapers, societies, etc., and many gifts were placed in our hands. One gentleman came to me and explained that though it was customary for the recipients of gifts to open the parcels so that all might see them there would be one gift of very small size, given by the Chosen Christian College, which I must not open there that night as it would get the donors into great trouble should it be seen by any of the many plain clothes policemen present. Of course, we followed his suggestion or his earnest request but opened it as soon as we got home. It contained two rings of Korean flag, one for each of us. Each had on it in colored enamel the old Korean flag, the exhibition of which would have meant very severe punishment to both givers and receivers. They had been made secretly, of course, and were intended to convey to us the fact that Korea was still engraved on their hearts and that they knew we sympathized with their loyalty to the land of their birth and that when we wore them in our own country we would remember that its people still cherished the thought that once again, at some time, they would be citizens of a free and independent country. Out of many, many expensive and beautiful gifts, none were more dear to us than those rings and that screen, I mention only those two out of many others from individuals, schools, colleges, hospitals, and churches because of their uniqueness.

"Now, in 1943, eight years later I am, as see Press of the Christian Friend of Korea, Pushing a movement in the U. S. A. and Canada to have the Allies declare the immediate independence of Korea while World War II is being fought."

After all other speeches had been made the Chairman, Baron Yun Tchi Ho, on behalf of every one present and the people a whole, made the speech of the evening, It was given in English, although the speaker was more than seventy-as five years of age and had learned the English language when he was but a very young man. Asa tribute to Baron Yun and the braininess of his countrymen, I append it without any changes or corrections:

"Dr. Avison, you see we are here assembled tonight, two hundred and forty men and women, representing practically every walk of life in the Korean community, to bid you farewell. I can assure you that there is not another person in the whole of Korea whose departure would have evoked such a unanimous sentiment of love, gratitude and regret.

In bidding you good-bye we are losing two personalities in one: a great public benefactor and a great personal friend. As our benefactor, you are leaving behind you Monuments of which anybody may be proud. In the first place, we have your bronze statue on the Severance Compound erected by the Alumni Association. When you are gone and we can see you no more in the flesh, we shall look at that statue with a degree of affection that none of us may realize at this moment. But a better monument than a mere statue we shall have in your two sons, one in the Y. M. C. A. and the other in the Medical College, who will continue the work you have begun in these two branches of the missionary enterprise.

Nobler even than these monuments, you leave us three great institutions, the Severance Hospital, the Medical College and the Chosen Christian College, to perpetuate your memory to the end of time. Your greatest monument, however, will be the never ending stream of graduates from the Colleges who will multiply your good work a thousand-fold, and the patients who will be benefitted by the healing ministrations of the hospital.

But as our personal friend your departure will create in our hearts a void that nothing can fill - neither your statue nor even your sons, nor your graduates, nor the beneficiaries of your hospital. As it would be a mere mockery for me to try to fill up an unfillable void with meaningless platitudes, I shall close by simply saying: God be with you till we meet again."

When we left Seoul on December 6, 1935, at least eight hundred people were at the railroad station to bid us "goodbye and come back" in the beautiful Korean phrase, "Kata Osio."

I am writing this at the age of more than eight-one years, wars are rending the world and breaking up relationships and I have not gone back to Korea. I probably will never do so but my heart is with its people as was that of my wife as long as she lived.

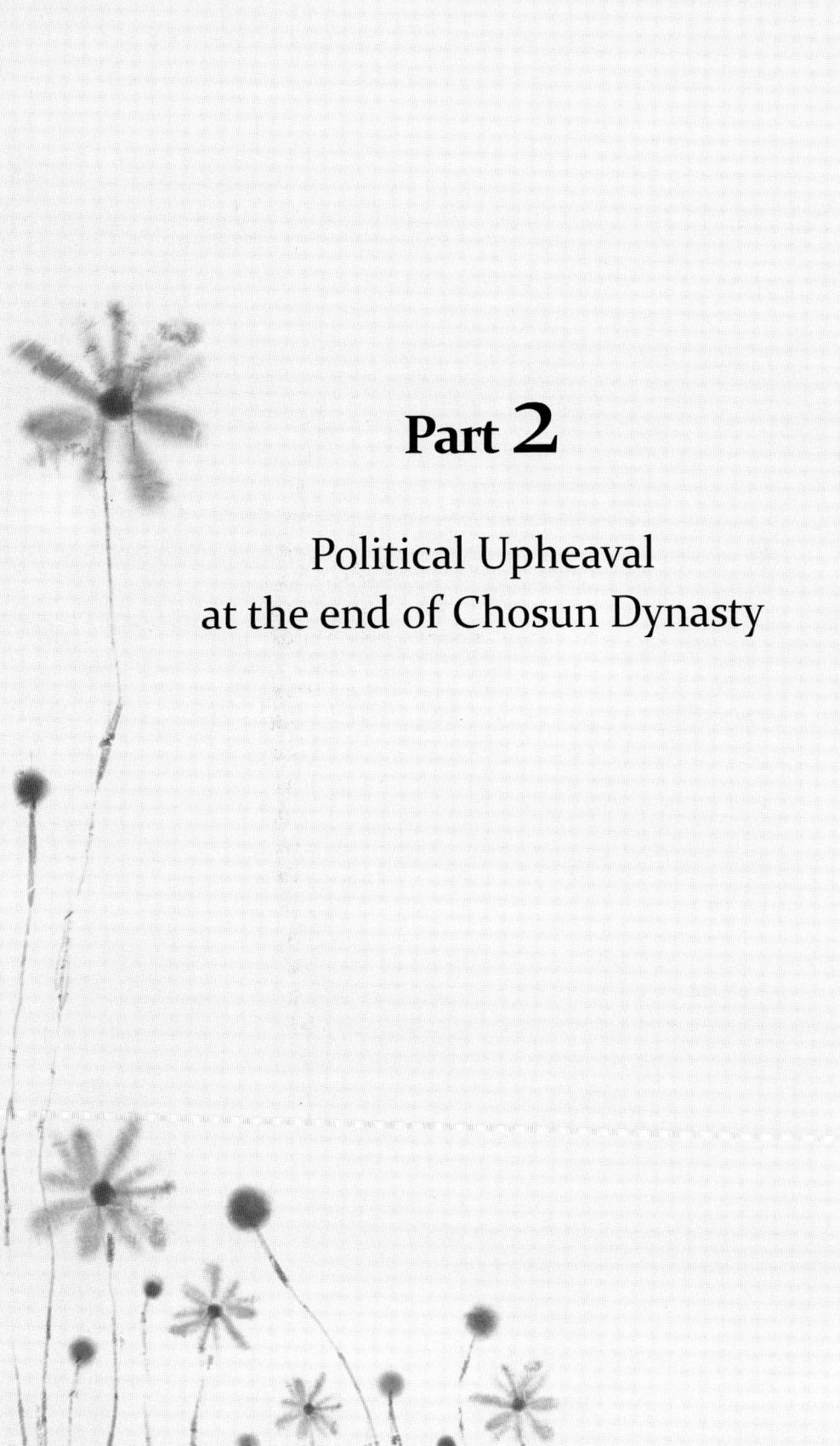

Part 2

Political Upheaval
at the end of Chosun Dynasty

Chapter 1

Korea's Royal Family

As said elsewhere the Yi dynasty was founded in 1392 A. D., the first king being Tae Cho. This dynasty lasted till 1910A. D., a period of 518 years, when Japan formally annexed it and brought its separate existence to a close.

In the year 1863 King Chul Chong died without an heir and it became necessary for the Queen Dowager to adopt a son to succeed her husband and maintain the dynasty intact. A formal search was begun for a suitable person with all the qualifications for such an important position. Certain characteristics were essential. He must be of high birth, bear the family name of the dynasty (Yi), be intelligent, and be young enough to be trained as though "to the manner bom." After a careful search the officials charged with this task recommended the youngest son of Yi Heung Sun, a boy of 12 years of age named Yi Myung Bock.

As the lad was too young to carry the responsibilities of government a regent had to be appointed to serve during the young king's minority and his father was selected. He became known as the Tai Won Kun which means the "Great Ruler of the House." Probably he was the best available person for he was a man of great strength of mind, capable of carrying on the affairs of government and able to secure the cooperation of his fellow nobles in his flames to compel the acceptance of his ideas by those whose help was necessary to the smooth running of the government which was then an autocracy.

In due time the young king reached the customary marriageable age, which, in Korea at that period, was from twelve to fourteen, and it became the duty of his parents to select a wife for him. I have said "parents" but in this case this prerogative was undoubtedly exercised by his father alone for his will was law in his own home as it was in the palace of his son.

The choice fell on the niece of Min Yung Choon, the wealthiest and most noble of all the noble families of Korea and the brother-in-law of the Tai Won Kun himself. The regent knew the haughty pride of the Min family and their reputation for always getting their own way and this should have made him hesitate to make such a choice since the King's nature was pliant and the proposed bride had the self-reliance and determination of her family. No doubt, however, Yi felt that during the minority of the young couple he could depend on them to do his will as all young people in Korea are taught to honor their parents and follow their advice, especially that of their father and, when a girl marries, her duty is transferred to her father-in-law. Though this was a fact, the daughter-in-law in this case developed to the full the characteristics of her family and, as her will ran counter to her father-in-law's in many instances, the Tai Won Kun learned he had been entirely wrong in his estimation of her cleverness and persistence.

During the earlier years of his regency, he had his own way in practically everthing, but as the couple grew older he found it more difficult, for though the king was happy to be free from responsibility, the Queen had quite different ideas. She wanted to be Queen in fact as well as in name and, as her husband reached maturity, was not satisfied till she had persuaded him to end the regency and take upon himself the full duties of the kingship. That was in the year 1873.

Though the regent should have recognized the inevitability of the situation and yielded gracefully to this natural development, he resented her attitude and became her bitter enemy, I was told by one of the King's chamberlains soon after our arrival that the Tai Won Kun had made many attempts to have her assassinated but she had always been too subtle for him and had foiled each one in turn. Just a short time before our arrival in Korea, he, under the guise of a desire to gain her friendship, had sent her another present but she having previous experiences in mind directed the parcel to be opened carefully and it again contained an infernal machine which was intended to kill her. These stories, told me 1893,of attempts made twenty years after his deposition, show how strong was his hatred and how great his pertinacity. Many who knew him as regent spoke well of the way in which he had governed, saying he had been a successful ruler; that though he was a thorough autocrat and always insisted on having his own way, he was just; that, though the people feared him, they were contented because they realized that as long as they obeyed him they were comparatively safe. Possibly a strong ruler, such as he, might have saved Korea from many of the disasters which resulted from the combination of the King's weakness of character and the Queen's self-will. That, however, is but a conjecture. His displacement was but the natural outcome of the passage of time and probably they did the best they could with their small resources when faced with powerful enemies outside and many disturbance within.

An Army Insurrection in Im-o Year (1882)

In May and June, 1882, Korea signed treaties with the United States and Britain, and negotiations were on with Germany and France. The Korean people, evidently aroused by the pro-Chinese leaders, attributed the making of these treaties to Japanese influence and, mobbing the Japanese legation, destroyed it. The Queen, fearing the palace would be attacked, fled secretly to Chung ju, many miles south of Seoul, and had her death announced in the capital. Secretly she appealed to Li Hung Chang, Prime Minister of China, for help and he sent a fleet of ships over to Chemulpo on a pretended visit of friendship. The commander called on the Tai Won Kun and in the name of Li Hung Chang invited him to go to Chemulpo to inspect the ships. Thrown off his guard by this apparent friendliness, he did so. A great dinner had been prepared in his honor and as soon as the inspection had been completed, it was served. Beautiful dancing girls entertained him and liquors were provided in abundance. While the merriment was proceeding the ship's anchor was quietly weighed and the ship started on its way to China. When their partly befuddled guest realized the ship was moving and asked what it meant, he was told they were taking him for a little trip to let him see how well the ship could sail. He grew sleepy and was put to bed and when he awoke next morning they were well on their way to China. He naturally became alarmed but they assured him he was only being taken to China on a brief visit to the Emperor, the great friend of Korea, and that they would speedily bring him back. As he could do nothing about it he settled down to await the outcome. This was August 30, 1882.

The Japanese made use of this opportunity to compel favors from the King, the first of which was an agreement to compensate Japan for the recent destruction of their legation property and to have fourteen Korean young men sent to

Japan to pursue military studies.

On October 9 the Queen returned to the palace under the protection of 3,000 Chinese troops led by Yuan Shi Kai and for the time being she eliminated the Tai Won Kun from any participation in his country's affairs. This act of deception did not improve their relations with each other and he was more than ever determined to get rid of her. Twelve years afterwards, in 1895, by his joining in a plot with the Japanese who were as anxious to dispose of her as he was, her death was actually brought about.

Princes

At the time of our arrival in Korea the King and Queen had two sons, the first being, unfortunately, a moron. He was already an adult and physically strong except that he was undeveloped sexually and, though twice married, had no offspring. His face was almost expressionless and he seemed to take but little interest in anything going on around him. Though I saw him every time I visited the palace he spoke tome very seldom. However, in spite of his mental dullness along usual lines, he seemed to have a wonderful memory for the shapes and names of things, I was told he had learned many thousands of the Chinese written characters and could name them instantly as he saw them written but that he had no knowledge of their meaning. Though he could write them as they were dictated to him he could not combine them into sentences so as to express a thought. As for those persons he had met only once, he always remembered them and could name them without hesitation. He never expressed an opinion on anything going on around him except to manifest his liking or disliking for it.

Because of this condition, when the Japanese in 1904 came to the conclusion that their plans for the control of Korea were being foiled by the stubborn refusal of the Emperor to accede to their demands, they decided to secure his abdication in favor of this son whose absolute unfitness for the position was well known to them. I will not inject the details of this into my story at this point but will leave them to be described in their proper setting.

The second son, named Eui Wha was very different from his older brother, being both mentally and physically alert and capable. Unfortunately his surroundings were not such as to ensure the best development of his abilities and his life cannot be regarded as a successful one. He has had no career except that of a Korean noble with nothing particular to think of ordo. He too will be referred to at another time.

Chaos after Entering into a Treaties with the Powers

Going back to the point where we were considering what might have happened had the Tai Won Kun continued to rule Korea, we must see what really did happen after the young King and Queen took over the responsibilities of government. Between that time and the date of our arrival in Korea they had been faced by many serious questions. Both Japan and China had thrown aside their efforts to maintain their isolation from the rest of the world by making Treaties of Commerce and Friendship with many Western powers and in 1879 those powers began to ask for a similar treaty with Korea. Korea had long followed a policy of nonintercourse with other nations even to the point of joining China to make a certain tract of country between Korea and Manchuria, a NO MAN'S LAND in order to make it difficult for any other nation to reach China via Korea. When the United States sent envoys requesting the opening of Korea to the "Western Barbarians" for mutual trade, the Korean King spurned all friendly overtures and went so far as to engage in combat with several American ships that had entered the mouth of the Han River and were making their way up the stream towards the capital, In the end, however, she followed the example of China and Japan and signed a similar treaty in 1882.

This gave Koreans and Westerners free access to one another's territories for purposes of mutual trade. No mention was made in the agreement, however, for missionaries to enter and carry on their religious propaganda though freedom of religious worship was specifically agreed to. However, the Boards of Foreign Missions in the United States and in some European countries immediately began to appoint missionaries.

A gift of money for opening work having been received by the Presbyterian Board of Foreign Missions, North, Dr. J. W. Heron was appointed as its first missionary. As he could not leave immediately the Board, taking advantage of the presence in Shanghai of Dr. Horace N. Allen whom they had sent to China as a medical missionary but had not yet assigned to any particular station, asked him to go to Korea instead of remaining in China. He cabled acceptance and crossed to Korea at once, leaving his family in China.

He arrived in Seoul September 20, 1884, and at once became a problem to the American Minister, General Foulke, because missionaries as yet had no legal status there. The Minister got rid of the problem by appointing Dr. Allen physician to the United States Legation. The doctor returned to China for his family, and arrived again in Seoul with them in December, 1884.

Events that followed almost immediately after Dr. Allen's arrival showed that his presence at that particular time in Korea was propitious. Soon after the making of the treaty with the United States, a group of Young Koreans, in most part scions of nobility, who had been studying the forms of government as practiced in other countries, began to feel that the autocracy of Korea was detrimental to the highest welfare of the country and its people. They organized themselves into a league to bring about a change. The story of this episode, known as the Emeute of 1884, is told in another chapter.

The years following the Emeute were stormy ones for the King and Queen, following as they did the opening of the country by the Treaty of Commerce and Friendship which brought into Korea foreign merchants from many lands, missionaries of different churches and creeds, travellers in search of knowledge of a country that had been closed for centuries to foreign intercourse, tourists looking for new interests, etc. Moreover, the King was beset by all kinds of new problems as he found himself presided on all sides by the messengers of foreign governments demanding this and that; this if granted, creating complications with other countries and that, if consented to, causing him to fear undesirable results. Here he was, entirely ignorant of foreign affairs but responsible for the good and bad results to come from those contacts with powers of whom he had hitherto known nothing.

Treaties of Friendship and Commerce! Often they were made a means of despoliation. China claimed a degree of suzerainty and insisted on being represented by a Resident rather than a Minister! Japan resented China's claim, and demanded a treaty with that country which would prevent her from sending any troops into Korea without previously notifying Japan! Japan also demanded special treaties with Korea, intended to improve her trade with that country even though such might in some cases be detrimental to Korea! Poor Korea! She needed a leader well acquainted with foreign diplomacy, wise in the ways of foreign diplomats, suave but firm when unfair demands were made and, withal, wise advisers and an army strong enough to uphold her decisions when once made. None of these requirements did she have.

And at home, what? Antiquated methods of government, an entire ignorance of Western knowledge on the part of both king and advisers, an ignorant and poverty-stricken population with the one redeeming feature of an intense love of their country but with neither knowledge of what was needed under the new conditions nor power to use the knowledge if they had had it and all the wealth in the hands of a comparatively small number of families who kept the masses busy working to support them in idleness and luxury.

Here was a chance for moderation on the part of foreign powers, for magnanimity on the part of the favored families, for a wise ruler to direct the thoughts and energies of his people and meet with firmness and discretion the demands of all outsiders who wanted to enrich themselves at the expense of those so much in need of help. But not one of these chances materialized, so the history of the country and the destiny of its rulers was written in blood and marked with failure.

Chapter 2

The Emeute of 1884
(Kap-sin Year)

Testimony by Philip Jaisohn

This event was coincident with the beginning of Dr. Allen's work in Korea. My account of it is factual, being based on the written statement of one of its leaders, Dr. Philip Jaisohn (Suh Jai Pil, his Korean name), in a letter tome and is here given by his kind permission. As I pen it he is still living and practising medicine in Media, Pa., U. S. A.

The Treaties of Friendship and Commerce between Korea and several Western nations were signed and promulgated in 1882, following close on a series of similar treaties between Japan and the same Western powers. Before the signing of those documents, Korea had had but few official relations, even with China, for a long period of years though both these countries still recognized a degree of suzerainty of China over Korea. About the only outward evidences of this were.

1. The yearly visitation of Korea by a deputation of Chinese officials to collect the small annual tribute which Korea paid to its suzerain, supposedly for protection of its vassal.

2. The continued use of red as the royal color by the Korean court instead of the imperial yellow which, in the Orient, is a sign of the absolute independent status of a country.

There was no particular relationship between Korea and Japan except the establishment and continued use of the port of Fusan by a colony of Japanese which had existed over a period of 400 years without any treaty concerning it. It was just spoken of as "the Japanese Settlement."

It was significant of Korea's attitude toward the rest of the world that she was the last of the three countries, China, Japan, and Korea, to sign a treaty with the Western nations. China signed in 1860, Japan in 1879, and Korea in 1882.

Korea is geographically separated from the Manchurian province of China by the Yalu River, but as that had not proved itself a sufficient barrier to incursions from the north, a tract of country, twenty-three miles in depth immediately north of the Yalu River, was set apart by China and Korea to be known as "No Man's Land."

This tract had been completely devastated so as to make it uninhabitable and render it difficult for either country to take an army across it. As a result of this determined policy on the part of Korea to avoid any communication with the outside world, it became known as "The Hermit Nation." No Man's Land continued to exist until 1867. Korea's hostility to Japan had been very bitter ever since the invasion by Hideyoshi in 1592, and that feeling was still evident even when we went there in 1893. The Koreans called the Japanese "little barbarians," a name suggestive of their small size and the low opinion the Koreans had of their characteristics.

Korea had but one great desire - to be left alone - as is shown by the following quotation from Dr. Jaisohn:

"In spite of their wish to be left alone, the world would not let Korea continue her dream of a hermit. Foreign nationals began to come to Korea, secretly at first, but later they arrived in merchant ships and war vessels and demanded that her door be opened to the commerce of the world. With a feeling of misgiving Korea finally opened her gates, first to Japan, then to the others, but there was not a man in the government or outside of it who knew anything about diplomacy or foreign relations. The treaties were written by the foreign envoys and the Korean representatives simply signed them on the dotted line."

- Advent of Progressive Group

Some of the brightest young Korean nobles, realizing their inadequacy as compared with the greater knowledge, military strength and wealth of the outside nations, formed themselves into a group to study all the available books and current literature of foreign lands. They called themselves the Progressive Group. Its leader was Kim Ok Kyun, and some of the others were Prince Pak Yung Hyo, Soh Kwang Pom, Hong Yung Sik, and Suh Jai Pil. To quote from a letter written by Suh Jai Pil (Dr. Jaisohn),

"The objectives of this group were: Reformation of governmental administration in taxation, justice, education, and selection of officials according to their qualifications, elimination of favoritism, waste of the government revenue in superstitious practices, abolition of class distinctions and strict enforcement of the old law against corruption, graft, and extortion of money from the people on trumped up charges of crime; sending of a large number of bright and promising young men to foreign countries to be trained in modern arts and sciences; employing of foreign instructors and advisers in the different departments of the government; improvement of sanitation in the cities and villages: encouraging the people to be thrifty and industrious and to see that their rights are respected by the government; establishment of a trained police force for the preservation of law and order and the organization of a modern army for national defense. To attain these aims the members of the Progressive Group must meet together frequently and consult each other as to the best means to be employed."

Kim Ok Kyun was given the responsibility of interesting the Queen, the most powerful personage in Korea, in their plans for improving their country. She was in favor of all their ideas except those of certain governmental reforms which she did not like because they would curtail much of her unlimited power. She agreed, however, to send some fifty young men to Japan to study in the schools there. Ten of these entered a military school so that on graduation they could teach Korean officers in a military school which was to be established in Seoul.

- The Emeute of 1884

They studied two years in Japan and on their return found the older and more conservative officials strongly opposed to their proposals for improving the conditions of the common people as they foresaw that that would in the end lessen the power of the royal family and seriously endanger its influence. These ideas had been instilled into the mind of the Queen so that the students, whose plan seemed to themselves so right and clear and simple, found a coldness to their suggestion of reform that was thoroughly disappointing for even the proposed military school was never established.

The representative of China at that time was General Yuan Shi Kai (Pronounced Yu-an She Kye) who, because of the still existing suzerainty of his country over Korea, held the position of Resident while representatives of other countries were only Ministers. He was also military commander of about two thousand Chinese soldiers and was held in high esteem by the King, the Queen and the Cabinet of Korea, so that his advice was always taken and he opposed the plan for reform.

The Progressive leaders had hoped, when they should return to Korea, they would be in a position to advise the King and Queen and they expected to introduce the various reforms gradually, but the hardened attitude of the royal family was so discouraging that they changed their plan for as low and peaceful reform and set about to accomplish their purpose by force. We, in this way, wonder why they did not exercise patience and gain their ends by a gradual education of the people until, by sheer force of numbers, they could compel the government to yield to their demands. The people, however, had never known anything of a free government and their minds were so fully occupied with the struggle for a bare livelihood that these young reformers, filled with the zeal of a new ambition, could see no chance of accomplishing anything except directly through their Majesties who could only be influenced by fear. So they made a plan to seize the King and Queen by force and compel him to put his seal on certain decrees which they would present to him before others could intervene. These were prepared and made ready for his signature while they were awaiting an opportunity to carry out their project.

In the meantime, the Queen's cousin, Prince Min Young Ik, a former member of the Progressive Group who appeared to have deserted them in favor of less radical methods than theirs, had used his influence to develop certain modern ways, among which was the adoption of a new postal system. Hong Yung Sik, another former member of the reform party, was appointed as Postmaster General and, a new post office building having erected, all was ready to put the new system into operation. This was done on December 4, 1884, at a banquet given in celebration of this important event. Prince Min attended as did all the high governmental officials. Other guests were the representatives of the foreign countries which had entered into treaty relations with Korea.

Strange to say, the Progressives, who, one would think, should have rejoiced at this excellent innovation, regarded the banquet as offering an opportunity to the palace and seize the persons of their Majesties while the officials were all at the opening ceremony. I quote here from a paper written by Mr. Suh himself, describing just what happened:

"--- they sent a few students who had studied in Japan to the neighborhood of the new post office to set some empty houses on fire and at the same time create a great commotion by firing a few shots of revolvers. The idea was to draw the banqueting government leaders to the scene of the fire as was the custom in Korea. One of the first who came upon the scene was Min Yong Ik,[26] the cousin of the Queen and general-in-command of the royal guards. He was immediately attacked by the students with a sword and one of his ears was slashed off in the scuffle while another general was seriously wounded. This news soon spread and the whole city was in an uproar because of all sorts of wild rumors which alarmed nearly every person inside of the city walls, including the royal family in the palace. The Progressives, headed by Kim Ok Kyun, rushed to the palace and demanded an immediate audience with the King, which was granted. Kim told the King that it was prudent for the royal family to leave the palace and go to a secluded building near the North Mountain in the back of the palace for safety, as he did not know when the mob would invade the palace grounds. Of course, the King and Queen were greatly frightened and docilely followed Kim to the small detached palace known as Keydong Koong, situated in the rear of the home of the King's brother, Prince Yi Chai Myen. As soon as they reached the building the royal family was put in a small apartment with only one door leading to the hall and this door was guarded by two students who had just finished military training in Japan. These boys were armed with revolvers and carried rifles with fixed bayonets. No one was allowed to enter or go out from the royal apartment without a written permit from one of the Progressive leaders. To all intents and purposes the King and his family became captives of the much maligned reformers whose advice they had to follow under the circumstances.

A new cabinet was formed with several well known scholars of that period as the members of the State Council and with leaders of the Progressive

26   Referred to above as one of the could-be reformers who had left that group as being too far-advanced but who still favored gradual reforms.

party as the heads of executive departments including such men as Kim Ok Kyun, Pak Young Hyo, Soh Kwang Pom, Hong Young Sik, Yun Chi Ho and others whose names I cannot recall. At any rate, the King was willing to sign all the decrees drafted by the members of the State Council and the Cabinet, and the Queen was as docile as a well-behaving child. Numerous reform measures were decreed and promulgated as the laws of the country during the three days the King and Queen were under the control of the reformers but we all know that none of these was ever observed after that. I cannot recall all of the new laws but the most outstanding ones were the abolition of class distinctions among the people, such as different kinds of yang bans, the middle class and the commoners: the reorganization of law courts; the army; the tax office; the treasury; all appointment of government positions to be made through examination of the candidates' qualification; establishment of public schools in every district in the country ;improvement of public sanitation, highways, better housing for the poor; Prohibition of devil worship and other similar superstitious practices; cutting off the topknots; wearing of foreign style clothes; stabilization of national currency; abolition of slavery and many others. Of course, these reforms were desirable but it was not the time to stir up the ignorant masses with such radical and impractical laws. These young Progressives had the right ideas but they lacked the wisdom of statesmanship or political experience. They were patriotic and progressive but, at the same time, were hot-headed and impatient.

While they succeeded in capturing the King and Queen. they had no armed force to protect themselves from a possible violent opposition from the Koreans or from the Chinese general who had some three thousand soldiers under his command. So the new Cabinet invited the Japanese Minister, Takezoi, to come to the temporary palace with legation guards, about 125 men, to protect the royal family and incidently recognize the new cabinet as the de facto and do jure government of Korea. Takezoi accepted the invitation and arrived at the temporary palace with his guards and quartered in one of the buildings adjoining the apartment where the royal family was confined. Whether he accepted the invitation and its implied obligation with the knowledge and consent of his government or not, I do not know, but it is hard to imagine that he had assumed the responsibility by himself alone. At any rate he came and stayed there for two or three days for the purpose of affording protection to the King and his family and moral support to the newly organized reform government. In fairness to him I want to say that at no time did he attempt to interfere with the matters of internal reforms which the new cabinet proposed or enacted into law. Takezoi was an old fashioned Japanese scholar, well-versed in Chinese classic, and fond of writing poetry, but otherwise he was a timid and inexperienced diplomat, lacking the fighting spirit which all Japanese were supposed to have.

The old Korean army was said to have had some two thousand soldiers divided into four regiments, 500 in each, and though they were supplied with rifles of various types they had no ammunition and, having had no training they knew nothing about military discipline. The officers were no better than the men under them in either education or military training and were absolutely useless for the purposes of the work for which they were organized.

It was my duty to guard the gates of the temporary palace against a possible intrusion of the enemies of the new government but I could not use the old Korean soldiers for that purpose. None of them had a cartridge in his belt and, besides, I could not trust their loyalty to the new cabinet, so the duty of guarding the palace gates was entrusted to a dozen students who had been trained with me in the Japanese military school. Even they had very little ammunition but they were better equipped than the old Korean soldiers. Moreover, they were loyal and were filled with the fighting spirit against the corrupt conservatives whom they considered as their personal enemies and the betrayes of their land. So poorly equipped and scanty in number as they were, these students did a fine job in keeping out all undesirables from the palace.

For two days the royal family had no communication with the outside but then the wicked but resourceful Queen succeeded in doing so and the result of that communication brought about the downfall of the reform government. The manner in which the Queen sent a note of appeal to Yuan Shi Kai, the Chinese general in Seoul, was very clever. She wrote a note telling Yuan of the scanty number of Japanese soldiers on the palace ground and asking him to come with his soldiers and rescue her from detention by the Progressives whom she designated as the 'rebels' or 'traitors.' She sent this note out from the kitchen by placing it in the bottom of one of the empty dishes on the table when her meals were served to her apartment. The guard at the door had evidently overlooked this empty dish which was taken out with other dishes after the meal was finished The note was discovered by a kitchen servant who rushed it to the Chinese camp on the other side of the city and handed it to Yuan. When Yuan knew just what forces were there to detain the Queen, he did not hesitate to go to her rescue.

With three thousand men he marched to the temporary palace and opened fire on the guards at the gate. This happened about four o'clock in the afternoon of December 7th and it was a surprise to us all. Our boys at the gate offered the best resistance to the invading Chinese they could, but they were overwhelmingly outnumbered. We had to retreat to the hill back of the palace where we fought back by firing several volleys into the Chinese rushing into the gate in a compact formation, I do not know what their casualties were but undoubtedly they were heavy for I saw many of them keel over after each volley we fired. The Japanese did not join us in this fight at the beginning, but later they did so after our appeal to the captain of the guards. Takezoi was not willing to continue the fight on the ground that he had no authority to start a war with China and ordered the captain to cease firing, but the captain kept on until the ammunition was exhausted. As soon as our firing ceased the Chinese rushed in and carried the royal family to the old palace. Many of our men were murdered by the Chinese at the request of the King and Queen and the only ones who escaped alive were Kim Ok Kyun, Pak Young Hyo, Soh Kwang Pom, Yun Chi Ho, and myself. There may have been one or two others but I do not recall who they were.

We escaped through the back gate of the temporary palace and walked through the foothills of the North Mountain and finally reached the Japanese legation which was then located in the central part of the city. As night was pitch dark the directions in which we had to travel were not clear and we arrived there physically and spiritually sore and tired. Personally I did not care what might happen as I was sick at heart. The people of Seoul were hostile and even the Japanese were not too friendly toward us. After a terrible night at the Japanese legation we walked to Chemulpo in the midst of rocks and tiles thrown at us along the streets of Seoul. Leaving Seoul at four o'clock in the afternoon we reached Chemulpo at dawn next morning, four weary souls without friends, without money, and without country. We were thrown into the hold of the bottom of a small Japanese steamer, Chitosei Maru[27], and carried to Nagasaki where we were sent to the shore without much ceremony and told to shift along as best we could. After some days we reached Tokyo and tried to find out what Japan was going to do in Korea and with China but all the information we could get was that Japan was not ready to do anything at that time."

Thus ended the well-intentioned but poorly timed effort to convert, in a few years, one of the oldest autocracies from its age-long way of thinking and doing into a limited monarchy, a system that calls for a citizenry prepared by gradual processes of education, not only to exercise a degree of self-government

---

27   "Chitosei" was the name of the ship and "Maru" meant 'ship.' The Japanese always use the term "Maru" after the name of any ship referred to.

but also to exert the will to support their demand for it. Some of the group lost their lives, others fled to different countries. As for Suh Jai Pil from whom the writer obtained the details of this remarkable bit of history, having fled to Japan as related he went from there to the United States as determined as ever to work for the better conditions in Korea that he and his fellow patriots had envisioned. I cannot do better than to give a brief summary of his career in his own words:

"When we reached Tokyo after many narrow escapes we found ourselves homeless, penniless, and friendless. The Japanese treated us shabbily and were at times actually hostile. I will never forget the terrible experience I had during my few months' stay in Japan. I often went by two days without food and occasionally without shelter. Had it not been for one or two Americans in Yokohama, I would have perished from hunger and exposure.

I was disgusted with the Koreans and equally disappointed at the treacherous behavior of the Japanese so I decided to leave the Orient and seek a new life in America. Prince Pak Young Hyo and Soh Kwang Pom came to America with me and Kim Ok Kyun stayed in Japan.

Our life in San Francisco was anything but happy. We had no money, no friends, and could not talk English. We received some financial help from one or two Americans interested in the mission work in the Orient but this was uncertain and often inadequate to meet our expenses.

Prince Pak returned to Japan and Mr. Soh Kwang Pom went to New York at the suggestion of some American friends whom he met a year before when he had come to America as secretary of the first Korean ambassador to the United States, so I was left alone in San Francisco for a year or more during which period I worked most of the time for a livelihood. One of the best jobs I had was distributing advertising circulars of a furniture store at the doors of the houses in the residential district of the city. While this job required no linguistic ability or salesmanship it was very trying to the legs and feet as I was obliged to walk about ten miles a day. My reward was $2 per day and I worked five and a half days a week. In the evenings I went to the Y. M. C. A. school to learn English.

The following year I had a chance to enter a school in Pennsylvania through the kindness of an American so I left the Golden Gate for the anthracite coal region of the Keystone State, where I spent three years in preparing for college, I was well treated and my living expense was paid by the American friend who had brought me to his city. By the time I graduated from the preparatory school this gentleman asked me to become a minister of the Gospel as he was a very religious man. If I would agree to do this he would send me to college and then to the theological seminary.

I thought the matter over for several days, but felt that I could not give him a definite promise for various reasons. In the first place, I was not sure that I would make a good minsiter and secondly, I could not tell whether or not I would ever be able to return to Korea under the then existing conditions. I explained this to him and said I could not make a definite promise but if the conditions should change in Korea and if I should feel like taking up the ministry four years hence I would then give him the promise he wanted. He was not satisfied with this conditional promise and told me that he would not continue his financial help for my further education. There was nothing else to do then but go out find some other means which would enable me to get more education so I went to Washington, the nation's capital, and searched there for an opportunity. Fortunately I found one and for nine years I worked for a living and at the same time was able to finish my college course and graduate in medicine.

While I was busy working and studying in America the expected war between China and Japan occurred and a few months after a disastrous defeat, China signed the treaty of Shiminiseiki and formally renounced all her claim of suzerainty over Korea. A new government was organized in Korea and all former refugees of 1884 were recalled. Pak Young Hyo was asked to be Minister of the Interior, but refused in favor of a friend, and Soh Kwang Pom became Minister of Law. If Kim Ok Kyun had been alive he would no doubt have been Prime Minister but unfortunately he had been killed by an assassin sent by the King from Korea. The assassin, Hong Chong Oo, was afraid to commit the murder in Japan so helured Kim to go to Shanghai on the promise of turning over to him a large sum of money which he said he had deposited in a Shanghai bank. As soon as Kim reached Shanghai the double-crossing assassin killed his unsuspecting victim, In the absence of Kim Ok Kyun, it was natural for Pak Young Hyo to become the most influential manin the country.

I also received a request to return to Korea to become Minister of Foreign Affairs but declined for two reasons. I thought that the new government would not last long ac Japan had the dominant influence, I did not see much difference between the conservative government under Chinese influence and the new one under Japanese domination.

The people of Korea had not changed one bit since 1884 and so no government could depend on them for support, no matter how good its intention might be. The only power in Korea at that time was exercised by the King and his crafty Queen, and I knew that both were against any new ideas and both hated the Japanese like poison, I did not think the combination of the King and Queen and the Japanese sponsored new government would get along even under Japanese duress. This surmise soon proved to have been correct because the Japanese found it was necessary to liquidate the Queen by another foul murder which they instigated.

Besides, the Japanese found Pak Young Hyo did not act as their rubber stamp for he asserted his right as minister of state of an independent country to act according to his own judgment. The Japanese knew that Pak had no other support in the government except their own so they told the Queen that she could discharge him if she desired. The Queen had always hated Pak but could not do anything to him for fear that the Japanese might resent it, but as soon as she heard the Japanese were not interested in him she immediately ordered his arrest. However, Pak got away from Korea for the second time before he could be captured. Soon after, the Japanese got rid of the Queen by murdering her through a mob acting at their instigation.

These events demonstrate how helpless the people of Korea were. They showed no interest when the Queen murdered hundreds of their innocent countrymen and, when the Queen was herself murdered by the Japanese, they were equally indifferent. When the people of any nation reach such a state of impotence and indifference it is no longer a nation. A land without law, without sentiment, without voice and without physical and moral force is just a place where any crook or criminal can ply his evil trade. Korea was just a space filled with people who were physically alive but spiritually dead. No wonder the nation perished."

- ## Return of Philip Jaisohn

"It serves no useful purpose to cry about what has already happened, but it is the duty of every decent man to do his best to rekindle the decadent nation to which he belongs with the revivifying spirit of enlightenment, moral and physical courage, the love of liberty and self respect. With this ideal in view I went back to Korea after eleven years of exile in America, not as an official of the government but as a private individual with the spirit of an evangelist. Although I spent only two and a half years in Korea during this visit, I saw some very exciting and dramatic scenes, It is my intention to relate some of the experiences in subsequent articles."

While studying medicine at the Washington Medical College, Suh Jai Pil anglicized his name to Philip Jaisohn by which name we will designate him in the rest of our story. After his graduation as M .D. he worked for a time in the Research Department of the American Navy Medical Service and was married to the daughter of General Armstrong of the American Army. When he decided to return to Korea after along absence, she accompanied him, showing herself to be both a devoted wife and a brave woman for the career of are former in an autocratic country is very likely to be strewn with thorns rather than roses.

He reached Seoul January 1896, unannounced, though his return had been expected, and was soon made Adviser to His Majesty's Government for a period of ten years with the expectation that he could be of assistance in the remodeling of governmental procedure and helping to solve the many difficult problems of the country. His task was going to be a difficult one because he was sure to be hampered by the efforts of the King and Queen to maintain their autocratic privileges, the jealousies that would surely be developed in the minds of the cabinet ministers who had not forgotten his connection with the plot of ten years before, and the ignorance of the 12,000, 000 people who could understand neither his background nor his intentions but he was full of enthusiasm at the apparent prospect of a free land in the work before him. He called on me several times, knowing of my relationship to the King as physician and friend and, among other things he had in mind, revealed his intention to have me appointed as Surgeon General with power to direct the medical policies of the country and of the army in order to introduce measures of hygiene and sanitation that would improve the vigor of the people and prevent the great loss of life that was retarding the growth of population. Quite naturally, however, he found many obstacles to his plans and methods for he himself was not a placater. Indeed, he was a bit hot-headed as he and his fellow reformers had been in the days of the Emeute. He saw an end to be attained and set about its speedy attainment by the most direct method. He might have got further by trying to introduce one improvement at a time and not even pushing that much faster than it could be understood and come to be desired.

- Publishing Tongnip Shinmun(The Independent)

Soon after his arrival he began to edit and publish a small newspaper called the "Tongnip Shinmun" (The Independent). Each edition was published in both

Korean and English as he wanted the English speaking members of the community to know just what he was advocating, in the hope that they would support him in his policies. The first issue made its appearance on April 7, 1896, and it was published three times a week. As it was the first newspaper of its kind to be edited, Published and financed entirely by Koreans and because it was printed in the simple Unmun script, native to Korea, which could be read by Koreans in general instead of in the Chinese characters which could be read only by a few, it created quite an excitement, especially when it was sold on the streets by newsboys at the price of only a Korean cent a copy, the equivalent at that time of half a cent of United States currency.

At first 2,000 copies were issued but soon the demand of it was so great that 4,000 had to be printed. As one copy would serve for several people who listened in while one good reader read it aloud, its real circulation was probably about 20,000. When we think of the population, about 12,000,000 this attempt to educate the people in an absolutely new form of government seems very small indeed but surely it was a brave effort. There is now no doubt that, though it was defeated at the time, it served to inform and arouse many who afterwards became leaders in more widespread movements for reform.

The editorial of the first edition set forth fully the aims of the editor and was as follows:

"The time seems to have come for the publication of a periodical in the interest of the Korean people. We do not mean merely the residents of Seoul and vicinity, nor do we mean the more favored classes alone, but we include the whole people of every class and grade. To this end three things are necessary; first, that it shall be printed in a character intelligible to the largest number; second, that it shall be put on the market at such a price that it shall be within the reach of the largest number; third, that it shall contain such matter as shall be for the best interest of the largest number.

To meet the first requirement, it has been printed in the native character called Unmun, for the time is shortly coming, if it is not yet here, when Koreans will cease to be ashamed of their native character which for simplicity of construction and phonetic power compares favorably with the best alphabets in the world. Difficulty is experienced by those not thoroughly acquainted with the Unmun from the fact that ordinarily there are no spaces between words. We have, therefore, adopted the novel plan of introducing spaces, thus doing away with the main objection to its use. We have made it biliteral, because this will act as an incentive to English speaking Koreans to push their knowledge for its own sake. An English page may also commend the paper to the patronage of those who have no other means of gaining accurate information in regard to the events which are transpiring in Korea. It hardly needs to be said that we have access to the best sources of information in the capital and will be in constant communication with the provinces.

To meet the second requirement we have so arranged the size of the sheet as to be able to put it on the market at a price which will make it unnecessary for anyone to forge its advantages because of inability to buy.

To meet the third requirement is a more difficult matter. What Korea needs is a unifying influence. Now the old order of things is passing away, society is in a state which might be described as intermediate between two forms of crystallization. The old combination of forces has been broken up or is rapidly breaking up and these are seeking new affinities. The near future will probably decide the mode of arrangement of the social forces.

It is at this moment, when Korean society is in a plastic state, that we deem it opportune to put out this sheet as an expression at least of our desire to do what can be done in a journalistic way to give Koreans a reliable account of the events that are transpiring, to give reasons for things that often seem to them unreasonable, to bring the capital and provinces into greater harmony through a mutual understanding of each other's needs, especially the need that each has for the other.

Our platform is - Korea for the Koreans, clean politics, the cementing of foreign friendship, the gradual though steady development of Korean resources with Korean capital as far as possible but under expert foreign tutelage, and the speedy translation of foreign textbooks into Korean that the youths may have access to the great things of history, science, art and religion without having to acquire a foreign tongue."

Up to that time all books printed in the Korean language followed the Chinese method in which there were no spaces between words and no punctuation marks, The reader had to depend entirely on the connectives to enable him to read it understandingly. Even the books published by the foreign missionaries followed the custom of the country in this regard. Dr. Jaisohn, knowing how difficult it was for an uneducated person to catch the full meaning under such a method, decided to space the words and double space the sentences and this made his newspaper all the more popular, for it was easier to catch the meaning of the writer. This method was soon followed in the publication of missionary literature most of which was printed in the easy script known as Unmun rather than in the Chinese characters known as Sinmun ("Jinso" instead of "Sinmun" - editors). This way of writing was followed by all publishers until the Japanese, feeling that the use of the native script was one of the pillars that upheld the Korean national feeling, began to use the Japanese script in all the literature they published for the Koreans, including all school textbooks.

- Korea Royal Refuge at the Russian Legation(A-kwan Pa-chun)

Soon after Dr. Jaisohn's arrival in Seoul the city was thrown into consternation by a report that the King, who had been kept practically as a prisoner in his palace, had escaped and taken refuge in the Russian Legation. Dr. Jaisohn feared there might be a disruption of the agreement he had with the cabinet because, of course, the old cabinet would be at once dismissed and a new group of politicians would be installed who might regard all agreements made by their predecesors as voided by the changed conditions. As a matter of fact, however, the new Minister of Foreign Affairs was a man of considerable vision and saw the advantage Dr. Jaisohn might be to the country and he at once assured the doctor that no change would be made and so the good work of educating the public in the art of good citizenship and good government went on. After nearly two years, in the latter part of 1898, he was able to see a change in the attitude of the people.

"They began to consider me as their champion and many sought my help when they were unjustly treated by the provincial officials. Adverse comments began to form against the encroachment of Russia on the rights of the nation and the character of men appointed to high places at the instigation of the pro-Russian crowd surrounding the King. These signs of awakening of the people seemed to worry the Russians and in the course of time their anxiety was shared by the King and his ministers. They all blamed me for the forming of public opinion and adverse criticism for official edicts affecting the interest of the nation. The officials gradually dropped out of the public lectures and debates and the Russians were cold toward me. Even some of the Americans thought I was unwise in making open criticisms of the Russian representatives and the actions of the King's closest friends. Dr. Allen, who succeeded Mr. Sill as the United States Minister to Korea, often cautioned me to be more diplomatic as he said that I could not Americanize Korea. If I persisted in my efforts, he said, I would not only fail but would also likely bring injury to my family and myself. He said the King was against me, the Russian Minister was against me, and the Japanese did not like my criticism of their high-handed policy toward Korea, Particularly the murder of the Queen and driving out Pak Young Hyo for not acting as their rubber stamp. While the Korean people generally seemed to have confidence in me and respected my motives they were powerless to give me either protection or help. He, therefore, advised me to return to America for the sake of my family. I told him I was not going to give up as there was no one to take my place after I had left."

However, the feeling against him on the part of the authorities became so strong that even the newspaper became taboo and the post office was ordered not to transmit it, and the people of Seoul became afraid to read it lest they be reported to the police. Under all the circumstances, he felt that he could not at that time serve the Korean people and after resigning his position as Adviser to the King, here turned to America with his family. At this time of writing, October, 1944 he is still living and practising his profession as a physician in Media, Pennsylvania.

Kim Ok Kyun

The actual leader of the Emeute was Kim Ok Kyun. He fled to Japan where he was followed by Hong Chong Oo who was sent by the King to bring Kim back to Korea alive or dead. Hong long sought an opportunity to carry out his task but Kim was wary and though the two men often fraternized as though they were friends a good chance for Kim's arrest or murder did not occur, It was less easy than one might think because Kim was really a political fugitive and was entitled, according to the law of nations, to the protection of whatever country he sought refuge in. It seems, from testimony given by his friend, Dr. Jaisohn, that by some means Hong gained Kim's confidence in him as a friend and when he invited the latter to go with him to Shanghai where he had some money transaction to attend to, telling him also that there was a plot of Japan to take Kim's life, Kim thoughtlessly accompanied him. Almost as soon as they had arrived Hong stabbed his unsuspecting friend to death while he was standing in the doorway of the hotel, obtained immediate passage on a boat bound for Pusan and took the body with him where, by the order of the King, so the story goes, the body was cut into eight pieces and one part sent to each of the eight provinces into which Korea was at that time divided. The story then says the pieces were paraded through the provinces to let people see what punishment came to a traitor.

Japan expressed its abhorrence at this but apparently most disturbed over the open violation of the law of nations which guarantees protection of a political fugitive who gain sits shores. This incident was one of several causes that led to the war between Japan and China shortly afterwards.

So Kim Ok Kyun paid for his good intentions toward his much loved Korea nine years after the frustrated attempt he had led in 1884. He was a true patriot, though rash and impatient in his desire to see his country take the place it was capable of taking in the forward march of the world.

General Yun and His Family

During a visit to his home shortly after I arrived in Korea, I was introduced to old General Yun who had been Minister of War many times and was one of the strongest supporters of the Korean King. He was the father of the Yun Chi Ho already referred to as a member of the Reform Party headed by Kim Ok Kyun.

I found him to be a very interesting character. He had had a checkered career and on at least two occasions when His Majesty's position had been imperilled by revolutionists, he had had to flee for his life because of his loyalty to his sovereign. In spite of his being Minister of War he was a soft spoken gentleman and I admired him immediately.

- Conversion of Gen. Yun's wife

Contrary to Korean custom, he brought his wife into the room and introduced her to us. Dr. Underwood and myself. She too had a fine personality and was quite at ease though, in accordance with Korean etiquette, she intruded herself into the conversation only very occasionally. We talked of their son, Chi Ho, who was then a refugee in China, and who had already professed himself a Christian, a fact which did not seem to disturb them at all. Mr. Underwood, who had introduced me to the family, talked of this religion, so new to them, and they listened with apparent interest. Not long afterwards Mrs. Yun professed her conversion and was baptized by Mr. Underwood who, though he was a Presbyterian, advised her to unite with the Southern Methodist Church because her son, who had been converted in China, had there joined that body.

- Sons of Gen. Yun

The General, following a very old Korean custom, had taken a second wife or concubine, who had borne him two sons who, at that time were boys of about five and six years. He was fond of them and proud of them as sons of his later years and dressed them as little army officers. Later on he often brought them to our home and no better behaved lads could be desired. Years afterwards one of those boys went to Scotland for a medical education and graduated as M. B. from the University of Glasgow. On his return to Korea he applied to me for a position on the staff of the Severance Union Medical College and was appointed as Assistant to Dr. J. W. Hirst, head of the department of Obstetrics and Gynecology. There he soon distinguished himself and when Dr. Hirst retired and returned to America, Yun succeeded him as Professor of those subjects as he possessed the essential requirements - Christian character, medical knowledge, surgical skill, and teaching ability. His success had abundantly justified the estimate the officers of the institution made of him and it was a satisfaction to me to entrust so much to one whom I had known when he was still a small boy.

- Yun, Tchi Ho

The estates of the Yun family were some distance south of the capital as were those of the majority of the men who were active in the government of the country. When Chi Ho, the eldest son of General Yun, was still young his father sent him to Japan to learn the English language and this gave him an eye-opening knowledge of how western countries were governed and he became quite democratic in his ideas. He was still in Japan when the treaty between Korea and America was signed, May 22, 1882, and when Lucius H. Foote, first United States Minister Plenipotentiary to Korea, arrived in Japan on his way to his post, young Yun was recommended to him as the best prepared Korean to be his interpreter, understanding as he did, all the three languages - Korean, Japanese and English. In that capacity he went back to his own country with the American Minister.

As already related Yun was connected with the Reform Party and after its failure to gain control of the government, he fled to Shanghai, China. (See story of the Emeute of 1884.)

When he reached China he fell in with Rev. Dr. Young, the president of the South China College for boys in Shanghai which was carried "on by the Mission of the American Methodist Episcopal Church South and soon became a student in that institution where the teaching was given through the English language, already partly familiar to him. During his stay in that school he became a Christian not only by profession but also as a sincere believer. He soon made his way to the head of his classes and, when he graduated, the Mission sent him to the United States for further study. He entered Vanderbilt University in Nashville, Tennessee, and after spending two years there, transferred to Emory University in Decatur, Georgia, where he graduated with the degree of B. A.

Returning to China, he became a teacher in the College in Shanghai. There he met and married a charming Chinese woman - a teacher in the Mission School for girls. Though she did not understand Korean she had studied English and as he could use both Chinese and English, they got along well in conversation and the marriage was a happy one. He remained in Shanghai till the war between Japan and China began. Then the Korean King, realizing he needed the counsel of just such young men as had taken part in the Emeute, recalled Yun and appointed him Vice-minister of Education. His wife accompanied him to Seoul and, since both of them understood English and were earnest Christians, they soon became friendly with the missionaries and it was then I just came to know him. Some of the missionaries feared that his position in the cabinet might detract from his Christian mode of life but they were mistaken. Paying strict attention to his government duties during six days of the week, he attended church faithfully on Sundays and often preached in the Korean churches. Though they naturally united with the Southern Methodist Episcopal Church in Seoul, they were never strong denominationalists.

He was soon advanced to be Minister of Education in which position his democratic faith and his penchant for reform asserted themselves. He became leader of the liberal group of his countrymen and when Dr. Jaisohn returned to Korea, Yun became a leading member of the Independence Club which Dr. Jaisohn had developed. When Dr. Jaisohn was forced out of Korea because of his intense campaign for reform, our Mr. Yun became President of the Club. For a time he carried on the little newspaper, the "Independence," and led the reform movement with much vigor. He lived with his Chinese wife in a small house on a hill outside the West Gate of the city that had been occupied by an American member of the group that had come to Seoul to build and operate the Street Railway which was jointly owned by the King and several Americans.

One day a company of Korean police visited the Yun home with orders to arrest him. The door was opened by Mrs. Yun who was told they wanted to deliver a message from the King to her husband. She asked them to wait while she called him. He was asleep in bed but she awakened him and told him of the coming of the police. He dressed quickly, climbed over the brick wall that surrounded the place and fled to the foreign settlement in the city while she conversed with the policemen and engaged their attention. The ruse succeeded for when the police became uneasy and pushed their way into the house their man had already gone and had reached a place of safety. From that time he remained in the foreign section and from there conducted his reform work. The constant interference of the police with the distribution of the little paper caused him to give up that aid to reform but he continued various other agencies.

In the course of time he ventured to go out in the city where he was always protected by a group of his sympathizers and, in lieu of the defunct paper he made speeches to great companies of people at the crossroads of the two main streets of the city. He explained the need for changes in th methods of government and urged them to join him in the movement for reform. Old General Yun, having again been appointed Minister of War, endeavored to disuade his son from his endeavors but with no avail. Young Yun's following rapidly increased and the place of meeting was changed to an open space near the new palace in Chong Dong. There I used to see him sitting at a table with a gravel in his hand which he used occasionally when someone in the crowd became noisy. One tap brought all into order again, thus showing the marvellous power he exerted over the thousands who gathered there.

These meetings were carried on continuously - 24 hours a day - with interchange of speakers and also, of course, of listeners, and the whole city was agog. The alarmed King called on the Peddlers' Guild to disperse the crowds of people and they came in full force from all part of the country but those attending the meetings drove them out of the city to the banks of the Han River nearly three miles away.[28]

It was rumored that the peddlers had secured arms and ammunition and intended to attack the reformers by force. While these preparations were going on, many refugees came to the hospital either sick or feigning sickness. A telegram was sent by the British Minister to every British home in the city directing all to pack their suitcases made be ready to take refuge at the legation if the disturbance should become more threatening. However, during the evening word was spread abroad that His Majesty would hold an audience on the street just outside the palace wall at which he would receive petitions from the two parties, each party presenting its ease in a written document which he would study and then announce a decision - for or against the reformers. This set everybody on the alert. What would he do, and how would it all end?

In preparation a throne was built just outside the palace gate and large tents were erected alongside, one of which next the throne was for all the foreign ministers, their wives and their staffs. By the hour set for the reception of the petitions the streets were packed with unlookers for such an event had not occurred within the memory of any living Korean. As physician to His Majesty I was admitted to the quarters prepared for the foreign representatives which was next the throne. The King was plainly visible and we could see all that happened.

The waiting seemed to be unreasonably prolonged as it generally does in such occasions. No seats were provided as it would have been disrespectful for any to sit in the presence of royalty. After the King had taken his place there was a stirring far down the line and then three men appeared - slowly and with marks of respect, making their way toward the throne. Who were they? First came Yun Chi Ho bearing the petition of the Progressives on a plate, Immediately behind him walked his two companions, Ye Won-Keung and Min Young Whan. Two of them, Yun and Ye, were notable Christian leaders and the third, Min, a non-Christian, was a high nobleman closely related to the Queen so that two out of the three were members of the higher class and the third, a Christian, was a member of the literati but not of a noble house. As they approached they showed the greatest respect to their king, who, stepping from his throne accepted the petition from Mr. Yun as he deeply bowing his head, offered it to His

---

28   See article elsewhere about this guild.

Majesty. They then retired to one side, and the King resumed his seat.

Then came three men representing the conservatives, Hong Chong Oo, the man who had killed Kim Ok Kyun in Shanghai, Kil Yung Soo and Ye Ke Dong, but, instead of walking, they were on hands and knees and in that posture they slowly neared the throne. His Majesty rose, and as before, accepted the paper they offered him. Then as the King resumed his throne, they retired, still creeping, It was a striking manifestation of the different attitudes of the two parties - one was respectful but manly, the other respectful but servile.

We had not long to wait for the King's decision. Apparently he had been previously made acquainted with the contents of both documents, for soon all the petitioners were recalled to hear his decision. He granted that of the reformers and advised those in opposition to return to their homes quietly. He then addressed the peddlers, who had been preparing to attack the reformers according to his own previous orders, and directed them to go back to their markets and refrain from any opposition to the new order that his decision provided for. That ended the episode, except that before retiring to the palace His Majesty gave audience to the assembled foreign representatives, including myself.

It looked like a great victory for the reformers but only time would tell whether it was a real victory or only one scene in a farce. Without asking my readers to wait and see, I will at once relieve their curiosity by saying it turned out to be the latter, because, of course, it still remained the privilege of the King to accept or refuse any or all of the propositions that the leaders might make. Flushed with success the reformers propounded reforms in many directions till the King and Queen, alarmed, began to seek ways of curbing them. Although all the plans proposed were for the betterment of the people, the overenthusiasm of those making them again caused them to go too fast for those who were not yet at all sure of the value of the changes or who were loath to yield privileges they had so long had that they were not more privileges but actual rights. As I said before, a longer period of education and the attaining of one reform at a time would probably have brought about more rapid advancement during a given number of years.

Pak Young Hyo

A fourth very important member of the group of early patriots who were involved in the Emeute of 1884 was Pak Young Hyo who, next to the occupants of the throne, was the highest noble in the little kingdom, being closely connected with Queen Dowager, Cho, relict of King Yi Chong Chul, who had adopted the youngest son of the Tai Won Kun when her husband died, in order that the Yi dynasty might continue.[29]

Pak is still living (in 1941) a retired life in Seoul. He was and is a real patriot. He always had high ideals for the betterment of his country so he joined heartily with the little group of reformers who, after Korea entered into treaty relations with the western powers, set themselves to free their land from the deadly grip of autocracy. When it failed he fled to Japan with Kim Ok Kyun, Suh Jai Pil, and others, but soon went to the United States with Suh and Soh Kwang Pom but did not stay there very long. Returning to Japan he continued to reside there until the invasion of Korea by the Japanese on their way to Manchuria to attack the Chinese in 1894. When the Japanese army had taken possession of the Korean palace the King recalled Pak along with others who had taken part in the Emeute, hoping they could help him retain his hold on the throne. In forming a new cabinet the King asked Pak to be its leader and to take the position of Minister of Home Affairs. Pak declined to take an official position but recommended the appointment of his close friend Ye. It was generally known that, while avoiding personal responsibility for the conduct of affairs, he could, through his influence on Ye, actually control the situation.

Ye was a Korean of the old type without any special knowledge of modern methods of government but willing to carry out the suggestions of the man to whom he owed his position. I got to know him quite well as I attended him from time to time as his physician and so had a fair opportunity to judge his lack of qualifications for such an important post.

Pak had the close friendship of the Queen whom he rightly regarded as the real ruler of the country. He hoped through her to carry out many of the ideas of government he had gained during his period of residence in America and Japan. While in Japan he had learned that the politicians there had a strong desire to gain control of Korea, in fact, to replace China as Korea's mentor and suzerain.

---

[29] Editor's note: Chong Chul actually refers to Chul Chong.

They foresaw the danger to Japan if either China or Russia should be in control of Korea. Japan needed Korea because of its value as provider of food to make up their lack and they also wanted the coal and many other minerals, which Korea could provide and they wanted it also as a buffer between those countries and their own comparatively small island country. He regarded the present partial subjugation of Korea and the war going on to break the dependence of Korea on China as but steps to gain complete control of the peninsula. All this information he communicated to the Queen and pointed out that one of the first steps that Japan would take after the war would be to get complete direction of Korea's school system so that the youth might be brought up to regard Japan as their guide and to accept dependence on Japan as their only safety. He told her that in his opinion the religion and culture of Japan were not suitable for Korea and that it would be a good thing for Korea to have at least one good educational institution of the type conducted in America or England in order to train at least some of its young people on different lines from those that would be followed in Japan-controlled schools. To this end he proposed that she establish a private college with her own funds in which to give education such as he had in mind to as many young men as circumstances would permit. As to the method by which such a school could be established, he recognized the fact that should it be known that it was being done at the instance of the Queen and as a national project, it would be suppressed by the Japanese even before it could be organized, so he suggested that the carrying out of the project and the money for it should be entrusted to one or more of the missionaries as a Mission Enterprise. After it was all completed and was in running order the real facts might be divulged at whatever time was deemed advisable. To this the Queen assented and the Prince at once consulted Rev. H. G. Underwood regarding the plan. Mr. Underwood consented to undertake it on condition that I be associated with him and that the Mission Board in New York, after being privily made acquainted with the facts, should agree to it. The Prince saw the wisdom of the suggestions and Mr. Underwood communicated with the New York Board and received its approval. Then we began to make plans for the buildings, the curriculums, and the teaching staff.

A site was selected on the slope of the hills north of Seoul and east of the palace, a locality favored by the Queen who could at any time look at the College as it carried on its work. But, alas, how could such a project be even dreamed of without its becoming known in a land of spies where every rock had ears, and every tree had eyes?

One day the Prince came to my home to ask me to relieve some tooth trouble.[30] He was to return in a few days to let me see the result of my work but did not come when he was expected. Indeed, he never came. Instead I received a note from him containing a liberal fee and saying he would be unable to see me again as circumstances required him to go at once to Japan. What had happened? We soon found that the Japanese had learned of the proposed College and, not desiring to come into open collision with the Queen, had told her that the Prince was conspiring to get rid of her and the king and place himself on the throne. Though this was not true her Majesty understood it as a veiled suggestion to her to get rid of the Prince.

Then they told Pak that the Queen, believing he had been conniving with certain persons to assassinate their Majesties, was looking for an opportunity to bring about his death and it would be wise for him to return at once to Japan where he could be protected.

So, willy nilly, he had to go and the whole idea of Queen's College fell to the ground.

Conclusion

This story of the Emeute of 1884 carries the story of three of the men far past the occurrence itself and relates some of the things they afterward did to turn the immediate failure of that effort into eventual success. The leader, Mr. Kim Ok Kyun, paid the penalty of death within a few years of the event but three others are still living in this year of our Lord 1944, sixty-eight years after that early attempt. Dr. Jaisohn never renewed his efforts to reform Korea except as opportunities came to him in America to help forward the same end. Prince Pak, now known as Marquis Pak, tried again later on to help in the saving of his country to an independent existence, the story of which will be told in due order. Mr. Yun Chi Ho lived a very adventurous life and his later efforts will also be related as these memoirs proceed.

---

[30]   No dentists had then reached Korea and doctors had to do the work dentists could have better done.

▸ Chapter 3 ◂

The China-Japan War and Syngman Rhee

The China-Japan War

In 1892 and 1893 disputes sprang up between Japan and Korea that led to the China-Japan War of 1894 and 1895.

Japan, finding herself unable to produce all the food needed for her population, had some time previously entered into a treaty with Korea by which the latter promised to sell to Japan every year a certain quantity of beans. This agreement, of course, was advantageous to both countries but there came a year when Korea, having a shortage in her crop of beans, felt she could not carry out the agreement without depriving her own people of needed food and so notified Japan. In spite of the limited crops in Korea, Japan threatened reprisals if the agreement was not carried out but the Korean government redeclared it to be impossible under the circumstances. This created much irritation and about the same time a second cause for Japan's displeasure occurred.

Japan having threatened retaliation on Korea because of its refusal to send beans to the former, the Korean king, in great fear, called on China for the assistance implied in that country's suzerainty though that was of a very limited type.

China and Japan had previously entered into a mutual agreement that neither country should send troops into Korea without notifying the other of its intention to do so but, on this occasion, China disregarded that agreement and, without any notice to Japan, sent a detachment to Korea in response to the king's request. Japan, therefore, had a quarrel with China as well as with Korea and ere long the China-Japan War was begun.

The story of the war is related in another section of these memoirs but is referred to here because most of it was fought in Korea and its aftermath completely changed the whole course of Korea's history and affected Rhee's after life.

Early in the war Japan's troops reached Seoul, the capital, and, in order to frighten the King into becoming their ally against China, seized the palace and demanded permission to pass freely through Korea to Manchuria where they expected to meet the main body of the Chinese forces.

Our home was on a hill from which we had a full view of the attack on the palace which, of course, lasted but a short time for the Koreans had neither armaments nor trained soldiers with which they could oppose the well-armed and well-trained attackers.

The king yielded to their demands but the queen, much more determined and subtle than he, did all she could to hinder their progress and in this she was supported by the king's father, the former regent, who was in all other respects her arch enemy as already related.

The Japanese promised to set Korea free from the suzerainty of China and guarantee her independence if their army was granted the right to pass through unopposed.

Finding the Queen obdurate they compelled the King to deprive her of all her rights as queen and reduce her to the rank of a common peasant woman.

The Japanese defeated China completely and, declaring the independence of Korea, raised it to the position of an Empire. All this looked very nice till their "friends" told them they would handle all Korea's foreign relations for her. Later on they also took over the management of her internal affairs so that she was independent in name only and her very limited dependence on China was changed to a very definite dependence on Japan which was very much disliked by all Koreans.

This introduced another grave issue for the would-be Korean reformers and interfered with their program for furthering democracy. They felt compelled to oppose the schemes of the Japanese to get complete control of Korea's affairs and at the same time they had to push on with their plans for governmental reform so that they were doubly menaced. The king regarded them as his enemies and the Japanese looked on them as their most dangerous opponents.

Our story must now deal with the relation of the reformers including Rhee, to their own king and government, leaving the story of the efforts of the Japanese to bring the people to accept their control to be told in another chapter except as it affected Mr. Rhee.

Yi Seung Man[31]

First President of the Republic of Korea.

When Dr. Georgiana Whiting arrived in Korea in 1895 to collaborate with the writer in the Royal Korean Hospital in Seoul, her first need was a language teacher and Yi Seung Man, a young student in the Methodist School for boys was selected for this duty. The son of a Korean scholar but a poor man he had, on the opening of Korea to foreigners, entered the M. E. Missionary School for Boys to learn English and whatever else the school offered that might help him to understand Western thought and fathom the designs of those who were thrusting themselves on his country. I say "fathom the designs" because the Oriental people very much mistrusted the motives of the Western politicians who had forced them to open their hitherto closed doors. The Missionaries too were under suspicion of having ulterior motives - they were inclined to regard them, also, as emissaries of their governments.

This distrust was not unreasonable. Had not the Hawaiian Islands been but recently absorbed by the United States after years of what seemed to Eastern observers to have been a process of undermining by the business men and missionaries who, when the time seemed ripe, had petitioned the American Government to annex them? And had not India suffered a like fate at the hands of the British? This fear of missionaries was felt by Rhee though he did not at first let me know it.

Rhee (as he now calls himself) kept all these misgivings to himself and, as far as we were concerned, seemed to be very friendly to us all. He came every day, outside of his school hours, to supervise Dr. Whiting's studies so he and I became very intimate for he was always eager to discuss with me the differences between Western forms of government and those that prevailed in Korea.

---

31   He now signs himself Syngman Rhee.

His own country's government was autocratic, the king's authority was absolute and, as he compared it with what I told him about the democracy of the United States and Great Britain and Canada, his mind became obsessed with a desire to work for such a change in the government of his own land which, it was plain, he dearly loved, In this love for Korea he differed in no respect from the rest of his fellow countrymen. At that time it was known to its people as Chosun "the land of the morning calm" and indeed, so far as its natural aspects were concerned, it was and is a land to beloved but its government was an autocracy as were the governments of most Oriental countries. Though the King had a cabinet of advisors they were appointed by himself and were subject to dismissal if they failed to please him or to provide him with all the funds he wanted so he had all authority in his own hands.

Such a system is good or bad according to the wisdom or lack of it in the reigning monarch. As this particular autocrat's physician I had opportunities of seeing many kind acts done at times to even the lowliest of his subjects and yet, one morning, I saw evidence of the danger any man was in if he were so unfortunate as to antagonize the king. As I was taking a stroll in the city that morning I was startled by seeing the decapitated heads of two men, each on a stick setup in the ground by the side of the street. The two men had been behead-ed during the night and their heads placed there to let the people realize what might happen to those who incurred the king's displeasure.

Nine years before Rhee came on the scene, treaties of trade and friendship had been forced on Korea by some of the Western nations, While most of the people had greatly disliked this disturbance of their customs by the outside "Barbarians," a small group of young men, sons of some of the highest nobles in the country had been trying to learn why foreign countries were so much stronger and richer than their own and they thus learned something of democracy.

Forgetting that a democracy requires an educated populace capable of understanding the principles of government they determined to act without any delay and so, in 1884, made the great mistake that many reformers make- that of acting precipitately instead of preparing both the ruler and the ruled by the preliminary process of education.[32]

On the failure of their first attempt the leaders fled to Japan, China and America but some seed had been sown. Mr. Rhee had come into contact with

---

[32]   For the details of this effort see the Chapter on The Emeute of 1884.

some of their followers and the idea of democracy for his own country had taken possession of his mind.

During one of these conversations he grew quite excited and told me he had decided to devote his life to helping change his country's form of government. I pointed out to him the dangers of such a course, showing him how in every country where men had attempted to change a long-established form of government too quickly it had resulted in blood-shed and often in the death of those engaged in it. When I asked whether he would be willing to face such an eventuality my question sobered him up for a bit but, after some reflection, he said he would be willing to undergo whatever might come to him in the pursuit of so great an objective. His after history showed that he was, indeed, in earnest, for he remained faithful to his ideal during years of the most severe trials, the keenest sufferings and the threat of death.

However, in actual life we not infrequently find our highest ideals at least temporarily forced into the background by unexpected occurrences of a grave nature and this became true in the experience of Mr. Rhee.

• The Ordinance Prohibiting Topknots

Soon after the end of the war the queen was restored to her former position and privileges and became an Empress instead of a Queen and that was probably not a help to the reformers.

The Japanese met with many difficulties in their efforts to bring the people to accept their rule. Looking around for ways in which to break down this stubbornness they realized that the Korean custom of men wearing their hair in the form of a topknot was closely associated with their nationalistic feelings. In the long age the Koreans had not worn topknots but the Chinese, at the end of a victorious war against them, ordered them to assume this form of hairdressing as a sign of their submission. Though at first a mark of degradation as time passed they came to think of it as a special symbol of their nationality and so it became very precious to them. A similar thing had occurred in China. When the Manchurians conquered China they ordered the men to wear the queue as a sign of their subjection and, after a long time, the Chinese had come to regard it as a symbol of their nationality and so clung to it in spite of its shameful origin and it was just the same with Koreans and their top-knots.

The Japanese, realizing that the Koreans regarded their topknots in that way and that as long as they wore them they would remain Korean at heart, ordered all the men to cut them off and dress their hair in the Western style.

The Korean men did not openly refuse to do this - they just ignored the order. Those living within the walls of the capital could be easily dealt with. But how were the police to enforce the order all over the country and especially amongst the farming population which constituted more than 80% of the people?

Policemen and soldiers were stationed at the city gates, each armed with a pair of long scissors kept concealed until they were to be used. The countrymen coming into the city were allowed to enter without being disturbed but every man going out had his hat pulled off and, if he still had his topknot, out came the scissors and off came the topknot.

When orders for all the city people to get rid of their topknots were promulgated even those within the palace were not to be excused. I was in attendance in the palace almost daily at that time and every day his Majesty anxiously asked if I knew when the order was to be enforced. Of course I did not know but one day, as I was leaving the palace, he told me not to come the next day but to come again the day after and, as I looked into his white face, I knew that tomorrow was to be the dreaded day, the day on which he was to be subjected to the greatest indignity that could be put on him.

When I entered the palace on the second day, as requested, I found a very sad-looking group and as I walked through the anteroom to His Majesty's apartment I could see he was watching me with a greater interest than usual. After greeting me he said, "Your hair looks all right, who cuts it for you?" Then he ordered one of his attendants to be called and as the man entered he directed him to remove his hat, saying to me, "Look, they have made us all into Buddhist priests." This was the lowest epithet he could use because for a period of more than three hundred years Buddhist priests had been regarded as the most degraded of all the people and had not been allowed even to enter the capital and, as everyone knows, they were marked by closely shaven heads.[33]

The sight of the attendant's hair would have been laughable had the matter been less serious. His topknot had been snipped off and the remaining hair left straggling. This enforced hair cutting added a quite unnecessary indignity to the enmity already engendered by various other acts of the Japanese.

---

[33]   See detailed account of this in another chapter.

You will wonder why the Buddhist priests had fallen into such disgrace in a country which had formerly held them in the highest esteem. The story is as follows:

Some 300 years ago Japan, which had long wished to conquer Korea, decided the time had come to do it. To make it easier she sent spies to learn about their defences and, knowing the esteem in which Buddhism - as it was practised in Korea - was hold, sent them disguised as priests.

The visitors were hospitably received and entertained as guests of the king. They lived at the capital and were given access to every part of both city and country as they professed a desire to study Buddhism as practised in Korea. But later on it turned out that they were not priests but officers of the Japanese army whose business was to learn all about the defence of the capital and prepare the way for an easy capture of the city when the army should arrive. From that time Buddhist priests were taboo at the capital. They were forbidden over again to enter its gates and became, to the Koreans, the most despised of all people so that when the Emperor spoke of being made into a Buddhist priest by the cutting of his hair he was using the most contemptuous term he knew. As a matter of fact, the order for their debarment from the capital still held good when I reached Korea in 1893, three hundred years later. Though sick priests did at times come from outside the city to the dispensary they always came disguised and the above story was told me to explain why this was necessary.

Returning now to modern times, during the progress of the China-Japan war and for sometime afterwards the members of the reform party were too much concerned with the danger of the complete loss of their country to push their own ideas of government very strongly but they did not forget and in time began again to promote their views as opportunity offered, though in doing so they faced a double hazard for they were as much opposed to Japanese rule as they were to the autocracy of their own king, as already mentioned.

One Sunday afternoon, soon after the cutting of the king's hair, Rhee called at my home and surprised me by asking me to cut off his topknot. "Why?" I said, "Do you really want it off?" "Of course not," he answered, "but, as it has to be done, I want it done by a friend and not by one who will take pleasure in doing it." We went to the dispensary where I cut it off in one piece, and, laying it on the table, trimmed off the remaining hair with whatever skill I possessed which was not much but, to say the least, I did a better job than had been done on his Majesty.

When I had finished, Rhee took up the topknot, wrapped it in a piece of gauze, and, while the tears ran down his cheeks, said he would take it home to his mother. Of course, why not? She had given it to him as a sign of his coming manhood and marriage and had, by so doing, made him into a full-fledged citizen of his country. At that moment, more fully than before, I understood the sentiment wrapped up in that little bunch of hair and realized to some degree the depth of the antipathy that Korean felt for their Japanese masters.

From my personal contacts with the Emperor I knew him to be a man of good heart, with the welfare of his people much in mind and I think if he had been left to himself he would have yielded to the demands of the reformers but the many officials and nobles and all others who were dependent on the royal treasuries knew such a change would be a menace to their privileges and it was easy for them to use the police in their efforts to prevent the success of Rhee and his friends.

·   Imprisonment of Mr. Rhee

One afternoon Mr. Rhee and my own language teacher of the same name came hurriedly to my home saying they had heard a notice was being posted asking for the arrest of a Mr. Rhee, a teacher of one of the missionaries. Neither of them waited to learn particulars but, as both answered to the description, both came to us for at least temporary protection. During the afternoon word was received from their friends that it was the younger man, the subject of this story, who was wanted and so my teacher returned to his home.

They came to us for protection because of the system of extraterritoriality then in force which precluded the property of a foreigner from being entered by a Korean or Japanese policeman without the written permission of the Minister representing that foreigner's country. They knew they would be safe with us at least until the machinery of the law could be set to work and that might take considerable time. Of course, under the circumstances, we could not refuse to shelter them for they were our friends and, from our point of view, were not criminals.

However, as we could not expect to keep Rhee in our home very long, we had to consider what steps to take for his safety, In conference with him it was decided that he should go far into country to stay with some friends. So we dressed him up as a Korean woman, borrowing necessary clothing from our Korean amah, called a woman's sedan chair and, before day break, sent him out of the city with the strict injunction to stay away long enough to let things blow over. Of course we made no enquiry as to where he was going as it was better that we should be ignorant of his whereabouts.

Men like Rhee, however, are not easily kept down and, within two weeks, he returned to Seoul and even ventured to call at our home. We scolded him but without avail - his whole soul was in the movement.

Within a short time he was arrested and jailed but managed to escape. In some way he had obtained a revolver and, when the police attempted to rearrest him, threatened them with it. They overcame him and soon had him in prison again and this time the charge against him was the serious one of having attempted to shoot a policeman. He was speedily tried, condemned to death and put in the death cell to await execution.

Day after day passed without the order for his execution corning and every day he was put in the stocks in an effort to break his spirit. Stocks are now a thing of the past in all civilized countries but at one time even in England and America they were frequently used. If you have read the story of the Pilgrims in Massachusetts or of Bunyan in England you will remember that Bunyan in England and the supposed witches in New England were put into the stocks in an effort to get them to recant or confess.

One can see that unruly prisoners might be quickly reduced to submission by the use of these contraptions but although Rhee was placed in the stocks every day for as many hours as he could endure it without fainting he remained uncowed - even this did not make him swerve from his life's purpose.

One day a request came to me through a confidential messenger to send him an English Bible and this was soon afterwards followed by a request for a dictionary. At this point I will let Rhee relate what followed just as I heard him tell it in several American churches.

• Mr. Rhee's Story of His Imprisonment

"Soon after the American missionaries began coming to Korea, we Koreans learned how, long years before, missionaries had gone to the Hawaiian Islands and that large numbers of the natives had accepted the Christian faith. The missionaries were soon followed by American business men who grew rich trading with the natives though the natives themselves were not much profited.

Then, a short time before the missionaries first came to Korea, we learned that the American government had, at the request of the Americans in Hawaii, annexed all these islands and made them a part of its territorial possessions and this, of course, necessitated the abdication of their queen. We Koreans naturally thought that a similar fate was planned for our country. Had not America forced Japan and China and Korea to open their doors to foreign trade and was not that soon followed by the corning of missionaries and had we not reason to think as we did? We could not help regarding the missionaries as agents of the American Government to prepare the way for future annexation.

At that time I was a very young man, I had received the usual education in the Chinese Classics but this did not prepare me to understand the ways of the West or the workings of the foreign mind and, as there had been developed in me a strong distrust of the missionaries and a hatred for their religion and for everything foreign, I decided to go to Seoul and enter amission school, there to learn all that might enable me to discover the secret of the Westerners' power and at the same time find out just what the missionaries had in mind in corning to our country and opening schools for the children and young people.

As I needed money to do this I accepted a position as language teacher to one of the missionaries and this brought me into close contact not only with the lady whom I was teaching but also with Dr. Avison and many of his fellow-workers, I was surprised to find in them only apparent goodwill to our people but still I continued to distrust them, thinking this seeming good will might be only a pretense in view what I had believed was their real motive in coming to our country.

In Seoul I soon fell in with a group of young men of my own country who were endeavoring to introduce a new form of government. They were being led by a rather young man of high station, the son of the Minister of War, who had had a minor part in the disturbance of 1884 and had left the country when that effort failed. He had studied with missionaries in China and had graduated at an American University in the U. S. A. During the China-Japan war he had been recalled to his homeland and given a position in the government. While in China he had become a Christian and was not only a firm believer in the good intentions of the missionaries but stronger than ever in favor of a constitutional form of government though he hoped this time to bring it about without bloodshed by educating the people and at the same time favorably influencing his Majesty and the members of his Cabinet.

I decided to cast-in my lot with this group. While we felt bound to work for the abolition of the autocracy that Korea, along with other Oriental countries, had been under for ages, we were at the same time opposed to domination by the Japanese who were trying to absorb our country after defeating China. So we found ourselves in a very difficult situation, being under the enmity not only of the conservatives in Korea, but of the Japanese also. It was not long, therefore, before many of us found ourselves in jail with dark days ahead of us and perhaps death. But during all those hard days I knew myself to be in good company for amongst us were some of the best minds in Korea. Some members of our group had become Christians but along with many others I still clung to my old religious beliefs and to my distrust of the missionary body though my contact with many of them had, in spite of myself, forced me to believe in their sincerity and, in the case of Dr. Avison, a real love had developed between us. When it became impossible to avoid the loss of my topknot I begged Dr. Avison to cut it off - it was too precious to permit it to be done by someone who I know would be happy in doing it. Later when an order for my arrest came out, I went to his home for temporary protection and he sent me to a safe place in the country. Within a short time, however, I returned to Seoul because I could not be happy away from my comrades. I was soon arrested and jailed as a traitor. I managed to escape, and getting possession of a revolver I threatened the policemen who were trying to arrest me. For this, together with my efforts at reform, I was sentenced to execution by beheading and was put into the worst of all the bad cells into which all prisoners condemned to death are committed. The cell was not more than 7 feet square, and was very dark and dirty and poorly ventilated. For some reason the order for my execution was delayed from day today but I could only live in expectation that the next day might be my last. Each day I was put in the stocks for as many hours as I could bear it.

I had not the solace that a good book might have given me, so I sent to Dr. Avison for an English Bible and a dictionary, thinking these at least might be allowed, I read the Bible whenever I was alone in my cell and, though it had not meant anything to me when I was in the mission school, it now had a deep interest for me. One day I remembered how one of the teachers in the school had said if we would pray to God He would hear our prayers and answer them so, there in my cell, I prayed to God for the first time in my life and said,' o, God, save my soul ; o, God, save my country I Immediately my cell seemed to be filled with light, a joyful peace came to my mind and I was a changed man. The hatred I had felt for the missionaries and their religion and all my distrust of them passed away. I knew they had come to give us what they themselves valued highly.

In my joy I told the jailer about my experience and when his brother came to the jail, as he often did, the jailer told him about it, and said I had been a different man ever since. Both these men were converted as a result of the change in me. My life in the jail became very different for I was given a better cell and they stopped putting me in the stocks. The jailer gave me permission to start a school for days in the jail for, sad to say, there were many young boys there. He allowed me to write to my missionary friends asking them to send me a copy of every publication in the Korean language they had in the Tract Society and these were eagerly read by the prisoners who had nothing else to divert their attention. The jailor's brother began to study for the ministry. Later on he went to America for further study and then returned to Korea to give the gospel to his fellow countrymen. I was soon happy to find many of the prisoners professing their faith in Christ and I became glad and contented. Life had a new meaning for me.

The cholera epidemic which was then rampant in the city invaded the jail and it is impossible to describe the horror of the conditions there, I gave up all my time to waiting on the sick, most of whom died, however, and, at my request, Dr. Avison came to the prison and left with me the medicine to be administered. The epidemic passed away after several weeks and I was indeed thankful to have been spared and enabled to be useful as there was so much to be done to comfort and help the others."

I now resume the story where I left off. There were many men of prominence in the jail as political prisoners, most of whom were as strongly opposed to Christianity as Rhee had been but the occurrences just related and the great change in Mr. Rhee induced them to read the Bible with amore sympathetic mind and many of them were converted. After their release these joined one or other of the churches and became active cooperators in the missionary work.

Amongst these was Yi Sang Chai, the most noted Korean student of the Chinese Classics of his time, whose story will be told in another part of these memoirs.

I am thinking now of one of the prisoners, Kim Chung Sik, who after his release, became the first Korean General Secretary of the Seoul Y. M. C. A. and is now retired and living quietly in Seoul where he still serves as an Elder in one of the largest Presbyterian Churches there.

- Mr. Rhee's Visit to America

Rhee was in prison seven years, 1897 to 1904, and after his discharge August 9, 1904, the question of what he should do was discussed very seriously by his friends because his zeal for Korea's reformation was still manifest and it was feared he would get into trouble again if he would remain in the country. All united in an urgent plea to him to go at once to America for further study which might enable him to do even more effective work.

He was loath to do this but, in the end, consented though he insisted on taking his son with him. Unfortunately the boy before long succumbed to an attack of diphtheria in America.

It meant, however, another long separation from his wife and family immediately after a seven year break in his home life while in prison and also a separation from his aged parents whom he would probably never see again. Those hardships were among the many of which I had warned him, away back in 1894, if he persisted in carrying out his purpose to devote his life to the reformation of the government of his country. He left Seoul November 4, 1904, carrying with him eighteen letters of introduction. That of Rev. Dr. J. S. Gale will serve to show the esteem in which Mr. Rhee was held by the foreign group in Korea. The affection of his own countrymen was shown by the honors they bestowed on him in after years.

Dr. Gale's Letter

To Christian Friends in Washington, D. C. and Other Parts of America;

This will introduce to the reader Mr. S. M. Lee (or Rhee) a Korean born in Seoul in 1875. He was well educated according to the old methods of Chinese scholarship but, early feeling the insufficiency of this for the present age of the world, he bent his energies to the study of English and other branches that lay open to him through the Chinese. He believed in the independence of his country and not only that Korean should be independent but that the Korean people should awaken from their torpor and think and live. He started a daily paper, the Mai II Shin Mun (Daily News) first and later the Chay Kook Shin Mun (the Empire Newspaper)which contained translations from English and in them he preached his ideas of liberty. This was contrary to the ideas of the conservative government and they had Mr. Lee arrested in September 1897 and for seven years he lay in prison.

For seven months he wore a wooden collar weighing twenty pounds or more and during this time, to add to his agony, he sat with both his feet in stocks. He saw his companions taken out, beaten, tortured, hanged and beheaded. He knows all the sensations that go with the heavy thud of the sabres on the execution ground which fate he fully expected for his own. More than once the morning papers announced, ' It is reported that S. M. Lee was beheaded in the night.' He walked too in the coolie gang with a heavy iron chain fastened over his shoulders and padlocked at the back- all because he claimed the right of popular assembly where he and his companions might meet for debate, conference, and mutual improvement.

He heard the gospel before going to prison but only in his agony and loneliness did he learn to trust. He performed that most difficult of all acts for mankind, namely, he renounced himself and gave his heart to God, and then set to work to see his fellow prisoners saved. He had a library started in prison, a library of Chinese publications from Shanghai, and work went on.

Among those converted through Mr. Rhee's efforts were Mr. Yee Sang Jai, secretary to the first Legation to Washington; Mr. Yee Wun Cung, one of the most noted scholars in Korea, specially mentioned in literary work of the last century; and Mr. Kim Chung Sik, who was at the head of the Police in 1896. There are many others, some forty in all, who have been touched by his persistent efforts.

He was tried and sentenced to life imprisonment at hard labor and 100 blows and last summer (1904) on August 9, he was pardoned and set free. He can tell a wonderful tale, all true to life, of the sorrows of the yellow man. May he find many good friends among his white brethren in the free land of America and, during the three years that he proposes to spend there in study, observation and writing, may he be cheered and helped and be sent back to do a great work for his people.

He is altogether worthy of friends for he is a gentleman born, a scholar and a Christian whom God has used.

Jas S. Gale,

Presbyterian Missionary in Korea   Author of "The Vanguard"
Seoul, November 2nd, 1904 (A pamphlet accompanied)

As an instance of how his countrymen regarded him I quote from the record of his journal "On reaching Pusan I dined with the Governor of the Province." That was less than three months after his release from jail and was a mark of the honor in which he was held even then.

On reaching Kobe, Japan, he was joined by the brother of his former jailer, Yi Choon Hyuk (American name Howard Leigh), who had become a Christian under Rhee's teaching while in the prison, as already stated, and who, after completing his theological studies in Seoul, was on his way to supplement these in an American College.

On reaching Honolulu, November 29th, many Koreans who had received word of his coming met the ship and escorted him to a meeting in the Korean Church. During his short stay in that city, he spoke several times to Korean groups. Leaving Honolulu the same evening, he reached San Francisco December 6. It is interesting to note a statement in his diary saying a double room for himself and friend at a Japanese hotel cost them 80 cents and food cost from 10 cents a meal upwards. They were evidently avoiding extravagance.

They left the city of San Francisco, December 16, and his notes say "Mr. Vail bought our tickets to New York via Chicago at half rate." He arrived in Washington D. C. December 31 and the same evening presented his letter of introduction to the Rev. Dr. Hamlin.

This evidence of his forthrightness was seen in all his acts - if a thing was to be done he wasted no time in getting it done.

The next day being Sunday he attended morning service at Dr. Hamlin's church, lunched at the pastor's house, took his evening meal at the Korean Legation and attended church again in the evening.

On April 23 he received Baptism at the hands of Dr. Hamlin in the Church of the Covenant, that rite having been deferred until it could be done in America. His foreign friends in Korea had advised this so he could feel free to choose, without any pressure from his associates, with what denomination he would prefer to unite.

Though he was thus baptized a Presbyterian he ultimately united with the M. E. Church when he accepted an appointment by that body to take charge of the educational work for Koreans in Hawaii which had, by mutual agreement between the Mission Boards in America, been turned over to the M. E. Church. But this took place after he had completed his studies in the U. S. A.

- Granted a Ph. D. Degree

During his stay in America he attended the George Washington University from which he received the B. A. degree June 5, 1907.

My family and I (the writer of this memoirs) were in America on furlough in 1908 and it was a delight to me to meet him again and have him speak on the same platform with me. During the same year he also accompanied Dr. Underwood and Mr. H. B. Hulbert on speaking tours.

It seems strange that we three, Underwood, Hulbert and I, who together spent the night with the King of Korea when friends of the Queen were trying to break the hold the pro-Japanese Cabinet had gained over the government, should be the ones to have his help in our speaking engagements that year when we were addressing audiences all over America. Having obtained his B. A. degree, as already mentioned, he took up further studies at Harvard University where he obtained the M. A. degree in 1910.

Later he received the Ph. D. degree from Princeton University the subject of his thesis being "Neutrality as Introduced by the United States."

His scholastic success in America in only six years after he was released from prison in Korea, during which time he also earned his support by lecturing in churches and on public platforms, gave clear evidence of the complete equality of the brain power of the Korean people with that of white and other colored folks and showed that their misfortunes and failure to win their way to recognition among the nations was due to causes other than mental inferiority. After receiving his Ph. D. degree he visited his native land where his friends kept a close supervision over him to prevent him from again getting into political trouble. As one part of this endeavor as well as because he was fitted for the part, the Korean Methodist Church elected him as a Korean lay delegate to the General Conference to be held in Minneapolis, Minn.

While he had been a student at Princeton he had won the friendship of President Woodrow Wilson and his family and his diary refers frequently to his visits at their home in the years that followed his return from what proved to be his last visit to his homeland.

As one reads his notes of those days, to which I have had full access, one is struck with his rapid journeyings to and from his efforts to arouse the sympathy of the American people for Korea.

Returning to Hawaii he travelled many times during the next five years, all over the Hawaiian Islands in the performance of his duties.

- Provisional President of the Republic of Korea

When the World War was in progress and the Allies announced a program for giving the small nations an opportunity for an undisturbed national life the Koreans believed their political independence would be restored when the victory, which they fully expected, would have destroyed the power of the autocrats and established democracy. In preparation for that event, they set about organizing the Republic of Korea. Of course, it could only be on paper then, but they prepared a proclamation, named a President and Cabinet and got everything ready for action as soon as the war should end. And who was named President? Who but Rhee Seung Man? Had he not really given his life for the establishment of democracy in Korea? It was a great honor his countryman planned to bestow on him but he had earned their esteem and love and confidence.

When I heard of it I rejoiced with him and my thoughts went back to the conversations we had had more than twenty years before when he told me he was ready to give his life for the establishment of a freer form of government in his country and I had warned him that such a course was likely to lead him along a thorny road that might indeed cost him his life. He had then replied that he would accept whatever suffering it might bring, and even death itself if it would secure liberty and happiness to the people. The road had certainly been thorny and death had been at his heels all the way but success was now in sight.

- Paris Peace Conference

Of course all this had to be done secretly and much of it by correspondence for many of the patriots were living abroad. It was arranged that the President-elect and certain others should go to Paris to present Korea's cause to those who would have the responsibility for making the terms of peace and carrying out the promises that had been made to the small nations.

Suddenly, and without any preliminary explanation, I find in his notes, January 6, 1919, "I left Honolulu at 6 P. Mon the S. S. Enterprise." We are left to guess where and on what business. Farther on his notes say, "Jan. 12 ; Wired Ahn Chang Ho." One has only to put together the dates, his hurried departure from Honolulu and his wireless to Mr. Ahn, another earnest patriot who had been a refugee in China and America, to conclude that "The Republic of Korea" was about to make an appeal to the group working at Versailles on the Treaty of

Peace to give Korea its freedom from Japanese domination. This, in fact, was so. Dr. Rhee and Mr. Ahn hoped to go to Paris to join Mr. Kim Kyu Sik, a Korean patriot nationalized in China, in making Korea's plea. This proposed journey to Paris called for passports from the American Government which felt it could not grant the passports because these two men, though they had spent years in the U. S. A., had not become naturalized citizens.

Thus thwarted they could do no more than write earnest pleas to President Wilson to listen sympathetically to the pleadings and arguments of Mr. Kim who had actually arrived in Paris from China.

Rhee and Ahn, accompanied by other Koreans, went to New York to attend a conference of the representatives of other small subject nations which, like Korea, were anxiously looking to Versailles for freedom, It is not necessary to tell of all the many efforts that Rhee made to get to Paris, of his visits to American government officials, of a cable to Lloyd George in England, etc. until, at last, I find the following brief sentence, "April 10, then I dropped it." Bravely and conscientiously he had done all he could, but without avail.

Only Kim Kyu Sik was at Versailles when the Treaty of Peace was being discussed. He stayed there and worked until it was signed and all hope for Korea's independence had been shattered. The Koreans had put much trust in the statement of Dr. Rhee's friend, President Wilson, whom he had found to be very favorable to Korea's claims, but in the end, Wilson had to tell them that the situation had turned out to be a much more tangled one than he had expected it to be as so many countries were involved and so many divergent interests of those who had fought in the war were discovered that a solution, such as he had envisaged, had become impossible of achievement. In the case of Korea, for instance, the wishes of Japan had to be considered. Japan was determined not to give up Korea, which was her connecting link with Manchuria and China, and as all the other parties to the war were very much averse to doing anything that might bring on any more trouble, Korea had to be sacrificed.

For many years the Koreans kept representatives in Washington always hoping that something would happen to open a way by which they might regain control of their own land but, in the end, Dr. Rhee returned to Honolulu.

•   Mr. Chang Ho Ahn

In the meantime Mr. Ahn sailed for Shanghai, leaving his family in Los Angeles where they are still living, or were in 1931 when Mrs. Avison and I met them there as we were on our way to New York.

Ahn had received most of his education in the Presbyterian Mission High School in Seoul where I had known him well - a devoted Christian, a genuine patriot and one of the most effective speakers I have ever listened to. He continued his activities in Shanghai for many years and many of his compatriots regarded him as the real leader of the Korean people. This eventually led to a breach in the cordial relations that had existed between him and Rhee.

In June 1920 Rhee again went to Honolulu en route to Shanghai to confer with the Koreans there as to the next step to be taken in behalf of the independence of the Republic of Korea. In China he met Kim Kyu Sik who had been Korea's only representative at Versailles and had just recently returned from there.

Dr. Rhee's visit to China seems to have been an outcome of the lack of harmony between him and Mr. Ahn, already mentioned. Many of the Koreans in China having supported Ahn to represent Korea as, against Rhee, the original representative of the signers to the Korean Declaration of Independence, Rhee was trying to heal the breach so that all could again united. The China group asked Rhee to resign the Presidency which he was willing to do provided his successor could be immediately and legally elected and assured of support. Apparently this could not be satisfactorily adjusted and Rhee returned to America.

A few years later Ahn was arrested in China by Japanese police who had been long on his trail but had hitherto been unable to take him because of international relations. He was brought back to Korea and, after trial in a Japanese court, was declared guilty of treason and sentenced to several years in jail. On his release he came to see me at the hospital in Seoul and say good bye as one of the conditions of his release compelled him to leave the Capital and live in the country. He did not live long after that but his name is one of the most revered of all Korean patriots.

- Petition to the League of Nations

Going back now to Dr. Rhee, a note in his diary says, "The Korean Commission was known in Washington as the Korean Legation," indicating that the Republic of Korea had set up a Commission in Washington with Rhee as its head and that this was recognized by this government of the U. S. A.

Dr. Rhee, accompanied by Dr. Philip Jaisohn (Suh Jai Pil of the Emeute of 1884) and Mr. H. B. Hulbert, engaged in a speaking tour throughout the U. S. A. with the object of acquainting the American people of their government's breach of faith with Korea when President Theodore Roosevelt suggested that the Treaty of Portsmouth recognize the seizure of Korea by Japan in spite of the fact that in making the Treaty of Trade and Friendship with Korea, the U. S. A. promised to uphold its independence against any power that should attempt to violate it.

The years until 1932 were spent by Rhee in travelling back and forth to keep the fires of patriotism burning and then plans were made to go to Geneva to plead with the League of Nations to champion Korea's cause.

Although in 1919 the American Government had declared its inability to provide Rhee with a passport for travel to Versailles, the government in the meantime changed its attitude in regard to this and now issued what was practically a diplomatic passport. This was the first of its kind this government had ever issued but it was visad by all the other legations. Although he got to Geneva and was well received individually by the representatives of the several nations, he was unable to get any action because all seemed unwilling to disturb their relations with Japan in view of the many difficult international problems the League was facing at that time. To this question will probably remain as it is until that indefinite time when Japan may be reduced to such a state of military disability that Korea can with safety be detached from her and once more become a free land.[34]

•   Great Man, Dr. Syng Man Rhee

Rhee returned to Honolulu and again took up the school work he had been carrying on there.

Some time ago I received from a Korean friend in Hawaii an account of the erection in Honolulu of a new and much enlarged Korean church which is named in honor of Dr. Rhee to let him know that the people amongst whom he

[34] The present war(1944) may make this possible - indeed that seems now (August 1944) to the one of the certainties as the several countries have already stated that Korea's independence will become a fact at the end of the war.

spent so many of his later years love him and honor him for all he did and tried to do for the advancement of his nation and wha the is still doing for the education of Korean children and youth in Hawaii.

In the spring of 1939, I learned he was again in Washington and in late April, when he visited New York for a short time, I had the privilege of spending a few hours with him. He was then 64 years of age. Time had dealt mercifully with him for he had but few gray hairs and his mind was as active as ever.

On one of our furlough trips to America my wife and I had called on him at Honolulu and, going to his school, we sent in a message that friends wished to see him. When he saw us he ran to me, threw his arms around my neck and wept for joy as though I were his elder brother. I, too, was deeply affected as I remembered the past years, beginning with such deep hatred of those who he believed had gone to Korea to take away his country.

Now no more hatred but the deepest affection, no more anti-Christianity but a heartful of religious soul, no more narrow nationalism such as is yet keeping the people of the world apart and fostering wars and rumors of wars; still a loyal Korean but looking upon all men as brothers. This is no doubt what Christ meant when he told his disciples to go into all the world and teach the nations what he had taught them when, in the Synagogue at Nasareth, he set forth the program for his life's work - goodwill, and loving deeds, two forces that will ultimately bring all men into a loving fellowship.

A man is great, not only when he has succeeded in accomplishing the thing he aimed at, but also when, in spite of all obstacles, he has held to high aims even through suffering and in face of threatened death.

Rhee Seung Man was and is a great man - one of the coterie of great men Korea has produced.

Chapter 4

Tragedy in Ul-mi Year(1895) and an Incident of Choonsaeng Gate

Increase in the Power of Japanese after the China-Japan War

The China-Japan war, fought in 1894-95, destroyed the last vestige of China's claim to suzerainty over Korea which thus became an independent sovereign state, but during the process the Korean royal family suffered much. Though the King and Queen feared the Japanese and realized the Japan's war with China was but a preliminary to the seizure of Korea the timid and peace-loving King was inclined to follow the easy way of submission but his Queen, endowed with the first spirit of her family, used all her native strategy and stubbornness to oppose each step of their program. Realizing that she was to be their greatest problem, they ordered the King to deprive her of all right to interfere in governmental matters. Though he unwillingly did this she still found ways of exercising her influence through her rich and powerful relatives. They then compelled him to deprive her of all the rights and privileges of her position as Queen by reducing her to the rank of an ordinary peasant and practically making her a prisoner in her home. To get rid of her relatives in the country they brought about the banishment to China of all the chief men of the Mins.

The King was kept on the throne merely as an agent forgetting their orders out to the people through the only one whose authority all Koreans would recognize. When their war with China ended victoriously the Japanese declared the complete independence of Korea which thus became an Empire and its ruler an Emperor. This was in accordance with Oriental custom where the titles of King and Kingdom distinguish a state of at least partial vassalage while Emperor and Empire were used to designate the ruler and country heaving complete sovereignty. One of the first acts of the Emperor was to restore the former Queen at her full rank and she became the Empress.

This change to Empire status necessitated a change of color from red (the color for a kingdom) to yellow (the color for an Empire), not only of the clothing of the Emperor and Empress but also of the whole paraphernalia of, the court. But neither the change in color nor in status changed in any way the natural dispositions of the heads of the Empire. The Emperor had the same neutral characteristics of the late King- he was still a follower rather than a leader; the Empress was still as impetuous and determined as before and it was not long before she began to resume her former place of influence. One by one, her exiled relatives quietly returned and received reappointment to positions in the government where they could again take part in shaping the destiny of their country.

The Japanese saw all this with alarm. Though they had nominally restored the country's independence they had told the Emperor he must take their advice in all his dealings with foreign powers - in fact, they had kept to themselves the right to handle all the foreign relations of the country, thus restoring independence with one hand, taking it away with the other. The Empress, of course, could not oppose these schemes directly but she did use every indirect method her fertile mind could devise to put obstacles in the way of their accomplishment.

An onlooker was reminded of how troublesome a little mosquito can be to a big man till at length he determines to do away with the mosquito so he can with greater ease carry out the work he has in hand. So at last this big man who had in mind the ultimate absorption of Korea resolved to get rid of the little Empress who was hindering his plan by her continual pecking. A new ambassador, Count Miura was sent to represent Japan in Korea and completely enforce the purposes of his country, even though it involved the killing of the empress. Knowing of the long-standing enmity between her and the former regent, her father-in-law, he decided to use this as a means for the accomplishment of his purpose.

By careful management he established friendly relations with the Tai Won Kun and then suggested to him that they could, working together, destroy the Empress and a plot for doing this was concocted. The role of the Minister was to provide a body of assassins to do the job and that of the Tai Won Kun was to make it possible for them to gain entrance to the palace and access to her apartments. Then they, the assassins would do the rest. It is said that, in order to make sure the right person would be destroyed, a Japanese woman who had been attached to her entourage as a teacher of the Japanese language and customs was made aware of the plan and instructed to indicate to the assassins which of all the women was the Empress.[35]

Assassination of Queen and new Cabinet

The time chosen for the deed was a night in early November, 1895. At the time appointed Count Miura led the assassins to the place of meeting near one of the palace gates where he was joined by the Tai Won Kun with a band of Korean soldiers who were to attend the party. The Tai Won Kun, whose relation to the King gave him free entrance to the palace at all times, ordered the guard to open the gate and allow the party to file into the grounds. As they approached the apartments of the Empress the noise of their coming aroused her guard who gave the alarm and she, closely followed by the Korean noble, Min whose duty was to guard the person of the Queen, attempted to escape through one of the narrow alleys but the means taken for her recognition enabled the assassins to distinguish her and the shots fired killed her protector and presumably her also. This was about midnight as I know because my wife and I were awakened in our home by the noise of the shots. We remarked to each other that the reports seemed to come from the vicinity of the palace, and then, as no other shots were heard, we went to sleep again.

The next morning we received news of the assassination which of course stirred the whole foreign community as well as the Koreans of the city. The foreign legations were so disturbed by the affair that they organized all the men of the community for the protection of the Emperor. It was felt that if two foreigners were placed in the palace every night to be within call of the Emperor, no at-

---

35   It is said that the Queen, fearing her life might be in danger had selected one of her entourage who resembled her in face and figure, dressed her in robes like her own and taught her to imitate her in all her ways so that in case of any attempts to take her life her substitute might be taken for her and killed while she made her escape.

tempt would be made on his life, not because of any force they could exert, but because their witness to the making of such an attempt would probably deter those who might otherwise have made the venture.

I was one of this group of foreigners chosen to protect His Majesty. After the affair had occurred the Emperor's Cabinet was disbanded by direction of the Japanese and a new cabinet, favorable to them was formed so that their will might be carried out more readily. I regret to say the man who became Minister of Home Affairs was the Hon. Yu Kil Choon, the very man who, so short a time before, had commissioned me to take charge of the city during the epidemic of Asiatic Cholera, and the one put in charge of palace affairs was the Hon. Yi Chey Myun, the older brother of the Emperor, who, pragued at the elevation of his younger brother to kingship, as already brother can readily conceive how this feeling of irritation during a long period of years had prepared him to take sides against the younger brother when he was being humiliated and how his natural dislike of the Japanese might not be strong enough to cause him to throwaway such an opportunity to indulge this feeling.

The ministers of nearly all the foreign states untied in condemning the murder and decided not to recognize the new cabinet. They refused to deal with it in their communication with the Emperor, and asked the Rev. Dr. H. G. Underwood, Presbyterian missionary and close friend of the Emperor, to carry their messages to and from His Majesty. He agreed to do this and, as His Majesty was afraid to eat food prepared in the palace, lest it should have been tempered with by his enemies, his food was all prepared in the Underwood kitchen, placed in a locked cashbox, carried to the palace and delivered into the Emperor's own hands by the missionary himself, to make sure that no one could put anything harmful into it. The only other foreigner who had access to His Majesty was myself as his physician.

The Incident of Choonsaeng Gate

As no one, during the several weeks following the supposed death of Her Majesty, had been able to find any traces of her remains, her friends began to hope that, in some way, she had made her escape from the palace and found refuse in some home outside. This seemed quite possible because thirteen years before she, under fear of the ex-regent had fled from the palace and totally disappeared for several months only to appear again after having arranged for the kidnapping of her father-in-law and his removal to China where he was held under surveillance for a considerable time, while she once more became the leading figure in the government of Korea. So now, when a considerable period had elapsed without any news of her whereabouts, a rumor was spread that she had really escaped and that her place of hiding was known to some of her friends. One day a former magistrate, another Yi, who had for a time acted as language teacher to one of the missionaries in the Royal Korean Hospital, called on me to assure me that at last her friends had learned where she was. He said they had banded themselves together to kill all the members of the pro-Japanese Cabinet, and, after restoring the Empress to her rightful position they would set His Majesty more firmly on his throne.

This project[36] was to be carried out that very night. He said the captain of the guard within the palace was loyal to the Empress and that her friends outside had been in communication with him. He had assured them he would help them to carry out their plans by seeing to it that the attacking party would find easy entrance through a certain gate in the palace wall and that he would have the guards so scattered in various other parts of the grounds that they could cause no trouble. My visitor added that though they had obtained enough rifles to arm the attackers, they were still short of ammunition and he was now trying to gather enough to enable them to accomplish their purpose. Having heard that I was the possessor of a rifle he had called on me hoping that I would turn over to them my supply of cartridges. He was dressed in Korean costume and was wearing two long flowing silk coats.

Throwing back the folds of the outer coat he showed me that the skirt of the inner coat had been turned up so as to form a big pocket or sack all around him, temporary pocket held the rather heavy load of cartridges he had succeeded in collecting and, which were to be added to the supply they already had. I did own a rifle but as it was only a Winchester hunting gun the ammunition I had could not be used in their military rifles so it would be of no use to him. He then told me the plot to relieve His Majesty was planned to take place at midnight of that very day and as he knew the missionaries and other foreigners were friends of the Empress I was at liberty to tell them about it and to say

---

36   During the proceeding summer when Cholera was rife in the city this faithful servant and cousin of her Majesty had survived an attack of the disease but had recovered, Perhaps because of my treatment.

that if they wished to see the palace recaptured by the King's friends they could do so by going to a certain place at the time specified. He also suggested that if I cared to do so I might convey the information to the various foreign ministers who were, he knew, in sympathy with the royal family.

When my guest left I went to tell my wife about the affair and found the wife of Dr. Allen, former physician to the King and now a member of the United States Legation Staff, calling on her, so I acquainted them both with what I had just heard. Then I went to the United States Legation to report the matter to Mr. Sill, United States Minister. He had heard of it from Mr. Underwood who had just returned from the palace where a cousin of the Emperor, the fat prince, had informed him of what was to take place and Mr. Sill had sent Dr. Allen out to consult with the various Legation Ministers as to what they thought should be done. I then went to the British Legation where I found the Russian Minister, Mr. Weaber, in conference with Sir Walter Hillier, the British Consul. Possibly they were consulting over this very matter though they did not say so. Though they listened with interest to my story they decided it was a purely Korean affair for which they had no responsibility and there was no need for them to interfere. However, they thanked me for reporting it to them as it was a most interesting development in the Korean situation.

Then I went to Dr. Underwood's home and found him quite excited over what he had heard of the affair while he was in the palace. He asked me whether I had had a message from the Emperor and I said I had not. "Well," he said, "I overheard the Emperor directing one of his chamberlains to go to your house and tell you that His Majesty wished to see you.

Doubtless, the chamberlains had all heard of what was to occur and this one had taken the opportunity to flee to safety instead of delivering the King's message to me.

Dr. Underwood did not care to give me any advice about what I should do under such circumstances but I said that, as I now knew I was wanted, I should go to see what His Majesty wanted to ask me. When I asked him whether he was going in again that day, he replied that he had made no promise to return but would accompany me if I went.

So we decided to go in together and, having arranged to meet at eight p m at a certain palace gate, I left to go home for the evening meal and make my preparations for the enterprise. On my way, I met Mr. H. B. Hulbert, a close friend of the Emperor and a former member of the staff of the English Language School established by the King for preparing young Koreans for government positions but had recently joined the American N. E. Mission, and knowing he would be interested in what was going on I told him of it. He was interested and also excited for he was and still is a most intense person and he declared he would go with us if we would take him.

That evening after dinner my wife accompanied me to the outer gate of our compound, the oriental name for an enclosed space with several buildings on it, and bade me goodnight with considerable trepidation, but without expressing any opposition to what I was doing for she knew I felt it was in the line of my duty. On my way to the palace, I met Mr. Underwood accompanied by a Korean, half gateman and half soldier, whom U. S. Minister Mr. Sill had sent with him but Mr. Hulbert had not arrived even when we reached the great gate of the palace grounds. We found this closed and locked for the night and when we asked the guard for admittance he declared he could not open the gate for us. This seemed strange for both of us were known to the guards who knew that we had the right to admission at any time, Dr. Underwood as the messenger of the Foreign Ministers and I as physician to the Emperor. But the guard continued to say it was impossible to let us in because the keys had already been sent to His Majesty in accordance with the usual custom. Dr. Underwood produced the official his attitude. He seemed to forget what he had just said about the keys for he opened the gate and allowed us to pass in, quickly closing it again. We walked quietly over the half mile between this gate and the Emperor's apartments and when we were announced His Majesty at once received us.

I had taken a bottle of medicine with me supposing he might want to consult me about some illness. After enquiring as to his health I placed the medicine in his hands and instructed him how to use it. Because of the disturbed conditions of the times I always delivered his medicine to him in person so as to make it impossible for anyone to tamper with it and then, in case of his death, charge me with having given him a poison.

When those formalities had been completed and we were bidding him good-night, he asked whether we were returning to our homes or whether, in view of the lateness of the hour (about 10 p. m.) we would remain in the palace through the night. As we understood what was behind his question, we said that though we had expected to go home, we could remain if His Majesty desired us to do so. He replied that though he did not want to discommode us, he would be pleased to have us remain if it would not be too inconvenient. We accepted his invitation and went to the quarters of General Dye and the two other American officers who were connected with the training of the palace guard.[37]

Soon after our return to the General's rooms we were surprised at the sudden appearance of Mr. Hulbert out of breath. He said he had been unexpectedly detained and so had failed to meet us at the gate as he had said he would. He had told the guard at the gate that he was to have accompanied a party of two Americans who had already come but he had been late in arriving. He asked to be admitted so he could join them. Though the guard declared this to be impossible and much argument had ensued, he had, in the end bluffed his way in. When he got through the gate and out of sight, he began to fear they might realize they should not have let him through and might run after him and force him out, so he took to his heels and ran the rest of the way as fast as he could.

Shortly afterwards the Korean Captain of the Guard, the one who was to leave the gate but lightly fastened, called on us, saying he had heard of our arrival and had come to pay his respects to us. Not knowing the real object of his call and not wanting to disclose our knowledge of what was to happen, we made no reference to it and ere long he left us.

Then Colonel Nienstead suggested that if we had brought any weapons with us it would be well to see they were in good shape. Underwood and I each produced a revolver from our hip pockets but Hulbert regretfully confessed that in his hurry he had not thought of it so the Colonel said he would lend him his as he had a very short rifle that he could use if it became necessary. As a matter of precaution we cleaned and oiled our weapons and loaded them, though we had no real expectation there would be any need to use them.

About midnight we heard the report of a rifle shot followed by other and the five of us started on the run for the Emperor's quarters. As we approached the gateway to the compound where we had seen him but two hours before, a company of soldiers was forming in a double line from the gate outward. They were just in the act of crossing their bayoneted rifles between the two lines so as to prevent anyone's passing through them and entering the gate but as they had not yet had time to complete the formation, Underwood took advantage of the moment to press his way through the, as yet, loosly held bayonets while I followed him closely and Hulbert pressed on behind me so that, before the soldiers had time to realize what was happening, we had passed through the gate

37   General Dye, a retired officer of the American Army with Colonel Nienstead also of that army, as his assistant, was employed by the Korean government to train the soldiers of the palace guard according to American Army methods while another American officer, General LeGendre was employed as adviser to the government in regard to the internal affairs of the palace.

and were rushing up the steps to the Emperor's rooms. As we ran up the outer steps we heard his crying out, "Call the foreigners, call the foreigners!" We ran into his room saying, "Here we are" and he was much relieved. He urged us to go into his inner rooms but we said it would be best for us to remain in the hall in front of his apartments where we could better watch developments. There each of us followed his own bent in moving about.

It was the night before American Thanksgiving Day and the air was quite chilly. We had left our overcoats behind in the hurry to get to His Majesty and felt cold. Realizing that the Korean soldiers had no evil thought toward us, I walked to the gate through which we had just rushed and entered into conversation with the man nearest it.

He recognized me for he had been a patient in our hospital so I asked him whether they were not cold standing there at that time of night and he said they certainly were so I said I would have some hot coffee prepared for them.

He thanked me. and I made my way back to the great hallway and found a servant whom I instructed to have the coffee prepared and served to the men at the gate. There I met Mr. Hulbert, shivering where the Korean law could not reach them.[38]

While this was going on the servants had obtained coffee for the soldiers standing guard at the gate of His Majesty's Compound and had brought our overcoats. We soon felt warmer and stopped shivering, so perhaps the coldness of the late November night had something to do with the shaking that had seized all three of us! While the firing and general uproar was going on just over a wall from us, His Majesty with his son the Crown Prince, both greatly frightened, came out to where we were and begged us to go back into their private rooms but just then the members of the cabinet appeared on the scene. The Prime Minister told the Emperor that they were going to another part of the palace which they thought was safer and saked His Majesty to go with them. The Emperor turned to us and asked what he should do for Dr. Underwood said it was not our place to advise him what he should do but we foreigners intended to stay right where we were and thought no harm would come to him if he stayed with us. The Prime Minister then seized the Emperor by the arm to force him away from us but His Majesty grasped my arm. The Minister of War seized

---

[38]   The law of extra-territoriality, which the strongest nations enforced in favor of their subjects who resided in those countries, meant that those foreigners were not subject to local laws but only to the laws of their own lands and that was true also of the property they owned or occupied.

the Crown Prince who took hold of Dr. Underwood and there we stood, they tugging at the Emperor and Crown Prince in an effort to separate them from us, while His Majesty until his teeth chattered. He said, "I am either cold or frightened, I don't know which, but there is no place in the world I would rather be, right now, than here."

As I too was shivering, I remarked that we had made a mistake in coming from our rooms without our overcoats, but I would find a servant and send him to bring them. Just then Underwood came in from a tour around the compound and he was cold. We chatted each others saying may be we were more afraid than cold.

We were not far from the gate where the would-be relievers of their Majesties were to enter and already we could hear the noise of their efforts to open the gate.

Though the captain had promised to have the gate but lightly fastened and the soldiers well scattered over the wide grounds of the palace, they found the gates double-locked and a large company of soldiers defending them. Yes, at the last moment, the captain had turned traitor and turned over the whole correspondence to the cabinet. In a rage some of the attackers, boosted by their comrades to the top of the wall, began to jump down inside only to drop into the arms of the guards and find themselves prisoners, It was a fine moonlight night and as the light shone into their eyes the invaders could not see what was going on inside though the guards, looking in the opposite direction, could see the attackers distinctly so catching them was an easy job.

Ere long those outside learned the true state of things and rushed to another gate not far away which they found but lightly guarded. They broke it in but, finding themselves engaged there also with a superior force, all that could do so fled. Their leaders ran to the homes of foreigners and his son held on to us. We just stood firmly where we were. It would have made a fine scene for a movie film!

The Prime Minister asked us what business we foreigners had to seize their Emperor and keep him from doing what he ought to do and what he wanted to do. Dr. Underwood replied that we had not seized them, they were holding on to us, and went there he asked what kind of a Prime Minister he was to seize his Sovereign and try to compel him to do what he did not want to do. So there we stood until His Majesty said he would stay with us and the Cabinet members could go wherever they wanted to do. Then they loosened their hold on their rulers and at once departed while the Emperor and Prince, not letting go of us, practically pulled us into their private rooms and made us sit on the floor cushions beside them. In the meantime the noise on the other side of the wall had been lessened and soon it all ceased and we knew the effort of the King's friends had failed.

Just then Hulbert realized something he had not thought of in the excitement of those hours. When Colonel Nienstead handed him his revolver, it was in a belt and Hulbert had hurriedly buckled it on the outside of his clothing and there he was sitting in His Majesty's presence with a revolver not only on his person but in plain sight, though by a strict regulation, no arms of any kind should be worn in the presence of royalty. Hulbert suddenly asked to be excused and went out of the room where he removed the revolver, belt and all, and re-buckled it under his coat where it could not be seen. We never knew whether His Majesty had noticed it or not. If he had, he wisely refrained from remarking on it, realizing no doubt that he might have had reason for being glad that those around him had at least one revolver which could have been used for his protection.

After a time, when the outside noise had completely subsided, I noted signs of weariness in His Majesty who was sitting next to me, so I drew his head down on my arm and suggested that he stretch out and try to sleep for a while. He did so and in this position remained sound asleep until morning broke.

About seven in the morning the members of the cabinet returned in quite a different frame of mind. The Prime Minister came into the Emperor's presence on his hands and knees and, after finishing his obeisance to royalty, bowed humbly before the three foreigners and apologized for the rudeness he and his associates had shown them the night before, acknowledging that they had been in the wrong. He then drew attention to the fact that morning had already come and we must be tired, If we would accept their apologies and assurances that His Majesty would not suffer at their hands, he would be glad to relieve us and furnish us each with a military escort, not only to make sure of our safe arrival a tour homes but also as an indication of their gratitude for what we had done for their Emperor.

Our wives greeted us with a real sense of relief when were turned in time for breakfast on Thanksgiving Day.

Recovery of Remains of the Queen

This narrative would not be complete without relating some of the events that followed.

It turned out that the Empress had really been killed by the shots of the assassins who had taken her body into a nearby woods within the palace enclosure and, having saturated her clothing with kerosene, had burned the body to ashes. This accounted for the difficulty of determining her fate and for hope that she had escaped and was in a home somewhere. How her friends were deceived into believing she was alive and had actually been seen no one ever learned. The discovery within the woods of a pile of ashes in which a few unburnt bones were found together with a few unconsumed bits of the dress the Queen had worn on the night of her assassination settled the fact of her death and proved once more the dependability of the old saying "Truth will out!" The assassins had tried to obliterate all of signs what had happened to her but just enough remained to establish them quiet.

The ashes with the fragments of bones were collected and put into a coffin which was placed in a new building in the palace enclosure erected for the purpose of housing her remains for the months that must intervene before a "lucky" site could be selected for their burial and a tomb prepared for receiving the huge heavy coffin. Every day during that time the Emperor visited her temporary resting place, no one else being allowed to enter except the priests appointed to perform the ceremonies prescribed for the peace of the departed. I personally knew what went on in the palace during all that interval because I was in to see him nearly every day. During that interval a site for her grave was chosen by the necromancers whose business was to peer into the future and especially to select propitious locations where the bodies of the dead might rest in peace without any disturbance from evil spirits.

Then the grave had to be prepared. This required the raising of a great mound some forty or fifty feet high and of corresponding circumference. Time must also be allowed for the earth to settle into a firm mass, after which it was covered with green sod so that rain would not spoil its shape. Near the top of the mound an excavation was made which was formed into a room for the holding of the great coffin. Its ceilings, sides, and floor were lined with heavy cut stones to make it practically impregnable. Besides the coffin, this vault would hold all the furnishing and sacrificial offerings required for the deceased.

During those months of waiting I was the only foreigner permitted to enter the palace and see His Majesty and that only because of my special relation to him. I visited him almost every day and it was through me he kept in touch with the foreign community which had become, as it were, woven into the web of his life.

The Funeral of the Empress

When the date set for the funeral approached, the Emperor, remembering the happy relations that had existed between Her Majesty and the missionaries, and the services the latter had rendered him throughout his time of anxiety and sorrow, sent, through Dr. Allen, a special invitation to them to occupy a place in the procession from the palace to the grave at several miles east of the city. Dr. Allen who was at the time Acting American Minister, conferred with some of the older missionaries about this and all felt that this special mark of His Majesty's favor towards a particular group in the foreign community might place both himself and the missionaries in an embarrassing position so he expressed to him the deep gratitude with which they had received his more than kind message and explained that they felt he was honoring them too highly as they had only done what many others in the community had done and what still others would have gladly done to serve him had the good chance come to them. For this reason they humbly suggested that he withdraw this invitation, which they would feel bound to accept if he pressed it, and invite them rather to attend the obsequies at the grave and to this he graciously acceded.

The immediate surroundings of the grave had been converted into a small town by the erection of many buildings for the housing of the invited guests. In one section was a miniature palace for the Emperor and his attendants; another group of buildings consisted of a special one for the temporary housing of the coffin and several smaller houses for the usual large group of attendants of the Empress. Then there were buildings for the accommodation of the numerous guests, including all the other members of the foreign community and high Korean dignitaries in great numbers. These accomodations included bedrooms, dining rooms, kitchens, servants quarters, and all necessary outbuildings for the comfort of the guests though they would occupy them only from one afternoon till the next day but, as it was all being done for the unfortunate Empress, no expense was considered too great.

The funeral procession was like all those conducted for the rich and the great except that it was even more magnificent because of her high rank. A detailed description of such may be found in another section of these memoirs. I took place on a Sunday afternoon, the exact date and time, like the location of the grave, having been determined by the most experienced and noted diviners.

The foreign community did not join in the procession but found places where they could watch it pass and see its grandeur and in the evening many went out to occupy the places assigned to them in the funeral village at the grave. Here those who desired food were served with the choicest foreign foods, cooked by well-trained Korean chefs. It was all very wonderful to us. We spent the evening watching the final preparations for taking the coffin up the hill to the excavation in which it was to rest, and in looking at the gorgeous array of sacrificial offerings of foods, flowers and other articles made to the spirits whose good offices were to be invoked sometimes during the night. The actual burial was to take place but no accurate information was available concerning this except that it would be as soon as all the preparations had been completed. We were told it would be all right to retire because a gong would be sounded a short time before the preparations were finished so many of us took opportunity to rest.

When the gong sounded I arose and, making my way to the great mound, found many men tugging and pushing the heavy coffin, laid on rollers, up the steep hill. To my surprise, the Emperor was personally superintending this work and laboring as hard as the others. At last it was raised to the edge of the entrance to the excavation around which many spectators had gathered. Some of the missionary ladies standing there were trying to get into better positions for watching the coffin being pushed from its plat from into the walledin space where it was to remain permanently. Seeing this, a guard of Russian soldiers who were on hand, thinking they were in the way, roughly pushed them back.

His Majesty, however, invited the ladies to come and stand beside him so they could easily see the whole procedure.

This of course, surprised the soldiers but it clearly showed the gratitude the Emperor felt to the foreign community and also that he had absorbed the Western spirit of Chivalry toward ladies.

When the coffin had been properly laid in its last resting place surrounded by the customary furnishings, food and charms, all present were invited to participate in the farewell salutes, after which the heavy doors of the compartment were closed and firmly secured. The ceremony was thus brought to an end and all retired, leaving the workmen to fill in earth til the contour of the mound was restored and to cover it with sod so that the location of the entrance was completely covered and concealed.

We were then at liberty to return to our beds or spend the time till breakfast in any way we wished.

After breakfast it was announced that the Emperor desired to receive in audience the members of the foreign legations and their wives and members of the foreign community. All others could return to their homes as soon as they wished to do so. After a time we who remained were summoned to the temporary throne room where His Majesty expressed his appreciation of our presence and sympathy, wished us a safe return to our homes, and invited us to partake again of the special refreshments prepared for us. As we left for home we realized that we had been witnesses, at close range, of a scene which, though sad, was unique and such as we should probably never have an opportunity to see again.

What Happened to some of the Friends of the King and Queen

But what about the Koreans who had risked so much to serve the Emperor and Empress? Many had been captured that night and more were arrested afterwards. Little of what happened to them was ever heard. Several of the leaders including the Mr. Yi who had called on me that day in search of ammunition and general Yun and his son Yun Chi Ho, took refuge in Mr. Underwood's compound where they remained several weeks. Frequent efforts were made by the Pro-Japanese cabinet to beguile these refugees off Mr. Underwood's premises because, while they could not enter the premises of a foreigner, they could arrest their own people if they were caught elsewhere.

One day Mr. Yi received an urgent note purporting to come from one of his most trusted friends asking him to meet him at a certain place outside this compound and he felt he must comply with the request of his friend. It was pointed out to him that this was probably a ruse to get him out where they could arrest him and that his friend could easily come to him where he was. He said his friend would be compromised should he go in to the foreigner's property and he was sure he could disguise himself so completely that he could make the venture in safety. He went out on the street and was immediately seized by police-men detailed for the purpose. He was thrown into prison and in time banished to a small island off the west coast where he remained for some years but was fi-nally pardoned and is, so far as I know, still living in Seoul. He called on me shortly before we left Korea in December, 1935, but I have not heard any news of him since that time.

The friends of General Yun felt an effort should be made to get him away from Korea and, hearing of a Chinese boat about ready to leave the nearest port, Chemulpo, arrangements were made to disguise him and get him over the twenty-six miles between Seoul and the port. His long greybeard was shaved off, the first time he had. ever had that barbarous act performed on him, and then he was dressed in foreign clothes. As it was then winter they borrowed my Canadian winter cap of otter's fur that covered his forehead as well as his head and wrapped a heavy scarf around his face and neck so that only his eyes were left uncovered. They borrowed also my official covered sedan chair and placing him in it set off for the port with four stout Korean Chairmen who could travel carrying the chair. Two of the male missionaries walked in front of the chair to set the pace and answer to questions of any guards whom they might meet on the way. Such they did meet and some of them looked suspiciously into the chair but, seeing only an apparently sick foreigner, they let them pass. At length they reached their destination and without delay, he was put on the small Chinese vessel which was ready to weigh anchor, It carried him across the Yellow Sea and landed him in China where he remained until it became evident that he could safely return to his home in Korea.

General Yun had several times occupied the post of Minister of War in the Korean Government, had always been a staunch friend of the King and had sev-eral country in some sort of guise or other so this most recent experience was not new to him. His son continued to reside in the Underwood home for a con-siderable period until such changes took place as made it safe for him to return to his home.

▸ Chapter 5 ◂

Royal Family

A Royal Procession

In the days of royal splendor in Korea, the king seldom left the privacy of his palace. On important occasions, therefore, such as visits to the family graves to pay respect to ancestors and offer sacrifices, a royal procession was a notable event. Soon after our arrival in Seoul, it was announced that on a certain day His Majesty would visit his ancestral tombs. The procession was to leave the palace and pass through the great East Gate to the tombs of the Kings several miles outside the city walls at a given hour.

Determined to see this great sight, I found a place where I could watch every phase of the parade from the time it came out of the palace gate until it passed through the East Gage, some two miles away. It would come slowly down the broad avenue which was lined on either side by rows of government buildings, turn on to the East Gate Street, then pass through that gate and out into the country. I was near enough to get a good view of every part of the long line as it passed by. And, too, I could see the full length of the procession as it made its way along the East Gate Street.

From the early morning, sightseers, dressed in their finest clothes, crowded the streets adjoining the palace grounds. The men wore colorful[39] outer gar-

---

39   The ordinary Korean garments are white, but this was a very special occasion and holiday attire was donned by all except mourners.

ments, mostly subdued hues of blue, green, or yellow. Their horsehair hats were polished to a shiny blackness.[40] Women, excepting those of the lower social classes, were not allowed to attend such public occasions and had to content themselves with a view from behind the window curtains. The hour announced passed but the palace gates remained closed. I inquired of several Koreans who stood near me just when the procession would come. Each shook his head. Who could know what was going on behind the palace gates? Who could know the mind of the King? If we would wait we would surely see it when it came forth in His Majesty's own good time. Sure enough, after hours of waiting, the big central gate opened and the procession got under way.

First came a long line of royal guards on foot bearing bright banners. These made no attempt to keep step as they moved along very slowly. Next came the cavalrymen of Korean forces carrying ancient weapons - swords, spears, battle-axes. Another company of guards on foot bore still more gorgeous banners. Then came the heavy palanquin on which His Majesty sat in state, dressed in right regal fashion. Some twenty[41] or more men carried this palanquin. A heavy pole running lengthwise on each side was provided with loops of rope which the bearers slipped over one shoulder. They often stumbled as they jogged along. "Jogged" is the right word for the great palanquin was heavy. These men did not keep in any sort of step either but this did not seem to bother he king. One man held a long-handled, red umbrella over His Majesty. The king and all his attendants were dressed in robes of dark red, the distinguishing color of a king. In the Orient the term 'kingdom' is used for a country not altogether independent. At that time the ruler of Korea still acknowledged the suzerainty of China and, therefore, was not allowed to wear the imperial yellow of an emperor.

Following the king came the crown prince sitting on a smaller palanquin. Next came ladies-in-waiting carried in curtained sedan chairs. The ministers of state rode in gaudy chairs, each carried by four men. Finally a long body guard of foot soldiers brought up the rear of the procession. No haste was permitted, hence it took a long time for the procession to pass a given point. No one cheered as it went by-instead the people bowed their heads as in deep respect for their

---

40   These hats have crowns about 5 or 6 inches high but very narrow and shaped like truncated cones and have a brim which at that time was about 6 inches wide.

41   Ordinarily only two men, or at the most four, carried a sedan chair.

king, supposedly too much awed to even look at him. What a contrast to a similar function in a European country or in America!

During the long journey to the tombs the chair bearers were allowed to stop to rest at inns along the route and there they consumed much drink. Night fell before the return of the party to the city for everybody had to feast at the graves of the departed kings and, because of the intake of so much liquid refreshment, the long procession back to the city was anything but an orderly march.

An interesting incident occurred during a former royal procession. Dr. Horace N. Allen had won the favor of the king through his successful treatment of Prince Min. The next time a procession of state occurred, the king, naturally thinking that Dr. Allen would wish to view the spectacle and wanting to do the doctor a great honor in the sight of his people, ordered a platform to be erected at a good location along the main street and sent word to Dr. Allen that he was to occupy this place of prominence. When His Majesty reached this dais, he stopped the procession, rose from his seat and bowed to Dr. Allen. Probably no other person has ever been so greatly honored in Korea and it was indeed a magnificent testimony to the work of medical missionaries in winning the good will of high and low and securing a favorable hearing for the gospel message.

The Summer Palace

Situated in the lower hills just behind the north palace was a building, known as the summer palace, into which it was customary for the royal family to move when the warm weather set in. Though it was but a small building, compared with the main palace, it was located in the midst of nice surroundings and was admirably suited to its purpose.

The first time I visited His Majesty there I was especially interested in a sunken garden located just in front of the main building. This garden was divided into eight sections representing the eight provinces of the country.[42]

Each was cultivated as a paddy field and all received the same care. The rice in them was about half grown at the time of my visit. The Chamberlain ex-

---

[42] At that time the country was divided into only 8 provinces but later on some of the larger provinces were cut into two so that there were 14 provinces instead of 8.

plained its purpose to me. From the way in which the rice grew in each field the coming rice crop for each province was estimated. It was a pretty idea, one that I had never heard of before, but the Chamberlain smiled as he explained it to me, evidently not believing in it himself. I did not express my opinion except to say that if only it could be relied upon it would enable people to prepare in advance for short crops. When I asked if their Majesties believed in it he smiled and said it was an old custom that had come down from the far past.

King and the Bicycle

On one occasion, when I was calling on the King while he was residing at the summer palace, he asked me how I came, by what mode of travel. I said I sometimes walked, sometimes came in a jinriksha, sometimes rode in a sedan chair, but had come that day on a bicycle. He showed much interest in this latter mode and asked where I had left the vehicle. When I told him that, in accord with palace regulations, I had left it at the entrance gates he directed the chamberlain to send some one to bring it so he could see it. It was brought and, after looking it over carefully, he asked how the rider kept it from falling over. I explained that it was difficult at first to keep it balanced but that it became easy with practice. Then he wanted to see me ride it. Although I had on my prince Albert suit, there was nothing to do but to tuck its tails under me, bestride my bicycle and let him see it in action. As I rode round and round the courtyard, the king laughed and seemed to enjoy the spectacle. I had hoped, he might ask to try it himself but he failed to do so. As I rode past a window of the palace building I could see the curtains being shoved a little to one side and I knew that the queen was getting a private view. Of course, she could not come out where we were because it was not customary for a woman to be seen by any men other than the members of her immediate family.

When the exhibition ended the servant took it back and the king thanked me and told the chamberlain to accompany me the three quarters of a mile to the gate where I would find my "carriage" awaiting me.

I think Reverend D. A. Bunker imported the first bicycle into Korea. It was of the solid tire type for that had been used before airfilled tires were invented. But soon after our arrival in Seoul the F. S. Miller suggested to me that he and I order one each with the new soft tires from England. When they came they were the first of that type to enter the country. That was about 1895 and when he and I wheeled forth on the bumpy streets we attracted much attention.

Rev. H. G. Underwood used to tell how the first bicycle got its Korean name. He was one day talking with one of the Korean language teachers when Mr. Bunker went by on bicycle and he asked his friend what it would be called in Korean. Though the man had never seen one before he, without any hesitation, named it a "Pakwhee," the Korean word for "wheel." Mr. Underwood thought it was very clever of him to give it in Korean the exact name by which it was usually known in America - a wheel. The name did not stick, however, for a more descriptive name took its place - "cha jun cha" or "self propelling car."

Before long Dr. Allen, American Minister, joined the bicycle brigade and it was indeed a sight to see that very tall gentleman wheeling through the streets of the capital astride such a contraption to the upsetting of all our ideas of the dignity pertaining to a representative of great America.

Of course there were great drawbacks in that early day to having a bicycle. The streets were rough; sharp stones here and there were ready to cut through the rather thin outer tires. Accidents would happen to various parts and extra parts were no nearer than England, but in spite of all the drawbacks we got a lot of service out of our bikes. Others were encouraged to import them and ere long they could be brought in from the United States of America. In time the Japanese began to make them and that reduced the price and made it easier to get repairs done and obtain new parts.

- Bicycle Accident

As the years passed the streets were improved and later on paved and the number of bicycles made travel for pedestrians more and more difficult. As the riders paid no attention to the traffic signs put up especially for automobile drivers many accidents occurred.

After I became President of the Chosen Christian College, three miles from the Hospital and outside the city limits, it was necessary for me to have an auto and a chauffeur and only supreme confidence in the skill and carefulness of the driver enabled me to ride through the mass of city traffic - pedestrians in the middle of the streets, other autos apparently being driven with little care for themselves or others, street cars rushing past and almost innumerable bicycles winding their way in and out between all of these. I often wondered how our chauffeur managed to avoid crashes.

Once, while standing at a busy corner waiting for a street car, I amused myself by counting the bicycles that passed me in one minute. I hesitate to tell you the number I actually counted - 120 a minute or two every second. I repeated this counting at other times while I waited a chance to cross a street and nearly always the count was just about the same. Most of these bikes were ridden by errand boys carrying messages or delivering goods from the many stores that by that time lined the main streets of the city.

When an accident did happen one day I was not surprised, I will give the story here not so much to tell you how it happened as to tell you how the policeman, who had a stand nearby and saw it all, handled the case. A young lad who was on the opposite side of the street started to cross to the side we were on. He should have crossed behind us but foolishly thought he could go in front of our auto and get by. Our chauffeur saw what he was trying to do and put on his brakes as quickly as he could but not quick enough. The bike, crossing in front of us was struck sidewise by the auto wheel. The bike was knocked over and so was the boy. By that time our car had stopped and a policeman was on the spot. After picking up the boy, he set him and his wheel to one side with an order to wait there.

Then, turning to our auto, he took out of his pocket a piece of white chalk and drew a line around the auto on the pavement and then told us to drive to the side of the street and wait there. Then he took a stand inside the chalk line and looked around to note just where the boy and the auto were when the accident happened. He could see we had just passed across a street and were where we ought to be and that the boy was in the wrong place. He told me we were in no way to blame and then gave the boy a good scolding for trying to pass us as he had done. He then examined both the boy and his bicycle and found both slightly injured. Having learned who I was he suggested that as the boy was but an ignorant chap and poor, I take him to the hospital for a more careful examination and necessary dressings and show him our goodwill by paying for needed repairs to his bicycle which he had learned from a nearby repair shop would be about two yen. He smiled as he made the suggestion and ended by explaining that while we were in no way to blame the boy had got hurt and the two yen for the repair work would be a lot for him to obtain while we could afford to be generous. We smiled in return and giving the repair man two yen we took the lad into our car and carried him to the hospital where his wounds and his feelings were all made comfortable. He had suffered more from fear of the policeman than he had from his injuries and he left us with many expressions of his gratitude.

After all, the policeman had acted wisely, considering all the circumstances. He soothed us by laying the blame on the boy who certainly was in the wrong. Then he complimented us by suggesting that we could help the boy out of his trouble at very little cost, so all were made happy. I remembered then Shakespeare's wonderful lines - "Mercy is twice blessed. It blesseth him that gives and him that takes." Thus it is better than mere justice.

The Queen and the Seclusion of Women

Because of the custom of the seclusion of women Her Majesty the Queen never appeared at any public function. Though I always accompanied her physician, Mrs. Underwood, M. D., to the palace when she was called to seethe Queen professionally so that we might talk the case over before treatment was prescribed, I never did see her face to face. I had heard so much about her that I very much wished for such an opportunity so I could form my own conclusions as to her characteristics and the strength of will with which she was credited.

One morning it seemed as though my curiosity was to be satisfied. A messenger came to my home to inform me that Her Majesty was not recovering from an illness as speedily as she desired and had decided to put aside her scruples and ask the King's physician to see her himself. I was thrilled at the prospect and wondered whether or not this violation of the ancient custom might be a first step towards its abolition for, if the Queen could break it, her subjects would feel at liberty to do so too.

At the time set in the afternoon the messenger returned, but only to say the Queen's illness had taken a favorable turn, so she would defer the call, hoping the improvement would continue, I was glad Her Majesty was recovering, but I could not help being disappointed at my bad luck.

The Queen's birthday was to be celebrated in November and it became known that she was to give a party to which all the foreign representatives and their wives were to be invited. Undoubtedly Mrs. Avison and I would be included in the list of guests and my wish would, after all, be gratified. But this birthday party never materialized. Before the time for it came she had been foully murdered. Her premature death thus delayed the extension to the women of

Korea of that freedom of action without which they could not take the place in their homes and their country that they were as naturally fitted to occupy as were the women of the Western nations.

The Rise and Fall of Palace Favorites

Probably the quickest way to royal favor in Korea, as perhaps it is in other countries also, was to find a way to provide the ruler with money or in some way to enable him to rid himself of those whom he disliked or feared, In Korea there were many such instances of the rapid rise of men from the very lowest classes to wealth and important government positions by one or both of these methods.

- Kim Hong Nyuk

One of these phenomenal rises was that of Kim Hong Nyuk, erstwhile cook at the Russian Legation. After the close of the Japan-China War, 1894-95, Korea was in a state of turmoil. She had hoped the outcome would be what the Japanese had led her to believe it would be - complete independence - but that hope was soon destroyed as the Japanese immediately demanded the right to control all her international relations and very shortly afterwards took charge of her internal affairs also. Then other nations felt they had an equal right to have a hand in these matters and among those outside powers, Russia was not behind. Early she began her intrigues. She had seen the tendency of the Korean King to conduct many of his affairs through favorite individuals who had won his confidence or at least his favor by supplying him with funds and she was not slow to make use of such persons to gain his attention.

In their approaches to His Majesty the language difficulty always stood in the way of complete understanding so it was important to find a Korean who understood their language. They found such a one in the cook at the Russian Legation, Kim Hong Nyuk. They did not let his humble station interfere with the good use they could make of him and he was quick to see the great opportunity for advancement that was open to him. He was carefully instructed by the great men of the Russian Legation as to his and the Korean King found him invaluable to himself.

Apparently Kim found his path not all flowers, for I discovered in Dr. Allen's "Chronological Index" the following note: "February 22, 1898, Kim Hong Nyuk, Russian Legation interpreter, was attacked by ruffians, saved by British marines." What ruffians they were is not stated but my own knowledge of what was then taking place is that they were servants of the legation of another nationality which did not like the developments he was furthering.

On March 11 of the same year, only seventeen days later, Kim was appointed Governor of the Capital, the city of Seoul, a phenomenal rise - from cook to interpreter to the Russian Legation, to the Governorship of the Capital City. Then on July twenty-seventh Governor Kim was arrested and banished for the phenomenal gains made by the Russians with his aid had been but ephemeral. For a time they had displaced the British and American advisers to the Korean Government and replaced them by Russians and their influence was being exerted in matters of finance, including the transfer of money from other banks to a new one - the Russio-Korean Bank- and in many other ways. During that time Kim was riding high but the appearance of the British fleet off the port of Chemulpo produced a wonderful change and the predominant influence of Russia was almost immediately nullified so that the former cook's rise began to decline.

About the end of September I was summoned to the Korean jail one night to treat a man who had tried to take his own life by cutting his throat and when I reached there I found the man to be Kim Hong Nyuk. He had been arrested as a political intriguer and condemned to death. The sentence was to be carried out next day but he preferred to take his own life and, with a knife which he obtained in some unexplained way, he had cut half through his windpipe. He had missed the great blood vessels on either side so that the bleeding, though considerable, had not been fatal. There was only a small lamp and the light from it was meager. He lay on the floor as there was no table on which to place him so I had to kneel at his side and do all that was needed in that awkward position. I staunched the flowing blood with cotton sponges, sewed the cut edges of his trachea together, washed the wound out with an antiseptic solution and left him breathing normally. On October 12, after he had recovered, he and two companions were hanged. To let him die from his self-inflicted wound would not have vindicated the dignity of the law so his life was saved that he might suffer the kind of death to which he had been sentenced I.

- Yi Yong Ik

Another example of the rise and fall of royal favor is that of Yi Yong Ik who, born into one of the humblest families, grew up to be a water carrier, supplying the homes of the people by carrying water from the wells to their houses. Even here he showed his shrewdness by making agreements to supply many homes with water and then hiring other men to do the carrying at a price that would yield him a profit. Gradually he accumulated a small fortune which he cleverly used to obtain advantageous positions both for adding to his wealth and for currying favor with men having more influence than means.

The King was nearly always in need of either money or intriguers who could find money or win some other advantages from him and our man Kim was just such a one as he could use. His money enabled him to serve His Majesty who rewarded him with a magistracy. That gave him still greater opportunities for serving the King as well as advancing his own influence and lining his own pockets. In those days magistrates over country districts were appointed by the King - generally at a price. They received no salary but their position in a neighborhood and their authority to collect taxes for remittances to the palace in Seoul, enabled them to demand indefinite sums from the people, out of which they paid the King the amounts due from their district and, without much fear of prosecution, Paid their satellite just enough to keep them quiet while they kept the rest. As a matter of fact, His Majesty knew that the magistrates could not buy their appointments and live without salaries except by levying a large enough tax to cover his share and to fully compensate themselves who were supposed to be both enforcers of law and protectors of the King's subjects. Everyone else also knew it but only when the magistrates went so far beyond what might be considered a fair squeeze did any dare to complain. So the cautious Kim, by helping to keep the palace in funds, won the good will of all within it and also had the good sense not to tax the people so greatly as to get himself into trouble.

The King's need for more and more money grew so greatly that he called on Kim to be head over all his finances. In this position, he augmented the King's revenues by increased taxation of the people, by dismissing officials who had been bled to a point where they could pay no more and then appointing new men to their posts who could or would pay well for official positions.

It was this man the King sent out with me when I was searching for a site for a hospital. The story of his objections to every place I suggested is told elsewhere. Kim was also thoroughly anti-foreign as was shown by an incident that happened while he was acting as the King's confidential adviser.

Rev. H. G. Underwood, with his wife and young son, had gone on a prolonged evangelistic tour into the country. One Sunday his helper brought him a copy of a poster he had found on the gate of the city where they were staying. It was a denouncement of all foreigners and an order for their extermination wherever found and it was put out as the command of the King. The time set for the execution of the plan was but a few days off, December 6, 1900, and something had to be done immediately. There was not time to send a messenger to Seoul so Dr. Underwood went to the telegraph office to send me a message. But in what language should he send it? Korean would not do and English would most likely be understood. Why, in Latin of course! So that evening I received the message telling me the circumstances and asking me to get word to His Majesty without loss of time for he felt sure the plot had not been instigated with the King's knowledge.

I at once called on Mr. J. S. Gale, my Canadian fellow missionary, and together we visited the American Minister, Dr. Allen. He was greatly angered and at once asked His Majesty for an immediate audience. The urgency of such a request on a Sunday evening startled the King but, knowing the American Minister so well, he acceded to his request. Dr. Allen took with him Mr. Underwood's telegram which had been translated, first into English and then into Korean, and coming as it did from one in whom he had complete confidence. His Majesty knew there could be no mistake. He denied any knowledge of the matter, saying someone had forged his name to an order which was the very opposite of anything he desired to have done. Surely Dr. Allen would understand that. Dr. Allen said he believed that, as the date fixed for the wholesale murders was but a few days off it was necessary that an order cancelling the one already posted in all parts of the country should be sent out just as widely without a moment's delay. Just as widely it to say that the order did go out so promptly that the effect of the original one was nullified and no killing occurred.

And the instigator of the original order? None other than Yi, of course, who felt himself so necessary to the King that he could commit even so gross a crime without endangering himself. This aroused His Majesty to the peril he was in placing himself in the power of such unscrupulous men and ere long he rid himself of this particular favorite.

It would have been well had he taken the lesson more to heart but all his power to obtain money in large amounts was bound up in the long established custom of selling offices and cultivating men who could supply his needs and he had neither the wit nor the courage to reduce his expenses or to set up new methods of appointing men and collecting enough for the legitimate administration of the country. He was really in a difficult position. Beset by his own satellites and ignorant of how to rid himself of them ; Put to his wit's end to satisfy the demands of outside countries - Japan at one side, and Russia at the other - with countering claims from other Western nations, he was ignorant of ways and means of withstanding the pressure of outside governments. Had he but placed his faith in the men who - with more knowledge of other countries and undoubted honesty toward himself - would have advised him wisely he might have saved both himself and his country, but ⋯"

Yi was dismissed from office December 14, again pardoned December 16, and restored to his post as Director of the Imperial Estates December 17. No wonder the King's real friends decided that autocracy should be destroyed and a limited monarchy established with wise men at the helm of the Ship of State to prevent the terrible mistakes of a well intentioned but unstable and ignorant monarch. When that effort to establish a new order failed the stronger nations took advantage of the situation and Korea's progress m the world was still further blocked.

The King's Characteristics - Was He Good or Bad?

When one either sees personally or reads of the almost unbelievable cruelties practiced by many autocratic rulers he can hardly believe that such a man or woman has any sympathy at all in his heart but is entirely selfish. However a longer or a closer intimacy with such sovereigns lack of feeling makes it that all such apparent hardness and pitilessness is exhibited only when they feel their royal status and its perogatives are being endangered. So long as affairs of state pursue their regular favor all such rulers are generally thoughtful and kindly and as good as the average commoner is when he gets his own way. I had many opportunities of noting this in my years of service to the King of Korea.

I append here a few happenings that illustrate the inherent sympathy of this ruler who as an autocratic sovereign was sometimes very cruel but, as a man, could be just as kindly as any one of either his own nation or any other.

• The Emperor and the Boy Who Lost His Leg

One afternoon a small and very dirty boy, evidently a street gamin, was brought to the hospital after having been run over by a street car. Examination made it plain that a high amputation of the thigh would be needed to save his life and preparations for that were at once started, I was due to visit the palace at that hour so I left the case in the hands of my competent colleagues.

At the end of conference with my royal patient, he surprised me by making enquiries about the injured boy and, when I asked him how he knew about the matter, he explained that all such things were reported to him over the phone. He said the report mentioned that the boy had been taken to the hospital. Had I seen the case before I came to the palace and if so, how old was the lad, and was he seriously hurt?

The young prince was standing by his father's side so, putting my hand just over the boy's head I said, "He is just so big, and he will lose his leg." The Emperor's face became pale and he asked me to have everything possible done to save the boy's life. He also said that when the time for discharging the patient from the hospital came he wished us to obtain an artificial leg for him for which he, the King, would pay.

The boy made a good recovery and when the leg had been obtained and fitted on him I suggested to His Majesty that he be brought to the palace so that he could see the lad and receive in person the thanks he was due. His Majesty consented and, while the boy was overwhelmed when the King spoke to him and could say nothing but "Ko-map-sim-nai-ta,"[43] His Majesty looked pleased and happy.

• The California Earthquake

At the time of the San Francisco earthquake the Emperor was much concerned about the conditions of the Koreans in California. On one of my visits to him he asked me whether I had heard anything about them, expressing his fear not only as to their safety but also as to their need for food or medical care. He wanted to send money to be used for those who needed it if he could get it to them in

---

43 "I am grateful to your Majesty."

time and also could be sure it was properly dispensed. When I suggested that our Board of Foreign Missions had an office in San Francisco and their representative would be glad to receive the money and see to its actual distribution to those Koreans who needed help, he was much pleased and asked me if I would undertake to send it to the proper person. When I said I would gladly do so he directed his chamberlain to give me Y5,000 at once so that there would be no delay and the money was put into my hands with the statement that more would be forthcoming if it were needed.

The next day I deposited it in a bank and arranged for it to be cabled to the Treasurer of our Board in New York with a request to send it to their office in California with proper instructions. I received a favorable reply immediately by cable and, when I presented this to His Majesty, he appeared relieved and asked me to express his gratitude to the Board. Fortunately no further contribution was required as not many of the Koreans had been seriously affected.

• Skating in the Palace Grounds

On the occasion of one of my visits to the palace in the winter of 1894, His Majesty asked me to extend, on his behalf, an invitation to a group of the foreign community to skate within the palace grounds. As there was no other place for skating except the river which was four miles from the city those who received the invitation were only too glad to accept this opportunity - and perhaps, too, they might see the King.

Just in front of one of the private royal apartments was a large pond with a small island in its center on which was erected a beautiful pavilion in which their Majesties were wont to sit in the summer months. At that time, however, the pond, covered with smooth ice, made an ideal outdoor skating rink. We were met by the King's cousin, a fat and rather jolly man, generally spoken of as the fat prince, who had been appointed to see that the party had a good time. He could not skate but from the pavilion he could watch the skaters almost flying around and he was quite exuberant at seeing the evolutions some of them performed - and how he would laugh when any one chanced to fall!

After we had skated till we were tired, we were conducted to the pavilion and there delicious refreshments were provided, the prince himself serving us while he made joking comments on the afternoon's occurrences, apparently enjoying it all as much as we did. In the early evening, were turned to our homes very much pleased with our royal entertainment.

The next day I visited the palace to convey the thanks of the group to Their Majesties and tell the King what a very great pleasure he had given us. He smiled and then laughingly said, "The Queen and I placed ourselves where we could watch the skating and were much interested. At first, when we saw one and another fall on the ice, we feared they might be hurt, but, as they got right up again, we soon felt they know how to take care of themselves. As Mrs. Avison didn't fall even once, we decided she was the best skater among the ladies."

Of course I smiled at that and then said I felt the best way to express our gratification was to say we hoped he would give us another opportunity to skate while the ice was in such good condition. At that he laughed heartily and said he would do so.

A few days later he asked me to select a convenient date for the second party and, after conferring with a few of those who had been before gave him the information. An invitation was immediately extended and on that occasion the Queen set aside her own private apartments for our use as dressing rooms skated until we were weary and then enjoyed a bounteous repast in the Queen's apartments. Afterwards Their Majesties gave separate audiences to the ladies and men of the group, an honor which was greatly appreciated.

- Good-bye Dinner at the Palace

In 1899 the Mission recommended our return to Canada on sick leave. When the King heard of our decision to leave, he graciously invited our whole family to dine at the palace, including Baby Martin who was less than a year old. We felt, however, that our two youngest children would be better at home, so we put them to bed before going to the temporary quarters of the King in the Sontag Hotel in Chong Dong where he was living while the new palace in Chong Dong was being erected. This was just after his stay at the Russian Legation.

Shortly after our arrival an audience was granted at which the young prince was present, even though he was barely able to walk. The prince would toddle to our children and play with them, but would not come near us grown-ups and this greatly amused the King.

When dinner was announced we sat down to an entirely Western meal served according to our custom and not a Korean style.

The following day several jiggae loads of presents came to our home, with

His Majesty's compliments and a message conveying his best wishes for a pleasant voyage and the hope that our health would be quickly restored so that we could come back in a very short time. The presents included several bolts of silk, both Korean and Chinese; many Korean fans, Pieces of brass, sundry articles and food. We had to prepare special boxes for these as our trunks were already packed, but we were happy to receive this expression of the King's esteem. These gifts naturally impressed our American and Canadian friends amongst whom they were divided.[44]

The King's Chamberlain, Ko Hui Kyung

Soon after we had settled in our Pakdong home, a young Korean dressed in beautiful silk garments came to call on us. He had recently finished his study of the English language in the Royal English Institute which had been established by the King to train court interpreters. One of its most successful teachers was an Englishman who, having abandoned the life of a sailor when he reached Seoul, had there found this job.

The young man, Ko Hui Kyung, was the son of the Minister of Finance and had recently been appointed as one of the King's Chamberlains. Presumedly he had come to call onus mainly to practice his English but we welcomed him into our home and soon became one of our closest Korean friends. He knew much of the inner life of the palace and told us many stories of their Majesties and of doings within the palace walls.

Not long after our arrival in Seoul I became the King's physician and, to my delight, I found Mr. Ko was to be interpreter. Often when I visited the palace I had to wait on his Majesty's convenience and at such times Mr. Ko would come into the waiting room and he always helped me pass the time pleasantly. The youngest prince, son of Lady Om, often came in and sat with us for he liked the tea and cake which was served at such times.

Mr. Ko was one of his Majesty's favorites who did not fall into trouble; he

---

[44] A jiggie is a framework so constructed that it balances the weight over the strong muscles of the carrier's back. He places his arms through the shoulder straps and goes along swinging a staff which helps him to maintain his balance when he squats down by the roadside to rest. By this ingenius distribution of weight, a load of three or four hundred pounds may be carried on a man's back without a great deal of strain.

remained a faithful chamberlain to the King from 1893 to about 1906 and when Prince Ito of Japan, erving as Resident General in Korea, brought about the abdication of the King in favor of the Crown Prince and he had the young prince sent to Japan to be educated hoping thus to gain a more friendly relationship between the two countries, Ko went with him and continued with him until he, Ko, died. Prince Ito felt that if the young prince could be educated in Japanese schools amid Japanese surroundings he might grow up with a pro-Japanese attitude of mind which would aid in the ultimate success of his own plans for a close relationship between the two countries.

Mr. Ko was chosen to accompany the young prince to Japan as they had grown up together and were fond of each other but this made it easier for the Prince to retain his love for Korea and even though they gave him the rank of a prince of the blood of Japan and brought about his marriage to one of Imperial Japanese princesses he remained a true Korean at heart.

Whenever the young Prince, now the Crown Prince, returned to Korea for a visit I went to the railroad station to greet him and he always came to shake hands with me. On one occasion he passed by me without seeing me but, happening to look back he saw me in the reception line and walked back to shake my hand and smile.

Mr. Ko accompanied the Crown Prince in these visits to Seoul and always came to the hospital to call on me. He had to be careful when talking to folks in Korea but generally he was able to give me some interesting sidelights on matters concerning the Prince. During his stay in Japan he, on two or three occasions, acted as Korean Envoy Extraordinary and Minister Plenipotentiary when that official was absent. Shortly before we left Korea Mr. Ko returned to his home in poor health and soon died. His return to his homeland before he died made it easy for his body to be buried in the family plot in accordance with the desire of all Koreans as well as other Orientals.

General Min Yung Chu and Pak Bong Lai

A Korean young man, Pak Bong Lai, beautifully dressed and with an assurance that might have indicated a position in Korean society of great importance, came to call on me at Pak Dong. A really important man like the King's chamberlain, Koh Hui Kyung, was modest in manner as befitted a gentleman of culture but young Mr. Pak, born in a humble home, who had risen, by his very assumption of importance, to be used by other men as a messenger, Put on all the airs that he thought went with such a position.

He said he had come from the palace of General Min Yung Chu, a cousin of the Queen, who had fallen from his horse and been severely injured and that General Min desired the services of the foreign physician. "Could I come immediately?" "Of course," I said, "I would be very glad to accompany him to the home of the General." The district in which we lived was in the vicinity of the homes of the noble and wealthy families of the city and so, we had not far to go. I suggested we should walk there. That was not in accord with good Korean custom as Pak let me know.

When we reached the outer gates of the Min estate, they were thrown widely open for us and I saw an array of soldiers just inside, apparently waiting to accompany me to the General's sarang (gentleman's sitting room). I had heard how great men were escorted into the palace but this was my initiation into such pomp and ceremony. A soldier on either side of me, hands under my arms, almost carried me in. It was not as comfortable as plain walking but, as they were showing me extreme politeness, I accepted smilingly, I was surprised when the general met meat the door of his sitting room for I had supposed from the description given by Mr. Pak that he had been seriously hurt but I, too, could be polite. So I bowed low and inquired about his injuries. I could see that they consisted of nothing but mere scraches on his face but he expressed great fear they might leave scars if not properly cared for. I had my surgical bag with me so I dressed his wounds as carefully as though they had been serious injuries for I had my reputation to make and must act accordingly.

The General then invited me to sit on the floor with him and was sorry that I had not learned to smoke, I took special notice of the pipe he was smoking, It had a small bowl made of white metal, with a bamboo stem beautifully carved and about four feet in length and a mouthpiece made of shiny amber. As he sat on the floor and smoked, he let the bowl rest on a metal plate, It was evident that he could not light his own pipe - lighting his pipe would not be dignified for a really great man, hence the long stem f When he wished to smoke he called two servants to empty the ashes, Put fresh tobacco into the bowl and light it for him. All he had to do was puff slowly and gracefully as long as the small bowlful of tobacco lasted.

The bowl is only about one third the size of the usual American pipe but as compared with a Japanese pipe, it was very large. A Japanese pipe holds enough tobacco to last for only two or three puffs and requires very frequent refilling and its stem is only about six inches long so the smoker can refill it himself.

As I had already learned a few sentences in Korean, I was able to distinguish some phrases in his conversation. There was one expression that he used frequently : "oo-ree Cho-sun," the English translation of which is: "our Chosun." Chosun was the name of the country at that time. It can be translated as either "morning brightness" or "morning calm." Thus he was saying, "our country" over and over again and saying it with evident pride. The Koreans do love their country and often use this expression in their conversation.

According to good Korean custom I had to be feted before I left and I found the taste of good Korean food quite agreeable. When I left the General's sitting room I was assisted to the outer gate in the same manner in which I had come, a soldier at either elbow helping me along.

Ordinarily a patient with such minor wounds would not have required a second visit by the doctor but General Min was so afraid his face might be scarred that he begged me to come and see him every day until the scratches were completely gone.

I soon learned that this man, Pak, was well known to the Koreans and to the missionaries who had arrived in Korea before we did. When I spoke of him they all smiled and said : "He is always called 'Pak, the liar' because his statements are all so greatly exaggerated." I saw him often afterwards and he was always polite and pleasant to me, traits which doubtless recommended him to those who needed a messenger of combined dignity and servility.

‣ Chapter 6 ◂

Foreigners whom I met in Korea

An Early Experience with a Russian Lady

Seeing a large white building on a hill just inside the West Gate I asked an American Lady - "What is the big white house on that hill, the highest one inside the city walls?"

"That? Oh, that's the Russian Legation. Haven't you been there yet? Well, you and Mrs. Avison must go there next Wednesday afternoon - it will be Mrs. Waeber's 'at home' and she will be glad to see you."

"What do you mean by her at home? That's new to us."

"Well, it is the custom here for every lady in the foreign community to set aside one afternoon every week or every two weeks when she will be at home to receive or entertain guests by serving tea and cake. Wednesday afternoons are all reserved for Mrs. Waeber, the wife of the Russian Minister, and, believe me, no one misses calling on her unless it is absolutely unavoidable for she is in every way the leader of foreign society in the capital."

I reported this conversation to my wife and we decided to go the next week.

Wednesday afternoon came and we went with some hesitation, for we had never met any Russians, but with pleasant anticipation because so many had spoken enthusiastically of Mrs. Waeber. It is quite a climb for, somewhat Russian-like (The Great Northern Bear), they had selected the highest site in the city for their legation so that it can be seen from every part of the city. When we reached the building, somewhat out of breath, we were met by a smiling-faced servant and ushered directly into the great dining room - yes, it was a great room, for they had not only the most prominent site, but also the biggest legation building in the city. Mrs. Waeber sat at the middle of one side of the long dining table, serving tea with a charming smile that made all feel welcome.

Our rather flurried guide introduced us to the hostess - "Mrs. Waeber, we are so sorry to be a bit late but we had to call for our newly arrived friends, Dr. Avison and his little lady, whom, I am sure, you will like. May I introduce them to you?"

"Dr. and Mrs. Avison, I am so glad to see you," she said in the purest of English, "please sit there, right across the table from me, where I can talk with you while I pour your tea."

We took our places quite relieved by her graciousness. The chairs around the large table were nearly all occupied and our introduction to the hostess was considered as an introduction to all her guests - a very good custom that saved any interruption to the sipping of tea, eating of cake, and the vivacious conversation that was carried on by the company. The friends who had brought us sat next us and told us the name and business of each guest.

"That little Japanese couple? They are the Minister for Japan and his wife. We will call on them one of these days. You will like them; That little man over there? Oh, that's Mr. Waeber, Mrs. Waeber's husband, you know. Yes, he's all right. He understands English very well but his speech is a little broken, not like his wife's. He is rather reserved at first, but very pleasant when you get to know him."

"Who are the two rather foreign looking people sitting next to Mr. Waeber?"

"Oh, yes, they are Mr. and Mrs. De Plancy - he is the French Minister. Yes, they speak English too, but with a good deal of accent. You will soon get used to it, though."

So we quickly got to know the faces and characteristics of all the foreign ministers and their wives and also of the other missionaries, many of whom were there.

"Who's that other distinguished looking Frenchman?"

"That's Bishop Mutel, head of the Roman Catholic Mission in Korea. He has lived here since he was quite young and has never been back to his native France. That's the way the French Roman Catholic missionaries do. - No, he doesn't speak much English though he understands most of what we say.

"How do you converse with him, then?"

"Well, I happen to understand some French and so have no trouble. When you learn to speak Korean you will have no difficulty in talking with him for he speaks Korean fluently. In the meantime you can get along with him in English if you keep to the simple forms and do not speak too fast. I will introduce you to him as soon as an opportunity occurs."

So went the chatter.

I had been watching our hostess and wondering at her knowledge of so many languages. Her servants? One was Korean, another Japanese, another Chinese, and she spoke to each in his own tongue, for although each of them knew a little Russian none of them could use it as well as she understood and spoke theirs. She was indeed a remarkable woman.

Mr. Waeber, being the first of all the members of the consular corps then in Seoul to arrive in the country was the dean of that body, and so Mrs. Waeber was the 'first lady' among the foreign residents of the city and leader in all the social affairs of the community. No one else could have filled the position more graciously or more efficiently, If there was sickness in the home of any foreigner she was the first to call and offer symphathy and help and she always took with her some food delicacy or a bottle of wine. If there was a death she was the first to proffer help in the preparations for the funeral.

Thus our new life in Korea served as an introduction to people of several different countries and Seoul proved to be a really cosmopolitan center.

McLeavy Brown

One of the most interesting men of the foreign colony in Korea was McLeavy Brown, an Englishman who had served both England and China in the Chinese Customs Service and, after the opening of Korea to foreign intercourse, was engaged by the Korean Government to direct the customs service in that newly opened country. That post needed a fearless and honest man and in securing Mr. Brown, the government got just that kind of a man.

During the many years of my acquaintance with him I never saw him take advantage of a position that afforded innumerable opportunities for personal gains and I never heard any one, either native or foreign, say that he had done so. What greater praise could be given to a servant of the public? In doing as he did he added much to the already great prestige of the British in the Far East. He not only conducted his special department competently, but gave time and thought to everything likely to add to the beauty of the capital or the advancement of Korea.

As an instance of this, he joined the Mayor of the City - a very talented and honest Korean, Yi Chei Yang, in planning for better streets, better drainage, and a better water supply and they paid for such improvements by taking such good care of the city's funds that many other improvements as well were begun. Unfortunately, the young Mayor was drowned in the river by the upsetting of a boat in which he and young pastor Yi of the Yun Dong Church were taking a pleasure trip and the man who succeeded him as Mayor was an old time Korean who had no ideas of either beauty or sanitation, as applied to the city, and the improvements which would have made Seoul a place of health and a city beautiful were greatly delayed though many of them were introduced in later years.

As time moved on the King more and more trusted Mr. Brown's honesty and good judgment and put him in charge of the country's finances so completely that no order on the treasury, no matter by whom drawn, even though it were the King himself, could be honored without Mr. Borwn's counter signature. All lovers of Korea rejoiced at the opportunity the country had thus gained to place its finances on a sound basis. One of the first acts of the new Finance Director was to make provision for a sound tax system throughout the country magistracies which would enable him to know how much each district was to pay and then see that it was paid in full. Of course, only by such a system of regular payments could wise administrative plans be conducted. He made arrangements also for stopping the sale of offices, for the payment of salaries to magistrates and for a fair assessment of taxation on families or individuals according to a set standard instead of leaving it to the magistrates to collect as much as they could according to their own judgment, a system that opened the door to oppression.

But, alas, other countries were annoyed to see so much power given to a Britisher even though he took pains to appoint men of various nationalities to work with him. Especially was this true of Russia in whose Legation the King had been a refugee guest from February, 1896 to February 20, 1897. Russia naturally used that opportunity to strengthen her claim for a greater share of the posts of influence under His Majesty's disposition and just as naturally His Majesty felt himself under the necessity of yielding to these demands. It was still felt desirable that the Palace Guard should be in charge of Foreign Army Officers. Previously these officer shad been Americans but they were now replaced by Russians. On May 8th Russians sought to increase the number of

Russian military instructors but the Korean Foreign Minister, Yi Wan Yong, refused to sign the agreement and this brought the Russian Admiral Alexioff to Seoul on May the 10th. Then on September 7th the conciliatory Russian Minister Waeber was replaced by the sterner de Spoyer. On October 8th Russian financial agencies arrived and on October 24th were appointed to fill the places of men of other nationalities and we were astonished to learn they had actually persuaded His Majesty to dismiss McLeavy Brown from his service and appoint Admiral Alexioff in his place. This was immediately followed by the establishment in Seoul of the Russo-Korean Bank into which the government's funds here transferred. Thus they stepped at once on the toes of two powers which had long enjoyed the favor of the Korean King, Great Britain and America, and of a third which in spite of the will of the Koreans had acquired a definite stake in the country, Japan.

Ere long, eight British ships under Commander Admiral Buller appeared in the offing of the port of Chemulpo. The Admiral and his staff came up to Seoul to visit the British Minister and pay their respects to the King who received them in a special audience.

When some one asked the Admiral the object of his visit he said he had heard the fishing up around Chemulpo was very good and he had come to try his luck. No other reason was given and apparently he did not find the fishing as good as he had hoped for within a few days, he gathered his fleet together and returned to his accustomed station off China.

But, strange to say, there soon began a series of events which resulted in the closing of the Russo-Korean Bank and placing the money where it had been before (the Japanese Bank); the Russian army instructors departed; Mr. Brown returned to his post. Perhaps the fishing trip was more successful than had appeared on the surface.

It was not long, however, before other changes in the government occurred for there was nothing very lasting in those days of Korea's transition, each outside nation striving to obtain an advantage over the others and these in the end resulted in the cancellation again of Mr. Brown's engagement, and he then retired from his long years of service in China and Korea and returned to England where he spent his remaining years.

So passed from the Far East a real man who had done great things for the closely related Empires of China and Korea when they were suffering the birth pangs of emergence from the oldest of East Asiatic civilizations and the equally severe suffering during their efforts to find their way into the new civilization of the West.

Notes from the Diary of an American Business Man Living in Seoul

In reply to my request he sent me the following:

Sunday Work

The lady Missionary had bothered me about six months to give the husband of one of her bible helpers a position on the Street Railway. She lived at the time at the East Gate Hospital. After he had been working about two months she came to me and asked if he could be excused from Sunday work. I told her that it might be arranged but said to her, "Suppose all the Missionaries came to me and asked to have all the men that I had given positions to let off on Sunday, what did she suppose would happen?" I said a lot of the Missionaries going to Church would have to walk or engage a riksha. Seventy - five percent of the conductors and motor-men were from Mission Schools and were recommended by Missionaries.

Another missionary - a man this time - came to me to complain because a conductor who was one of his Christian converts had to work on Sundays. He too wanted him to be given a Sunday holiday. I asked the missionary how he got to the foreign church on Sunday for his home was about two miles from the church. He said he went on the street cars. "Well," I said, "is it not wrong for you to ride on a street car on Sunday when it makes men work on sunday so you can ride?"

When the Street Railway was started they had a private car for His Majesty, the Emperor. He never used it but one day we had a request from him to have the car near the Memorial Tablet on the corner of Department Street and the East to West Gate Street. The "Fat Prince" wanted to go out to the Queen's Tomb and he had a lot of servants with him. Well, as you know, at first we only had a single road track, with switches to allow cars to pass each other. I had the car there at 10.55 A. M. and we switched it up and down the line waiting for the prince to come out of his house which was near that point. He finally showed up with all his friends and servants at 2.45 P. M. They more than filled the car and I had to send one of the regular cars coming from West Gate with the servants that could not get on the private car, and I phoned the East Gate car shed to send another car in place of the regular one that would have to go out to the Queen's Tomb. It was after 11.00 P. M. before they were ready to return from the Queen's Tomb. Of course they had plenty to eat and drink and had a grand time.

George Washington

One evening I was coming up from the East Gate with the late Robert A. Mclellan, the Chief Engineer of the company, and the late Henry G. English, Chief Electrician. It was snowing and blowing heavily and at Department Street a well - dressed Korean got on the front car, came in with a great rush, and sat down on a seat opposite us. Mr. English said, "You must have been blown in with the storm." The passenger replied in perfect English, "I suppose you think I am crazy." Mr. English was very much surprised and asked him what his name was. He said, "My name is George Hong and he was the nephew of Yi Chai Young, who at that time was the Governor of the City.

Young Hong had run away to America and gone to school in San Rafael which is across the Bay from San Francisco. I knew him quite well for several years after this incident.

Escape of Two Nationalist Leaders

Here is one of the strangest things that I have ever experienced in Korea. I was building a house outside West Gate on the hill. This house afterwards was burned down while my wife was in San Francisco and I was on a trip to Unsan Mines at Hokuchin.

I had a Chinese contractor building the house. His office was in the old store that Steward Co. ran on Legation Street near the West Gate just about opposite where I had my office during the last few years I was in Korea. Two rooms were finished and I was living in them and looking after the building of the house night and morning. One morning at 2:30 a man came to the new house and handed me a note from Dr. -- that said, "I am in trouble and you are the only one that can help me out. Please come to my house at once." I got over there about 3:15 A. M.

Dr. -- was in his study and he had two young Koreans there. One of them was the nephew of a high official and the other man was from Pyong Yang. He was the greatest orator in the country and was a Christian.

Both had just been released from prison by the people who are now running the country. Dr. - said that they would be arrested again as soon as they went out. They had been warned by their friends to that effect and they had to get out as soon as possible. He could not keep them in the house as he would get into trouble.

Well this matter stumped me for some time, but finally I said, "All right, Dr. -- . I will get them out within two hours. I must leave now but I will be back as soon as I have arranged matters." He asked what I was going to do. I said, "Never mind, I will get them out safely and that is all that is necessary for the time being." So I went to my Chinese builder's shop and it was about 4:30 A. M.

When I finally got him up, I told him I wanted him to get two suits of Chinese carpenters' clothes, and find two Chinese carpenters and bring them with him. He was to follow me to Dr. - 's house Pig Tails and Chinese caps.

Well, when we arrived at Dr. - 's house he was more than surprised, The two Korean gentlemen did not like to put on the old Chinese clothes but as I said it was the only thing to do they finally let the builder dress them up and put some dirt on their faces. At 7:30 A. M. four Chinese carpenters went to the builder's place. Two days afterwards they took the train which at that time started outside the West Gate near the old pastor house and went to Chemulpo to take a boat for Chefoo. I was at the station. There were four Japanese police there watching all the passengers but they did not see anything wrong with the Chinese carpenters and about two weeks after that time Dr. - sent for me and said that a Korean friend had come to him and handed him a letter from the young men who landed safely in Peking.

They sent him 1, 000 yen to pay me for the expenses I had been put to and for helping them out. Dr. - always appreciated this and said time and again that he does not know what would have happened to these men if they had gotten out and that I was the only one that he could think of that could have put the thing over the way I did.

Another Strange Experience

I had been in Seoul about three weeks. We street railway men were all living in a house which we called the California House. It was just below the East Side of the hill that the Russian Consulate Building is on. A street ran in from the East Gate Street just about opposite where the Salvation Army Headquarters are.

At 3 A. M. I was awakened out of a sound sleep. I got up and lighted a lamp, as the men who knocked on the door nearly broke it down. I looked out and man who knocked on gun with a fixed bayonet on it and back of him a whole company of soldiers with fixed bayonets. The man at the door handed me a note and it was from W. F. Sands who had just been made advisor of His Majesty. He told me in the note of two Koreans who had been refugees in Japan for some years on account of being connected with the Murder of the Queen. The name of one was

Kwon and I think the other one was Youn. They had just returned from Japan and the Japanese had made His Majesty promise that he would not torture them when they returned. As soon as they landed, however, His Majesty had them arrested and taken to the prison just inside the little West Gate opposite where the late H. R. Boswick lived, and there had them hanged.

His Majesty was having a meeting in the palace that night and the Japanese were there accusing him of going back on his promise. They said that both these men had been tortured and made to confess a lot of things that they had never done. So Sands requested me to go with the company of soldiers, examine both bodies and report to him what I had seen. I went over. They were both fine looking men. Both were naked and the only mark on either body was a black ring around the neck of each made by the ropes that hanged them. I wrote out a report accordingly and sent it to Sands. Well, the Japanese claimed that they knew better and that they had proof that these men had been cut to pieces. They raised a big row about it. The next morning Sands had Dr. Baldock of the English Church Mission go in and examine the bodies. The latter had Dr. Wada, who was then a Navy surgeon with the Japanese, go with him. They both went and examined the bodies and made the same kind of a report that I had made so the Japanese could do nothing further. His Majesty had not tortured them - he just had them hanged.

An Occurrence at the Barracks

I suppose you remember the day at the old barracks inside the little West Gate, when you, Dr. Avison, with Dr. Hirst and myself were in there shortly after the Korean soldiers had opened the gate to the Barracks and set off a cannon, killing a bunch of Japanese soldiers, who were demanding their surrender. And also the soldiers that we saw with all the bayonet wounds who had hidden under the building, which was a good illustration of how cruel Japanese soldiers can be. Also all the wounded that you had taken to Severance. One officer had been shot in the abdomen and his intestines were all cut to pieces and you and Dr. Hirst were to do what you could for him. Worms were crawling in masses out of the holes in the intestines made by the bullets.

An Explosion

Another day when I went over to the old hospital, you were dressing up four men who had been back of a cannon when it exploded. I took a picture of them for you. Their heads, hands and arms were all bandaged up.

Smallpox

Perhaps you will remember something that happened about two weeks after I was married. A Korean boy was stealing a ride on one of the electric cars and just as it was passing a switch.

He jumped off right in front of another car that was leaving the switch, It ran over his right leg above the knee. They telephoned me and I went down at once. The blood was squirting out of his leg. I had an interpreter named Chang, whom I called Charlie. He went down with me and as soon as I saw the boy, who was about twelve or fifteen, I sent Charlie to a cloth store to get a yard of cotton cloth, I made a torque out of it, got a stick and twisted it up tight and told Charlie to get a riksha and we would take him to Severance. A big crowd gathered and insisted that he be taken home first, so we went to his house where they carried him into a room and put him on an old mattress in the corner. After about an hour, the people said we could take him to the hospital and just after leaving the house, Charlie said, "Well, Mr. Morris, this family is having hard luck today I" I said, "How is that?" He said that just about an hour ago they took the boy's older brother out to be buried. When I asked what had happened to him, he said, "Oh, he died last night with smallpox."

I asked where he died and he said, "In that room we were in - he died on that matress we put this boy on." When I got to the hospital and turned the boy over to you, I told you about the brother dying with smallpox on the mattress in the room where we put the boy with the injured leg and asked you what I had better do about it.

You gave me a basin with disinfectant in it and told me to wash my hands and face but to be careful of my eyes, and said that when I went home I should say nothing about the matter. Well that is what I did and nothing happened. In the early days, every day I saw women getting on the cars with infants on their backs with the infant's faces covered with smallpox and all scabby. Within a few years this was all cleared.

A Cholera Reminiscence

When the cholera epidemic struck Seoul one year, I had conductors and motormen go home to lunch. Later in the day, the parents brought back their badges and ticket punches, as they had died with cholera. Many of my men who, working on the track, went over to the side of the road and died. I counted 300 corpses being carried outside the small East Gate and piled up on the hillside.

Prince Ito

After Japan had signed its Treaty of Friendship and Commerce with the U. S. A. and other nations in 1882, she began to consider how she could best turn this move to her advantage. She sent men to observe the strong points and the weaknesses of the various foreign countries and, on receiving their reports, dispatched young men as students to the U. S. A., Great Britain, Germany and France to learn their respective languages and study the particular lines in which each country excelled. On their return she copied the educational methods and army regulations of Germany, followed the naval methods of England, and copied the legal code of France.

A young nobleman named Ito decided to go to England to study the form of government and Navy of Great Britain and then also visited the U. S. A. to compare its government methods with those of England. He returned strongly impressed with what he had learned and became the chief leader of the Japanese venture into the ways of the Western world.

My first introduction to this greatest of all Japanese statesmen was in 1895 when he was on his way to China to arrange for and sign the Treaty of Peace after Japan's victory over that country. On his way to China, he made a short stop in Seoul and the Japanese Minister gave a dinner party at the Legation in his honour at which I had the privilege of being a guest.

It was one of the hottest evenings of that midsummer season and I wore a white suit with a short naval coat such as was then commonly worn in the Orient as formal dress in summer. Dr. Horace N. Allen, Secretary of the American Legation, in whose company I had gone, was being sorry for himself because he had not worn a similar costume instead of the more formal black suit and tailed coat.

The Prince was a perfect example of courtliness and courteousness. Is there a distinction between these? Though dignified in his bearing he had a charming smile that made everyone with whom he conversed a friend. He spoke English almost perfectly, having acquired that language in England and America. His conversation gave evidence that he had made good use of his time while there and that he liked the Western people and admired their democratic institutions.

- Japan's first Resident General in Korea

Later, when peace had been concluded between Japan and Russia in 1905, he was sent to Korea as Japan's first Resident General and his desire to combine service to his own country with the improvement of conditions in Korea was very evident and I think sincere, but the hatred of the Korean Emperor and people for the Japanese, a hatred which had lasted ever since the Hideyoshi invasion in 1591 and had been intensified by the ruthlessness of the Japanese during the years between 1893 and 1905, stood in the way of any friendly co-operation on the part of Korea. The latter could not forget the degradation to which their queen had been subjected, the indignities shown to them in the forced cutting off of their topknots and the destruction of their political independence so they were in no frame of mind to even consider friendly relations with Japan.

The King had grudgingly yielded to their demands for this and that concession when heavy pressure was put on him for he realized he must either give in or lose his crown completely. So the Japanese government sent its wisest man over as Resident, as stated above, but even he found the difficulties almost insurmountable.

It was not long before he recognized that the influence of the missionaries on the people was greater than that of any other group and he set himself to the task of establishing friendly relations with them.

Just at that time the Hon. Wm. Bryce, British Ambassador to the U. S. A., resigned his post and, on his way to England, visited the Far East to make himself more familiar with its problems and especially to learn what might be done about the relations between Japan and Korea.

While in Korea he was the guest of Sir John Jordan, British Minister who called me to the Legation for a conference with him. At Mr. Bryce's request I talked frankly with him on that subject. Naturally I was pro-Korean and urged that England and America should see to it that Korea's freedom should be restored. He then called on Resident General Ito with whom he also discussed the same subject, and then he met me again. He told me frankly what he had learned from the Prince who had said that he was in quite friendly relations with the missionaries but feared them more than any other group. The reason he gave for this fear was that the native Christian group, under the. guidance of the missionaries had attained a degree of self-reliance and cohesion not to be found in any other body of Koreans so that the Christians could give the Japanese more trouble than any other group. He had no fear that the missionaries would interfere in the political situation but the Korean Christians had gotten, through their contacts with them, an ability to stick together in a way that was not found in others. He would certainly, therefore, in the interests of his own country, be glad if the missionary influence, indirect as he knew it to be, could be eliminated.

I asked Mr. Bryce his own opinion of the situation after hearing from both sides. His answer was politic. He took the view that as the Japanese had actually taken possession of Korea, it now had to be considered as "un fait accompli," in the phraseology of the diplomats meaning "a thing accomplished and presumably irrevocable." That being the case it was the part of wisdom for all parties to accept the situation and guide themselves accordingly. He said he did not wish me to infer that it was something that he personally approved or that he expected the friends of Korea to approve but, as nothing was to be gained by continued opposition to the ruling power, he hoped I would do my best to bring my fellow missionaries and the Koreans to regard it in that light.

I did not feel it necessary or wise to make any reply to that suggestion except to remind him that it was not the practice of missionaries to advise the people with whom they worked either pro or con on any political situation. He smiled the smile of the trained diplomat and the subject was dropped. I had the pleasure of meeting him again that evening at a dinner given in his honor by the British Minister. And next day he continued his journey to England where I suppose he gave his government the same service he had given me.

- First Graduation Exercises of the Severance Hospital Medical School

In the early summer of 1908, when I was preparing for the first graduation exercises of the institution which we rather presumptuously called a Medical College, I realized that I must get the approval of the Resident General before venturing to give diplomas to the seven young men who had completed the course of studies I had prescribed for them. By no other method could three young men gain legal right to practise as physicians, so I followed the only road open tome.

So one afternoon, after arranging for a conference with him, I met him at his home and was most graciously received.1 told him the whole story of the many years these young men had been studying medicine under my supervision and how they had covered all the courses given in medical schools in America; how they had successfully passed a thorough examination and were now, in my judgement, Prepared to practice their profession, and that to enable them to do this₁ would need his cooperation. Having listened with patience and apparent interest to my long story, he expressed his satisfaction at what had been accomplished, and asked "What can I do to help. What do you want me to do?" I said I felt this first graduation of doctors in Korea marked an epoch in the forward movement of the country and that I wished to make it a day to be re-membered, not only by the graduates themselves, but also by all who might come to see these first diplomas presented and he said that was a fine idea. I ex-plained that many invitations would be issued to the foreign representatives, to government people, to friends of the graduates and to many others who ought to be interested in such an event but we found ourselves without a room large enough for such a purpose.

"That is a fine plan but how can I help you to provide such a room?"

"We haven't a room but we could make one over the lawn if he would lend us army tents enough, when they were put together, this would cover the re-quired space."

He smiled at the idea but said he would be glad to arrange that for us." "Is there anything else?"

"Yes, I hope you will attend the function and let the young men and their friends see that you are interested in them."

"That would give me great pleasure." he replied.

Then I felt encouraged to ask him to present the diplomas and, when he agreed, I said, "I am making very bold your Excellency, but if you will deliver an address of advice and instruction to the young men I am sure they will appre-ciate it very much and I too will be grateful."

He fully carried out his promises to me when on June 8, 1908 the Korean young men who had been the first to receive a Western type medical examina-tion on their own land received their diplomas at his hands and, next day, at his direction, the Sanitary Department issued to each young doctor a license to practice his profession throughout Korea.

- Ito's View on Chosun and the Missionaries

When he smilingly promised to do this I arose to leave but he asked me to sit down again as he would like to talk with me about his plans for the Korean people. He said he knew that many influential men in Japan wanted to annex Korea and merge it into the Japanese Empire as a province, but he did not approve of that. He believed the best interests of both Japan and Korea, as an independent country, would be a friendly neighbor to Japan, he would do all he could to help her. He felt sure the Japanese Government would agree to such a course if he urged it but, he insisted, it would be absolutely necessary for Korea to be really friendly with Japan if it was to maintain its independence and it would be only on such an understanding that he, who had a real desire to see Korea become a strong power, could devote himself to this ideal.

This conference lasted more than two hours during which time he talked at length on the subject. Realizing that he was doing this in the hope that I would pass his views on to the rest of the community, especially to my fellow missionaries, I listened with the greatest interest for here was the wisest of all Japan's statesmen, the man who had really made the new Japan, wanting little me to be his mouth piece to the group of foreigners who he felt had more influence with the Korean people than any other persons, either foreign or Korean.

I explained to him that the missionaries had only one purpose in Korea - to win the people to the Christian faith by teaching and example and by convincing them of our desire for their welfare by helping them through our churches, schools and hospitals to a better mode of life. I further assured him that we were all firm in our decision not to interfere m any political matters. When he agreed this was a proper attitude, I talked with him at length about this question of missionary interference in foreign politics.

I referred him to a book recently published by Prof. Ladd of Yale University entitled "With Prince Ito in Korea." Prof. Ladd had spent some time in Japan where he had been in conference with Prince Ito and they had come to Korea together when the Prince took up his assignment as Resident General.

On reaching Korea, Ladd had asked the Y. M. C. A in Seoul to allow him to deliver a series of lectures to Korean young men in the Y. M. C. A. building. The "Y" Secretary, an American, having learned of his views concerning the future relations of Korea to Japan, said it would be difficult for him to allow Dr. Ladd to use the Y. M. C. A. platform for the delivery of lectures of a political nature because that organization was an entirely non-political institution. Only the directors, he said, could decide on his request and he would call a meeting at which he, Dr. Ladd, could present his request.

At the meeting of the Board, Prof. Ladd repeated his request. When the Board members questioned him concerning the topics he would discuss it was found all were connected with the relations between Korea and Japan and the Board decided that the platform could not be used for such a discussions. To give one person the privilege of speaking on one side of such a question would necessitate the granting of a familiar privilege to opponents of that policy Und serious trouble might ensue. The Board was very careful to remind Prof. Ladd that it was expressing no opinion concerning the matters in which he was interested and suggested that they would be glad to listen to his addresses if he delivered them from some other platform. As a member of the Board, I was present at the meeting and was much hurt to find Prof. Ladd not only disappointed but aggrieved at our decision. He really abused us a good deal and accused the missionaries of constant interference in the political situation. He claimed they urged the Koreans to refuse all Japan's efforts to bring about closer relationships.

The professor seemed to regard me as the prime mover in all this and declared that my relation with the King as physician was that of a spy against the Japanese and my business was less that of a physician than of a messenger to carry news to and from the palace.

I pointed out to the Prince that Prof. Ladd repeated those charges in a book which he published after his return to America. In it he claimed to be Prince Ito's adviser in matters connected with Korea, a claim that seemed to us ridiculous as we were well aware that His Excellency knew far more about Korea than the writer of the book could possibly do.

As for the charge he made that I was a spy on behalf of the King - that was something that must be amusing to His Excellency because all my relations with His Majesty or with any other persons in the palace were well known to him. I was sure he, the Prince, had ways of learning all about what took place there for I had had the honor of meeting him many times both in the palace and outside and I was sure he knew everything that took place there

His answer to all this was a most charming smile and the remark that of course he had means of knowing what was going on and was quite sure my relations with the palace were in all respects proper.

He went on to say further that, in the nature of things, many policemen and others, who desired his favor, were constantly bringing him reports of what they had heard this or the other man say but he knew that many of those reports were based on parts of sentence they had heard uttered and then filled in with their own ideas of what the people had been talking about. But, he said, he knew how to distinguish the false from the true especially as he knew the real character of the men being reported on. No one need fear that he would too readily accept what were clearly distorted statements.

"Do not be afraid that I shall misjudge you and your companions for I know you to be men of integrity," he said.

I thanked him and said that none of us ever replied to Prof. Ladd's statements. However, it was quite natural that the missionaries who were giving their lives to promote the welfare of the Korean people should sympathize with them in their sorrw though I was sure none of them ever transgrossed the bounds of propriety by interfering in any of their political affairs. They were keenly sympathetic toward the Koreans just in the same way that the missionaries in Japan were towards the people they were trying to serve.

Then I ventured to say that if Japan had lost the recent war with Russia, the Russians might have gone over and taken possession of Japan. If that had happened and the missionaries, dropping their interest in the Japanese people, should have helped the Russians what would the japanese have thought of them?

He said they would have lost all their respect for the missionaries, of course, and it would be difficult for him even to imagine such a possibility, knowing the missionaries thereas well as he did.

"Well," I said, "you won the war and took possession of Korea, and now you are expecting the missionaries in Korea to do the very thing for which you would have despised those in Japan if they had sided with the Russians. Is that fair?"

He was quiet for a moment or two and then said he saw my point and realized the missionaries in Korea were doing the only thing that could be expected of them.

Of course I reported all this to the other missionaries, who were much pleased with his statesmanlike point of view of the relations that might exist between the two countries and with his recognition of the correctness of our attitude.

• Ito's End

Unfortunately, a Korean patriot assassinated the Prince a few months later as he stepped off a train at Mukden in Manchuria. The man knew the Prince was the representative of Japan in Korea but did not know his attitude and that he was the best friend Korea had under existing conditions and the one best able to carry out his benevolent intentions. He only thought he was proving his loyalty to his country by this act. He must have known he would lose his own life as he could not expect to escape when the man he shot was surrounded by a body of policemen. As a matter of fact he was immediately arrested and speedily executed.

Sone Araske

The Vice-Resident General, Sone Araske succeeded to the vacant post. He held views similar to those of his predecessor but it is very doubtful whether he could have carried out the Prince's plans as he had not the latter's prestige in Japan. His health was even then undermined by an ulceration of the stomach and, within a brief period, he resigned his post and returned to Japan where he passed away soon afterwards.

His successor was General Count Terauchi, who, it is said, came to Korea with a mandate from his country to prepare the way for the annexation which actually did take place in 1910.

Governor General Saito (1919-1929)

At the end of the unarmed uprising of 1919 General Hasegawa withdrew from his position as chief executive of the government in Korea and was succeeded by Admiral Saito. When, following the usual custom, the men of the foreign community called on the new Governor General at his residence they were greatly astonished to find him dressed in an ordinary business suit, wearing no medals and with no even a sword at his side. All his predecessors had, on such occasions, appeared in full uniform with a sword dangling at their sides and their breasts covered with medals. But Governor General Saito wore nothing to distinguish him from his guests. He was very gracious in a simple way and all were immediately at ease in his presence.

After retiring from the residency guests of course discussed this and the explanation suggested by one of the men was that it had been observed that Japanese admirals were always more simple and courteous than were generals. Why? When Japan opened her doors to foreign nations in 1879 she looked carefully at the various Western nations and compared their apparent strength as regarded their navies, armies, educational systems, and law courts and selected England for the training of her naval officers, and Germany for her army officers - hence the difference. Her army officers followed the methods and characteristics of the Germans and her naval officers those of the British and even to this day those two different types of training are reflected in the two branches of the fighting force. So ran the comments. The German autocratic spirit is also exemplified in the educational system of Japan which was in that early day based on German ideas and ideals. Baron Saito was a fine example of the broader democracy of the British navy.

The Baroness too was a splendid companion for a man so trained. She had received her education at the Canadian Missionary School in Tokyo and was a fine sample of Japanese womanhood and devotion to the work of her husband.

In spite of the faithlessness of the Japanese in depriving Korea of its independence Saito had a genuine sympathy for the Koreans and seemed to understand their desire to regain their independence, In fact, he conceded it to be praiseworthy though, of course, he had to carry out the policies of his own government in all his relations with them. Because of this sympathy and also because of his efforts to be fair in all his dealings with them he won the admiration and even the goodwill of many Koreans.

The group of Koreans who were giving their best efforts to regain their country's independence recognized this fact and regretted it as was made apparent to me by a young man who had been a leader in the uprising of 1919. One day, while calling at my home, he said he and all the Koreans acknowledged that the governor was a really fine Japanese gentleman, a man to be greatly admired and even loved, but it was just those qualities in him that made them refuse to support him and to oppose all he did even what they knew was intended for the good of Korea. They felt his very goodness might lead the younger Koreans, as they grew up, to lose their natural hatred of the Japanese and begin to regard themselves as an integral part of the Japanese Empire and so Korea would cease to struggle for its independence. From that standpoint it seemed to them it would be for Korea's ultimate good to have the worst men sent over to rule them so that the desire for an independent Korea would continue to grow stronger.

At the time the baron came to Korea the policy of Japan in regard to Korean education seemed to be founded on the idea of limiting it to a much lower grade than was being given to the Japanese residents in order to keep the conquered people from competing with their conquerors and reaching a position where they might become more difficult to rule, while, on the other hand, the schools conducted for the Koreans by the missionaries were of a high order. Their religious teaching was considered by the Japanese as subversive of Japanese interest and so a ban was placed on all religious instruction, not only in the national schools but in all schools. That made it difficult to carry on the mission schools satisfactorily.

I was personally interested in this because I was in charge of two mission colleges - the Severance Union Medical and the Chosen Christian College, and so I took a considerable part in the efforts made by the Missions to have a more liberal interpretation of the educational regulations made. In a conversation with the Governor General about school matters on one occasion, I suggested that the regulations regarding schools be interpreted to mean that incase any school carried out in full the curriculum of the Educational Department, the government should not object to the addition of other subjects to its curriculum that were not in themselves objectionable. I did not say what the extra subjects might be but left it to him to draw his own conclusions.

This suggestion evidently bore fruit for one day a messenger came to my home to say that the Governor General desired me to meet him at his residence that afternoon for a conference on school matters. Of course I said I would go and then the messenger asked if there were any one I would like to have accompany me. I suggested Rev. Mr. Koons, principal of our Boys' High School who of course would be deeply interested in such a conference and the messenger said he would call on Mr. Koons at once and invite him. As soon as he left me I got in touch with Mr. Koons by telephone so as to make sure he would be in when the messenger called.

We went to the Government House at the designated time and were at once taken to a room in which we found His Excellency surrounded by all the members of his cabinet and other officials especially concerned with education. I supposed they wished to question us about same matters connected with education or perhaps warn us about some closer observance of the regulations but, instead of that, the Governor drew from his pocket a document and, spreading it on the table, began to read it aloud, It turned out to be a new interpretation of the regulations and it said that though all schools were expected to carry out in full the educational program of the government but schools specially recognized by the Educational Department as fully equipped and manned with satisfactory teachers, and as fulfilling all the requirements of the educational system should have the privilege of adding to their curriculums other subjects which they might wish to teach in addition. We listened intently, and when he had finished, he asked me what I thought of it. I glanced at Mr. Koons who nodded his head and I replied that we were both pleased with that liberal interpretation of the government's educational regulations. The conference then came to an end and we returned to report the matter to our co-workers. This, of course, greatly increased the popularity of the Governor General with both missionaries and Korean Christians.

His success in his administration apparently pleased his home government for he was soon afterwards elevated to the rank of a Viscont.

During the latter period of his Governorship, he was sent to London as head of his country's commission to meet with representatives of those countries that had been parties to the making of the Treaty of Washington in 1921 when Great Britain, the United States, France, and Japan settled the ratio of the naval power of each at 5, 5, 4, and 3 respectively. The Japanese naval authorities, feeling this ratio was unfair to them, asked for another convention to reconsider the question in view of the growing importance of Japan and its need for more ships. Unfortunately for Japan the other nations involved did not see eye to eye with them and the same ratio was extended to a further period of years, though certain minor concessions were made to Japan on the return of the Japanese delegation to Tokyo the matter was reported to the Diet and Matsuoka, a member of the commission, strove hard to have that body repudiate this decision of the London Convention. He failed in this but succeeded in forming a strong anti-Saito clique which did not rest until it had brought about the latter's death at the hands of the Japanese army officers. Admiral Saito had been given only a leave of absence from Korea to attend that Convention so on his return from London he resumed his duties in Korea, completing a period of years' occupanvy of his post. On his return to Japan he became the leader of the liberal wing in the Japanese Diet and within a dhort time rose to be Prime Minister On the occasion of a visit to Japan I gave myself the honor of calling on him at the Premier's office where he greeted me very kindly and offered me his help in the attainment of my purpose in visiting his country.

After serving in the position of Prime Minister he became keeper of the Privy Seal, an office that brought him into frequent personal contacts with the Emperor, thus giving him a great influence in the court. Then came a change in the spirit and aims of the Japanese, mostly due to the machinations of his co-commissioner Matsuoka who had never slackened in his efforts to arouse a strong military desire for the conquest of China, the first step to the bringing together of the yellow races of the world to take from the white races the world dominance they had long held.

General Ugaki was Saito's successor to the Governor Generalship and the friends of Korea feared that his appointment would bring sad results. But instead, the General became deeply impressed with the good qualities of the Korean people and did much to improve their conditions so that next to Saito, he was the best of all the governors sent over from Japan. He served several years and on his return to his homeland he, like Saito, became the Prime Minister, but in a government that was dominantly warlike. Apparently his military confreres expected him to hold views of world conquest similar to their own but he disappointed them and refused to cooperate in their plans even for the subjection of China, declaring he would rather resign his high office in the army than be responsible for the prosecution of their schemes. This, of course, under the circumstances, meant that his high place in the government would soon be taken from him. Before that occurred, however, a group of young and overenthusiastic officers in the army decided to do away with both him and Saito.

In pursuance of this plan some sought Ugaki and finding him, as they supposed, killed him without warning, It turned out that they had killed his brother and the General himself took his place in the sitting of the Diet the next day.

Others sought for Saito at his country home at midnight. When they called for him to leave his bed and come out to meet them. He, in spite of his wife's pleading, went out hoping, Probably to reason with them. She followed him and begged them to kill her instead as his country needed him. They, however, shot him as she pleaded. And thus ended a life that had meant much to his country. He had lifted the political life of his day to a high level and even in his old age increased the regard that some foreign countries had for Japan.

The following is a copy of the author's testimonial to Governor General Saito that was being published by the Japanese Government after his retirement to Japan.

Viscout Saito

Though I must write very briefly, my heart responds very full to the request that I testify to the goodness and greatness of Governor General Saito and his lady as manifested during their ten years' residence in Korea.

Viscount Saito came to Korea in succession to several governors who had been more concerned with the military enforcement of Korea's submission to Japanese rule than to winning the homage of the people to their new rulers. They always wore military uniforms when appearing in public and the sword was always in view as the emblem of their authority.

How surprised we foreigners were when - on the occasion of our first call on Governor General Saito - we were introduced not to an Admiral of the Fleet but to a benevolent-looking gentleman dressed in an ordinary American business suit, with no military emblems in sight and not even any of the many decorations which had been bestowed upon him by his Emperor! Naturally, our hearts warmed to him at once. From that time on, the sword was not manifest as the symbol of Japanese rule in Korea, at least during his reign.

A few years later, one of the most intensely patriotic of the young men of Korea said to me: Of course, we all know that Governor General Saito is a perfect gentleman, though he is a Japanese, and we recognize that he has the welfare of Korea at heart and that is why we do not like him as governor, If he stays too long, children will grow up contented to be subjects of Japan. This will make it more difficult for Korean patriots to keep alive the Korean spirit that will make it possible for Korea to regain her independence some day. So, while we admire the Viscount as a fine and noble gentleman, we do not want him as a governor. The worse the governor, the easier it will be to keep alive the Korean spirit.

When he took up his duties as Governor General, the missionaries were vainly endeavoring to obtain some concessions that would enable them to carry on their schools without giving up the right to teach the Bible and hold Christian services as a part of the regular curriculum. At that time this was forbidden by the educational regulations of Japan. But we found Viscount Saito very sympathetc and, in time, he promulgated special regulations which made it possible to carry on the evangelistic work in and through the schools. This understanding attitude towards the work of the missionaries won not only for himself but for the Japanese Government also a greater degree of cooperation from the missionaries and the Korean Christians than any other course would have done.

Throughout the entire period of his illustrious career, Viscount Saito's service was greatly enhanced by the gracious assistant and sympathetic understanding rendered on all occasions by his charming wife, Viscountess Saito.

Oliver R. Avison, N. D. C. M., LL.D

President Emeritus, Severance Union Medical College
President Emeritus, Chosun Christian College

The receipt of the above, sent from America after our retirement from Korea, was duly acknowledged by Mr. Oda. English language interpreter for the Government General, who had asked me to write a testimonial to be published in a book that was to be presented to the Viscountess, I fear it did not meet with the favor of the Japanese Government, for although ı received from Mr. Oda an acknowledgement of its receipt by him I heard nothing further from him although I had been given to understand that a copy of the book could be sent to each contributor. Apparently my commendation of him was not the kind that was desired.

Mr. Oda

The Japanese are not all bad. In these memoirs I have already told of Prince Ito who was a princely man and a real statesman, I have also mentioned Governor General Saito and his successor General Ugaki, all known by name and reputation at least.

Kagawa, the greatest Christian of Japan is probably one of the most devoted followers of Christ in the world today. Men of all nationalities living in Japan as representatives of States, Christianity, Learning and Science could tell of many other examples of fine Japanese and it is all that at this time, when the worst elements of Japanese politicians and militarists have brought their country into contempt, the world should be reminded that just now Japan is being misrepresented by those in authority. While she will have to suffer both the contempt of the other nations and the national punishment that those in control are earning for themselves and which all good will have to endure, we must stand ready to lend a helping hand when the time comes for correcting the political and economic abuses which we have all helped to build into the world structure.

In the meantime the fact that those who know Japan best can testify to the genuineness of many Japanese men and women should prepare us to give that country the same consideration that God is said to have given the world when at the pleading of Abraham, he spared the whole nation when only one man was shown to be worthy.

Mr. Oda, when a young man, went to the U. S. A. for a higher education than he could acquire in his own country. He studied at and returned in due time not only educationally fitted to serve his people but as a sincere follower of Jesus Christ.

When Saito brought him to Korea to act as his English interpreter he did Japan a real service in letting the Korean people see that at least some Japanese are kind and courteous and fair and, at the same time, he made it possible for foreigners generally and missionaries particularly to feel sure their views and wishes were properly presented when they had matters to lay before the heads of governmental departments.

Mr. Oda's knowledge of English and his conscientious desire to help both his own government and the foreigners made both sides sure that they understood and were understood. As already stated, he is a sincere Christian and has for many years been superintendent of the Japanese Methodist Church Sunday School in Seoul.

His whole time is given to two endeavors - first as a language interpreter for those who do not understand Japanese and for which his good use of English and the understanding of American ideals and customs which he imbibed during his long stay in the U. S. A. expecially fit him, and, second, as an interpreter of the intentions of both the Japanese Government officials and the foreigners in their dealings with each other. This second kind of interpretation is especially useful because much of the animosity that national groups of different countries feel towards each other is due to the mutual misunderstanding of each other's ideas. Misunderstanding of this kind underlies many disputes between the members of different national groups so that an interpreter who can clarify such unfortunate misapprehensions is especially valuable. Just such an interpreter is Mr. Oda.

On the other hand a government interpreter is sometimes placed in a very difficult situation and this happened to Mr. Oda several times during the years of my association with him. One such example will suffice.

During the fist Shanghai incident when the Japanese army and navy were bombing and burning the Chinese part of that city at the beginning of the war between Japan and China and shocking the rest of the world so deeply that Japan completely lost her reputation as a civilized nation, the then Foreign Minister of the Japanese Government in Korea felt it desirable to try to explain to the foreign missionaries that what Japan was doing in Shanghai was inevitable because the Chinese refused to accept Japanese domination peacefully. He, therefore, invited about a dozen of the older Protestant missionaries in Seoul to dinner at the Banker's Club in which group I was included.

After a sumptuous dinner, we were ushered into the beautiful drawing room where comfortable chairs and sofas were arranged by a wide fireplace. Some time was spent in general conversation between the Minister and his guests. Fortunately the host understood enough English for this butwe all knew this was only preliminary.

After a time Mr. Oda introduced the real purpose of the gathering which, as he put it, was to explain to us, as representatives of the missionaries, that the things that were occurring in Shanghai were unavoidable in spite of the good intentions of the Japanese government and also of the commanders of the army engaged in doing them.

He brought out photographs of the terrible doings of the Chinese in opposing the benevolent efforts of the Japanese to appease them and show their underlying good will to the people who were being so greatly abused by their own rulers. He had a collection of Chinese flags which the natives had been flying against the orders of their real friends, the Japanese, etc., etc., etc.

We listened quietly for a time and then I surprised them all by saying, "Well Mr. Oda, all you are telling is very instructive and perhaps the army had to do all those things that are shocking the world in order to gain the upper hand over the Chinese after they got to Shanghai, but we are not so much interested in an explanation of what is taking place now in that part of China but, in view of the fact that Japan is one of the members of the Nine Power Pact which guarantees the existing national status of the world, we are anxious to know why Japan is in Shanghai at all. Will you please explain that to us?"

Poor Mr. Oda was stunned by that question, but after some blushing and other blushing and other manifestations of uneasiness he resumed his former line of talk. Again we listened politely for a while. Then another guest repeated the question "But why is the Japanese army in Shanghai?" Again Mr. Oda showed uneasiness but went on with his story. Then a third guest repeated the same question. Mr. Oda, unable to longer maintain his usual equanimity, then said he was not now speaking for himself as a Christian man but was speaking on behalf of the Japanese government telling us what they wished us to understand.

In all the years since that time, he has been trying to do his duty towards his employers and at the same time to make the path of his foreign friends as free from snags as possible - a difficult but important task.

Even during recent events when the American, British and Canadian governments were practically ordering the withdrawal of their nationals from Korea Mr. Oda put forth his best efforts to obtain steamship passage for them and help them in every way possible. When trainloads of them were en route to the port of Chemulpo to embark on the S. S. Maripose, he accompanied them, both as an official of the Japanese government and as a personal friend of the retiring foreigners. He continues to help those who still remain in Korea and has enabled many of them to avoid pitfalls or get those out of them who had unfortunately fallen into them.

For what you are, Mr. Oda, and for what you have done for us all we thank you. We all love you and respect you as a Christian Japanese gentleman.

Part 3

Every Sides of Korea

Chapter 1

Women in Korea

Are we to write about women in Korea as conditions were in the end of the 19th century or are we to write of them as they became during the years we saw them advance? The difference is very marked so let us begin with the advent of Christianity as taught by the Protestant Missionaries in 1884. The only women of that time who were free to move about openly outside their own homes were those of the coolie class and the more or less public women, generally called dancing girls. All others were closely confined to their own homes or, if they went out at all, were covered by a sort of coat which, though it had sleeves and so reminded us that it once had been worn as a coat, is now worn as a cape, covering head and face and all the upper part of the body, leaving the sleeves hanging empty of arms. The wearer's face could not be seen by those who met her but she could see them or whatever was in front of her through the narrow slit left as she held the cape with one hand so as to permit this. As already suggested there had been a time when this article of dress was worn as a jacket and therefore a time when women could go about as freely as did men. The change is said to have been made long long ago after a war with the Chinese whose soldiers carried off all the attractive young women they met.

The change in manner of wearing the dress was intended to hide the faces of both the young and old women so the soldiers could not distinguish the young and pretty ones from the old and less pretty. This seclusion of the middle and upper class women reacted on the work of the missionaries in manyways. These women of course could not attend public gatherings where men were also to be present. Most of the contact of the missionary ladies with them could be made only in their homes and these were not always open to them, especially if the men of the house were opposed to their teachings or to what they had heard from the male missionaries.

Very young girls up to, say, eleven were allowed more freedom and were often to be seen on the streets playing but as soon as they approached their twelfth year they too were kept in their homes. They were then approaching the marriageable age and it was necessary to prepare them for that event by instructing them in housekeeping in all its branches - selection of foods, cooking, sewing and housework. This was the more important because a girl, when she married, became a member of her husband's family and lived in his family home, and her mother-in-law could expect her to do all or most of the housework she herself had previously done. She would become practically the servant of her husband's mother. If she proved herself inefficient she was just unfortunate - life would be made miserable or she might even be sent back to the home of her parents - a terrible disgrace.

It can be seen from this account of a Korean household that a young woman's chief desire was to please her mother-in-law. After that and perhaps even of greater impotance was her wish to bear a son and great was the disappointment of the whole family if her first born were a girl - only a girl- for one of the most important functions of parents was the continuation of the family line which could be done only through the male members - daughters would leave home after a few years to join another family and help maintain its continuity.

Therefore, there was not much, if any, opportunity for a girl to get more than a modicum in the way of book knowledge after her marriage and before that event she had had little chance to do so.

The result of these conditions was that women in Korea were generally unable even to read and were largely ignorant of anything outside of their own homes. To account for this ignorance the men were wont to say that women had no capacity for learning anything but housework, overlooking the fact that some women had been noted in their history as both learned and wise. Their own Queen, indeed, was a good example of great ability.

But it is still true that the general impression in Korea, as in other Oriental countries, is that women are inferior in intellect to men.

Development of Women in Korea

When the missionaries first came to Korea they opened schools for boys and also for girls, It was comparatively easy to get parents to allow their boys to attend these schools but when they were asked to send their girls there was no response. When fathers were pressed for a reason they said that girls had no brains and so could not learn, and as they had no souls what was the use? Besides, they said, the girls would have to marry when they were twelve or thirteen years old and it would take all that time for them to learn to do housework. If a girl couldn't do that, she would get no husband.

However, they offered to send their very little girls to school until they were old enough to begin to do housework and on that basis the schools for girls were founded. As a matter of fact those young girls learned quickly, but it was not till 1908 that the Northern Presbyterian Mission School for Girls had pupils ready for graduation from courses comparable to the first or second year of high schools, I remember that first graduation day very well because I had the privilege of being chairman. The exercises were held in the new Yun Mot Kol Church which was large enough to seat 1,200 people on the floor mats. The building was filled with about equal numbers of men and boys on one side and women and girls on the other, all filled with curiosity and interest.

As I went on the platform I was surprised to note the absence of the curtain which had heretofore separated the men and boys from the women and girls in accordance with the custom of the seclusion of women. From the beginning of mission work the curtain had held its place but on that day it was missing. When I asked the meaning of it, they said that this was a great day for the women of Korea - the graduation of girls who had studied the same subjects that only boys had heretofore studied and they, the men and women of the church, feeling it should be marked by a forward step, had decided to remove the curtain that had hitherto made an artificial barrier between the sexes. It seemed very strange indeed to look down from the platform on that sea of faces without the usual curtain separating the men and women.

However, the men were all seated on one side of the church as usual and the women on the other side, but they could see each other and this change marked the beginning of a degree of freedom for the women that had not before existed.

Then another break in custom was made - the graduates, all marriageable girls were seated on the platform in full view of the whole audience.

The usual Western commencement program was carried out even to the giving of a valedictory address. The girl who had earned the distinction of valedictorian was the daughter of a man who, a few years before, would not have been allowed to sit in a group of people such as those gathered there for he was a butcher, a member of a much despised class ; he was, to be specified, Pak the Butcher, referred to in a preceding section.

When she rose to deliver her address I fancied I could see the care of the men turn forward so as not to miss a word for it was a new experience to them to sit and listen to a mere girl. But as she proceeded the look of doubtful expectancy turned to one of interest as she told them things they had never heard before. My own interest was aroused too and I could not help thinking that when she married she would make a new kind of home and be a new kind of mother and that I fall the girls in Korea could be similarly educated and trained the need for foreign missionary work would come to a speedy end.

Miss Helen Kim

That was in 1908, just thirty-five years ago, and since that time grade schools, high schools and colleges for girls have been overcrowded. School teachers are no longer under the necessity of seeking pupils - applicants far exceed the capacity of every school. Only recently I received a letter from the President of Ewha College for Girls which said that the applicants at the beginning of the school term were so many that not more than one - sixth of them could be admitted.

The present President of Ewha College is a Korean woman, Miss Helen Kim, Ph. D. of Boston University, who received much of her schooling in Korea, even to graduation from the college of which she is now President. After that she studied in America, obtaining her B. A. and M. A. from Syracuse University, and her Ph. D. from Boston. There she received also the Phi Kappa Gamma Key.

On several occasions she represented Korea at meetings of the Pacific Relations Conference held by representatives of all countries bordering on the Pacific Ocean to discuss matters of interest to those countries. She also represented the M. E. Church of Korea at a General Conference in Kansas City, Missouri. During a debate on the question of discontinuing the appointing of a Bishop to Korea. the sentiment appeared to be swinging to the side of those who were opposing this custom. Helen obtained the floor and made such an eloquent and convincing plea for the continuation of the policy that, at the end of her address, almost unanimous decision was given in favor of her plea.

Again at the Jerusalem Conference of Christians sent from all the countries of the world, she was a delegate from Korea. A Japanese Bishop, representing his country, argued that Korea, having become an integral part of Japan, should not have its own separate representation at these World Conferences but should be represented by the Japanese delegate. Miss Kim followed him in defense of the policy then in force of allowing Korea to send its own delegates and won an almost unanimous vote for Korea.

Pak In Duk

Many years ago, a little girl, Pak In Duk, living in a country district where there was as yet no school for girls, heard of the Ewha Mission School (Methodist) in the capital where girls could begin in a kindergarten and go on up through all the lower schools and even through college. She was fired with an ambition to get an education, but her mother was too poor to send her to Seoul.

There was a school for boys in the neighborhood - if she could only go to that (A bright idea filled her mind and hesitatingly she confided it to her mother - could she not go to the boys' school dressed as a boy? Whew! Her mother was astounded but the more she thought of it the more she became ambitious for her daughter's education and at length gave her consent. How she gained the consent of the teacher I do not know but, dressed as a boy, she attended the school until she completed its courses and was ready for a higher grade. This meant she must go to Seoul. She was now old enough to venture a trip to the city so, resuming her regular girl's costume, she made her way to the capital and to Ewha School. Presenting herself there she told the story of her strong wish to get education, of how she had, in the garb of a boy, studied at the school near her home and, having graduated there, was now anxious to go on with her studies. Could they help her? Of course they could and would. Such a girl should be helped, so she entered Ewha.

She was as persistent as she was ambitious and also as bright so she passed from one grade to another and at last was admitted to the College. There, too, she shone as a brilliant student and after graduation from College became a teacher in the high school of the same institution.

In 1919 the people of the entire country rose as one man to manifest their unity as a nation and protest, without resort to arms, against the over lordship of Japan.

Already as apostle of the equality of women with men both in mentality and responsibility, she told her pupils that neither women nor girls should refrain from taking part in this patriotic protest so, each having made a small Korean flag to carry in the procession, she and they went out to one of the main streets where they waved their flags and, with all the enthusiasm they possessed, shouted, "Long Live Korea."

It was not long before the Japanese police, widely scattered throughout the city at the time, came up with them and arresting the whole class, marched them, with their teacher at their head, to the crowded detention station.

In Duk pleaded for the youngsters, saying they were but children and that she alone was responsible for what they had done. Would they not detain her and send the pupils back to their school? She also said the school officers knew nothing about what she had done.

Her plea was accepted and she was committed for trial. When her case came up she made no attempt to minimize her guilt but rather justified the action of the people who were simply making known their own country and protesting the action of Japan in annexing it.

She was, therefore, regarded as a leader meriting special punishment and was one of those condemned to solitary confinement for an indefinite period. The authorities realized that if she were confined with a group of other young women she would imbue them still further with her own determined spirit.

At a later period I obtained the special privilege of visiting one of the large prisons in which the chief leaders of that uprising were confined and, after I had seen all the men and been permitted even to speak to groups of them under the surveillance of police guards, they asked me whether I would like to see the women's side of the institution. Of course I would so I was taken there too. As we walked along a corridor the guide opened the doors of several cells, each containing four or five young girls many of whom I knew. They smiled at me as I passed and then two cells were opened with only one girl in each. One of these was Pak In Duk. She was sitting on the floor of a small room about seven or eight feet square, reading her Bible, which she had been permitted to keep. As she lifted her head and recognized me, she smiled but was not allowed to speak.

At the end of six months she was released and returned to her school but, in accord with Japanese law which forbade any one who had served a term of imprisonment teaching in a school, she had lost her position there.

Some one, conversing with her, remarked that she must have been very lonely during those months of solitary confinement. Smilingly, she replied, "Lonesome? No, why should I be lonesome? I could read my Bible and think over everything I had learned in school and college. No, I was not lonesome." What a spirit!

After a time she was sent to America to pursue her education at Ohio Wesleyan College in Delaware, Ohio, over which Rev. Dr. Herbert Welch, afterwards Bishop of Korea, presided. Many boys and girls from various Asiatic countries have there found sympathetic teachers and a golden opportunity.

In the College her keen ambition, her brilliance and a degree of persistence not always found in association with those qualities, carried her far. She won recognition as a brilliant public speaker with an unusually good use of the English language after her graduation. She was asked by the Student Volunteer Association, and an American body for promoting missionary zeal amongst college students, to travel amongst the colleges of the U. S. A. and Canada and address students in an effort to find suitable young people to join the ranks of missionaries. This often meant speaking before teachers as well as students. But who was more fitted than she for such an important task? She had come through all the ranks, she was a product of missionary effort, she could speak with authority and, as she spoke, her hearers had before them an actual example of what might be done by those just getting ready to do their part in making better world older.

I was then in Korea and was much interested in learning how she was received at that great but somewhat conservative institution, the University of Toronto, Canada. I was much pleased to receive a letter from a friend there telling me that her meetings had been attended by large numbers of students and also by many professors and that she was numbered amongst the most convincing speakers that had ever visited the University.

On returning to Korea she looked around to see what might be the most needy group of women amongst whom to work, for her former connection with the uprising of 1919 and her term of imprisonment made it impossible for her to resume her teaching work.

Her attention was drawn to the condition of the many women and girls of the farming communities who, as yet, had few opportunities for betterment. She decided that the readiest and probably the only way to help them as a class would be to improve their economic condition, and that her part in this should be to help them to be better farmers' wives and to make better use of what they had.

She planned a short term school for farmers' daughters, to be held at times when they could get away from farm work, where they could learn to read, to write and to figure, get practical instruction in animal industry, especially in raising better poultry, cattle and goats and in such hygienic and sanitary methods as they could practice in their homes, thus promoting health in themselves and in their children.

She made a beginning of this work and then visited America again in an effort to secure necessary financial assistance. While in America she was much sought as a speaker and was for several winters one of the most effective lecturers in the Florida Chain of Missions.

I spent the last five winters, 1937 to 1941 in that balmy state and one of the most common questions put to me by those who learned I had lived in Korea was "Do you by any chance know Pak In Duk?" She is again back at her work in Korea.

A letter recently received from my son and his wife in Korea spoke of her and said she was soon to address a meeting of the wives of the doctors on the staff of the Severance Union Medical College.

Kim Maria

Kim Maria (we would transpose it into Maria Kim) came to live on the Severance Union Medical College Compound when she was a very small girl and grew up to womanhood there so I knew her almost as well as I knew my own children.[45]

She attended the Presbyterian Mission Girls' School and on graduation

---

[45]   The Kim family had always lived in the small village of Sorai, in Whanghai province, far from the capital, and were amongst the first group to become Christians. In another chapter will be found the story of Suh Sang Yun who carried on a trade between Korea and the city of Mukden in Manchuria. Having been converted to Christianity through his contacts with the Scotch missionaries in Mukden, he carried the message and some of the scriptures (in Chinese Script which educated Koreans could read) to the people of his village. Kim Maria's uncle was a member of the first class of graduates from the Severance Union Medical College and was my principal helper in the translation of the medical books which the class needed during their course of study.

from it entered the Methodist Ewha College for Girls, from which she graduated with high honors.

After her graduation from College Maria was appointed as a teacher in the Presbyterian High School for Girls in Seoul.

Lady Kim or Kim Poo-In

Lady Kim was a member of a wealthy family with high social connections and at the time we first knew her had been a widow for many years.

As a member of high-class family she was naturally a Confucianist and as a woman she was just as naturally a Buddhist. This duplication of religious profession is common in nearly all the countries outside of the Jewish and Christian faiths for, where people believe in the existence of more than one god, Polytheism or the worship of many gods at the same time is but natural. Indeed this gives them a greater feeling of safety. It was in Korea just as Paul found it in Athens when he said to the people "I perceive that you are very religious for as I passed along and observed the objects of your worship I found also an altar with this inscription. To an unknown God." Even there they feared there might be a God of whom they had no knowledge who would be offended by their failure to worship him.

Lady Kim was one of the earliest women to accept the Christian faith and was already a devout follower of Christ when Mrs. Avison and I first met her.

Naturally of fine character, she became, under the influence of her Christian faith, such a one as Mary, the sister of Martha, beautiful of face and full of tenderness.

Her aristocratic friends did not approve of this change in her religion. They reasoned with her, pleaded with her and threatened her with expulsion from her family, but she remained firm and continued to give most of her time and energy to the work of evangelism amongst the women of her acquaintance.

To relieve her of embarrassment, her missionary friends urged her to accept the position of a paid bible woman, but she preferred to give her time to the work without compensation as long as her family connections remained intact, hoping that her example of loving patience would finally bring them to the Christian faith, but they continued obdurate and, at length, at a family council, declared her unworthy to be regarded as one of them. She was told to leave her home and look for support to those with whom she associated.

Under such conditions she reluctantly consented to become a paid bible woman but refused any remuneration beyond what was necessary to provide food and lodging. She had been allowed to take with her clothing and all her private belongings.

She never complained or spoke ill of her family but whenever an opportunity offered to meet them she quietly bore testimony to her faith.

One of her brothers once said to her, "You say your God is a God of love and that he was the maker of everything. If that be true, he made sin, too, and that is an evil thing. Why did your loving God make such a bad thing?" Unable to answer this question, a problem that has puzzled even supposedly wise men through the ages, she came to me greatly disturbed but hoping to get an answer.

1 knew my answer must be very simple so I said:

"There is a road to Chemulpo, is there not?"

"Certainly."

"There is another road to Songdo?" "Yes."

"But if, wanting to go to Chemulpo, you took the road to Songdo, what would happen?"

"I would not get to Chemulpo."

"Right. But if you did this knowing the right road to Chemulpo, what would you call it?"

"I would have made a mistake or else have been foolish."

"Certainly. But if after knowing which was the right road to Chemulpo, you persisted in taking some other road, what would you call such a course?"

"Well to say the least, I would be a fool."

"Well," I said, "There is a right way to do everything, is there not?"

"Certainly."

"If there is a right way then any other way is the wrong way, isn't it?"

"Certainly."

"Well then, was the wrong way purposely made in order to give you a chance to err?"

"No, it was probably the right way to somewhere else."

"Well, that is just the way it is with everything in this world. If there were only one way to act there would be no choice and there would be no errors and no sin for sin is choosing to do the wrong thing. But if there is something right, there is naturally something opposite to right and that is wrong. If there is a white there is a black, for if there were only white there would be no color at all. Things in this world always occur in opposites - there can be no alternative to that. God did not have to make sin. It is the opposite of the right and is just a natural consequence of there being a right."

"Men have power to choose what they will do and if, after experience and knowing the right, they choose to do the wrong, they commit sin. You can therefore tell your brother that God did not make sin - it just became."

Her eyes fairly shone as she said, "Oh, I wish he would ask me again." Her family at length became ashamed of seeing one of their own members dependent on foreigners so they set as idea small house for her use and gave her a monthly allowance. This made her very happy as it enabled her to do her evangelistic work without receiving pay for it.

One day she asked me to go to the home of a rich relative, a Korean banker, to see his wife who was very ill and steadily growing worse in spite of the attendance of a Korean doctor of the old school.

She had long pleaded with them to call me in but it was very difficult for them to do so because of the seclusion in which women of high class passed their lives and only when they thought she was going to die did they consent.

She explained to them that if they called me they must pray to the Christian God as I always looked to him for guidance and when she came to take me to the home she told me of this and asked me to offer a prayer in the woman's room as she hoped not only for her relative's recovery but also for the conversion of the family as a result of my visits. 1 was duly introduced to the sick woman as she lay on a comfortable padded mat on the floor of the small chamber. She greeted me with a smile that meant great hope.

After examination I told them she was suffering from an abscess in one of her lungs and that only an operation would relieve her and that for this she should be taken to the hospital at once.

The husband naturally objected strongly to taking his wife to the hospital and it required several more days of seeing his wife's suffering and thinking out the problems involved in such a violation of the social code to bring him to a decision.

At last sympathy for her and keen sorrow at the thought of her death won the day and Lady Kim, wreathed in smiles, brought me word and asked that a room be made ready. They brought her in the same day and she came feeling confident she would be cured.

 The next day the operation was performed. Lady Kim remained in the operating room to give the patient courage while the gray haired husband waited in the corridor. He was yet unconvinced that the doctor could know there was pus where none could be seen and certainly he was putting great trust in this stranger who was going to cut into her chest to let out pus which no one could see.

The necessary cuts were made and out poured a stream of pus. Lady Kim opened the door of the operating room that the husband might see the pus still escaping through the wound. His face shone with joy as he saw with his own eyes what the doctor had discovered with his fingers.

She was taken to her room under the care of the American nurse and a Korean assistant and kept quiet the rest of the day.

When the husband was permitted to go in next day she greeted him with a smile and as she was free from pain and fever he was a happy man. Her progress to complete recovery was uninterrupted.

Once, when I opened the door of her room rather too suddenly, I found her husband sitting cross-legged on her bed, holding her hand and looking at her very lovingly. As my unexpected entrance caught them in an unusual situation for Koreans, he blushingly dropped her hand and with some stammering said, "Well, you know, doctor, it is just like having a new wife."

After all, love is as powerful an emotion in Korea as it is elsewhere.

I assured him that what he was doing was all right and just what I would do myself. He then told me they both realized her recovery was a gift from God and they had decided to be Christians and train their children in that faith.

This broke down all opposition to lady Kim's Christianity and brought about her complete restoration to her former position in the family.

Banker Kim (for such was his position) opened his house to a weekly prayer meeting for the people of that well-to-do neighborhood and later on a survey of the city for new church locations indicated the desirability of that vicinity for one of them.

Mrs. Avison and I often visited the homes of the family group, (and there were many of them) and before Lady Kim died, after a long illness during which she manifested a beautiful spirit, she told me that all the members of the various branches of her family except one had accepted Christ and she was hoping for his conversion ere she died.

She quietly passed away during our next furlough and her body was given the simple burial of the Christian church instead of the gaudy, noisy and expensive funeral that would have been given to a non-Christian.

Conjugal Affection

In 1894 a call came to me from a family some twenty miles out of Seoul. The messenger said the lady of the house was very ill and her husband wanted me to go at once to see her.

As I had been in Korea only about six months, I could not yet use the language. I again asked Mr. Underwood to go with me and we accompanied the man who had brought the request.

When we arrived at the patient's home the husband metus and, according to the custom of the day, insisted on entertaining us with an elaborate array of food before allowing us to see the patient, an instance of Oriental courtesy that can scarcely be duplicated in the West.

Then, inviting us to follow him, he led us out of doors to the front of a window in a room in the women's quaters. Instead of glass, the panes were glazed (the word is used figuratively) with a paper which, though not transparent, admitted considerable light. A hole had been made in one of the paper panes and to my surprise, I saw a woman's breast pressed through the opening so that I could see the diseased part without the lady herself being seen.

The condition was quite evident, however. It was a case of cancer so far advanced as to be plainly inoperable.

When I told her husband this he was much disappointed, but choking back a sigh, he said he had expected such a prognosis, but wanted to get the foreign doctor's opinion before giving up entirely.

We returned to our homes with sad hearts at not having been able to help the family.

But I learned one thing that made me glad - in spite of all I had heard to the contrary - some Korean men do love their wives and do not regard them as mere slaves in the home. To get that new point of view made the visit worthwhile for me at least.

I was made conscious of this again by the evident grief of the King when his Queen was assassinated. During the weeks before her funeral he visited the special resting place of her remains every day to offer sacrifices and mourn her death and, as related in the account of her funeral, he did not merely stand by as an onlooker when the heavy coffin was being dragged up the high mound and into the vault prepared for it - he personally tugged and pushed with the workmen until it was placed in the stone walled room near the top.

Another example of similar devotion was given me when I found the rich Mr. Kim sitting cross-legged on his wife's bed in the hospital, holding her hand as just related. Though he blushed at being caught doing this, he said, "Well, you know, Doctor, it's just like having a new wife. I am so happy that she had been spared to me." Though nothing had compelled him to violate the custom of the seclusion of women except the conviction that the only hope of saving her life was to allow the foreign doctor to enter the privacy of the women's quarters to see the patient, he did that and went further by bringing her to the hospital and allowing her to be operated on by a male surgeon, making it plain that marital love can be as powerful in Korea as elsewhere.

However, so necessary was it that at least one son be provided that, if only daughters were born, it was the almost universal custom either to send the wife away and give her place to another woman or to take a second wife in the hope that she might bear a son, in which case the son was claimed by the first wife, if she had not been already cast off. This, of course, was hard on the second wife.

This custom had its counterpart in Judea. Abraham followed it when his wife Sarah, failed to provide him with an heir and later on his grandson. Jacob, took to himself several wives. And, just as Sarah be sought Abraham to take her maid Hagar to be his second wife, so the wife of the famous Korean scholar who for many years served Rev. Dr. Underwood as language teacher and literary assistant begged her husband to take a second wife when it had become evident that she doomed to a life of childlessness.

He finally did so and when this woman bore him a son, the child was at once laid in the arms of the first wife who claimed him as her own. But unlike Sarah, who grew jealous of Hagar, she lived in peaceful companionship with her youthful co-wife.

Chapter 2

Seoul and Fusan

Seoul, the Capital of Korea

Previous to the year 1392 A. D., the capital of Korea was Songdo, the center of the kingdom then known as Koryu.[46] In that day one of the most powerful generals had been sent by the King to punish the Chinese who had been raiding the northern part of the country.

But when his army got as far north as the Yalu River, he turned back toward the south to meet another Korean army which was following him with the intention of fighting him. He defeated this army and then declared himself King of Koryu, made Seoul his capital and changed the country's name back to Chosun, the ancient name (Pronounced Cho-sun), meaning "Morning Calm." The new King Yi started a new royal family which was destined to carry on a series of reigns known as the Yi Dynasty. Several sons were born to the new sovereign. He wished to make his fifth son his heir but the third son rebelled and made himself King. This third son abdicated in 1413 and built himself a palace at Yun Heui Dong, close to the present site of the Chosun Christian College which took the term "Yun Heui" as its Korean name.

---

[46]   The present name "Korea" is a corruption of Koryu.

- Construction of Seoul

Seoul was chosen as the capital because it occupied a site that could be easily fortified against an enemy's attack, It is situated in a rather extensive valley surrounded by mountains except in the narrow places between the hills where gates were erected. The new king ordered high stone walls to be built around the city extending over the ridges of all the surrounding mountains and hills with a gate at each mountain pass, so that the people might go in and out on every side.[47]

The work of constructing the wall around the city was begun in 1396 and completed within six months by a rather unusual method. Each family was assigned the responsibility of building a certain portion of the wall, the only specifications being that the wall should be thirty feet high, properly coped, and with an earthen embankment on the city side so that the defenders of the city could easily climb to the top of the wall. Naturally a section assigned to a wealthy family would be built of great stones properly chiseled, smoothed off on the outside and connected by well fitting joints, while the very next section assigned perhaps to a poor family which was unable to afford expensive construction might be built of undressed stones of varying sizes and put together with irregular joints with the spaces filled with clay. This division of labor accounted for the speed with which the wall was built and the differences in construction which often cause visitors to wonder. The wall lasted for five and a half centuries and would still be there had not the Japanese administration decided that a wall was no longer necessary as a protection against an enemy attack so it has recently been torn down in many places and the stones utilized for other purposes.

There are seven gates through this wall, of which the East, South, West and are the largest and most important. Then there is a somewhat smaller one called North Gate, another called Little West Gate lying between West and South Gates, the North East Gate and the Water Gate on the east side of the city and north of the large East Gate. All guests to Seoul are impressed by the South Gate for it is one of the finest expressions of Oriental architecture to be found anywhere.

While the architecture of Korea was suggested by that of China and is similar to it in many respects, there are distinct differences, It differs also from that of

---

47   Whenever I looked at the hills around Seoul I was reminded of the scriptures: "As the mountains are round about Jerusalem so is the Lord God round about them that fear Him."

Japan though some of the Japanese temples and palaces are replicas of the best types of Korean models. By comparing Hatamon Gate in Peking, China, the large gate which separates the new city from the ancient Tartar town, with the South Gate in Seoul, a clear idea of the differences between Chinese and Korean architecture can be seen. Whereas all the horizontal lines in Chinese architecture are straight, with the exception of an upward curving at the corners, all the horizontal lines in Korean buildings are slightly curved, even the main roof line.

In laying out the city of Seoul as the capital the first palace was built at the foot of the northern hills, It took its name, East Gate or Tong Kwan, because it was located not far from that Gate. When the King for some reason desired a change of residence a site on the northern hills somewhat west of the first location was selected for a second palace building. The streets leading from the main thoroughfare to these palaces are very wide, especially that leading to the second one. The main thoroughfare just mentioned is about 120 feet in width and connects the East and West Gates while another wide street runs parallel to it nearer the south side of the city. A few of the cross streets are also comparatively wide though much narrower than those just mentioned. All others are mere lanes, not even straight, winding in and out between houses already built. None were paved even up to the time of our arrival so after a rainstorm they were very muddy.

•   Chonggye Chun

One main canal for drainage purposes runs from east to west through the lowest part of the city. It is about 100 feet wide and some four feet deep, with stone retaining walls but only earth for a floor. It begins near the West Gate and, running east, empties into the Han River several miles from the city. A few narrower canals running north and south connect with this large central one. Into these all sewage of the city flows and the big canal carries it to the river.

Down each side of the narrow streets and lanes are open ditches which carry rain and filth into the smaller canals. All these canals, side ditches and sewers are uncovered. Perhaps this is a good thing from a sanitary point of view. Especially would this have been true if they had been kept free from rubbish so that the water could flow through them without being held up in foul smelling pools at short intervals. As a matter of fact, a covered sewer which has not been properly constructed is a greater menace to health than an open one because the sunshine can get into the latter and act as a disinfecting agent even though the hot sunshine in the summer does cause a good deal of fermentation and bad odors.

The servants' quarters of the big houses and all the houses of the poorer people are built close to the streets and the sewers ran along outside the foundation of these buildings. Doors to the Korean houses do not open from the streets but from lanes running from them, and only the small windows of the servants' huts or storehouses face on the streets. The occupants found the easiest way to dispose of night soil or household rubbish was to throw it out of these windows into the open ditches. Some of the liquids and even some semi-solids thus thrown out ran down the outer wall of the houses, often sticking there and giving it a very disagreeable appearance and emitting foul odors. The ditches were soon filled up with this refuse and were seldom cleaned out. It was easier to wait till the heavy rains came when all this refuse would be washed into the canals. So why worry! In hot and dry weather the stench was almost unbearable and at all times the appearance was bad. Regular coolies worked at carrying away these masses of filth but never succeeded in making the ditches clean.

Because of the obstructions in the ditches the contents overflowed during the rainy season making sewers of the narrow streets and then the only way to cross some of these lanes or streets was to use stepping stones placed at intervals along and across them. These conditions no longer exist in the principal streets though they are still found in some of the lanes.

One of the chief aims in building homes was to secure privacy and so were all enclosed by stone or mud walls and the roofs, being either yellow thatch or black tile according to the financial status of the occupants, the combination gave avery drab appearance to the city. Even the palaces were thus walled in and their architecture was visible only here and there from vantage points on nearby hills.

Night in the Capital City

Mention has been made of the seclusion of Korean women and perhaps readers about that have wondered, as I used to do, how the ladies could endure such constant confinement.

Two or three ways of overcoming this were open to them. They could go out on the streets in the day time if they rode in closed sedan chairs accompanied by female servant attendants who walked beside the chairs. The fact that the men carrying the chairs could see them when they alighted did not matter for those men were only coolies and seclusion[48] really applied only to meeting with men in their own grade of society.

A second way of getting out in the daytime was to wear a sort of coat which was thrown over their heads and shoulders and held over their faces by their hands in such away that, though their faces could not be seen they themselves could see where they were going. Women of the middle class thus arrayed might be seen on the streets at any time during the day. But for the higher classes social calls could be best made at night because men were not allowed on the streets after a certain time in the evening - only women accompanied by their female servants had that privilege. These regulations did not apply to foreign men who went about freely at any time. So as I went about the dark streets I often passed such groups of women. Generally a young girl, daughter of one of the household servants, walked a few steps in front of her mistress. Though as stated above there was a law forbidding Korean men to be out on the streets after night some ventured out and more than once I saw men who had done so arrested by the police.

The streets of the capital were not then lighted at night. Even the house lights might have made night travel a little safer had there been doorways open or windows uncovered but the whole front of every house was closed. Occasionally a beam of light shone through a crevice enabling one to detect the location of a house but that was all. A foreigner who had reason to go anywhere at night carried a lantern or more often was accompanied by a servant to go before him with a light to show him where he could safely tread.

The Wells of Seoul

A city of two hundred thousand people need plenty of water and Seoul has always had an abundant supply, for the hills and mountains that surrounded it ensured this. They she drain and snow enough to serve with water all the homes clustered in the valley. The people needed only to dig down a few feet into the

---

48 Seclusion was enforced only on higher class women. Women servants - families in the houses of the lower classes - moved about quite freely.

soil to get a steady supply while carriers distributed it to the nearby houses in buckets. These wells, however, for the sake of convenience were usually dug close to the narrow lanes which constituted the main lines of traffic throughout the greater part of the city and at the sides of the lanes were ditches into which the contents of the privies drained and most of them were so close to the ditches that contamination of the water in them was practically unavoidable, especially as the wells were lined with rough stones and the wide crevices between the stones permitted free entrance of the seepage from those drains.

The only way of getting water to the homes was to pay water carriers to deliver it as needed or for the women of the house to fetch it. If the women did it they raised the water from the well by means of a small dipper attached to a rope. This dipper was usually left on the well curb and was used by all comers. The woman, having filled her water jar, carried it home on her head. The regular water carriers, however, men who made this task their business, carried it in two buckets attached to a frame that rested on the shoulders of the carriers. Originally those buckets were made of wooden staves but by the time we reached Korea these had been to a large extent replaced by the five gallon kerosene cans which the Standard Oil Company of America had found to be the most convenient containers for distributing its products throughout Asia. Surrounded by a wooden framework that prevented easy destruction, these were being almost universally used even in the most distant parts of the country.

The water, thus carried to the house, would be poured into earthen jars similar, no doubt, to the jars mentioned in the story of the wedding at Gana of Galilee at which Christ turned the water into wine and this had to be dipped by small grounds that, when not used, lay around anywhere. One can see how easy it was for the water in the well or in the jars to be contaminated and be the means of disseminating intestinal diseases such as diarrhoea and dysentery.

As we saw these Korean wells, we were reminded of the wells of Biblical cities as they are described in the scriptures. The Jewish carriers were generally women who carried the water in pots on their heads, a method also common in Korea. Read Exodus, the second chapter, verses 15 and 18 - "And he (Moses) sat down by a well. Now the priest of Midia had seven daughters and they came to a well and drew water and filled the troughs to water their father's flocks."

The wells of all the towns and villages throughout Korea were similar to those just described in Seoul and they were a chief cause of the many sicknesses which made the death rate of the country greater than the birth rate so that it looked as though the Land of Morning Calm was doomed to almost complete depopulation if something were not done to improve these unsanitary conditions.

Of course there were some saving customs that had served to render many of the people more or less immune to the disease germs that were so widely distributed through these wells. Cold water, for instance, was not the most common beverage as it is with us. The most frequently used drink was prepared from the part of the boiled rice that adhered to the inside of the iron pots in which the rice had been cooked. The adhering rice, which had been partly caramelized, was softened and partly dissolved in the added water, Producing a liquid that was completely sterile, very palatable and a good substitute for the tea used in other countries.

Another saving factor was the partial immunity that constant infection gradually produced in some of the people so that many of those who had not succumbed in childhood lived to a ripe old age. The destructive death rate was found in the first few years of life.

To what more important work could missionary doctors devote themselves than to spread about the better hygienic knowledge they possessed? To this process of education and to the development of native doctors I decided to devote my time and energy. What use would it be to preach the Gospel of Jesus Christ merely as a means of spiritual salvation and leave the people to be doomed to disappear from the earth? Was not the Gospels of Christ, as he expounded it, devoted as much to the liberation of men and women from bodily affliction as it was to their spiritual betterment?

Fortresses of Seoul

Although the capital city, founded when the Yi Dynasty was established in 1392, is surrounded by mountain ranges over which it would be difficult to enter, there were depressions in them where a force might successfully attack the city. A high and almost impregnable wall was built around the city and strong gates erected at the lower places where entrance and exit could be made. Those precautions would seemingly make it impossible for an enemy to get into the capital, but there was always a chance that traitors within might make it easy for an invading army to force a way through the gates as had been the case not infrequently in other capitals in former times. So, with such a possibility in view, two mountain fortresses outside the city had been prepared to either of which the royal family might retire in case of an invasion.

One of these fortresses, Puk Han or Northern Fortress, was located immediately behind the palace in the recesses of North Mountain. This retreat was located high up on the mountain, surrounded by high walls pierced by two small gates which could be reached only by a difficult climb up steep hills. A gate through the city wall, back of the palace, led to this roadway.

In the days after Korea's treaty of friendship and commerce with outside nations, foreign residents often climbed this mountain in the summer time to get away from the heat and slush of the city and to breathe the cool air of the mountain top. Buddhist temples had been erected at various points on the mountain and the priests were always glad to open their temples as resting places for such excursionists and indeed, quite often they would move the idols into a corner or into another room to clear a space for the cots or sleeping pads of their guests. Always, of course, this was done with an eye toward the generous compensation which the guests would surely offer as they were departing. In one of these temples there were five hundred idols and it seemed strange to us to see them moved about from place to place in order to make visitors comfortable.

As a doctor, I was sometimes called during the day, or even at night, to climb that mountain to see a sick member of a missionary or business family. My first trip up that difficult path, winding between and over rocks, was made in the middle of the night. When I retraced my steps the following day and found it difficult, even by daylight, to keep on the winding and rugged path, I wondered how my guide had kept to it so easily in the dark of the night.

The view from the mountain top, however, was beautiful - as are all such vistas in Korea - and the summer breezes were cool, clean, and refreshing, making an ideal place for summer residents, particularly if they were satisfied to stay there after getting to the top of the mountain and providing they kept well and did not need the services of a doctor and also, were able to keep a servant to bring fresh supplies up daily from the city.

As a refuge for a fleeing king with his family and attendants, it would be also safe, Providing he brought along enough provisions to supply his needs indefinitely or until the beseiging army could be beaten off. If, however, his enemies gained possession of the place or of the pathway up the mountain so as to cut off needed supplies of food the fortress became a dungeon from which the only way of escape was capitulation or death from starvation.

Puk San (North Mountain) afforded a favorite climb for athletic young foreigners who found full scope between daylight and dark for all kinds of adventures.

The other fortress, Nam Han (Southern Fortress), was located some twelve miles from the palace and so could be reached in safety only if the king's retreat were made in advance of the arrival of the enemy. So it was used only when the coming of a supposedly invincible army was known long enough in advance for the trip to be amde in time. In someways Southern Fortress (Nam Han) seemed less safe than Puk Han. It was not so high, and as it is not so rocky, its approach is easier. But to offset this, the only available road up to it is easily defended from above. Forces attempting to reach the top of the mountain from other sides are exposed to attack by rolling stones and by gunfire on all sides from a well-protected army at the summit. The top of this rather low mountain is narrow and is almost entirely covered by a walled citadel. Here again the danger to its occupants is that of starvation, If the invading enemy can surround it on all sides and be patient until the food supplies in the fortress are exhausted, its ultimate surrender is inevitable.

I saw this happen in a year, when a company of Tong-haks took possession of the hill when they were hard pushed by the King's soldiers. We could see the fortress from our home in Seoul and, having spent a part of one summer there, we could fill in from our experience some of the details we could not see. Many wounded soldiers came to our hospital during those days. They had been sent up by their unwise commanders in vain efforts to get into the stronghold, only to be shot by its well protected defenders.

I remember one of those men who had been shot in the chest. His treatment had consisted in the applying of newly killed chicken's entrails to the wound and binding it in place by a bandage. So drained he had made his way slowly to our hospital, reaching it only after several days of difficult walking. You can imagine his condition. Weak with loss of blood and insufficient food as well as by the enforced walking during several hot summer days, he threw himself on the floor of the only small room we had to give him. Only a few times before had I been called upon to endure such a foul stench as came from the already putrid flesh of the chicken, combined with that of the pus from the infected wound, and together with the odor from the unwashed body of the wounded soldier who had probably not had a bath for weeks. We would forego the details and say only that his smile of thanks, after his wound had been cleansed and dressed and his body bathed, repaid us even more fully than would his money have done had he been able to pay for his treatment and food.

We got quite accustomed to the sound of artillery and gunfire during the weeks that followed, but at last a company of royal troops that had been drilled by British officers on the Island of Kang Wha were sent to relieve the attackers. They had learned much of strategy and, instead of vainly trying to capture the fortress, they simply camped around the foot of the hill, Preventing all communication between the attacked and their friends, and stopping all their efforts to obtain supplies. This policy was effective for, after enduring starvation as long as they could, the Tong-haks sent out a white flag and surrendered.

The Marble Pagoda

In the center of Seoul is a small public inclosure known as Pagoda Park because of the marble pagoda erected in the middle of it. The story of the pagoda is an interesting one.

It was erected in the capital of China. It was sent to Seoul by the reigning Emperor of China as a present to the King of Korea who had it erected on its present site in the heart of the capital. It is reported to have been sent from India to China.

The upper section of the pagoda stands on the ground beside the main structure. Why? Two different explanations for this are given. First, when it was being erected in Seoul, a Korean sage told the king that if it were completed the Yi Dynasty would come to and end and to prevent this disaster the upper sections were left on the ground. Second, though it was first erected in its entirely, the Japanese after one of their incursions removed the upper part and left it on the ground where it now stands as a proof of their capture of the Capital, but the date when this occurred is not given and such treatment of an emblem of Buddhism would be a questionable procedure for such strong Buddhists as the Japanese to be guilty of.

Whatever the case may be, the marble pagoda now stands with the upper part on the ground. It bears no resemblance to Korean architecture and the characters carved so beautifully in the marble are reputed by competent scholars to be Indian. However, it gives evidence of the influence that Buddhism exerted over the thought of both Korean and Chinese and clearly indicated the enthusiasm of early Buddhists priests to promulgate their faith in remote countries.

A Trip to Fusan

Shortly after our arrival in Seoul, I received a telegram one Sunday afternoon asking me to go to Fusan as quickly as possible to see Dr. C. H. Irvin who was very ill with a fever. Fusan is the most southernly port in Korea and it was not an easy trip from Seoul in those days. There were no railroad and only an occasional boat went there from Chemulpo, the chief port on the Yellow Sea Coast. If an overland trip had to be made it might require ten days on a pony and, even by boat, the fastest speed that could be made would require three or four days.

Telegraphing to Chemulpo for information about best sailings I learned that a boat was due to leave on Tuesday so I might be able to reach Fusan in four days, if good fortune attended.

What was the nature of the disease? Could we find out? A missionary friend who could speak the language[49] went with me to the telegraph office and for several hours a series of messages went back and forth between Seoul and Pusan. The doctor's home was at the top of a steep hill, half a mile from the telegraph office and it took a long while to get answers to my questions. However, after several times of telegraphing to and from I was able to make a tentative diagnosis of Relapsing Fever and prescribe treatment. Then telling them I would go as soon as possible, I called off the telegraphic conversations.

First of all I had to arrange a mode of travel over twenty- six miles of mountain roads between Seoul and Chemulpo. Horses of the size to which foreigners were accustomed did not then exist in Korea. The so-called horses were all about the size of Shetland ponies and the donkeys were correspondingly small so that a tall man could almost touch the ground with his feet when seated on a saddle. But one of the missionaries owned a Manchurian pony which was about a hand taller than a native Korean horse and so was regarded as a real horse and my friend allowed me to use it.

In my eagerness to make speed I must have urged the pony to go faster than its usual gait, for before I had gone far, its knees buckled and I was thrown over its head. Fortunately I was not hurt and the mapoo[50] in charge of the pony came running up to help me remount. Usually the mapoos lead their ponies by a hal-

---

[49]   I was then but a beginner in language study.

[50]   A mapoo is a man in charge of a pony and each pony has a mapoo. He gravely leads the pony by a rope attached to the bridle.

ter but as this pony had been broken to a bridle rein the Korean man had lagged behind us. After that we made slower progress but still reached the port before night fall. That evening I arranged for my passage to Pusan and then went to Steward's Hotel to secure accommodation for the night?[51]

Next morning when I boarded the small steamer it was still being loaded with rice for the Japan market. The tide at Chemulpo sometimes rises to a height of twenty or more feet being, I believe, the second highest in the world.[52] Because of this tide, there is an outer and an inner harbour. It is more convenient to lead boats in the inner harbour which is near the shore and so saved both time and cost but, when the tide is out, only the smallest boats can remain afloat there. My steamer was anchored in this inner harbour and the stevedores were hurrying to complete their work before the tide would go out but, when the loading was finished the boat was found already grounded. Two courses were open to the captain. He could wait for the next tide to float the vessel or some of the cargo could be unloaded in order to permit the boat to float and be taken to the outer harbour. He ordered part of the cargo to be removed but much time elapsed in the process and we were unable to weigh anchor until the following day.

Though I could not help feeling uneasy about the sick man in Pusan, I could do nothing but exercise patience because this boat still offered the quickest way of getting there.

On the way down the west coast we wound in and out of the many small islands which stud the coast and cause Korea to be sometimes called "the land of ten thousand islands." As often happens on that coast a heavy fog compelled us to slow down. Suddenly a black shadow loomed ahead of us - the high rugged outline of an island. The steers man saw it just in time to signal the engineer to throw the engine into reverse and order the anchor to be lowered. How perilously close we had come to being wrecked! (See note on preceding page.)

We anchored there until the fog lifted and so lost another day. Not till one week from the time the first telegram was sent did the boat reach the harbour of Pusan and I wondered what had happened to the patient in the meantime. As

---

51 This man [Steward] had the only place in any of the port cities of Korea where a foreigner could get anything like foreign lodgings. See another chapter concerning him and his hotel.

52 Rev. H. G. Appenzeller of the American Methodist Mission (North) lost his life on that coast when a boat on which he was travelling collided with another boat under similar conditions. He was the first missionary to represent the Methodist Church in Korea.

there were no docks yet, even at that important port, I had to board a sampan which was propelled to shore by sculling.

A servant met me as I went ashore and, to my great relief, told me the doctor was convalescing.

My diagnosis of relapsing fever had proved to be correct and we had now only to wait to see whether a relapse would occur. Fortunately this did not happen and I was free to go back home as soon as a ship bound for Chemulpo should come into the harbour.[53]

The homeward journey was uneventful but when we reached Chemulpo, I learned that the river boat would not sail for a day or two, so as Seoul was only twenty-six miles away I decided to walk home over the hills. I was the more eager to reach home quickly as the war between Japan and China was about to break out and it would be fought mainly in Korea and certainly around Seoul. I left the port at two in the afternoon but an attack of my old enemy, migraine, slowed me up and made a rest at the halfway tea-house necessary. Then one of my knees gave way. Walking became painful and slow and the effort to tramp over and through a mile of softs and before reaching the river bank almost broke my spirit. Finally, however, I reached the river, hoping to find a ferryboat there but that hope was vain. Night had already comedown and business on the river had come to an end.

The river at that point is some 300 yards wide and I had to make my voice heard across that "waste of water" in order to arouse the ferry-man on the other side. At length an answering voice was heard and I sat down to wait the coming of the boat. How slow! How slow! But, as the dawn comes to a sick man in the end, so the boat at length drew to the shore and I could travel and rest at the same time. Still, when I reached the other side, I was three miles from the City Gate and my aching knee made every step a groan and progress too slow.

After what seemed an interminable distance, the City Wall did loom in the darkness and Gate was really there but it was locked, for it was long after closing time. The guard was inside but he dared not open the gate. The wall was thirty feet high but my home was on the other side and I had to get there for a smiling

---

[53]   The cause of relapsing fever was unknown at that time and treatment could only be symptomatic. Later a specice or spirllum was discovered in the blood which was found to be the cause of the disease. This could be detected under the microscope and in time it was learned that a comparatively small dose of salvarsan would destroy the spirilla and, within a short time after the administration, not only would all the distressing symptoms cease but the usual relapse was prevented. That was a great discovery for us in Korea.

wife and a comfortable bed would welcome me and make me forget the hard road, the expanse of sand, the migraine and the painful knee.

I knew that belated travellers had found a way of scaling the wall not far from the gate by getting fingers and dees into niches that had been made between the stones and that a rope let down from the top of the wall by waiting friends or by someone hoping to make a fee, made climbing possible, but how was I to get such help! I called several times the usual call of Koreans to attract attention: "Yuh-bo. Yuh-bo-"[54] and ere long a voice asked "Who is there?"

"Dr. Avison of the Jejoongwon" (hospital), "All right I am letting down the rope. Tie it around your body and then find the niches and I will help you." So in a short time I was at the top. I looked at my succorer but could not recognize him so I asked him who he was and why he was so willing to help me, a stranger. His answer was surprising. "Oh! my brother was cured in your hospital, I often went there to visit him so I know you well though you may not know me. You were very good to my brother and I am very glad to help you." It was now my turn to be grateful and I thanked him heartily. I would have paid him but he refused to receive anything.

Once over the wall, it did not take me long to get to my home, but alas! It was empty! And it was eleven o'clock at night! A Korean neighbor hearing my rapping, opened his door and told me my family had moved to the Mission Girls' School. It was not very far away - perhaps half a mile - but my knee felt worse and that half mile seemed longer than any one of the other twenty-six miles I had travelled.

When I did arrive all had gone to bed but I was soon admitted by Mrs. Avison who told me that the British and American ministers, realizing that war would soon break out, had ordered all their nationals to leave their homes in various parts of the city and find accommodations near the legations. Fortunately she had been given two or three rooms at the Girls' School but, as there was no way of communicating with me, all she could do was to move and await my return. My knee speedily recovered!

---

[54]   See here! See here!

Chapter 3

Korean Society

White Hair and Black

When I was a young boy in England (I left there before I was six years old) my hair was almost as white as that of an albino. Nearly all whom I met stopped to look at it and feel it for it was just as silky in texture as it was white. Then they would remark on it as unusual and pass on. I grew tired of their attention and one day when a man stopped me and asked for a look of may hair I became enraged and kicked him on the shin. My anger was not appeased when he laughed heartily and I kicked him still harder. After a bit more teasing he passed on much amused.

As I grew older my hair darkened perceptibly but was always unusually light and continued to attract attention, but fortunately I grew accustomed to this and was able to smile and even ignore people's remarks.

It is white than ever as I approached my 82nd year, but no one seems surprised now at the absence of color. One does get rid of troubles by the passing on of years.

The hair of most Koreans is black like than of the Chinese though it is quite often tinged with brown, showing an admixture from a race of red-haired people such as the Huntribes of Northern Manchuria and Mongolia. Their whiskers too are seldom black. They are more apt to be brownish.

But Koreans with white hair, pink skin and blue eyes are sometimes met with just as they are occasionally seen in all countries. These are examples of the almost total absence of the pigment that produces the shades of brunette with brown or black hair and brown eyes. Without doubt blond men like myself and blond women such as are quite common amongst the missionaries were regarded by the Koreans as albinos. Many however took us young folks to be old people and much wonder was expressed that such old men and women should be as active as we were.

A strange result of this attitude was that even though two Westerners might have different complexions and hair of different colors the Koreans often regarded them as brothers, being at first unable to see anything in them but that they were both Westerners. Rev. Dr. Underwood had brown eyes and hair almost black while I had a blond complexion, light hair and blue eyes but when we were in the country sections together we were looked on as so much alike that we must be brothers.

Korean Agriculture

Farming in Korea can never be conducted according to American methods. The topography of the country has settled that.

There are few extensive plains and one never gets away from the mountains that tower around on every side. The valleys are generally so narrow that fields have to be made in terraces one above the other as far up as cultivable land can be found. These terraces must be held up either by strong earth embankments or by stone walls to keep them from being washed away. A newcomer, when he sees the curving boundaries of the fields wonders why they make them that way. Why do they waste so much land in the lay out of fields? Why are they not laid out in straight lines? When the questioner has passed two or more summers in the country and experienced the heavy rainfalls of July and August, he begins to see the reason. The rains fall so copiously on the surrounding hills that the soil is in danger of being all washed down to the lower levels. Straight lines in the embankments would weaken them and long experience led them to the present system of curves.

Of course the fields are not all in such steep places but even in plains, there is some slope and the same method is followed.

These slopes, whether steep or gradual, serve a good purpose in the irrigation which is so greatly needed in the cultivation of rice because water may be introduced first into upper fields and then allowed to flow from one field to another lower down so that the same stream, led into the upper fields can be utilized for all the fields of that valley. The embankments are used by pedestrians as well as farm animals as pathways to cross the valley walking single file.

Agriculture has always been the mainstay of the greater part of the population. Some years ago the ratio of farmers to all other classes was 85 to 15, but in later years this has changed somewhat as the great increase in population has made it necessary to establish and foster many other industries.

Now much less than 85% of the people are engaged in farming and the rapidly increasing population call for a greater increase in farm products so that better farming methods have become necessary.

These products consist of rice, barley, corn, buckwheat, oats, millet, rye and many kinds of beans with some Indian corn, much cotton and, lately, soy beans. Native fruits are crab apples, pears, peaches, grapes, and persimmons. walnut, pine, chestnut and hazel (filbert) nuts are plentiful. Vegetables - native cabbage similar to what is known in America as Chinese cabbage, beans (many varieties), potatoes, and in the North many kinds of roots.

- Irrigation

In a rice growing country a water supply for irrigating during dry seasons is a necessity and the Koreans have done their best to develop wells and irrigation ditches close to their rice fields. Their irrigation systems are simple - consisting of a well dug at the highest point at which a sufficient supply could be found; ditches leading from the well to the nearest fields and from the higher fields to the lower; and of course a method of conveying the water from the well to the ditches. One system for doing this consists of a water wheel some six or eight feet in diameter, located at the edge of a pool of water, and driven by one or more men on a treadle. Then water being filled up into the buckets on the wheel which was driven by one or more men on a treadle. A second method was still simpler - a frame from which a large wooden scoop hung like a dipper was erected over a shallow well. The workmen seized this by its long handle, tilted it so as to dip water in the scoop and then emptied it into the ditch. It was slow work, but why hurry? It took time for the well to fill anyway.

Of late years streams have been dammed, small lakes created and gates placed to hold the water back till it is needed. These are then opened to let the water flow into a system of ditches which serve large tracts of land by being divided as the number of field increases.

The credit for the introduction of this larger system must be given to the Japanese who have done a great deal to make farming more productive. The Koreans many years ago made an effort to improve their agricultural products and their method of production by establishing a school of agriculture but it was unsuccessful. The farmers were uneducated: few of them could read the Chinese characters or understood either English or Japanese; no books had yet been published in the easy UNMOON script; missionaries, who had been the first to give any effective leadership along agricultural lines, knew very little about the subject and had not enough funds to do anything on a large scale; (and in fact, many of them would have objected to devoting the funds given for evangelism to these nonevangelistic projects).

But when the Japanese took the country into their own hands they did several things that made the farmers see the need for changing their ways of doing things.

They encouraged farmers from their homeland to come to Korea; they helped them to obtain farming land (the best in the country of course) by money grants and loans, subsidizing them in various ways. They were even accused of encouraging Japanese money-lenders to lend to farmers in difficulties who, when the time for repayment came, could not pay and so were compelled to give up their farms and emigrate to Manchuria. Whatever may have been the truth about that (and the evidence for it was very strong) many Japanese overload farmers now exist in the country. Those Koreans who wished to hold their lands had preferred to improve their methods.

The Japanese authorities prescribed the kind of crops that should be planted and the varieties of rice and other grains that should be sowed. They sent inspectors to see that these orders were carried out and that the exact rules for cultivation which they had promulgated were being followed.

Though the Koreans resented this close supervision of their methods of work they found themselves reaping greater and more valuable crops and gradually adopted the newer ways of doing things. This was not a democratic method but, under the circumstances, it brought results more quickly. The Missionaries and the Boards behind them began to realize that, if self-supporting churches were to be developed, the financial conditions of the people must be improved so an era of agricultural education through schools and through agriculturally trained missionaries was opened up. These did a great deal toward improving

the financial status of their converts enabling them to support themselves better and to send their children to the schools that were becoming more numerous.

- "Paddy" Field

This name is applied by Westerners to the rice fields of Korea. As the word "pat"
in Korea means "field" I wondered whether there was any connection in deriva-
tion between "pat" and "paddy." On looking up the word "paddy" in an English
dictionary, I found "paddy or padi" defined as "A Malayan word meaning un-
milled rice or rice in general." So the term "paddy field" appears to be properly
applied as a name for a rice field.

The rice fields of Korea are of two kinds - dry and wet. Dry rice fields are
similar to other cultivated fields for grains like wheat, oats, etc. These are fewer
in number than wet fields, because the rice that can be grown in dry fields is
much more glutinous than that grown in wet fields and, for general use as a
food, the latter is preferred, the former being used for special purposes.

The term "paddy fields" is used only of the wet fields in which rice is
grown. In Korea a similar distinction is made between dry fields or PAT and wet
fields or NON. The above description of rice fields applies only to the NON or
wet fields.

As a large and continuous supply of water is needed for the growth of this
type of rice, the fields must be located near a body of water which need not be
large but must be constant. A valley is therefore chosen which begins well up in
the hills and slopes down to the lower section not too rapidly. Terraces are made
all the way down, each terrace being banked with earth so that it can retain a
sufficient supply of the water that flows into it from the next higher field. A
small cut is left in the embankments so that water can flow down from field to
field, the cut being controlled to regulate the supply so as to keep each field
provided with just enough water for its needs.

Usually there are no roads across these valleys and use is made of the embankments as footpaths from one point to another.

When it comes time to sow rice seed one of the terrace slow down is specially fertilized and filled with water. The seed rice is then sprinkled thickly on
the surface of the water. It absorbs water, sinks and sprouts. The roots penetrate
the soft soil, the leaf stems lengthen upwards and emerge from the water. By the
time for transplanting arrives the plants cover the field like a grass lawn except

for the water in which they are growing. During all this time the other fields have been under preparation to receive the young plants. The fertilizing material, of which plenty must be used, has been well incorporated into the plowed and harrowed soil which is kept covered with water. Then a transplanting bee of all the neighbors gathers and divides into three groups, one to pull up the rice plants in small bunches, one to gather these and carry them on their JIKAES to their destined places and the third to plant these bunches several inches apart and in straight lines so that only straight lines can be seen from whatever angle they are viewed. Only bunglers will plant the rice so as to show other than straight lines. The bee continues its work until the rice fields of all the neighborhood have been planted. Weeding time comes and the Bible injunction to let the tares grow with the grain is violated. These are pulled up by the roots and left in the water to rot and make fertilizer for the rice. Throughout the summer the fields require careful attention. The weeds must be kept down, the amount of water regulated and, when ripening time comes, the water must be drained off and no more allowed to run in. It is then cut just above the roots with sickles, tied up in sheaves which are stood up to dry just as grain sheaves are treated in America. In due time it is carried to the village homes of the farmers where it is thrashed out with a flail very much like the flails American farmers used before the era of threshing machines.

As will be observed, the whole process of nice growing involves hard individual work and, for several reasons, it is likely to continue so for a long time. The fields are small because of the formation of the valleys and only plowing and harrowing can be done by the use of animals - cows or oxen attached to the simple implements. Seeding, transplanting, weeding, harvesting, threshing and winnowing are carried out by either men or women or both.

•   Fruits

Through their[55] influence many native fruits have been supplanted by improved Western varieties and fine apples are being exported to Britian.

When we first entered Korea (1893) no Western species of apples were being grown there - only crab apples. Now, because Korean climatic conditions for

---

[55]   Missionaries

apple cultivation are better than those in neighboring countries, Korean apples are being shipped in barrels or boxes to Great Britain via Canada, the land of good apples.[56]

Strawberries, raspberries, better kinds of peaches and Western vegetables were introduced. Better farming methods had to be followed and now in the vicinity of large towns the markets are supplied with many improved varieties of fruits and vegetables.

One summer I accompanied one of our Educational Missionaries on a trip through Whanghai province. Arriving at one town we called on one of its leading men who was an Elder in the Church. He had just moved into a fine new home and he ushered us into what was a very large room for a Korean house. Of course we sat on the floor on mats with our legs crossed, Korean fashion, I wish I could show you just how a Korean sits on the floor, but you will most easily understand it if you try to do it yourself as I describe each step.

Sit on the floor; bring the right foot up to rest on the left knee and the left foot so it will rest on the right knee. Of course you have to practise it a long time before you can do it comfortably. The Japanese first kneel on the floor and then sit back on their heels. The Chinese follow another method, but they are apt to draw their feet up under them. A Korean, coming into our home will at first sit on our chairs as we do but, ere long, one foot will be drawn up when we are not looking and, a little later when our heads are turned, up will go the other one. Though they try to do it surreptitiously we of course see it but do not remark on it. While we were sitting and talking with our host a large tray of fruit was brought in and placed before us. On it were peaches, apples and tomatoes! - a large, smooth tomatoes, to be eaten just as one would eat an apple. We expressed our surprise at seeing these for the Koreans, like most others when they ate this fruit for the first time, had not liked them "Well," said our host, "we were told that tomatoes are very wholesome so we began to cultivate some and have grown to like them." "Yes, we generally eat them as we do other fruit. Please eat many of them," And we did, though we preferred the peaches.

They have a very delicious native fruit - the persimmon- of which there are many varieties. Those have the same basic flavor that the American persim-

---

[56]   Naturally, they cannot be profitably shipped via the ports, the Red Sea and the Mediterranean, because the distance is great and the fruit would be spoiled by the heat so they are being sent across the Pacific, Canada and the Atlantic Ocean to England. It was a great surprise to the Canadians to find the Koreans so soon beating them in supplying the English markets with the quality fruits they thought could be grown only in Canada.

mons have, but the best specimens are as large as our biggest tomatoes. There are two shapes, flat ones like tomatoes and others like inverted pears and there are two types of consistence - one that continues hard even after ripening and one that gets soft and pulpy. Some prefer one variety and some the other. When tomatoes were first introduced by the Missionaries, the first question was "What do you call them?" We told them "tomatoes" but that was a hard word for them to pronounce and it was not long before we heard them called "il-yun-kam" (which means "one-year-persimmon") from the similarity in form and color they bear to their flat persimmons. The persimmons grow on rees, which of course bear fruit annually, but tomato plants are annuals so they made their name accordingly - "one-year persimmons." Persimmon trees have been introduced in America and nice large specimens are now found in many markets, especially the inverted-pear-shaped variety. They appear to be grown best in Texas and California.

Persimmons can be dried and then they are a fair substitute for figs. The drying is done by exposing them to a hot sun which causes evaporation to take place before fermentation can begin. As they dry they flatten, and are sold ten in a bunch. Two methods are followed. The best fruits are dried individually and packed ten in a roll. These are served in the homes of the richer classes. The poorer fruits have a stick about one-quarter of an inch thick passed through them - ten on one stick. Less care is taken to keep these clean, but they are sold in larger quantities because they are cheaper.

Generally these dried ones are eaten just so, as we often say of uncooked food, but when cooked by boiling in water they make a good substitute for either prunes or figs. While cooking does not make them more palatable, it does make them safer from the hygienic stand point.

Rice is their most important grain and the prosperity of most farmers depends on the yield of their rice fields and their conversation about weather conditions always bears are reference to the effect the abundance or absence of rain is going to have on the rice crop.

So important is this crop that a man's wealth in old Korea (and this is still true to a large extend) was reckoned by the extent and fertility of the rice fields he owned. Though I say extent, I use that word only to fit the thought into the thought of my Western readers, In Korea they do not think of fields as measured by their area, but by the average yield of rice they may be expected to produce. A man is said to have land yielding a certain number of bags of rice.

There are, of course, different kinds of rice in Korea just as there are varieties of wheat in America. The best Korean rice is generally admitted to be superior in quality to that of its neighboring countries so that it always finds a good export market and when the crop is not up to the average in quantity, the home growers are often reduced to eating the cheaper grades - nearly all the best having been exported. As a matter of experience there are years when the cheaper grades are also sought after by exporters because of scarcity in the total yield and then still cheaper qualities are imported from other countries for home consumption. Then there is much complaining by the people.

So far, I have referred only to rice grown in water fields, but they also have another kind that grows in dry fields. When this is cooked, it is more mucilaginous than the other and so is not used for ordinary consumption but is reserved for boiling into a semitransparent paste that is used in the making of several varieties of candy[57] as well as for making a paste for use in wall-papering because it is so strongly adhesive.

Next to rice the most commonly used grain is barley, which is much cheaper and can be more abundantly raised in the north. It is used as food instead of rice by many in the north and by poor people generally though all who can afford it prefer rice.

Wheat was one of the least grown of all cereals until after Westerners introduced wheat bread. During the last thirty years wheat bread has become a recognized food and much flour is imported from Manchuria. Smaller amounts are imported from Canada.

Indian corn of poor quality has long been grown for feeding cattle, but since Westerners introduced the finer qualities much more of this has been cultivated especially to be eaten as green corn. The climate and soil of northern Korea are very suitable for the growth of corn and some years ago the Corn Products Co. of the U. S. A erected large mills at Pyong Yang for the preparation of its many corn products. The company supplies seed to all who would promise to grow it as a regular crop and guaranteed to purchase all the corn produced each year. So far, Korea has not been able to supply the great demand of this company and it imports a great deal from Manchuria in order to keep the ex-

---

[57]   Sugar was not used for candy-making either in Korea or Japan until the practice was introduced by Westerners. Even yet, the people generally prefer the candy made with a paste prepared from rice or barley, either as a semi-liquid substance resembling non-granular honey, or a more nearly solid kind that is quite elastic. These pastes do not consist of cane sugar such as Westerners use so plentifully but of a species of grape sugar or maltose which is much less sweet. One form of it is on sale in America - the Japanese ame wrapped in soluble rice paper that can be eaten with the candy.

tensive mills working. The fact that this American Company "feels obliged" to employ Japanese supervisors almost entirely has kept the Koreans from dealing with it in a large way. This attitude is a manifestation of the national dislike of their conquerors.

Millet is one of principal grains grown and there are several varieties of it. It is used in place of rice in some parts of the country, especially where water is scarce. Its small yellow seeds are cooked in the same way as rice is prepared and it makes a very palatable and wholesome food. It is also used to some extent for feeding cattle. Beans are next to rice in extent of production. They constitute the greatest of all the crops grown in dry fields. Their variety is legion and the uses to which they are put are many.

The soy bean has been largely cultivated in recent years, though formerly it was not widely grown in Korea. The great demand for soy products in America as well as in Japan and China has stimulated the farmers to put larger fields into this very useful bean.

Many varieties of legumes are grown each of which has its own special uses. Many of the so-called beans are really peas, but no distinction is generally made between them and real beans.

Green beans were not eaten until westerners introduced the custom. The ripe seeds are cooked in a great variety of ways. They are often roasted and eaten just as we eat roasted peanuts. Horses are fed almost entirely on a mixture of beans and chopped straw boiled together and fed to the animals while still hot.

Rye and buckwheat are occasionally seen but are not important.

Tobacco is widely cultivated for nearly all the people smoke it, except many of the converts to Christianity and all the younger girls. Most Missionaries frowned on its use, coupling the use of tobacco[58] with that of alcohol, so that in the earlier years but few of the Protestant church members used it. Gradually its use among Christians has increased as they have come into contact with tobacco-smoking members of the Western nations and learned it is, not taboo in most of the American and European churches.

---

[58]   As in Europe tobacco was not native to Korean. It was apparently introduced from Europe after Raleigh took it to England for its Korean name "Tambai" is not derived from any Chinese words, but seems to be corruption of the word "tabacco" by which it was called in the Spanish- speaking countries from which it first came.

Markets in Korea

When we arrived in Korea in 1893 there were no good roads from one city to another, the widest being only sufficient for two-wheeled ox carts to travel on and most of them were deeply rutted. The only ways of traveling were walking, boating, riding in sedan chairs, and riding on the backs of ponies, donkeys or cows. There were no steam trains and no electric cars. All walked except the gentry who rode in covered sedan chairs carried by four men if they could afford it or if their station in life called for it; or by two men if they were poorer or less proud. The only difference between donkey riding and pony riding was that gentlemen rode donkeys and common people rode ponies. There were, however, but few saddle horses, Pack ponies being commoner. Their mapoos (horse caretakers) walked beside them and controlled them by means of a halter.

A pack pony did not carry a regular riding saddle but had instead a sort of rack on its back on which the traveler's baggage was placed so as to provide a comfortable seat for the rider who sat on top of the pack with his feet hanging in front, one on each side of the pony's neck. The rider need not to be concerned about inequalities in the road or guiding the pony into smooth places - the mapoo looked after that. It was the rider's business to keep himself evenly balanced on his high seat so as not to distress the pony. When he got tired of riding he could get off and walk, without in any way slowing up the rate of travel. Ladies rode the same way.

As a matter of fact, however, most travellers walked at that time. The Koreans are great walkers. They do not setout at a fast gait and slow up later on. They travel steadily all day long. Day after day they will average 100 li, thirty miles, even with fairly heavy packs on their backs. Because of these primitive means of travel, it was desirable that the village dwellers should be able to purchase supplies not too far from their homes. Farmhouses were generally grouped together in small villages for the sake of greater safety and companionship. One of these villages would, for one reason or another, grow to be of town size and, to make trading easier, markets[59] were held in such towns every five days. Peddlers travelled from one market to another carrying wares on their backs and the villagers too to the market home-made products which they did not need. In order to accomodate the peddlers as well as the purchasers, markets

---

[59]   Markets were held every day in large cities like Seoul and Pyong Yang, and regular stores in these places kept a fair amount of stock on hand.

were held on successive days at different villages at least a day's walk apart.

I found those village markets very interesting. The main streets were lined along both sides with stalls displaying a variety of products and the middle of the street was generally occupied so that carts and other vehicles could pass along them only with great difficulty. It reminded me of trying to drive a car through a traffic jam in a large city in America though the slowness of Oriental travel greatly reduced the danger to both the travelers and the merchants. The resulting delay was not then considered of great importance. On the roads leading to and from the markets nearly every traveler would be carrying something on his back or be leading his ox or pony loaded with wares.

At the market place food stuffs of all kinds were displayed in shallow straw baskets arranged on the ground. These baskets, several feet wide and only four to six inches deep held rice, beans, barley, and other grains; fresh and dried fish; all kinds of vegetables and nuts; fruits in season such as persimmons, oranges, Pears and apples. Animals were also brought to the market to be sold - cattle, ponies, horses, donkeys and oxen; chickens, geese and ducks. A variety of household wares were offered for sale - iron kettles, tin vessels, earthenware, carpenter's tools and farm implements; in fact, anything from notions to pine coffins.

A traveller could always tell when it was market day as he approached a village for early in the morning he would see a steady stream of people loaded with goods, all travelling toward the town and in the afternoon and evening there were just as many lines of travelers making their way back to their homes, loaded with their purchases.

As there were no newspapers in those days, the markets were used for gossiping and the dissemination of information. Speakers on various topics could often be heard presenting their ideas to all who would listen. The missionaries took advantage of this opportunity to widely proclaim their message, to sell tracts and bibles, to distribute free pamphlets and to invite the people to religious services being held in a nearby house. Many listened to the good news and thus the Christian message was widely spread.

These markets not only served for the exchange of goods locally made but also made it possible for the country people to buy many things that the small village traders could not handle. Traveling peddlers visited the markets carrying silks, hats, shoes, and many kinds of manufactured goods from the stores in the larger cities. These merchants, in order to limit their number, forced themselves into guilds which allocated the territory in which each member might travel and determined the kinds of goods each might sell. To prevent the organization of too many guilds they made an arrangement with the king to license them and make it illegal for any unlicensed peddlers to do business, in return for which favor they agreed to serve his Majesty as soldiers whenever called upon in any emergency or uprizing against him. By this means they created a very lucrative monopoly. During all my years of service in Korea, however, there was only one occasion when the king called on them to perform military service in his behalf. That story is told in another chapter.

The unit for measuring distance on the road was a li (lee). Ten li would equal about three miles but a li was not exactly a measure of distance, It was rather a measure of the time it required for a man to walk in a given length of time and that would vary according to the character of the road. Ten ii on a comparatively smooth and level road would be longer than ten li on a rough mountainous road. The average distance that a mail carrier, always on foot in those days, could walk in one hour was called ten li. This method of calculating distance enabled the postal authorities to equalize the rate of wages to be paid to mail carriers in different parts of the country which was based on the time it took them to cover their different routes. Though it took some time for foreigners to get accustomed to this method of measuring distances, because in Europe or America a mile measures a certain distance whether it is on a plain or over a mountain, the Korean method had its advantage in that in a country where most of the travelers walked one could always know about how long it would take him to reach his destination whether it was across a plain or over a mountain whereas, if the number of li were determined by the actual length of the road, he would have no way of reckoning how long it would take him to reach a given place.

The Korean Fire Pot

The native name of this indispensable article is wharo. This word of two syllables is a combination of two Chinese words Wha and Ro, each of which means "fire" so that the English name, if literally interpreted, would be fire fire instead of fire pot. It is quite common for Korean words derived from the Chinese to be thus duplicated apparently for the sake of emphasis so that instead of saying as we would "bring in the fire" they would say "bring in the fire fire" by which they mean the fire in its container. So we in translating the term Wha-ro simply interpret it so as to fit better into our own language forms and call it a fire pot. This method of making a name for an object is quite a common thing in the Orient and its effect is to draw the attention to the real meaning of the object - in this case fire. Even we do this occasionally in English. For instance we often speak of group singing as Sing Song. Another instance of it is to describe something worth seeing as a Sight See. Korean Wha-ros are of innumerable sizes and shapes an dare made of many different materials - pottery, brass, bronze, nickel, etc.

The Wha-ro is prepared for use by half filling it with fine sifted ashes on which is placed a glowing piece of charcoal. Other bits of charcoal are laid on this and soon enough heat is developed for the immediate need. If haste is necessary a fan is used for increasing the speed of burning.

If the charcoal is of good quality scarcely any smoke comes from such a fire though of course the colorless carbon monoxide and carbon dioxide are formed and escape into the air of the room. If the fire is brisk, the amount of carbon monoxide given off is very small as the monoxide is converted by the extra heat into carbon dioxide which is comparatively harmless, but good ventilation of the room is always desirable. A grid laid across the Wha-ro will hold anything that needs to be heated and the man with the pipe can easily light it at the red hot place.

In Japan each room of a house is heated separately by placing a Wha-ro in it, but in Korea more effective methods of heating are generally used, as described in another chapter.

Charcol in Korea

Much charcoal is used in Korea, so the production of charcoal is almost a major industry.

Of course, you all know that charcoal is partially burned wood - wood partially converted into coal by a process of charring or slow burning. The process almost completely burns up those parts of a piece of wood which produce smoke leaving the heat producing parts unburnt but charred. When it is being burned no flame results - the charcoal burns slowly and produces an almost smokeless red glow. Various kinds of wood are used in the making of charcoal but hardwoods, especially oak, are preferred.

As good charcoal can be made from the roots of trees one finds charcoal makers located on hillsides on which are the stumps of threes that had been cut down so that the roots are readily available and the cost of production is thus greatly reduced. So much of the cooking of foods is done in wha-ros over charcoal fires and so many rooms are heated by those same things that Korean modes of living would have to be greatly altered should the supply of charcoal fall short. Blacksmiths and workers in metals of all kinds use it constantly also so that wha-ros and charcoal contribute in avery large way to the welfare of the Korean people.

They are movable, they are efficient, they are cheap, flues are unnecessary and they are invaluable on picnic excursions.

Signal Fires

One of the first objects that attracted my attention in Seoul was a bonfire that burned every night for a short time on the top of a mountain near the Pekin pass. I was told it was a signal fire. "A signal fire?" I asked. "Yes, it brings news to the King every night of the conditions existing in the farthest parts of the country. In the absence of telegraphs there was no way of getting early information of the conditions existing in the sections far from the capital. Even invasions might be in process or uprisings amongst the people might be going on for days before any news of these could become known to the central government. So a system of these signal fires was devised to give the government all necessary information promptly.

All over the country on certain mountain tops a large mound of stones was built on which one or more flaring "fires could be built, the number of fires indicating either that all was well or that some uprising was occurring or some other very important disturbance was taking place, In whatever district the trouble was one fire or more fires would indicate the nature of the affair and its location. This fire would be seen at once by the watcher at the next station on the way to Seoul, and the signal being repeated there would be at once seen by the next watcher and so on to the central one at the capital and within a few minutes, the condition of affairs in any part of the country would become known at the palace almost immediately. These signals would reach Seoul almost as quickly as telegraphic messages could have done because the wood for the fires was put in place every day and those in charge were at their posts waiting at a given time every night to light them. It was literally true that the news was flashed to the capital.

I wonder whether this wording, "the news was flashed," may not have had its rise from this very system of beacon fires.

One of the interesting relics was located at our summer resort at Sorai beach. It consisted of a large mound of earth on the top of which was a pile of large stones and we made it serve a useful purpose as a guide to any of the pleasure seekers overtaken by a dark night while still too far out on these a to be able to distinguish land. Anxious friends would hang a large gasoline lamp on a high pole on the beacon mound and those out in the boats would know just how to steer their craft and at the same time could relieve the anxiety of their friends by signals from an electric flashing lamp that was always part of each boat's equipment.

Thus, even yet, is the ancient signal mound a useful part of the equipment of a modern summer resort.

Clothing of the People

For the most part, the people of Korea dress wholly in white. The farmer who ploughs in his rice fields binds his brow with a white head band, wears a white jacket and white beggy pants rolled up above his knees. So it is with the "yangban," or scholar, whose long fingernails indicate that he does no menial labor. His fine silk vest and jacket, his long coat and bulging trousers bound neatly at the ankles, all are white. The women too, whether rich or poor, wear shor tjackets and long pleated skirts of white material. One interesting fact concerning the women's clothing stands out in contrast to our Occidental usage, In Korea. the more brazen a woman is, the more she covers her body and the better dressed she is from our standpoint. The common women will go about with a gap of several inches between their skirts and jackets, thus exposing their breasts to public gaze without any thought about its indelicacy but a keisang (dancing girl) would not leave her room without having her skirt tightly bound around her chest, high up under the armpits, and her short jacket coming down well over the skirt band. I was told that as long as a married woman gave birth to daughters she did not expose her breasts - they were without honor - but as soon as she bore a son her breasts were exposed as having become very honorable - they were suckling a son.

Because so many of the people wore white clothing an idiom for describing a crowded street came into being. "How crowded the street is today - it is just white with people!"

However, although the majority of people still wear white, bright colors which were fomerly reserved for royalty and officials are beginning to come into the commoner's wardrobe. Little children have always been garbed in brilliant and, to our thinking, strange color combinations. Bright purples and cerises - greens, reds, and yellows help to brighten up the drab little homes with their brown mud walls. We read in our Bibles of Joseph's coat of many colors and find small Korean boys today wearing coats with sleeves of many colored strips quite like Joseph's of so long ago, I should imagine.

Perhaps you are wondering how these white clothes are kept clean. They aren't. One suit may sometimes be worn as long as several months without being changed, It is used for work, sleep, and recreation. And even now, after Western ideas of hygiene have been introduced and clothes are in many homes changed more frequently, if one is next to a man who has toiled and sweated and eaten in one outfit which has not been changed for two or three weeks the odor is not to be spoken of as pleasant.

In thinking of the Korean white clothing as being dirty from long wear, we must not forget we too wear our clothing for long periods and it is only because ours are generally not white that we are regarded as being clean. Ours, however, does not give off a dirty odor because we wear under-clothing that is frequently washed.

Computing Time

Soon after our arrival, we noticed that the Korean calendar differed from ours. While the years were practically of the same length they began and ended at different times. Our years begin in midwinter, theirs began in the early spring. Their months were nearly all of 28 days each (29 days, in truth - editors) but, as twelve didn't fit into the normal year by a matter of 29 days (30 days, in truth - editors), some adjustment had to be made and every so often they had an extra year of thirteen months instead of twelve. We too could not make our year of 365 days fit exactly - every year was 1/4 day ahead - so every four years we have a leap year when one day is added to the month of February. In the long run eigher way will do but we had to learn their way of doing it and as, in all our dealings with the Western world, we had to use the Western calendar, we had always to state which Calendar we had in mind when making a date.

Korea used the Chinese cycles of time which consists of sixty years and, doubtless, the idea was gained from their experience of the average length of life of human beings. Each cycle has a name which distinguishes it from other cycles in the histories of those countries that use this method of calculating the passing years.

Each year in a cycle also has a name so that those familiar with these names know just how far the cycle has advanced.

This calendar was used by China, Manchuria, Korea and Japan until the making of treaties of Commerce and Friendship with the Western Nations made it more convenient- necessary indeed - for all the nations thus brought into cooperation to have one standard. Naturally that of the West was adopted.

It is not difficult for us to calculate just what Western date corresponds to any given Oriental date. As our year 1944 A. D. is the 21st year of the Chinese Cycle, we have only to subtract 21 from 1944 to give us the first year of this cycle 1923, or add 43 to 1940 to get the date when the next cycle will begin, 1983.

You may remember the title of a book about China entitled "A Cycle of Cathay." Cathay is an old name for China and therefore the title meant "Sixty Years of China" or the story of the sixty years of that land about which the author was writing.

Chapter 4

Athletics in Korea

Outside of archery there seems to have been few if any outlets for activities on the part of the so-called higher classes and their women had no participation in any kind of athletics.

These were nearly all relegated to the lower classes though some of the women of those groups, or perhaps one should say the girls, took part in certain kinds of games.

The most common village sport was the annual tug of war that every village put on. For weeks before the date for the tug, a great rope was in preparation. As practically all the men and boys and perhaps the girls of the village would participate it must be long and strong, It was made by combining a great many strands of the straw rope that every village makes for itself in various thicknesses for general use. When finished the rope is several inches thick and long enough to enable all the male members of the community to take back in the pull. You can imagine for yourselves the great weight of such a rope. The rules for the game are practically the same as in Western lands. When the umpire signals for the tug to begin it takes some time for the long line of competitors to get into action. Not only those doing the pulling shout and yell to their fellows but all the onlookers shout for them. So that, if noise can add strength to those doing the work, the competitors must grow wonderfully strong while the contest is on.

Traditional Sports

Korea was not without its own sports even before foreigners entered the country and introduced those of Western nations. Among these native sports were wrestling, rope walking, archery, and dancing.

- Wrestling

Wrestling was quite different from what we Westerners were accustomed to seeing. The naked bodies of the wrestlers, barring a loin cloth, had a belt around the waist and another passing from the belt between the thighs and wound around the wrestler's other thigh. The match was begun by the judge placing the two wrestlers in position, one hand grasping the belt and the other the thigh band of his opponent. To win it was necessary for one contestant to lay the other fairly on his back on the mat which was spread over a cushion of sand used to soften the fall for the unfortunate loser. Each man tried in every way he could to throw his opponent by lifting him and throwing him over his shoulder, by tripping him by all sorts of foot and leg combinations. If, during the scramble, one lost his grip on the belt or thigh cloth of his opponent, and so they were separated, each stood watching for a chance to get a first hold on the other and thus throw him down before the other could regain a hold. To Western onlookers, it often appeared to be rather fearsome, and of course accidents did sometimes happen though but few of them were serious.

Since my return to the United States I have watched the modern developments in wrestling into which the methods of the Japanese judo have been incorporated and there certainly is no comparison between the methods of ancient Korea and those of modern America insofar as possible injury is concerned. The American are much more brutal.

In recent years Japanese judo had been introduced into Korea and is now taught and practised in the athletic departments of all schools and colleges. Severe accidents are infrequent because the man who is receiving punishment can always give the sign of defeat in time to prevent the fracture of a bone or the snapping of a tendon.

In the use of judo the Koreans are rapidly becoming as expert as are those from whom they but recently learned the art.

- Rope-Walking

Rope-walking is quite a common part of the exhibitions given on the streets and commons of the villages and cities by traveling troupes. The ropes are not taut, but hang loosely from the posts to which they are fastened. On these ropes the showmen and girls walk, run, dance, and turn somersaults, carrying on with apparent ease. They generally use no poles with which to balance themselves. Though I have watched them quite often, I have never seen a performer fall.

- Archery

Archery is a sport of the higher classes who have plenty of time to practice it. As in other countries it was formerly a chief arm of the military department before the invention of gun- powder and the consequent change to guns. It was also the principal weapon used in hunting.

Now, however, it is only a game of skill practiced by people of leisure in Korea as elsewhere.

I saw more of this game in the palace than outside for here were more people of leisure and also there was more room for target ranges. The king, though I never saw him participate in any form of athletics, was very fond of watching his high class attendants at this sport.

The Korean bows are famous for their strength, their durability and beautiful lines. They are made of hickory, or similarly tough wood, and covered with the thick, tanned skin of hogs tightly stretched and firmly glued to the wood. When the string is released, the bow does not merely straighten, it turns back on itself, until its ends nearly touch, so that when it is strung its driving force is more than doubled. The arrows are made of bamboo stems about one-quarter to three-eighths of an inch in diameter; the nodes on which have been scraped to an even smoothness. They are from eighteen to thirty inches in length and have a metal head and the usual feathers and notch.

I often wondered at the accuracy of their shooting. The target, not less than one hundred yards' distant, was marked with circles just as in other countries. The contestants stood in line, each shooting in turn. With apparent nonchalance, the shooter would draw his bow to the full length of the arrow, swing it up to the side of his head and let it go, seemingly without much aiming. The arrow would soar to a considerable height and then, falling in a beautiful curve, would nearly always strike the target and stick in it. sometimes making a bull's eye or coming very near it. Seldom did a shot miss the target. It was a fine sight to watch the arrow soar in an arc and then drop down the other arm of the arc to its rooting place and one could but wonder how the archer could so gauge the pull on his bow and so direct the arrow in its semicircular flight so that, judging the force and direction of the wind, he made it fly so accurately to its goal.

- Dancing

Dancing was regarded by the Koreans as an art rather than as a means of taking exercise. It was practiced only by young women and usually for the entertainment of man.

The young women were selected, first of all, for their beauty and their grace of motion. Other important attainments were a sweet voice, a pleasant laugh, and an ability to sing. They were educated in special schools where they learned to read and write, to talk interestingly, and to be charming.

The King had his own troupe of girls - the best that could be selected from many applicants - who entertained him and his guests as occasion arose. They danced to the music of a native orchestra. This music is always in a minor scale of only five tones and so sounds very monotonous to Western ears but it delights the ears and stirs the emotions of Orientals. Eastern dances always illustrate some fancied subject, or at least, they are supposed to, though I never reached the place in all my hearing of the music and seeing the dances where I could recognize what it was all about without being told.

This same illustration of a fancied subject is also true of a great deal of the instrumental music of Western countries. It is intended by the composer to suggest some subject such as "autumn leaves" or "spring" or something which usually does not mean a thing to an audience until it is explained. Oriental music is like that to the ears of a Western audience only mere SO.

However, when the meaning of an Oriental dance has been explained to a person one can follow the movement of the dancers and imagine what they are trying to interpret. These performances of dancing girls are usually a part of every entertainment given by people who can afford to provide it. There is no reason why those dancing girls should become harlots though generally they are considered to belong to that class, or they eventually drift into it when the charms and accomplishments for which they were selected and trained have diminished through the passing of the years. The danger to the morbidity of the girls, however, is very great when they are at the height of their career. The entertainments to which they are most commonly called are marked by the serving of plenty of wine and usually the best girls are brought into the dining hall toward the end of a feast when all the men are excited by drink. They are served freely with wines and the feast often degenerated into ribaldry. These girls do not all become prostitutes but the danger is obvious.

It must be stated, however, that a dissolute life is not inherent in Korean dancing. It is very graceful and calculated to inspire the best of emotions. When Western dancing was introduced into Korea both men and women participating - the latter of whom appeared to Koreans to be most immodestly dressed it created quite a scandal. To them it seemed very immodest to see those so lightly dressed ladies gliding around in the arms of their partners and they turned their faces away from the scene. So, there! What shall we say?

Other Sports

- Stone Fights

We had not been in Seoul long when one evening, as I was leaving the dispensary for home, I noticed a crowd of men on the street. They were in two groups facing each other and it looked as though a riot was in progress. Each group was throwing stones and other kinds of missiles at the other. The street was so filled with men that I could not pass through so I stood at the side to watch what was going on. Some of the onlookers who were near me explained that it was an annual affair, a kind of sport, which took place at that season in nearly every town or hamlet throughout the country.

When I asked my language teacher about it he said that the custom had been begun long years before during the prolonged absence of war. One of the old kings wanted to keep up the fighting spirit of his people and so each village was divided into two sides or one village was pitted against another and a day for a fight selected. During the days preceding the fight each side collected stones, bricks and other things they could use as missiles. At first it was intended to be a game only though a dangerous one for some were likely to be hurt or even killed, but it was understood that no matter how badly a man might be injured, or even though he were killed, his family or relatives could make no complaint. So, in some cases, a person who had a spite against another would try to get on the opposite side to him and thus have a chance to get even by injuring him or even killing him without danger of punishment. I never heard of anyone's being killed in Seoul in one of these fights, but many were brought to the hospital for treatment after the fray. This led to conversations with my teacher about what appeared to me to be a strange custom. Then he told me of another custom that was prevalent in the city of Pyong Yang.

The Pyong Yang men, he said, were reputed to be very brave and were considered the best fighters in the whole country. Strange to say they fought principally with their heads, bending their necks and butting their opponents, often killing them in that way. Of course, they needed very hardheads for such work and, when there was no fighting going on, they had a habit of butting their heads against the houses or even the city wall in order to keep their head hard.

He went on to say that he expected the missionaries who were then just opening work in Pyong Yang would find it very hard to get converts because, he said, the Pyong Yangites were so antiforeign that they would oppose the introduction of a foreign religion but, on the other hand, if they once took up with Christianity they would persevere against any amount of persecution.

As a matter of fact the early missionaries to that city were stoned and made to feel anything but welcome but they continued their work and, in the years that followed, those who became Christians made that city, reputed to be the most wicked place in Korea, noted for the strong character of its Christians and it became the leading center of evangelism in the country.

•   Kites

Korean kites are made in all sizes from a few inches square to very large ones several feet square.

When I say square I mean that and not some other oblong. The frame is made of bamboo strips of a thickness proportionate to the size of the square, - the greater the length of the sides the thicker must be the strips of the supporting frame. Two cross bars form a background to support the paper which covers the frame to offer resistance to the wind. Strips fastened to each end of the cross bar meet together at a point several inches from where the bars cross and to these at their meeting point is attached the string which is to connect the kite with its owner who may be either a man or a boy.

You will note this kite has no tail to hold it in balance. It is so skillfully constructed that a tail is not needed to make it keep its face to the wind.

The flier's end of the string is attached to a reel in the hands of the boy and the boy whirls it in his hand when he wants it to go higher or to pull it in. This reel gives the flier much greater command over his kite than the American flier shave when they merely wind the string around a stick.

The absence of the tail also permits the kite to be manipulated to a much greater extent than is possible with an American one.

As a matter of fact the Koreans can bring their kites around in the air so as to fly them either with the wind or against it.

One of the most exciting spectacles during the flying season is a kite fight. A kite spreads itself in the breeze and makes the fingers of its owner tingle with pleasure as he send sits off in one. direction and then in another. Yes, that's good, but there is another lad getting ready to send his kite up to compete with it. Now it is up and the contest begins. Which one can make his kite fly in greater circles? Then comes the great test - the kite fight. Each is trying to cross the other's string so that he can by a see-sawing movement cut the other's string. Away goes the freed kite and away goes the owner and away go all the boys who have been eagerly watching for this very thing to happen to one of the kites, no matter which. Whoever can first catch the fly-away can claim it as his own. Often not one of these running so eagerly can catch up with it. Quite frequently a boy far away from the scene finds it dropping in his direction and gets possession of it long before the others can reach the spot. Well, there is no use crying over spilt milk. No, I mean water because they haven't milk to spill in Korea or didn't have in those days of which I am writing. Away, therefore, they go again all the time on the look out for a runaway kite which they may follow this time with success perhaps, for hope never dies in the heart of the Korean boy during the kite flying season.

In preparation for kite fighting, either as an attacker or defender the boys prepare their strings for the contest by a very simple process. They break up pieces of glass or porcelain and pound for fragments almost to powder. Then they make a strong glue and while it is still hot stir into it the broken glass or porcelain and rub this mixture into the fibres of the string and let it dry.

When a string, thus treated, crosses another string that is not so fortified it will immediately cut it and win the battle for its owner, but if both strings have been thus treated, the battle will be prolonged until a weak spot in one is found when a few see-saws will finish the struggle.

My own sons, who passed their boyhood days in Korea, still take pleasure in recalling the hours spent in making kites and armoring them for the fights. Each of them had his own Korean chums, who came to our house and helped the boys prepare their kites. Such companionship kept our boys from developing that feeling of snobbishness that white children often have for those of another color and so my wife and I encouraged it.

Foreign Athletics

The custom of the annual village tug of war became one of the annual events on the Chosun Christian College campus. Being so near the big city, it was not necessary to make the rope - it could be purchased - and as hemp cables were by that time available, a much lighter rope served. The College provided the long cable two inches thick and, because it was made of hemp, it lasted several years. As there were three departments in the College, the trial of strength was made between two of those and then between the winners and the members of the third department. The winners of two out of three pulls were awarded the prize. As members of the faculties added their strength in the struggle, great enthusiasm prevailed and a feeling of community fellowship resulted that was very much worthwhile. The President was there to give encouragement but as he was a member of each of the departments he could not get into the pulling though he could and did cheer all the participants. This one game always took up a half day in preparations, in actual tugging and in getting the cable back to its resting place till the following year.

It was the aim of the College to keep up all the national games that contributed to good sportsmanship and to the improvement of the health and strength of those engaging in them.

When the Westerners (government officials, missionaries, and business men) arrived in Korea they organized the Seoul Foreign Club, membership being open to women as well as men.

The club bought a piece of ground in the district in which the foreigners then lived and erected a clubhouse. Inside the building were several rooms for various social purposes besides a library and reading room and outside several tennis courts were prepared. Both men and women played tennis and the club-rooms became the social center for all the foreigners in the city.

As one would expect this became, for the Koreans, what they called a great "Kookyung" which, translated literally, means a "Sight-See." Strange to say we have in the term kookyung a combination of two syllables "Koo" and "Kyung" each meaning "to see" and presumably the duplication is used for the sake of greater emphasis just as in English a sight-see (same kind of a combination) means something especially worth looking at.

Often the losers either wept or wanted to fight the winners. As doing either of those was contrary to all the spirit of play the teachers had to include talks of sportsmanship into their lessons on "reading, writing, and arithmetic." This effort to arouse a spirit of fair play and a respect for good sport recurred every year as each new class was received until the high schools, where the sports were soon made popular, had time to impress on their minds the true spirit of sportsmanship.

But for years the desire to either fight or cry broke out on occasion and showed itself even in college students. If college students who had already had several years of athletic practice and exposure to lectures on sportsmanship could occasionally break down under the strain of great disappointment, is it strange that the members of teams that began to be organized in other groups outside of the schools and colleges and had no training in self-discipline should often end their contests in a free-for-all fight or that the fighting forces should sometimes be augumented by the entry into it of onlookers who sympathized with one or the other team?

It was sometimes necessary for the police to interfere and then the on-lookers were disappointed at the breaking up of the fight or chagrined by the unwelcome sight of a bunch of young fellows weeping and sobbing over defeat.

One game after another was added to their list of sports - basketball, association football or soccer, skating, hockey, swimming, etc. Schools and colleges employed athletic teachers and all students had to participate in at least one kind of sport unless they were excused by the head of the school for sufficiently good reasons.

These outdoor games were followed by the erection of indoor gymnasiums where basketball could be carried on during the winter months and where wrestling and judo and various other physical training exercises could be carried on under supervised. It was not long before some of these sports were introduced also into schools for girls, especially tennis and basketball played outdoors in summer and gymnastic exercises and basketball indoors during the winter season.

But what use was all this physical effort to students who were in desperate need of instruction in class room work of all kinds?

In the first place they received a grand training in self-discipline, the supreme need of all who have to live with others and who should do so in harmony and with due respect for the equal rights of others. In the second place they got the physical exercise they had formerly failed to get and also the blood cleansing that came from the greater inhalation of good clean air. This was, and still is, necessary for the avoidance of that greatest of all scourge of students in Korea, lung tuberculosis.

But time changed this idea, for the mission schools put athletics into their curricula. The first game the male students learned was American baseball and it set the boys on fire!

- Tennis

One hot summer afternoon one of the members had invited a young nobleman who, having gained a fair talking use of English, cultivated acquaintance with Westerners, to visit the club and watch the play. He showed great interest but when at the end of a hard fought game that had called forth all the energies of the contestants, they returned to their seats near him, wet with perspiration, breathing heavily and red in the face with their exertions they asked him how he liked the game, he smiled and said he thought it very interesting and then naively asked why, if all that effort had to be made, they did not let their servants do it for them. This question indicated exactly the attitude all Koreans of his class had at that time, toward all athletic activities that called for exertion. To him it had looked just like so much hard work.

- Wrestling

Wrestling had, throughout the long past, been a favorite sport in both Korea and Japan, as in nearly all countries.

The methods of grappling and the rules of procedure differ greatly even in those two neighboring countries and this difference is even greater when compared with those of most Western countries. I will not try to describe these events as I saw them practised in Korea for they must be seen to be appreciated,

It was, of course, necessary that the students should become familiar with all the methods of both Korean and Japanese wrestlers and they were anxious also to learn all their coach could teach them about the rules and procedures of Western wrestling.

Since returning to America I have seen several bouts but, after having watched American professionals wrestle, I am certain that the combination of wrestling with judo as practised in America is much more savage than anything I saw in the East.

- Judo

When the Korean athletic coaches suggested the inclusion of Japanese judo into the college calendar of sports the Western members of the faculties, including the president, expressed a fear that it might not promote the objects the colleges were aiming at but the students were practically unanimous in their desire for it. As a matter of fact they wanted to be in a position to take their own part on equal terms with any possible Japanese contestant in their sports so it was soon included and a special room with soft straw mats two inches thick was prepared in which both judo and wrestling could be practised.

- Ice Hockey

Ice hockey is of course a real test of courage, speed, dexterity and quick thinking and this sport attracted many of our students so that when the Chosun Christian College was laying out its athletic grounds, it did not forget either skating or hockey. It arranged for a large outdoor skating rink in the center of which was a fenced-off hockey rink.

- Foot Racing

Foot racing was always a favorite pastime. A good Korean walker could make better speed on long journeys than the best Korean ponies could make. It was a real pleasure to see a young Korean walking on a country road. With his body erect, his head held well up and his arms swinging, he would take long steps and without any apparent effort at haste would cover a great distance in a day. The usual walking distance for a day was 90 li, about 30 miles but in case of haste that could be much increased.

- Running

In the school sports running also held a foremost place. The Chosun Christian College put on a yearly athletic contest open to students of any high school in the country and in it these foot races were preeminent. They were scheduled in distances from 100 meters to eight miles. The eight mile race was dignified by calling it a Marathon.

One high school in the capital had its buildings on the side of a hill and a general athletic field could not be laid out on its site, so foot races became that school's specialty. Every year it sent running teams to our college and year after year these outsiders carried off nearly all the prizes given for that sports. They were especially good in the long distance races and one of their boys won the Marathon each of the four years - he was a student in that school.

In the last Olympic contest before the war, held in Germany, the winner of the International Marathon of 25 miles was a member of the Japanese team. The Japanese were very much gratified to have won an event where they, because of the average short stature of their nationals, were unlikely to be a head of the taller men of other countries but the winner of the Olympic was a Korean, the very man who had been the star runner in the 8 mile Marathon at the athletic contests held at the Chosun Christian College.

The sad sequel to this was that the racer when he was interviewed after his victory, told reporters that he was a Korean and not a Japanese and gave them his Korean name instead of that given on the program by the Japanese. For this he underwent severe punishment after his return home, the Japanese military governors not wanting the world to know that a Korean, one of a country they had conquered had carried off the honors, and then made the mistake of letting it be known he was a Korean.

Tennis soon became a great favorite in Korean student circles and naturally they often played against teams from the Japanese schools of both Korea and Japan. Tennis was already a well-established sport in Japan long before it found its way to Korea so for years they were the winners of nearly all their contests with Koreans but at last found themselves outclassed.

- Basketball

On one occasion a basketball team made up of students in the University of Hawaii in Honolulu visited Japan. This group was practically international, having as its members natives of Hawaii, Negroes, Japanese, Koreans, Americans and Canadians, all citizens of Honolulu.

They played all the principal teams in Japan and won every game. Then they came to Seoul and, after winning all their games with various teams, including that of the Japanese University of Korea, Played the team of the Chosun Christian College all of whom were Koreans. I watched that game with great interest and it was a fascinating one. First one team was ahead and then the other until at last it ended with the victory of our Korean College team by one point. It was so close that the losing team lost nothing of the glory it had already gained but, for the Korean College team, it was unexpected glory they had held their own with a team from America and a bit more!

That experience with the Koreans led to a mutual friendship between the winners and the losers that lasted through all the following years - a friendship based on a better understanding of the fact that true sportsmanship and sporting ability are not confined to any one nationality.

In a later interview with Dr. Crawford, the President of the University of Hawaii, during one of my visits to Honolulu, he referred to this game with satisfaction because it had broadened the international thinking of his own young men.

- Soccer

I might go on writing of other types of athletics in which the Koreans proved themselves equal to members of other races, but I will only mention some of them briefly.

Soccer was a favorite sport in the colleges and high schools and in this the Koreans proved themselves able to meet other nationals as equals.

It was always a pleasure to me to watch their agility and their dexterity in the use of their feet and heads in this game which, of course, is the real game of football for in it the ball must always be kicked and never carried in the hands or even touched by the hands of any of the players except those of the goal keeper.

Chapter 5

Missionary Works

An Easy Way to Dispose of a Year's Accumulation of Sins

If one can sin many times in a day how great is the guilt of a whole year of sinning!

Surely there must be some way of getting rid of such a burden on one's conscience. As the old year according to the lunar calendar is nearing its end, straw dolls begin to appear in the shops. Why? I wondered.

Some clever person won the gratitude of all sinners by making these dolls of straw to be used for this very purpose. At the end of the Korean year, which occurs usually in the early spring, all one has to do is to make a list of one's evil deeds on a piece of paper, fasten it to the little mannikin, attach the mannikin to a kite and send it up in the air. When it has gone as high as you think necessary you cut the string of the kite and away it goes, wheresoever the wind lists, till it finally settles on the ground far away. It has taken your sins with it and you are free but it is really too bad for the unlucky person who may pick up the kite and the doll for all the sins with which it was burdened will go to the finder. One can imagine that but few will venture to gather in these lost babies and if one does happen to make such a mistake, he will hurry to send the doll up again on another kite and so get rid of his acquired misdeeds. As a few small coins are generally hidden in the doll some needy beggars will the more readily try to capture the kite and risk the danger.

Decrees against Christianity

As has been mentioned before, the French Roman Catholics had been the first Christians to carry their religion to the Far East and had had a good footing in China as far back 1286. There were Roman Catholic Christians in Japan too, at least as far back as 1586 A. D., for history says that when the Japanese Daimio, Yasuhiro, failed to force Korea to resume the neglected custom of sending envoys with tribute to Japan, Yoshitose, Daimio of Tsushima, a Christian, was sent to do what Yasuhiro had not accomplished. Another note says that in the war that followed the Japanese troops were commanded by Konishi, a Christian general. Still another note says that in 1604 A. D., a Jesuit priest and a Japanese Christian came from Japan to Korea to work among the Japanese troops and the natives.

Not long afterwards, in 1603 A. D, a Korean prince who had been baptized in Japan, tried to get to Korea via Peking but failed and returned to Japan. Then persecution of the Christians broke out in Japan and this prince was killed at that time.

- Introduction of Roman Catholic

In 1784, in Korea, a royal decree issued against Christianity and Thomas Kim, a Korean who had been converted in Peking and had returned to his home as a missionary, was killed. Again in 1793 two Koreans named Kim came from Peking and suffered a like fate and in 1794, a Chinese Christian, Jaques Tsui, arrived in Korea, and in 1801, he too was beheaded.

In 1802 a new edict against Christianity was issued and the note says "Christianity began to spread rapidly. This, the new edict, added much to knowledge of the faith." Thus persecution helped the general cause at the expense of individual lives - just as it has always done.

In 1811 the Korean Christians applied to the Pope for aid.

The notes say, "In 1853 Bishop Ferriel died a natural death and Priest Jansen also died a natural death in 1864." Because so many had been killed for their faith the word "natural" had a special significance in these records.

In 1860 four more French priests arrived and the number of Christians was reported as 18,000. This number would include all the infants and children of Christians, in accordance with Roman Catholic custom.

In 1863 King Yi Chul Chong died and his adopted son became King at the age of eleven years and his natural father, Prince Yi Heung Sun, was appointed to act as Regent. He is generally referred to in the record as the Tai Won Kun, which means "The Great House Ruler." The Tae Won Kun's wife was reportedly a Roman Catholic Christian but he himself was strongly opposed to the introduction of the faith into Korea and, in 1866, began a severe persecution of Christians and of all foreigners by ordering the death of Bishop Bernoux and eight priests.

- Arrival of the First Protestant Missionary

1884 marked the arrival of the first Protestant missionary, Dr. H. N. Allen, an American Presbyterian, and the first hospital was opened in February, 1885. It may be noted here that the King, on the occasion of his twenty-first birthday in 1873, had assumed the reigns of government and the records do not tell of any particular cases of persecution up to the time of the coming of Protestant Christianity in 1884. In that year Dr. Allen, by saving the life of the Queen's cousin, Min Yong Ik, gained the favor of the King so no objection was taken to the coming in of Protestant clerical missionaries which began the following year by the arrival of several Presbyterian and Methodist clergymen and another physician, Indeed the King's attitude to these new comers was shown by his request in 1886 to have three American teachers selected by the Foreign Missions Board of the Presbyterian Church in the King's patronage to teach in a government school for English and also a request for a lady physician to treat the Queen to be selected and sent out in the same way.

But in 1888 a decree was published against Christianity. What had happened to change the attitude of the King who had surrounded himself with Christians as doctor, teachers and friends?

The Roman Catholic had purchased a hill site inside the city on which to erect a large church. Though it was across the city from the palace it was on higher ground and these standing on the hill top where the church was to be erected could see the inside of the palace enclosure and with field glasses might even see the royal personages themselves. As this was contrary to all Korean ideas of propriety the church authorities were asked to exchange their site for another differently located. But the church men, regarding the church as higher than the government, refused the request and the decree against Christianity was the answer to that.

The fear that the coming of so many American and English missionaries might lead to the overthrow of many customs and ideas to which the people were attached was also propagandized as a means for arousing public sentiment against foreigners, but in 1887 some Korean officials demanded that all foreigners should be forbidden to reside in the capital and be compelled to live in a foreign settlement at Yong San on the bank of the Han River three miles from the city. It was then that this incident of the Roman Catholic Church's planning to build its cathedral on a site overlooking the palace occurred. The Methodists had built also on a prominent hill but as it did not overlook the palace little objection had been made.

But in spite of this decree against Christianity, the Roman Catholic authorities stuck to their determination to build on the site they had purchased and as Korea's treaty with France granted the right to purchase land, without specifying any restrictions, there was no legal way of preventing their buying any sites that the owners were willing to sell, so the cathedral occupies its prominent place in the capital and the people have become so accustomed to seeing it there that it no longer assails their sense of propriety.

Probably the Christian converts, not to mention the missionaries and other foreigners, brought on themselves much of the opposition of the people by their too rapid erection of big buildings of foreign style and the flouting of many Oriental customs which held a firm place in the thinking of the people.

Story of Kim of Cheju

About the year 1903, while the hospital was still being carried on at its old site within the city, a young man applied for treatment of empyema of his right chest, It was an old chronic case with foul smelling pus and the process of erosion had already involved several ribs. Treatment had to be carried on, of course, over a long period and recovery did not take place until all the ribs of that side had been removed so that the outer wall could fall in and adhere to the inner wall of the chest so he was with us for about two years.

During that time he became interested in religious matters and when he returned to his home in Cheju he told his friends he had become a Christian. He explained to them what Christianity is and told them all he had learned about

God and Christ. The story spread and aroused much interest and a group of believers resulted. Up to that time, as far as I can learn, no Protestant Christian work had been carried on in that island.

Though we had news of him from time to time, we did not see him again for many years. In the meantime the General Assembly of the Presbyterian Church had sent a pastor and bible-woman to the island to follow up Kim's religious work and a church was organized and in time more churches came into existence.

Then one day while Mrs. Avison was sitting on the porch of our home a stranger called and asked for Dr. Avison. She said he was out then but would be back soon and while he waited he said to her, "Why, lady, do you not know me?" She answered, "I'm sorry but I do not remember you." "Why, I was in your hospital about 30 years ago and as all my ribs of one side were taken out I was there for two years. I have been well ever since. My home is in the island of Cheju. We now have a great many churches there and I am on my way to attend the General Assembly in Pyongyang as a delegate from there" Of course she then remembered him. When I returned you can well believe with what a feeling of gratitude I met him and learned that his two years' stay in the hospital had led to such good results.

He had come up to the house with an elder of the South Gate Church (Hospital Church) who had been born in Cheju and, becoming a Christian through Mr. Kim's teaching, had later on come to Seoul where he attended the church connected with the Hospital and had become one of its Elders. Mr. Kim asked many questions about the student assistants who were in the Hospital when he was a patient and was told that all of them had become doctors and one of them was still a teacher in the medical college while others had hospitals of their own in the country. We sent him down to the hospital where he met this doctor and other workers who had been in the former dispensary. Photos of him and of his formerly diseased side were taken to be put in the hospital records.

This is one story out of many which could be told of how the missionary hospital, while caring for the physical needs of the sick, gives the spiritual influence which changes the lives and aspirations of those who come at first only for bodily ills. Many of the churches throughout Korea grew out of the medical care received by individuals who, while they were being treated, received religious instruction and became earnest disseminators of their faith.

Sorai Village

When Mr. James S. Gale went to Korea under the auspices of the Y. M. C. A. of the University of Toronto he wanted to go deep into the country where he could learn the language by constant contact with the Koreans without any opportunity to talk in his own English tongue. He was told of Sorai Village, two hundred miles from the capital, the home of the first Christian Church in Korea, and went there to pursue his studies. He lodged in the home of Mr. Suh, the first Protestant Christian in Korea and there obtained an unusually good use of the language. He came to be regarded as the best foreign linguist in Korea and his knowledge of the Chinese written characters was probably unequalled by any other foreigner. Moreover, he then lived entirely on native food.

Mr. Malcolm Fenwick of Toronto who came soon after Dr. Gale, followed the example of Dr. Gale in going to Sorai to study the language where he also learned to speak idiomatic Korean and he also lived on native food. Both of these accomplishments brought both Gale and Fenwick into closer relations to the Korean people than any other two things could have done.

- Rev. W. J. McKenzie

Rev. W. J. McKenzie of Nova Scotia came to Korea for a visit during our first year there and as I was a Canadian, came at once to our house. He had heard of the work in Korea when he was a pastor in Nova Scotia and had made up his mind to come out and see it for himself. At that time he was engaged to a young lady from his own town but she did not feel the call to Korean and refused to come with him. After he arrived in Korea he wrote another young lady whom he had known in Canada who was working under the Missionary Alliance Society in China, asking her to become his wife. She consented but as she was already serving as a missionary in China it would take a little while to arrange to change her work and break her connections with those who were supporting her there so the marriage could not take place immediately so, after conferring with some of the missionaries in Seoul, Mr. McKenzie decided to settle in Sorai Village for language study. I believe he was not under appointment by his Church Board at that time but he wished to take up work in a territory that might later be assigned to his church and so asked that the selection of his field should be decided by Inter-Mission Committee in Korea appointed to determine the allocation of missionary responsibility to the various denominations. His denomination was the Presbyterian church of the Maritime Provinces in Canada. He, as Dr. Gale and Mr. Fenwick had done, decided to reside in the meantime in the Suh household in Sorai where he became greatly beloved by all the people.

At that time a group of Koreans called "Tong-haks" was very active in Whang Hai Province in which Sorai was located. They stressed the importance of maintaining their own Korean culture and preserving the Orient for Orientals name, "Tong-hak" means "Eastern Culture." In common parlance it was understood to stand for a Korea for the people. They often burned villages and threatened communities opposed to them. When they threatened the village of Sorai, Mr. McKenzie volunteered to go along to meet them and plead with them not to molest the Sorai villagers. His friends there were fearful for his life but he went alone, refusing to allow any one to accompany him. He was a very tall man and heavily built and had a very pleasing smile and when he reached the camp of the agitators and began to talk with the leaders he quickly won their confidence and was able to arrange with them for the safety of his village. Afterwards he visited the group frequently and won their leader and many of the men to Christianity.

Typhus fever was very prevalent in Korea at the time and McKenzie took the disease, It was in the summer of 1895 just after the victory of the Japanese over the Chinese and great feasts were being held in Seoul by the Japanese to celebrate this victory. During one of those functions, I received a letter from Mr. McKenzie which said he was very ill and begged me to go to see him. I conferred with Mr. Underwood about the request and learned that he too had received a letter urging that I be sent immediately to him. A meeting of the Seoul station was called to consider the advisability of my taking the trip in view of the heavy medical work I was then responsible for in Seoul. A young doctor just arrived in Seoul from Portland, Oregon, Dr. J. Hunter Wells, who had no family and as yet no assignment of work was asked by the station to go instead of me. He consented but as he did not yet know any of the language Rev. F. S. Miller was asked to accompany him. They left the following day but the journey required several days and when they reached Sorai Mr. McKenzie had already passed away. Apparently he had become delirious with the severity of the fever for he got up from his bed on the floor, secured a gun belonging to one of the Suh brothers and, before any one was aware of the situation, took his own life. Thus, in so short a time, one of the most promising young missionaries had been lost to the work.

The people of Sorai would not permit his body to be brought to Seoul for burial, saying he belonged to them. They prepared a grave just outside the church property, interred his body there and erected a monument on which an epigraph was carved, both in Korean and English. Though he had been with them so short a time they loved him greatly and throughout the years that have passed since his death they have kept his grave in fine condition.

When word was sent to Miss Louice H. McCully in China of this unfortunate death of her fiance she decided it was her duty to leave China and come to Korea as she had intended to do, and there carry on the work which Mr. McKenzie had been assigned to do. Shortly afterwards the Presbyterian church in the Maritime Provinces decided officially to begin missionary work in Korea and Miss. McCully was appointed as their first missionary there. The northeastern section of the country, beginning at Wonsan and extending northwards to the border of Manchuria was assigned to them by the Intermission Committee as their evangelistic responsibility. The Southern Methodist Church of the U. S. A. had already started work in that district but they withdrew so as to give the Canadians a free hand, except that both missions should have the right to work in the city of Wonsan.

- Songchun or Sorai

The village referred to above has two names, both words meaning exactly the same thing. Every place in Korea has this duplication of names, one being the Korean pronunciation of the written Chinese characters and the other the Korean name itself.

The Korean name of the pine tree is So and that of a stream is Rai and the name of the village is So-rai but the Chinese characters are pronounced song for the pine and chun for the stream and the name of the village is therefore also Song Chun, each name meaning the same thing. But by whichever name it is called it is indeed a lovely hamlet from the Korean point of view, though we might say "picturesque" from the American viewpoint.

It is located near the center of a plain that stretches from the foot of the Tai Kyung San (Great View Mountains) to the Yellow Sea - very fertile and beautiful to look on.

A winding stream flows from the mountains, flows through it (the village) at one point in its course, right in the middle of the stream and for some ten or more feet in diameter, bubbles can be seen rising briskly as though it were water boiling in a pot. Day and night it has been doing this as far back as people can remember but it is not hot water, it is as cold as though it came from a deep spring, as no doubt it does. It is a great boon to dwellers there who daily fill their water pots from its very center. It needs neither to be boiled to make it pure nor iced to make it cold. It is nature's gift of pure cold water. Doubtless it was this that attracted people to build their homes there in the first place and perhaps it has had its due effect on the mental and spiritual up building of the villagers for from that place came many of the most intelligent, most vigorous and most devoted men and women who made the church at Sorai noted throughout the whole country.

Even before the missionaries came to live among them and teach them they were devoted to religion as they had learned it from Confucius, from the priests of Buddhism and from the spirit worshippers of their own antiquity.

One of their number named Suh Sang Yun, a gentleman farmer and student of the Chinese Classics, after travelled to the far north, across the Yalu River into Manchuria and onto Mukden, its capital, taking with him goods produced in Korea and returning with Chinese goods valued by the people of his neighborhood. On one of those trips to Mukden he fell in with the Scotch Presbyterians who had established a Mission there and became especially attached to the Rev. John Ross with whom he could converse through the knowledge of Chinese both he and Mr. Ross had. From Mr. Ross he learned of the Christian religion and took back to his home a copy of the New Testament printed in the Chinese script, which he could read. He was thus led to believe in Christ and so it was that a new religion came to beautiful Sorai and, when American missionaries first went there, they found the seed had already been sown and some of it had already begun to germinate.

On one of his visits to Mukden, Mr. Suh traded his load of Korean goods for Chinese Bibles and carried them on his back to the Manchurian border town of Anturn on the Yalu River. As the customs officer there would not permit him to take them into Korea, where Christianity and its books were yet taboo, he loaded them on a boat that was sailing down to the mouth of the Yalu Riber and South to the Korean port of Chemulpo. On arriving there, he again found himself unable to get them past the customs house and they were stored there until, through the friendly intervention of the American Minister, they were released. The energetic and devoted Mr. Suh then took them to Sorai where he disposed of them to the readers of Chinese in that community.

Thus the names of Suh and Sorai will be forever connected with the beginning of Protestant Christianity in Cho-sun.

Mr. James S. Gale and Mr. Malcome Fenwick, both of Toronto, Canada, and both unmarried, went there to live during their early years in Korea where, with no English people to talk to and divert both of them from their studies, they could the more readily learn the language and at the same time get accustomed to Korean ways of living and where also they could be sure of the sympathetic attitude of the people.[60]

That territory had been assigned to the supervision of Rev. H. G. Underwood who made it the center for his country work in the Yellow Sea Province - Whang Hai Do. When Mrs. Avison and I arrived in Korea, the converts there included nearly every member of that community and the need for a large church had become evident. By vote of the residents it was decided that the best and most logical site for the church would be the very spot occupied by the village temple so that building was torn down and the site made ready for the erection of a Christian Church.

Having decided the question "Where" the question of "How" had to be considered. At other places, where churches had been established by Roman Catholic missionaries, buildings had been erected by Mission funds so the Christians of Sorai, having provided a site, visited Mr. Underwood to report this, naturally expecting the money for the building would be at once forthcoming. What was their surprise at hearing Mr. Underwood express his gratification at their progress and then ask when they thought the building would be completed and ready for dedication.

"Why," they said, "we are expecting you to supply funds for that - we have no money for it. The materials will have to be bought and workmen paid."

"Oh," said Mr. Underwood, "how do you build your own houses? Who provides that money?"

"Why?" said they, "each one buys the materials and the neighbors join together and help him with the work."

"Then," was the answer, "why not follow a similar plan for the church? You will need wood - doesn't the village own woods around the neighborhood? And aren't there plenty of stones to be picked up without cost and also the clay and sand needed? Have you no carpenters and stoneworkers in the village who are

60   See the preceding section titled 'Sorai Village.

members of the church? Will they not help by giving their services?"

At first they gasped, then their leader began the smile and at last exclaimed, "Of course we can do it that way" and off they went. And they did it. And so was the first protestant church in Korea built and that settled for all time the way of building churches in that land.

The building was of purely Korean architecture and large enough to accomodate all the residents of the village.

When it was completed Mr. Underwood and some of his fellow-missionaries dedicated it to the worship of God and all the more joyfully because it was the first church building erected entirely with Korean funds, and would, in this respect, be an example to every other community that might need, or wish, to have a church of its own.

In the year 1896 I visited the village for the first time and, in company with Mr. Underwood, had many unique experiences. After calling at many villages and towns en route we arrived at Sorai at dusk on a Saturday evening. On reaching Mr. Suh's house we gave special cough used by Koreans to announce the coming of a visitor. The door was quickly opened, revealing a sight most surprising to both of us. We were startled to see them sitting with their hats off -quite contrary to Korean etiquette and, wonder of wonders, their top knots had been cut off and their heads closely shaved. I know I caught my breath at such an unexpected appearance for they all looked like Buddhist priests.[61] Later on, when the formalities of arrival had been observed, we asked, "Why?"

"Well," they said, "the Japanese authorities who have seized our country have ordered all Koreans to cut off their topknots. We do not like it but we discussed it and studied our Bibles to see if there was anything in its teachings to guide Christians under such circumstances. There we found Paul's direction to his converts in Rome - Romans 13, 1-7 and we decided that the orders of our present rulers should be obeyed by us as Christians."

1.　Let every soul be subject unto the higher powers. For there is no power but of God: the powers that be are ordained of God.

2.　Whosoever therefore resisteth the power, resisteth the ordinance of God: and they that resist shall receive to themselves damnation.

---

[61]　Buddhist priests always have closely shaven heads.

3. For rulers are not a terror to good works, but to the evil. Wilt thou then not be afraid of the power? do that which is good, and thou shalt have praise of the same:

4. For he is the minister of God to thee for good. But if thou do that which is evil, be afraid; for he beareth not the sword in vain: for he is the minister of God, a revenger to execute wrath upon him that doeth evil.

5. Wherefore ye must needs be subject, not only for wrath, but also for conscience' sake.

6. For, for this cause pay ye tribute also: for they are God's ministers, attending continually upon this very thing.

7. Render therefore to all their dues: tribute to whom tribute is due, custom to whom custom; fear to whom fear honor to whom honor.

We couldn't object to that attitude of course. On Sunday Mr. Underwood conducted the service and at its close I witnessed a very unusual ceremony.

The leader of the church, though not then an ordained minister, was Mr. Suh Kyung Jo, brother of the Mr. Suh who had brought the first Bibles into Korea from Mukden. He had lost his first wife and had afterwards taken a second wife. Following the custom of the country at that time he had taken her into his home without any marriage ceremony. She had borne him several children of whom two were sons, thenabout 12 and 14 years of age.

Though his second marriage had been without a ceremony it had the sanctity of common usage and the children were all legitimate in their country and the question of its validity had never arisen but now that he was to be ordained as an elder in regular charge of a Presbyterian Church, he himself suggested that, as a matter of example to the members of his church, he and his wife should be married in the church according to the Christian formula, so Mr. Underwood, without in any way minimizing the legality of the relationship already existing performed the regular marriage ceremony. It was of course a very unusual event and the first instance of such an occurrence in Korea. They stood before the minister with their children at their side, thus including them in what they were doing. I said this was the first instance of such an occurrence in Korea. If another did occur, I did not hear of it, though I lived in the country for forty years after witnessing it. Their children too were all baptized at that time.

That evening, while Mr. Underwood and I were sitting with Elder Suh and his family in their home, the subject of his boys' future was discussed. Mr. Suh said he wanted his eldest on to be a minister of the gospel and the other to be a physician, I turned to the boys who were, according to Korean custom, listeners without joining in the conversation unless directly spoken to and asked them if they were of the same mind as their father. They said they were except that the older boy wanted to be a doctor and the younger one a minister. We talked the whole question over, the father saying little but we could see that he still expected to have it go his way. However, when the boys were older and the matter had to be decided, the father sent the older one to our Medical College and he became one of the first group of seven doctors to be graduated in Korea. The father, you see, had learned some things in the meantime. The other boy set out to be a preacher but because he became involved in plans for regaining the independence of Korea and fled to China to escape capture by the Japanese and, up to this time, has never returned to his much loved land, his original desire has never been attained. The father, Elder Kyung Jo Suh became a student in the Theological School the Presbyterian Mission established in Pyong Yang and in 1908 was a member of the first group of its graduates. He was then ordained as the first regular pastor of the Sorai church over which he had presided as leader from its very beginning.

The fact that Sorai was the first place in Korea where Protestant Christianity gained a foothold led some of the early missionaries (as already stated) to go there to live while they studied the language so that close contact with the people in a locality where no one understood English might give them amore intimate understanding of the language and a greater freedom in speaking it than most others gained, the church, because of their presence, grew all the faster. The community established a modern day school which became as famous as this church.

From it came one of our early medical students (Kim Myung Sun) who after his graduation was appointed as an assistant to the American Professor of Physiology in his Alma Mater.

He did well in that position and the College, after a few years of testing in that position, sent him to Northwestern University in Chicago to study Physiology as a specialty. There he took the degree of Bachelor of Physiology. Continuing his studies, he gained his Master's degree and then proceeded to the degree of Ph. D. in Physiology.[62]

Returning then to Korea he was given the rank of Professor of Physiology in his own college where he has successfully served ever since. Recently he was named by the Japanese as Superintendent of the large hospital in Pyong Yang, nearly 200 miles North of Seoul, which duty he carries on in addition to his teaching in Severance. He spends half of every week in Pyong Yang and the other half in Seoul. Thus Sorai became a leader in modern medical education as well as in religion.

The Sorai community now has a large church building and a flourishing public school and still maintains the enviable position in Christian leadership it gained in the early days of Mission Work in Korea.

Founding of a Church

The Rev. D. L. Gifford was one of the earliest of the Presbyterian missionaries to Korea and about the same time Miss Mary Hayden arrived to assist in the educational work for girls, It was not long before these two became man and wife, having decided they could do better work as a team than singly. I wonder after all whether this rather overworked idea of doing better work in double harness really determined this or whether it was not the same old cupid, old but ever young, that did it.

They lived in the eastern part of the city of Seoul in the district known as Yun Mot Kol, the lotus pond district, so named from its proximity to a beautiful lotus pond. Their home became the center of the Presbyterian work in that part of the city, he working with the men and she with the women. He selected a young Christian named Yi as his Korean helper and ere long a small group of men and women formed the nucleus of a church destined to become one of the most influential in the city. The few members of this group me teach Sunday for a church service and each Wednesday evening for prayer meeting, with Mr. Yi as their leader.

His contacts with Americans interested him in their ways of thinking on other subjects besides religion and especially matters of government and this led him to associate himself with the group of young reformers who were arousing their people to try to bring about a constitutional monarchy. Many of the

---

62   During a conversation with the Professor of Physiology in the University, shortly before the completion of those studies, Dr. Ivy assured me Dr. Kirn was fitted to become a teacher of Physiology in any College in the United States of America.

men had taken part in the Emeute of 1884. After a period of exile most of these men had been pardoned and some of them, having returned to their native land, were again advocating the substitution of a constitutional form of government for the autocracy which had so long existed. This time they were carrying on a campaign of education amongst the people instead of attempting to get forcible possession of the government as they had tried to do in 1884.

However, the King and Queen, still urged on by those of their subjects who profited from the autocracy, Pursued a policy of repression that often took the form of imprisoning the leaders of the movement and, the time Mr. Yi began to take an interest in the question, some two hundred of the reformers had been incarcerated. When he heard of this he became greatly excited and, Presenting himself at the jail, demanded that he too be imprisoned as he was a reformer and a member of that group.

The jailer urged him to return to his home, saying that only the chief of the City Police could put any one in prison. Yi then went to that official who also refused to accomodate him as no complaint had been laid against him. The young reformer persisted, however, and at length an order was issued for his arrest and imprisonment with the others.

The news was received with consternation by his little group of Christians and when they met for their weekly prayer service they, like the Christians of old when their leader, Peter, was in jail, Prayed earnestly for his release.

As Wednesday came around, Yi, in the jail, thought of his little flock and asked the jailer to release him for that one evening that he might go and meet with them as usual but naturally his request was refused.

However, after much pressure from Yi and his solemn promise to return the same night, the jailer reluctantly allowed him to go. You can imagine the surprise and delight of the little congregation when Peter Pastor opened the door of their meeting place and stood before them. Delight? Yes, but why surprise? Had they not just been praying for it? Yes, but - well, weren't the few believers gathered in Mary's house in the long ago to pray, surprised when Peter arrived? They had just been praying for this but, when the maid opened the door and ran in to tell them it was Peter, the record says, 'And they said unto her, thou art mad.'

At the close of the meeting to the great relief of the jailer, Yi returned to the prison.

Before long an order for the release of the whole group came and Yi was again free to pursue his Christian work. Unfortunately, he was drowned in the

Han river not long afterwards by the upsetting of a boat. His death was a great loss to the little group in the church, but the spirit of the members was such that its growth continued as before.

In that summer Mr. Gifford, while itinerating in the country outside Seoul, was taken ill with dysentery. He was too sick to be brought back to his home so his wife hastened to his dido but he died before medical aid could reach him. She then contracted the disease, which was evidently of a very virulent type as she also died within a few days.

The little church was thus triply bereaved. It survived and continued to grow so chat a larger meeting place had to be found for it. The supervision of this church was given to another missionary and its next move was into what had been a large Korean residence made up of a series of small rooms surrounding a central court yard. The walls separating it into rooms were torn out leaving a large number of posts many of which were but seven feet apart. When the open central courtyard was also roofed in and floored a very remarkable structure developed such as no architect had ever conceived. It, however, met the immediate need as two hundred people could sit on its floors.

You may be interested in seeing the accompanying photograph of its interior with Mr. L. H. Severance of New York and the writer standing in the building. I imagine the wealthy Mr. Severance, accustomed to worshiping in the noble sanctuaries that adorn the larger cities of America, was very strangely affected by the sight of this makeshift church building but I can vouch for it that, during the several years it was occupied, the growth of the congregation and the religious enthusiasm of its members would have surprised the rather careless and often small congregations in the grand churches of U. S. A. No pews were needed - for Korean homes have no chairs - all sit on the floor and in this church, the only seat an attendant wanted was a circular mat about 18 inches in diameter made of straw braids spirally rolled around a center and sewed together. In the way mats of braided rags are made in this country. By this method two hundred people could be accommodated where only sixty or seventy could have found seats in pews such as are used in Western Churches.

Rev. J. S. Gale, a Canadian graduate of the University of Toronto who had come to Korea as the representative of the university's Y. M. C. A. but had later joined the American Presbyterian Mission, was appointed as pastor of this growing congregation. He brought with him as his assistant, a Korean named Chay who, before his conversion, had been probably the most depraved man in the city of Pyong Yang in the North.

When Rev. S. A. Moffett first went to that city to open Mission work there this man, with others like him, stoned the missionary in an effort to drive him from the city, but instead of accomplishing this, he was conducted.

He had been a drunkard, gambler and companion of prostitutes, but after his conversion he used all his energies to preach to his former pals and with such success that he was soon given recognition as a missionary helper and put in training for the ministry.

In time he became Mr. Gale's co-worker and came to Seoul when Mr. Gale was appointed to the church of which I am writing.

There were many rather wealthy people in that church, some of whom had been or were then government officials and it was a question whether this man could make good as a co-pastor in such a church.

The sequel showed that he did make good. He was a marvellous preacher and all the more honored because in his youth he had gained great skill in the writing and reading of the Chinese Script which was then a sufficient guarantee of scholarship and was the "open sesame" to a respect akin to reverence.

Mr. Gale too had a fine command of the Korean language and also of the Chinese characters so these two made a very strong combination, just suited to that congregation which had in its members also the students of the Mission High Schools for boys and girls which were situated near the church.

Under these two workers the church prospered even more rapidly than before and it became necessary to plan for a still larger building. A nearby site was secured and a building erected that would accomodate 1,200 people. While this building was undergoing construction the large congregation worshiped in a large tent.

In the midst of this great success Mr. Chay, the helper, died. At once a dispute arose as to where and under what auspices his body in Seoul should be buried. His congregation claimed the right to decide this but the Christians of his native city, Pyong Yang, where he had been so notorious as a sinner and so revered as a saint, were so determined that his body should be taken there for interment at their expense that the Seoul group at last yielded, recognizing the oriental custom that a person's birthplace has always a prior claim on him whether alive or dead. So he was born and sinned, was converted and buried in his own city. The Seoul congregation sent a large deputation of its members to participate in the burial service and all was peaceful.

One can not but wonder at the spiritual force that turned so depraved a man so suddenly from his career of vice and transformed him into so great a power for the uplift of his follow men.

The church at Yun Mot Kol continued to flourish even after it lost its foreign pastor also when at the age of 65 he left Korea to live in England and spend the rest of his life in literary work.

In the course of time the church celebrated the thirtieth anniversary of its founding. I had the honor of being invited to be one of the speakers on the occasion presumably because I was one of the few missionaries left in the city who had known the church from its very beginning.

The celebration was held on a Sunday afternoon and the platform was filled with a group of elderly people including the then pastor and the elders of the church, while not a fort of seating space was left empty in the body of the church.

When it came my turn to speak I told of the very beginning of the church in the little 7 x 14 ft. room where Rev. Mr. Gifford and Mr. Yi gathered together the first Christians in that district; of the imprisonment of Mr. Yi, of his unexpected release to lead the prayer meeting and his return to the jail afterwards; also how their present pastor, while he was still a non-Christian judge in the city of Seoul, had entered our hospital with a severe disease of one of his leg bones which required a long time to heal and how, while there, he yielded to the influence of his surroundings and became a Christian: of his resignation from the judgeship to study for a time, he became pastor of the church that had grown up around the hospital where he had become a Christian ; then of his becoming pastor of this the largest Presbyterian church in the city, now celebrating the 30th anniversary of its founding, I also told how Elder Kim Chung Sik, then seated on the platform, had been a political prisoner in the early days and of his conversion while in the jail ; of how, after his release from the prison he had joined the Y. M. C. A. and later was the first Korean to become General Secretary of that flourishing organization. I spoke of how I had watched the growth of this church and had been present at the dedication of the building we were then in and of what a privilege it was to me to be a participant in this day's proceedings and the more especially so because of my long association with its present pastor and Elder Kim.

When I sat down Elder Kim arose and told us he was the Chief of Police in Seoul who had carried out the order for the imprisonment of the two hundred reformers and the first Korean assistant pastor of this church, Mr. Yi, as just related by Dr. Avison. Can you imagine the effect of this announcement on the congregation?

But when the pastor arose and said that he was the judge who had ordered the arrest and imprisonment of those same men and afterwards had been converted in the hospital as just told by me, you can hardly realize the enthusiasm of the great congregation.

Now, as I am writing this several years after that anniversary occasion, I know, though I am in America, that that church is still a great force in the Christianizing of the people of Korea. The same pastor is still its guiding spirit and my mind often dwells on the young judge I had known in the hospital as a non-Christian, on how he was converted there, how he became a minister of the church that had grown up out of the hospital work and then, years afterwards, when, with head grown grey, he had become and still continues to be the pastor of the great church which had had such a humble beginning in the early years of mission work in the "Land of the Morning Calm."

Foreigner's Summer Resorts of Korea

Really the summer resorts of Korea should be described by several persons rather than by one. There are many of them and they are all different in kind. As is usually the case the occupants of each think they have chosen the most desirable place.

My first experience in selecting a place in which to spend the summers was an interesting one. It was in 1894, the first summer after our arrival. Most of the foreigners in Seoul felt it necessary to go away from the city in July and August for those were the months of the rainy season and of the highest temperatures, both of which facts greatly increased the danger of sickness to those who resided in the city where the lack of those modern sanitary measures to which they had been accustomed in their homelands debilitated them and menaced both health and even life. Especially was it necessary for those who had children to seek a summering place away from the cities.

Some families went to the mountains of Japan where summer resorts had already been established, others sought immunity in China, but the majority of the foreigners, for various reasons, had to remain in Korea. Among these my family had to be counted. We then had four small children and as both my wife and I were in poor health some special precautions must be taken. As I was tied up to the care of the little hospital - the Royal Korean Hospital or Chayjoongwon we were compelled to seek a temporary place out of the city but near enough for me to make a daily trip to the hospital. Many of those who remained in Korea went to Buddhist temples in the mountains but the difficulties of such travel made that impossible for our family.

- The River Han

My friend Rev. H. G. Underwood was somewhat similarly situated, as was the Rev. F. S. Miller, so we three got together and set out in search of a suitable location on the bank of the River Han which ran in a semicircle around the city at a distance of about three miles. That short distance from the city fitted in well with our need to make daily trips and it was also a fond for us to be near a body of water for the sake of coolness and the facility for bathing and boating. After a rather prolonged search we found a place on the river named Han Kang that suited us exactly. Mr. Underwood was deputized to deal with the several owners and ere long we became landowners.

We formed a company of three members, each having a third interest, and attended to all legal requirements. Each paid an equal share of the cost and then three building sites were laid out, one for each. Each built his own summer house and each was allotted a garden plot. The rest of the ground was to be used in common by all. Legal matters and unfortunate local animosities caused us much concern, but as these are referred to in another section, they may be passed over here. We hurriedly planned our cottages and by August they were built and ready for occupation. It was none too soon for our youngest child, Douglas, the one born in Pusan soon after we arrived there, was like to die with intestinal trouble and my wife and I were both ill with the same trouble.

The very first day after we moved out there I hired a boat and took the family for a trip up the river and the result was almost like a miracle. All slept well that night and each day a similar trip was followed by improvement and we felt that the change from the city had really saved the lives of half the family.

Feeling I must visit the hospital every day I bought a horse on which to ride there and back thinking that offered me the easiest method of travelling but experience proved it would have been better for me to have used a swining sedan chair with four men to carry it. The jog trot of the horse along the rough paths and up and down the hills shook me so much that I found myself less and less able to make the trips, weakened as I had been during the preceding hot months in Seoul. However, the coming on of the fall months with their gradually increasing coolness restored us so that, at the mid of the summer, we were able to carry on our work in the city with less distress.

We used this river beach for years and our children grew to love it so much that even now all of them still speak of these summers at Han Kang as the most pleasant memoirs of their early days although the first two to leave there did so forty years ago.

- Sorai Beach

Passing years brought changes of many kinds. Other summer resorts were found and opened. Among them one of the first was Sorai Beach.

In another part of these stories of Korea you can read of the little village of Sorai where the first Protestant church building to be erected without financial assistance from a mission is located, the place where Rev. William J. McKenzie lived and died and is buried, the home of the Suhs whose name will always be revered by the Christians of Korea.

Sorai is situated in the mid-southern part of Whang Hai Province only about two miles from the Yellow Sea.

Rev. Dr. H. G. Underwood was for many years the missionary in charge of that district and he frequently took walks to the sea shore to look at the beautiful scenery from a promontory which at that place jutted out far enough to make a sheltered coast line of several miles of sandy beach. As he sat there he began to dream of that promontory and beach as a summer resort for missionaries who needed to get away from their stations during the two hottest months of the year. As he daydreamed he could see the high promontory covered with cottages and feel the sea breezes blowing over it from whatever direction. He saw the tide coming in from half a mile out till it covered the smooth hard sand, making, a bathing beach sloping so gently toward deep water that it would be safe for children too young to swim and for older persons who could go through or over the rollers into the deep waters.

To ensure the corning of his dream into actuality he bought the whole promontory together with a large adjoining pine grove in which children could play while their elders wandered amongst the trees; fields beyond where playgrounds could be arranged-fields for baseball, tennis and golfing; fields for cultivation of vegetables such as the summer colonists would like. He then had it surveyed, a map of it made and the promontory divided into house plots to be sold at cost to all who might be admitted into the Association of Householders which he foresaw coming into being. He then invited half a dozen others (of whom I was one) to join him in the organization of a governing board to make regulations by which all who bought lots must agree to be governed.

He began the colony by building a house for himself, several small houses for rental and a building to be used for church services and entertainments.

At one side of the promontory which rose to a height of about 80 ft, was an arm of the sea several miles wide and, on the other side, the promontory gradually lowered to the level of the sandy beach. A large island known as White Wings spread out to a length of several miles at a distance of twenty-five miles from the promontory and other smaller islands curved gradually shore wards, making a sort of inland sea beyond which large ships plied and whales were to be found.

This shut in area of water could, under provocation, become too rough for the small craft which we summer residents sailed but generally our rowboats or small yachts or outboard motor boats found it safe and pleasant sailing. The tide there was fifteen high and when it ebbed it left more than a quarter of a mile of fine hard sand. When the tide came in it was usually in the form of great rollers which afforded swimmers both exercise and pleasure. Yes, it was a perfect beach and safe for in all the years I summered there not one case of drowning occurred though even babies played in the surf under the care of members of the community who took on in turn the duty of watching the bathing of the small tots.

To encourage long-distance swimming a one-mile course was laid out along the shore and prizes offered to different groups. It was surprising at what an early age the youngsters were able to make the mile swim. The nearest island was three miles away and, after gaining courage and strength to make the mile course the children began training for the three-mile one. They all loved the water. As they grew older they found other games to spend time at such as tennis which attracted large numbers of those of teen age and on up to 45 and 50 years while the boys and men played baseball. A golf course appealed to many, both old and young, male and female.

The neighboring farmers soon learned what kinds of vegetables and fruits we liked best and grew them for us. We established a market where they could put them on sale and this made the matter of sale and purchase simpler and did away with the constant stream of peddlers who had gotten into the habit of coming to our homes. Committees on recreations and on religious and literary meetings provided plenty of opportunities for us to put our time to the best uses and the weekly editing and mimeographing of the "Sorai Blow" gave some members of the community a chance to air their views and publish the news to the rest of the community.

Sunday services for old and young and younger still were provided by the religious committee and these were well-attended but, without doubt, the one service that proved most attractive was the evening meeting at the Point.

This was at the very end of the promontory, facing South and sloping gently towards the sea. It had been terraced and grassed to make sitting more comfortable and was mainly a service of song. The time of meeting coincided with the setting of the sun and generally the sunsets over three or fou miles of water and then over a range of mountains were glorious. To sit in the hush of evening with the sun setting on one side and the moon rising on the other side over another series of hills and miles of sea was in itself a delight and as we quietly sang "The Sun is dying in the West," our emotions were deeply stirred.

Those of us who have been retired by age and are now again in the Western world think back on those privileged moments and are ready to sing as we had so often done while there "Sorai, Sorai, Sorai by the Sea !"

•   Wonsan Beach

But even Sorai did not attract all the holiday makers who needed a period of rest and escape from the sultry heat of the cities. Some business men could get away only for weekends so that a nearer place was desirable and some preferred a different kind of outlook, so a second resort was built up on the east coast of the country near the big port of Wonsan, the Korean name or Gensan (hard G) the Japanese name. The cottages were all built on the sand just a little above the level of the sea. The tides were only a couple of feet high and drinking water was more readily available than at Sorai. It was only necessary to drive an iron pipe into the sand to a depth of 8 to 12 feet, attach a simple pump to it, and lo, an abundant supply of water was obtainable as near your cottage as you cared to have it. At a certain depth the water obtained might be salty and brackish, but by driving the pipe just a little deeper, it entered a layer of cold freshwater that never failed. The Sorai water supply was not like that. Deep wells had to be dug and quite often solid rock was struck or water was not found within reach, or what was found was not drinkable. So there most of the drinking water was brought from those never-failing cold springs in the stream running through the village of Sorai, two miles away, and the water carriers were kept busy all day delivering it from tanks hauled by oxen. It was good water, but it wa shard to get. Each of these places had its individual advantages and disadvantages and there was a constant rivalry between the two which added to the intererst taken in both.

As the Wonsan Beach faced East they could have glorious sunrises, but the "sunsets of Sorai" were not available there and Sorai being on a promontory jutting out into the sea had both sunrises and sunsets. Both had boating and swimming, different of course at each; both had tennis, baseball and golf. Each had a pavilion for church meetings and entertainments and both had goodly communities of satisfied summer dwellers. All the people were alike in both character, and aims and visits were frequently interchanged. But, alas, the government (Japanese) looked enviously on that fine level tract of land at Wonsan, so near the big port and so well fitted for a naval airport, and at length announced its intention to utilize it for such a purpose. A time for evacuation was set, values were placed on all the buildings, and a promise given that a new site to be selected by the cottagers would be given by the government. Such a site was found on the east side of the Diamond Mountains. Indeed it pleased the residents even better than the old one had done. Though not directly on the seashore it included a beautiful inland lake around which the cottages were built while behind them rose the famous range known as "the Outer Kongo" or "the Outer Diamond Mountains." The only drawback they have so far complained of is the comparative absence of these a breezes which, after all, constitute one of the most desirable features of a summer resort.

- A Mountain Resort at Chiri (Cheeree) San

The members of the Southern Presbyterian Mission live in the southern part of the country and both the resorts just described are considerably farther north than halfway up the peninsula, so a few years ago they sought for a location that would be nearer to their homes and yet cool enough to be refreshing. Rather than another seaside resort, they chose one far up on Chiri Mountain and, year by year, the number of cottages increased though the difficulty of reaching it, because of the steepness of the only road up, the fact that the amusements are much restricted because of the absence of sufficiently large level spaces and also because most people prefer the seaside with its bathing and boating facilities, will keep it from becoming a serious competitor of the other two. I am sure those who go there, however, will strongly dispute this opinion.

As the number of foreign business men and foreign missionaries in Korea is likely to decrease rather than increase in the years to come it is quite unlikely that these various resorts will grow larger - they are more likely to become smaller.

The Koreans do not build up summer resorts for themselves - they betake themselves to the temples in the mountains, not in large companies but a few here and a few there, or they go in picnic parties to a nearby river or to a seaport, so at present at least little will be done by them in similation of those resorts for foreigners I have described.

The Japanese have already established a few resorts for themselves but they do not go to them for long periods at a time - they go generally for week-ends and prefer places where they can bathe in hot mineral springs.

Appendix **1**

Vitae
Oliver R. Avison. M. D., LL. D.

- born in Yorkshrie, England, on June 30, 1860

- arrived in Canada in 1866

- taught three years in public school in Canada

- graduated from Norman School in Ottawa (similar to U. S. Teachers College)

- three years' apprenticeship in pharmacy

- graduated from Ontario College of Pharmacy --- 1884 Pham. B.

- taught microscopic materia medica and botany --- 1884-1892

- graduated from Victoria University, Toronto --- 1887 M. D. & C. M.

- graduate student in medicine at University of Toronto --- 1887 M. B.

- taught Pharmacology and Therapeutics in Medical School of the University of Toronto, Canada --- 1887-1893

- practiced medicine in Toronto, Canada -- 1887-1893

- accepted appointment under Board of Foreign Missions of the Presbyterian Church in the U. S. A. as "Medical Missionary" (was a member of the Methodist Church of Canada) --- 1893

- physician to the King of Korea --- 1893-1903

- appointed by the British Government as physician to the British Legation - 1895 - 1935

- granted license to practice medicine and pharmacy by the Japanese Government

    organized the Severance Union Medical College* in Seoul, Korea (seven men graduated in the first class, 1908)[63]

- organized the Chosun Christian College* in Seoul, Korea in cooperation with its first president in 1915

- became president of Chosun Christian College in 1916

- with the permission of Edward VI, received from the King of Korea the decoration of the Fourth Degree of Yang Ban

- with the permission of George VI, received from the Emperor of Japan the decoration of the Fourth Degree of the Sacred Treasures

- granted degree from the University of Toronto --- 1924 P. D. hon. causa

- granted degree from the College of Woester (Ohio) --- 1925 LL. D.

- granted second honorary degree from the University of Toronto (on fiftieth anniversary of graduation in medicine) --- 1937 LL. D.

---

* These two colleges have full recognition by the Japanese Government as equal to their own colleges. They are not universities in the sense in which that term is used in Japan. A college course may be completed after fifteen years of study a university course may be completed after seventeen or eighteen years of study. Graduates of the Severance Union Medical College do not have to pass a government examination they are licensed to carry on medical practice in any part of the Japanese Empire.

Appendix 2

Synopsis
Autobiography of Oliver R. Avison, M. D- LL. D

- **Early Life** - parentage; boyhood days; emigrating to Canada from England; school life; influence of self-educated father.

- **Work** - entered woolen mills where father was employed; taught night school at age of twelve to working boys who had no chance of an education. Author determined to get an education in order to make a living "without taking my coat."

- **School Life Resumed** - entered high school: decision of one of high school masters to go to India as an evangelist broadened author's horizon; greatly influenced by teaching of principal who presented historic events from the standpoint of a liberal in politics, author made aware of the social significance of history. Attended Model School to get a teacher's certificate; taught three years in a country school; attended Normal School in Ottawa to get a higher grade teacher's certificate.

- **Apprenticeship** - determined not to make teaching his profession, author entered a drug store to become a pharmacist; studied assiduously and manufactured many of pharmaceuticals used by doctor who owned drug store; served three year's apprenticeship.

- **Career as a Pharmacist** - entered the Ontario College of Pharmacy in Toronto and graduated with highest honors in a class of fifty, winning four gold medals. Former employer offered partnership in drug store, but author decided to accept teaching position in the Ontario College of Pharmacy. Having much spare time, thought of entering a prosperous drug store to supplement income but was strongly advised by principal to enter medical school.

- **Medical School** - work in College of Pharmacy counted as one year toward medical course in Victoria University. At end of first year in medical school, ranked first in class and won scholarship; same was true at the end of second year. Studying and teaching in Pharmacy brought about weakened physical condition, hence decided to work less strenuously last year in medical school, dropping to third place in class but with much improved health.

- **Teaching in Medical College** - after graduation from Victoria University, offered instructorship in pharmacology and therapeutics in the Medical college of the University of Toronto. Continued teaching at College of Pharmacy, and accepted this position-making a total of thirteen hours of teaching per week. During the summer gave a special course to young physicians called "Elegant Prescribing" - the writing of prescriptions which would produce pleasant looking and pleasant tasting medicines.

- **Practicing Physician** - after teaching in College of Pharmacy for five years, gave up instructorship to devote entire time to practicing medicine. Appointed to Examining Board of faculty in School of Medicine. Served as physician to the mayor of Toronto. Numbered among pupils in medical college are such famous doctors as Thomas Cullen and Liewellyn F. Barker of Johns Hopkins, and Herbert Bruce - leading surgeon in Toronto and until recently lieut. governor of the Province of Ontario.

- **Medical Missionary** - at the end of the sixth year on the staff of the medical college at the University of Ontario, appointment was renewed for another five-year period. The author decided to resign and accept the challenge to become a "medical missionary" under the Board of Foreign Missions of the Presbyterian Church in the U. S. A. although he had been brought up in the Methodist Church of Canada. Sailed with his wife and three children from Vancouver in 1893; one week after the family landed in Fusan, Korea, another son was born. About a month later the family arrived in the capital city Seoul, where they were to make their home.

- **Medical Work in an Oriental Country** - brought author in touch with all classes of people, from the king down to the lowliest of his subjects. Three months after arriving in Korea, became physician to the king-a position held for fifteen years. Then political upheavals and national and international complications compelled His Majesty, the King of Korea, to use Russian, German, and Japanese physician in turn as their rulers gained ascendancy in Korea.

- **Early Korean History** - origin of the Korean people; founding of Korean more than 4,000 years ago; early knowledge of the arts and sciences; Korean literature, inventions, such as the use of movable metal type long before Gutenberg's time, first suspension bridge, first iron-clad boat.

- **Medical Education** - introduction of modern medical knowledge; establishment of first medical school, graduation of over 500 doctors and nurses - the latter taken from an environment than had no schools for girls as they were regarded as soulless and brainless. Modern education has proved that Korean girls are fully as able to acquire knowledge as are Korea men; and as opportunity offers, the young Korean women of today compete with women of other nations in the pursuit of higher education.

- **Severance Union Medical College** - founder and only teacher for "early fifteen years": now a well qualified staff of both native and foreign doctors and technicians. A Korean became president of this institution when the founder retired.

- **Chosen Christian College** - established in cooperation with its first president in 1915; author became president in 1916 and served until his retirement in 1934; college consists of three faculties; liberal arts, science, and commerce; on author's retirement, an American missionary succeeded to presidency and a Korean became vice-president

- **Population and Medical Education** - from a population of 12,000,000 in 1893, spreading of knowledge of sanitation and treatment of disease, especially improvement in treatment of contagious diseases, changed the statistics for Korea to approximately a population of 23,000,000 in recent years. Enforcement of sanitary regulation by the Japanese is a contributing factor. Medical missionaries in all parts of Korea and modern-minded Korean doctors and nurses scattered throughout the country have aided in promoting modern medical science.

Appendix 3

Summary from Chronological Index

The following selections from Dr. Allen's "Chronological Index" are here introduced because they seem to me to have had some special historical connection with the development of Korea and especially to show how determined they were to keep foreigners out of their country thus acquiring the significant appellation - 'The Hermit Nation.' The notes are injected by the author of this book.

The first few of these happenings appear to show that the Koreans in early times desired to have friendly relations with their neighbors.

(This part was omitted.)

Appendix 4

1. Regarding Chinese Characters:

How many? According to William E. Griffis "The Great Dictionary of Kang-Hi in 1704," contains 44,449 words and 80,000 characters in modern Chinese repertoire. How many are in general use for newspaper work, for most books?

Opinions are different on these matters because there is not statistical report. Some one said 8 or 9 thousands are in general use for newspaper and 7 or 8 thousands for most books. When they designed and what led to their peculiar formations?

It is a tradition that Chang Hil invented characters. He got the idea from the bird's tracks. The script, though less archaic than that of the earlier bronzes, is of an exceedingly free and irregular type. Some attributes them to the Shang, or Yin dynasty (1766-1122 B. C.) in accord with Chinese tradition. Others think that they represent a mode of writing already obsolete at the time of their production, and retained of set purpose by the diviners from obscurantist motives, dating them about 500 years later, or only half a century before the birth of Confucius, long after the appearance of a new and more conventionalized form of writing, called in Chinese 篆, chuan, which is commonly rendered by the word seal, for the reason that many ages afterwards it was generally adopted for use on seals.

In Chinese writing, a few characters, even in their present form are pictures of objects, Pure and simple. Thus, for the "sun" the ancient Chinese drew a circle with a dot in it, ⊙, now modified into 日; For "moon" ☾ now 月; for "God" they drew the anthropomorphic figure, which in its modern form appears as 天; for "mountain" ⛰, now 山; for "child" 윳, now 子; for "hand" ✋ now 手; for "well" 井, now written without the dot. These picture-characters, then, accumulated little by little, until they comprised all the common objects which could be easily and rapidly delineated-sun, moon, stars, various animals, certain parts of the body, tree, grass and so forth to the number of two or three hundred. The next step was to put together a few compound pictograms; 旦 the sun just above the horizon - "dawn"; 林 trees side by side - "a forest"; 舌 a mouth with something solid coming out of it - "the tongue," etc.

While writing was still in its infancy, it must have occurred to the Chinese to join together two or more pictorial characters in order that their association might suggest to the mind some third thing or idea. "Sun" and "moon" combined in this way make the character '明' which means "bright"; woman and child make '好', "good"; "fields" and "strength" (that is, labour in the field) produce the character '男' "male"; the "sun" seen through tress '東' designates the "east"; a "woman" under a "roof" makes the character '安' "peace," etc.

The whole body of chinese characters may be divided up into pictograms, ideograms and phonograms. The first are pictures of objects, the second are composite symbols standing for abstract ideas, the third are compound characters of which the more important element simply represents a spoken sounds.

2. Reason for the wearing of so much white clothing by Koreans?

White clothing was largely due to the mourning purpose, and also due to the influence of Tang dynasty, regarded as the golden age of the Oriental civilization. During that period men wore white as Li Po, the poet, appears in picture in loose white garment. Korean men copied from that. Since the Manchus conquered China, they forced the Chinese to adopt their customs and wear the quine. But the Koreans were left alone to retain the Tang style.

3. Have you any pictures of yourself?

Will try to find them, 1904, 1918, 1919, and present, in files.

4. Have you any pictures of some of the men connected with reform in Korea?

Yes. Pak Yung Hyo, Yun Chi Ho, etc. Yes.

5. Have you any pictures of celebrated places in Korea?

Yes.

6. Do you think it would be possible to get Koreans as actors, etc?

Yes, we have some of them and will try to secure them and may be able to get some of them from Hawaii and to make some of them.

7. Have you pictures of a royal procession, etc?

Yes, I think we have it.

8. Was a treaty signed between China and Korea about the time treaties between Western countries, etc.?

February 26, 1876-Between Korea and Japan.

(Chosun being an independent state enjoys the same soverign rights as does Japan.)

July 14, 1894 - Between Korea and Japan.

(The object of the alliance is to maintain the Independence of Korea on a firm footing - Korea will undertake to give every possible facility to Japanese soldiers regarding their movement and supply of provisions. This Treaty shall cease and determine at the conclusion of a Treaty of Peace with China.

September 11, 1899 -Between Korea and China(Treaty of Amity and Commerce was made by Korea with China in substantially the same language as the Treaty with the United States.)

9. What missionary wrote the book "A Cycle of Cathey etc.?"

Sorry, I do not know

10. Date of Washington Convention regarding Naval matters, etc.

November 11, 1921 to February, 1922. Washington Convention
March 25, 1936 on London Convention at which time Saito and Matsuoka represented Japan.

11. Who is the Princess Min who was at your Korean Liberty Conference?

Queen Min who was killed by the Japanese is Princess Min's great aunt.

12. Name of the youngest prince who taken is Yi Kuen Name of his father is Yi Hei.

Index

South Norwalk__34
Stainland__29
Stanley Park__77
Steadman, F. W.__204
Steward, E. D.__85
Steward's Hotel__358
Stewart, Isabel M.__186
stone fights__383
Suh, Jai Pil__224, 268
Suh, Kyung Jo__403
Suh, Sang Yun__340, 400
summer palace__288
summer resorts__410
suspension bridge__21

T ai Won Kun__142, 217, 272
Tangun__17
Tate, Martha__109
Taylor, James H.__149
tennis__185, 388
Things Korean__100
Thoburn, James M.__149
Tong-haks__398
Tongnip Shinmun__235
Tories__33
Toronto Medical School__71
Tsui, Jaques __393
typhus fever__130, 152, 398

U nderwood, Horace G.__3, 74, 107, 273,
401, 411, 412
Underwood. John T.__5

V ancouver__76
Vinton, C. C.__4, 87

W aeber, Karl Ivanovich__306
Webster, Elizabeth__186
Welch, Herbert O.__339
Wells, James H.__398
Weston__36
Whiting, Georgiana__117, 251
Wilkie, John__51
Wilson, Woodrow__264
Winnipauk__34
Wonsan beach__414
wrestling__388

Y . M. C. A.__69
yangban__110
Yi, Chei Yang__308
Yi, Chey Myun__273
Yi, Choon Hyuk__263
Yi, Heung Sun__217
Yi, Myung Bock__217
Yi, Sang Chai__260
Yi, Soon Sin__22
Yi, Yong Ik__295
Yokohama__79
Yong San__142
Yonhi College__5
Yonhi University__3
Yonsei University__3
Yorkshire__27
Yorkshire pudding__28
Yu, Kil Choon__127, 167, 273
Yuan, Shi Kai__220
Yun Mot Kol__405
Yun Mot Kol Church__335, 409
Yun, Tchi Ho__203, 213, 241